The New
Republic of Childhood

The New Republic of Childhood

A CRITICAL GUIDE TO
CANADIAN CHILDREN'S LITERATURE
IN ENGLISH

Sheila Egoff and Judith Saltman

Toronto
OXFORD UNIVERSITY PRESS
1990

Oxford University Press, 70 Wynford Drive, Don Mills, Ontario, M3C 1J9

Toronto Oxford New York Delhi Bombay Calcutta Madras Karachi
Petaling Jaya Singapore Hong Kong Tokyo Nairobi Dar es Salaam
Cape Town Melbourne Auckland

and associated companies in
Berlin Ibadan

PR
9193.9
.E34
1990

CANADIAN CATALOGUING IN PUBLICATION DATA
Egoff, Sheila
The new republic of childhood
ISBN 0-19-540576-5
1. Children's literature, Canada (English)—History and criticism*
2. Children's literature, Canadian (English)—Bibliography.*
I. Saltman, Judith. II. Title.
PS8069.E34 1990 C810.8'09282 C90-093226-0 PR9193.9.E34 1990

This book is dedicated to the memory of ROSE and STANLEY ARKLEY in gratitude for their gift of early and rare children's books to the School of Library, Archival and Information Studies, University of British Columbia—a gift that has enhanced the status of children's literature at the university.

Contents

Illustrations

Acknowledgements

For various forms of research assistance, the authors wish to thank Irene Aubrey, Chief, Children's Literature Service, National Library of Canada; Margaret Burke, former administrative assistant at the School of Library, Archival and Information Studies, University of British Columbia; Terry Clark, Head, Youth Department, Vancouver Public Library; Corinne Durstson, Branch Head, Vancouver Public Library; Sarah Ellis, author and reference librarian, District of North Vancouver Public Library; Kit Pearson, author and reference librarian, Burnaby Public Library; Linda Stanfield, Vancouver Public Library; Margaret Johnston, former head of Children's Services, Toronto Public Library; the Canadian Children's Book Centre; and Vancouver Kidsbooks. We are grateful to Rolf Roth, President, Creighton MacKay Management Inc., for computer services, and to our editor William Toye, Editorial Director, Oxford University Press Canada, whose help extended far beyond the call of duty.

Preface

By WILLIAM TOYE

Wishing to have someone other than themselves introduce this third incarnation of *The Republic of Childhood*, Sheila Egoff and Judith Saltman very kindly asked me to write a Preface. The publisher's editor for all three books, I was a member of a group called the Children's Recreational Reading Council of Ontario when, in the winter of 1964, it was decided that the Council should sponsor the first serious study of Canadian children's books as a Centennial project and Sheila Egoff was chosen to be the author. Oxford Canada was designated as the publisher—partly, I suppose, because I was a Council member, but also because for over a decade Oxford had been endeavouring to make some contributions to the then-sparse field of quality Canadian children's books. Thus began my long publishing association, and friendship, with Sheila Egoff, which among other things greatly enlarged and sharpened my knowledge and appreciation of children's books—a service she has performed for countless others. In 1964 Sheila Egoff had behind her ten years as a librarian at the internationally famous Boys and Girls House of the Toronto Public Library, under the dean of children's librarians, Lillian H. Smith. After five years as an editor and conference organizer for the Canadian Library Association in Ottawa, she was invited to become a member of the founding faculty of the School of Librarianship at the University of British Columbia, under the directorship of Dr Samuel Rothstein. She was the specialist in children's literature, and as the School developed she probably became the first full-time professor in this area in Canadian library education. She retired in 1983. Her co-author on *The New Republic of Childhood* is one of her brilliant former students, Judith Saltman, who (after working as a children's librarian at the Toronto, West Vancouver Memorial, and Vancouver Public Libraries) succeeded her in what is now called the School of Library, Archival and Information Studies at UBC.

The Republic of Childhood: A Critical Guide to Children's Literature in English was indeed published in Centennial Year, 1967. (The title was suggested by Paul Hazard's statement about the international reach of children's books in his *Books, Children and Men*: 'Every country gives and every country receives—and so it comes about that in our first impressionable years the universal republic of childhood is born.') For its discussions of Canadian children's books—a not-very-large collection that included many works of interest, though few of lasting value—*The Republic of Childhood* was welcomed. But it did more than draw attention to them. It brought to bear on Canadian children's books high critical standards—formed by Sheila Egoff's learning and by her acquaintance with the best children's books from other countries—and revealed a knack for summarizing plots and describing contents readably and trenchantly. In 1975 a longer Second Edition was published. But as Sheila Egoff wrote in her Introduction:

> Although there has been a sharp increase in the production of Canadian literature for adults, there has been no corresponding increase in books for children. In fact, depending somewhat on how one classifies, the number of children's books issued per year may have actually declined in absolute terms in relation to population growth. However, there are some offsetting factors. Much more *attention* is now devoted to Canadian children's books than was evident before 1967.

This increased attention was no doubt partly due to the publication of her first book.

By 1988, when a Third Edition was begun, there had been an explosion in Canadian children's books. It was agreed that much of the text of the Second Edition would have to be rewritten from the perspective of today, and that some abridgement was called for, omitting discussions of various titles that time had winnowed out, along with the chapter on history and biography. But when, as the book neared completion, it was clear that about seventy per cent of the titles discussed were published in the 1980s, something more than a Third Edition had evolved. It had become *The New Republic of Childhood*.

Sheila Egoff and Judith Saltman demonstrate that Canadian realistic fiction, particularly young-adult novels, represents only one of the genres that have advanced so far in the last decade or so that some recent Canadian books vie with the best in the international field. It is joined by fantasy and science fiction. Of course other categories of fiction are also treated in depth, and firmly placed in their cultural background. These include two that are quintessentially Canadian, the realistic animal story and native legends, along with folk and fairy tales, and novels with a historical setting—in all of which there are at least a few works of genuine distinction.

In the treatment of fiction there is the constant aim to recognize and appreciate works of *literature*. These are books that rise above the commonplace formulas of writing for children and young people and convey—through invention, wit, style, and a profound identification with the subject matter—a truthful handling of character, emotion, social environment, and sometimes moral dimensions. Though formulaic books are not ignored, particularly when they are entertaining—and in the discussion of picturebooks the quality of illustrations is given precedence—the presence or absence of these literary qualities is emphasized.

The sudden leap of Canadian children's books onto the world stage is perhaps best exemplified in the 38-page chapter on picturebooks and picture-storybooks. (The equivalent chapter in the 1975 Second Edition of *The Republic of Childhood* was only 15 pages long.) Here we are presented with a liberation of the Canadian picturebook. This is a form that requires not only artistic and storytelling skills, but a balance between the two: story and illustrations should be inter-dependent. New artists and writers have let themselves loose on a variety of subjects, producing, in a wide-ranging display of graphic and verbal imagination and playfulness, more than a few books that will undoubtedly last. All are described in such sharp and sympathetic detail (in many cases with evident enjoyment) that one wants to experience them for oneself. The chapter 'Poetry and Verse' reveals another facet of the authors' critical sensibilities.

The feelings of confidence and illumination one derives from these discussions of a multitude of books stem partly from the realization that the critical context is enriched by frequent references to the history of children's books, as well as to English, American, and European classics and to key works intended for adults. As a result, the high praise of certain books by Canadians is raised from the level of providing chauvinistic encouragement to placing them convincingly, without disadvantage, among the best international works of their genre.

One can object that critical studies of this kind simply express what adults, and not children, gain from the books described. It is surely undeniable that an informed adult sensibility is required to separate the wheat from the chaff. But it is also undeniable that children have a keen instinct for quality—for the truest claims on their imagination and their openness to delight. This belief colours all the critical writing of Sheila Egoff and Judith Saltman, who— formerly as children's librarians and even now as occasional storytellers—have never removed themselves from the intended readers of the books they discuss.

Here, then, we have evocative, acute, and often lengthy discussions of an enormous array of books and authors—spanning more than a century, against a background of historical development and standards—that earn for this book a place among the significant critical studies of Canadian literature itself. Given the present high creativity and production rate of Canadian children's books, which will presumably continue, one wonders if *The New Republic of Childhood* will inevitably be the last attempt at such a thorough single-volume overview. The very thought makes one appreciate this study all the more, as a milestone in the consideration of a literature whose possible exciting future may be signalled by the exceptional recent works described in the pages that follow.

1

Canadian Children's Literature and How It Grew

Canadian children's literature of the home-grown variety—that is, created by Canadian-born writers—did not make an appearance until the second half of the nineteenth century when there was more to living than the pioneer struggle for bare survival. The first piece of printing for children in Canada may well be lost, but it is safe to assume that it would have been religious and instructional in nature, such as an abridged version of the Douay catechism published in Quebec in 1778 that is held by the National Archives. The gap between this (and possibly other such early publications) and the beginnings of a national literature—seen in the works of James De Mille, Egerton Ryerson Young, Marshall Saunders, and James MacDonald Oxley—was filled by a few English writers who never set foot in Canada, by visitors, and most importantly, by one of our well-known literary pioneers, Catharine Parr Traill.

It was natural enough for such writers to follow the pattern of children's literature already established in their home country, as did writers for adults. When Frances Brooke, the wife of an English army officer at Quebec, wrote *The History of Emily Montague* (1769)—considered the first Canadian, indeed the first North American, novel—she modelled it on the epistolary form of Samuel Richardson's *Pamela; or, Virtue Rewarded* (1740). Similarly, books for the young were didactic, purveying Christian doctrine and bald information—hallmarks of the separate stream of literature for children initiated by the Puritans in the seventeenth century and still prominent in the nineteenth.

This represented a new school of thought that eschewed the

romantic heritage of the English oral tradition—legends of King Arthur and Robin Hood, folktales, and ballads—and was firmly grounded in the Puritan concept of religion rather than romance: it extolled death rather than life, as in the title of a book that became the apotheosis of such writing, James Janeway's *A Token for Children: Being an Exact Account of the Conversion, Holy and Exemplary Lives, and Joyful Deaths of Several Young Children* (1671-2). The religious tone of books for children softened in the next hundred and fifty years, but they were still little more than exhortations to children to be good, obedient, kind to those less fortunate than themselves, and accepting of the station in life to which they were ordained. As well as precepts, there were punishments. No fictional child was allowed to escape the consequences of even the slightest mischief. Many of the books were informational with religious overtones; many were thinly disguised as fiction and were condescending to other races and cultures.

With books for children first in the control of the Puritans and then of a group of Evangelical writers, it was inevitable that works of the imagination would be considered detrimental to children's spiritual health and therefore forbidden to them. Educators from Roger Ascham to John Locke to Sarah Trimmer (from the sixteenth to the nineteenth centuries) railed against the literature of the oral tradition—myth, legend, and folklore. Although such pronouncements were few in terms of recorded criticism, additional evidence can be adduced from the manner in which the literature of 'faerie' was treated. Even John Newbery—who was the first commercial dynamo in children's book publishing in the eighteenth century, and certainly had the interests of children at heart, since he printed attractive little books and sold them along with toys—trod carefully with 'Jack the Giant-Killer' in his *A Little Pretty Pocket Book* (1744). Here the hero of the folktale is reduced to explaining the use of a ball and a pincushion. Mrs Sarah Fielding and Mrs Mary Sherwood, both prolific writers in the Evangelical tradition, made use of the elements of the fairy tale, but turned them into moral tracts—and then issued warnings to their young readers about the dangers of believing in imaginary persons.

Eventually, however, old stories—'The Babes in the Wood', 'Tom Thumb', 'Cinderella', and others—proved tougher than their detractors. The chief reason was a publishing phenomenon: the printing and distribution of such tales in the form of little chapbooks (cheap-books), which were among the wares of the travelling pedlars of the period, and sold for a penny throughout the British Isles. But the stories themselves were so compelling in their plots, and in their air of wonder, that they could not be destroyed—even in a crude format, or in cut and mangled versions. And of course there were children who pleaded for a story from their old nurse, or somehow had access to the chapbooks. In the eighteenth and early nineteenth centuries such children were akin to those of the seventeenth century, who read the greatest Puritan book of them all—John Bunyan's *The Pilgrim's Progress*—as a marvellous fairy tale. It is probably more than a sidelight on the development of English literature itself that most of the outstanding writers of the period—Henry Fielding, Samuel Johnson (and his Boswell), Joseph Addison, Richard Steele, Charles Lamb, Samuel Taylor Coleridge, William Wordsworth, and Charles Dickens—revealed in their own writings, letters, articles, and autobiographies a knowledge of fairy tales, and in many cases remarked on their love for them as children. Dickens, for example, wrote that marriage to 'Little Red Riding Hood' was his childhood dream.

In 1839, two years into the Victorian era, Catherine Sinclair's *Holiday House* heralded a change in the concept of childhood. Her two young children, presented in a domestic situation, are allowed to be noisy, frolicsome, and mischievous without receiving punishment or sermons on misbehaviour. They suffer only gentle chidings from their older brother, a more typical child of his period. They also hear a fairy tale—'Uncle David's Nonsensical Story of Giants and Fair-ies'—which is the first literary fairy tale in the English language. To many critics, *Holiday House* represents the true beginnings of children's literature—that is, one of delight rather than of didacticism.

Still, in the public view books for children were considered chiefly as tools for bending the child mind to the adult will. Although this attitude was doubtless carried to Canada by the early settlers (as it was to the United States, which has a more fully documented early history of children's literature than Canada), a new land and a new set of circumstances did make some difference, not only in content but in the attitude to the young. Our early literature veers far more towards

Catherine Sinclair than to James Janeway! With the aim of describing a new environment to English readers, the writers—whether absentees, visitors, or pioneers—cut down on the heavy doses of moralizing in favour of imparting local information (flora, fauna, and native life).

One of the earliest examples of absentee writing (perhaps the earliest) was *A Peep at the Esquimaux* (1825) by an anonymous English 'lady'. Told in verse, but based on the journal of the explorer George Frederick Lyon, it is an accurate picture of some aspects of the everyday life of the Eskimos of the Eastern Arctic and, for its time, is less condescending towards natives than many other English books of the period. It seems prescient of Catharine Parr Traill to have written a book about Canada before emigrating in 1832: *The Young Emigrants; or Pictures of Canada. Calculated to Amuse and Instruct the Minds of Youth* (1826). Though heavily didactic, it is accurate in its portrayal of pioneer life, being based on actual letters received from Canada. British writers of boys' books in the late nineteenth century—notably Mayne Reid with *The Young Voyageurs* (1854) and the equally prolific G. A. Henty, who based his *With Wolfe in Canada* (1887) on the work of the American historian Francis Parkman—continued to find our forests and Indians and history exotic enough for an adventure story.

The wife of a British army officer, Mrs H. Bayley, resident in Canada for perhaps ten years, may have produced the first piece of Canadian fiction. Her *Improvement; or A Visit to Grandmama* (1832) is a little moral tale completely in the English tradition of the period. So is her *Henry; or The Juvenile Traveller* (1836), travelogues being considered a cunning way to impart information to the young; this has a fair amount of Canadian content, since it apparently retraces the Bayleys' voyage from England to New York, to Île-aux-Noix, and finally to Montreal. Once in Canada, young Henry is informed that Canadian ways are superior to those of the Americans, and English-Canadian ways are superior to those of French-Canadians!

Frederick Marryat and R.M. Ballantyne exemplify the more typical visitor's contribution to our early literature, but in very different ways. In Marryat's *Settlers in Canada* (1844) a family of immigrants, learning that their fallen fortunes have been restored, hastens home to ease and comfort; but the youngest son enjoys the outdoor life, as well as his woodsman friend and the natives, and elects to stay in the new country. Marryat, who falls into Northrop Frye's category of those foreigners 'whose most articulate literary emotion was their thankfulness at getting the hell out of Canada', did not spend his brief time in Canada in the wilderness but with the Loyalist forces in Lower Canada during the Rebellion of 1837.

Ballantyne began his long and highly successful career as a writer of adventure stories for boys with two 'Canadian' books: *Snowflakes and Sunbeams; or the Young Fur Traders* (1856), later republished as *The Young Fur Traders*, and *Ungava: A Tale of Esquimaux-Land* (1858). He had spent six years (1841-7) working for the Hudson's Bay Company, which he joined when he was sixteen, in the Northwest (later on the St Lawrence) and had an affinity for the vast lands he served in. *The Young Fur Traders* shows most clearly and happily what it was like to be young when Canada was young. Its old-fashioned style and Christian ethos do not diminish its exuberant quality, especially in the portrayal of the young hero, who kicks over his accountant's stool for the freedom of the wilderness. Ballantyne seems to be saying 'Boys will be boys.' His considerable influence on the adventure story—in Canada as well as Britain—lasted well into the present century.

When the first contributions of the settlers appeared they were meagre and predictable. Philip Henry Gosse, the English naturalist who spent some years in Newfoundland and then farmed briefly in Lower Canada, produced *The Canadian Naturalist: A Series of Conversations on the Natural History of Lower Canada* (1840). The information is presented as a dialogue between the omniscient adult and young Charles, thirsty for knowledge, a standard format in English informational books of the period. A similar but less intrusive technique is used in *Little Grace; or, Scenes in Nova-Scotia* (1846) by an unknown Miss Grove, in which a little girl learns the history of her province. The first Canadian children's magazine *The Snow Drop* (1847-53), and its short-lived competitor *The Maple Leaf* (1852-4), contain the obligatory moral and religious tales and indifferent verse and could just as easily have been published in London as in Montreal. Canadian content consists chiefly of snippets of history and animal lore. The serialization of *Uncle Tom's Cabin* in *The Maple*

Leaf adds a welcome amount of drama and emotion to an otherwise bland publication.

While these little periodicals did not break new ground, they provided an outlet for local writers such as Susanna Moodie (the author of *Roughing it in the Bush*) and her sister Catharine Parr Traill, to whom belongs the honour of writing the first Canadian children's novel. Its title, *Canadian Crusoes* (1852), is an open declaration of its subject-matter as well as a salute to the greatest survival story of all time, Daniel Defoe's *Robinson Crusoe* (1719). Its sub-title, *A Tale of the Rice Lake Plains*, indicates its setting—the Ontario town of Cobourg and the unexplored forest that spread to the north and west behind it.

Although the setting is not as exotic as that of a desert island, *Canadian Crusoes* contains the irresistible stuff of the isolation story: the procuring of food, shelter, and clothing and the need for protection against the elements, wild animals, and unfriendly natives. It also has three young characters (two fourteen-year-old boys and a twelve-year-old girl, all cousins) who conduct themselves with the same courage and equanimity as the great Crusoe and look for the same spiritual guidance. The book was later republished with the title *Lost in the Backwoods* and, in 1923, reappeared with its original title. Its descent into oblivion is probably due to its flowery nineteenth-century style (Defoe's plain eighteenth-century diction still appeals to the modern ear); however, in 1986 it was reissued in a scholarly edition, edited by Rupert Schieder for the Centre for Editing Early Canadian Texts.

Traill's potential as a novelist for children, which *Canadian Crusoes* hinted at, was dimmed in her next two books as she reverted to English conventions of the time. In *Lady Mary and Her Nurse; or, A Peep into Canadian Forests* (1856) an English child questions her nurse about life in the Canadian woods. Its one appealing—probably unintentional—childlike note comes at the end of the second chapter when Lady Mary says: 'Indeed, nurse, I have learned a great deal about squirrels, Canadian rice, otters and Indians; but, if you please, I must now have a little play with my doll.' Traill's *Cot and Cradle Stories* (1895), edited by her great-niece, is a mish-mash of nature stories, heavily laden with anthropomorphism—again a characteristic of the period.

Our first major Canadian-born writer, James De Mille, gave children an opportunity to see more of Canadian life than the forests and pioneer ways of Upper and Lower Canada. He drew upon his personal knowledge of a boys' boarding school in Nova Scotia and his own youthful adventures around the Minas Basin in the Bay of Fundy for *The B.O.W.C.* (Brethren of the White Cross), the first book in a series, published in 1869. Other titles are *The Boys of Grande Pré School* (1871), *Lost in the Fog* (1870), *Fire in the Woods* (1871), *Picked Up Adrift* (1872), and *The Treasure of the Seas* (1873). These are insouciant stories of boy life, carefree and amusing, as opposed to the usual survival stories that concentrated on the cult of 'manliness', and they are noticeably free from didacticism, both religious and instructional. It is interesting that the school story appeared in Canada considerably before it became so popular in England, constituting a separate genre of the realistic story. The famous *Boys' Own Paper*, which glorified the schoolboy (and manliness), did not begin publication until 1879. De Mille's boys do not live by the Christian ethics of Tom in Thomas Hughes' *Tom Brown's School Days* (1857), nor do they display the intellectualism—and cruelty—of Rudyard Kipling's schoolboy trio in *Stalky and Co.* (1899). De Mille, however, did indulge in typical stereotypes of the time. The boys have a flunky, a stupid but good-natured 'darky' who always had to be rescued from some disaster but who could produce a delectable meal under the most adverse circumstances. Their other companion in their adventures is an equally obtuse sea captain who is always at their beck and call in his unseaworthy boat *The Antelope*.

Like his contemporaries, whether they wrote for children or adults, De Mille provides accurate and lovingly described backgrounds that draw upon personal knowledge. His style gives rise to the greatest surprise; it is chiefly staccato and conversational, quite in keeping with his boyish characters and unusual for its time. The Young Dodge Club series—*Among the Brigands* (1872), *The Seven Hills* (1873), *The Winged Lion* (1877)—in which an ineffectual adult tries to act as a tour guide for a contingent of schoolboys, was based on De Mille's travels in Italy. These books, however, lack the sure-footedness and authenticity of his Canadian-based stories.

While De Mille extended the light-hearted tone of *The Young Fur Traders*, James MacDonald Oxley, a native of Halifax, wrote simple, straightforward adventure stories with such titles as *Up Among the Ice Floes* (1890) and *The Wreckers of Sable Island* (1894), in which the physical environment is a testing-ground for the young heroes. But they do not have De Mille's contemporary ring. Oxley's only claim to importance now is as proof that it was possible to live in Canada in the nineteenth century and make a living by one's pen.

Unlike De Mille and Oxley, who wrote primarily to entertain, Egerton Ryerson Young, an Ontario Methodist minister, was as keen a religious proselytizer as any writer of the English Evangelical school. Nevertheless, his experiences as a missionary and his knowledge of Indians, combined with his obvious love for life in the Northwest, appeared to keep his Christian uplift in check. Spirited adventure is the main thrust of his *Three Boys in the Wild North Land, Summer* (1896), in which an English boy, a Scottish boy, and an Irish boy (artful conjunction) spend some time in Canada as the guests of a former member of the Hudson's Bay Company. *Winter Adventures of Three Boys in the Great Lone Land* (1899) is a sequel. *Children of the Forest: A Story of Indian Love* (1904) has an unusual and absorbing plot with a Romeo and Juliet motif; only towards the end of the story does Young remember his missionary purpose and hastily convert a tribe or two.

No development was shown in the boy's adventure story in nineteenth-century Canada. Such works as C. Phillipps-Wolley's *Gold, Gold, in Cariboo: A Story of Adventure in British Columbia* (1894) or John Burnham's *Jack Ralston; or, The Outbreak of the Nauscopees: A Tale of Life in the Far North* (1901) are realistic enough in their settings but extremely wooden in characterization and predictable in plot. Poet Marjorie Pickthall's attempts at boy's adventure stories, *Dick's Desertion* (1905) and *Billy's Hero* (1908), are as flat and uninspired as their titles.

The most noticeable characteristic of early Canadian children's books—whether written by absentees, visitors, settlers, or those 'born in the briar patch'—and one that distinguishes them from early English children's books, is a fascination with, and a love and respect for, the land itself. This was well expressed by Frances Brooke, who wrote in her *History of Emily Montague* of the 'thousand wild graces which mock the cultivated beauties of Europe'. While the English landscape had a defining quality in many major adult works, such as the moors in Emily Brontë's *Wuthering Heights* or the county of Dorset in Thomas Hardy's novels, only Charles Kingsley in *The Water-Babies* (1863) made the natural world an integral part of a children's story as opposed to a lesson in nature. In nineteenth-century Canada, however, the setting becomes almost the most important part of the story. As Northrop Frye has said of Canadian literature in general, early writers tried to make novels out of 'knowledge and observation, but had no story in particular to tell'; their material did not come to them in the form of a story, 'but as a consolidated chunk of experience, reflection and sensibility'. The pouring of the 'new wine of content into the old bottles of form' had to wait for writers in the modern era, such as James Houston or Monica Hughes, who at times perceive the landscape in metaphorical terms.

Yet if not great storytellers, writers such as Marryat, Ballantyne, Traill, De Mille, and Young evoked a spirit of youthful freedom in their characters. It is no accident that all the English boys' adventure stories of the nineteenth century were set in the colonies or on exotic desert islands. Class-conscious England was no place for younger sons or for those intent on improving their lot in life. But in Canada's forests, fields, and rivers only skill, courage, and ingenuity counted—not birth and breeding. Moreover, the youthful protagonists are at home in their environments; they exhibit none of the 'garrison mentality' of Frye's observation, nor do they fit into Margaret Atwood's 'survival' theory. If the wilderness provides danger and drama, it can also be benign and fruitful, as Ballantyne described it in *The Young Fur Traders:*

> All nature was joyous and brilliant, and bright and beautiful. Morning was still very young—about an hour old. Sounds of the most cheerful, light-hearted character floated over the waters, echoed through the woods, as birds and beasts hurried to and fro with all the bustling energy that betokened preparation and search for breakfast.

Catharine Parr Traill's young trio do not despair at their plight but turn their energies to storing up food for the winter. Even Miss Grove's Little Grace shows more spirit than most English girls as she thoughtfully questions what she had been told about the expulsion of the Acadians.

All in all, nineteenth-century Canadian children's books were less pietistic than their English counterparts; the exigencies of the natural world take precedence over the spiritual one. Philip Gosse's young Charles and Traill's Lady Mary may get more information about nature than they want, but unlike English children they are subjected neither to sermons nor to the anthropomorphism that are so evident in Mrs Gatty's *Parables From Nature* (1855). Still, despite their relatively liberated tone, no nineteenth-century Canadian children's book has leapt the time barrier into the modern age. Characterization, plot, and a strong moral stance—as exhibited by the American writers Louisa May Alcott in *Little Women* (1868) and Mark Twain in *The Adventures of Tom Sawyer* (1876)—are more enduring than setting.

The greatest change in children's literature took place in England in the middle of the Victorian era when a wave of fantasy arrived, which became an irresistible force—Charles Kingsley's *The Water-Babies*, Lewis Carroll's *Alice* books, and the works of George MacDonald allowed children the release of their imaginations and proved that children's literature could be *literature*. It is not surprising that fantasy did not take root in the frontier society of Canada. No other country produced anything even comparable to the great English fantasies—except for the later, and inexplicable, appearance of Collodi's *Pinocchio* (1883) in Italy.

In the first two decades of the twentieth century sentimentality towards the young was the most obvious characteristic displayed by children's writers in England, the United States, and Canada. It was the age of 'sweetness and light', a phrase of Jonathan Swift's used by Matthew Arnold in *Culture and Anarchy* and by the English critic Edward Salmon, who wanted more sentiment in books for the young. He would have been delighted with the Edwardian penchant for angelic heroines. In strong contrast to the books for boys of some sixty years before, there came a flood of books with girls as the chief protagonists: from the United States *Rebecca of Sunnybrook Farm* (1903), *A Girl of the Limberlost* (1909), and *Pollyanna* (1913); and from England *The Secret Garden* (1911), among many others. In these rhapsodic narratives the young heroines not only solve their own serious difficulties by their incredible charm, but eventually those of all the adults around them.

Canadians eagerly contributed to this wave. Our first sentimental 'hit' was about a dog rather than a child. *Beautiful Joe* (1894) by the prolific Nova Scotia writer Marshall Saunders, was cast in the form of the famous English *Black Beauty* (1877), in that a mistreated dog relates the story of his life, just as Anna Sewell's horse tells of his fortunes and misfortunes. Like its forerunner, *Beautiful Joe* made a tremendous impact on its wide audience and did much for the prevention of cruelty to animals. However, even its popularity was insignificant in comparison with L.M. Montgomery's *Anne of Green Gables* (1908), still our best-known children's book. Of all the girl heroines of the Edwardian era, Anne was to be the only one with staying power. Eighty years later the red-headed orphan from Prince Edward Island is even popular in Japan and has gained new audiences through television adaptations of the Anne books. Her despairs and triumphs have been re-enacted yearly in Charlottetown since 1965 in a musical based on the first book. *Anne's* seven sequels, written under pressure from Montgomery's publisher, never capture its freshness, originality, and humour, but they are still devoured by adoring fans around the world.

Twelve-year-old Pearlie Watson of Nellie McClung's *Sowing Seeds in Danny* (1908) is closely related to Pollyanna. The daughter of a poor section-hand in a town in Manitoba, she goes into domestic service to repay her father's debt and with her lovable nature conquers everyone she meets. Thanks to her a young doctor faces up to his responsibilities, an old doctor is rescued from habitual drunkenness, and into her young brother, Danny, are sown the seeds of goodness. Like her contemporary, Ralph Connor, McClung wove her strong beliefs into her episodic plot. She was active in temperance and suffragette organizations and both causes are evident in *Sowing Seeds in Danny*, along with her militant Christianity: the local children, though enticed by gifts of candy to attend Sunday School, never know on which Sunday the treat will be distributed.

Ralph Connor (the pseudonym of the Reverend Charles William Gordon) did not write specifically for children, but his *Glengarry Schooldays* (1902) had enough childhood scenes in it to make it part of the then small stock of Canadian children's books. Excerpts from it were printed in school readers for many years after its publication. The scenes of school and pioneer life in Glengarry County, Ontario—the spelling-bee, the swimming hole, 'sugaring off', barn-raisings, and other social customs of pioneer days—have an authentic ring. The force and emotion of the book come from Connor's arrant proselytizing and particularly from his idealization of womanhood, evident in his portrayal of the minister's wife Mrs Murray.

Montgomery, McClung, and Connor wrote out of their own experiences as Canadians, but because their sentimental tone matched the mood of the times, their works crossed international borders to an extent that has probably not been matched since. They also had an eye for their environment: Connor for the towns and countryside of the Ottawa Valley, McClung for the small towns and farms of Manitoba, while Montgomery exulted (often to a tiresome extent) in the beauties of Prince Edward Island. They also provided their readers with a rare opportunity to see Canada as something more than a wilderness or 'a few acres of snow'. Most noticeable, in comparison with the typical boys' outdoor adventure story, were their insights into the adult world, which in other children's books of the era were seldom more than shadowy. Montgomery in particular had an eye and an ear for the eccentric adult and the social milieu of a small country town.

While these three writers were working the rich lode of sentimentality, the traditional pioneer characteristics of observation, reportage, and first-hand knowledge of wild life were presented in an intensified form in the works of Ernest Thompson Seton and Charles G.D. Roberts. With Seton's *Wild Animals I Have Known* (1898) and Roberts' *The Kindred of the Wild* (1902) a new genre was formed—the realistic animal biography. Quite distinct from the talking-animal tales of Marshall Saunders, the new form was to be Canada's major contribution to world literature.

Roberts' and Seton's animal stories appealed to both adults and children. Seton's one book deliberately written for the young, *Two Little Savages* (1903), is in many ways the apotheosis of the outdoor adventure story. His two boy heroes, Sam and Yan (Seton himself), are archetypal Canadian boys of the period who play at being Indians. But the play is serious, and the knowledge the boys gain from it will serve them in their adult life. Seton was an idealist who loved to learn concrete skills and to impart his knowledge to others. As a naturalist and conservationist he was a forerunner of such writers of the modern period as Roderick Haig-Brown, Farley Mowat, and James Houston, who brought the environmental story to new heights.

Norman Duncan's *The Adventures of Billy Topsail* (1906) achieved considerable popularity in its time, chiefly because Billy's adventures on the waters and coasts of Newfoundland were dramatic. Episodes from the book were reprinted in school readers, and generations of Canadian children grew up knowing about Billy's escape from the giant squid and the loyalty and bravery of his Newfoundland dog. Although Duncan was only an intermittent visitor to Newfoundland, he captured the essential qualities that enable men to face the sea and wrest a living from it. At the end of the story Billy has passed the tests of manhood; his rites of passage are over and he is accepted as a full member of the crew. Duncan followed this with several other juveniles, including two more Billy Topsail books. But Billy in the first book is the most memorable of the hundreds of young males who move through the early outdoor adventure story, whether Canadian or British. In his appealing boyish qualities he is akin to Twain's Tom Sawyer and, as with Tom, it is almost with reluctance that we see him enter manhood.

Only a few books of the next thirty years are worthy of mention, but they are significant in heralding a concern with Indian and Inuit culture. Native peoples were certainly not neglected in early adventure stories; nineteenth-century writers treated them with respect as woodsmen and guides and frequently allowed them to mock the ineptitude of the white men. But their beliefs, tales, and legends did not make an impact on writers for children until Cyrus Macmillan, born in Prince Edward Island and a professor of English at McGill, collected and retold many of them in *Canadian Wonder Tales* (1918) and *Canadian Fairy Tales* (1922). The titles are indicative of the romantic European flavour of his retelling of indigenous tales—a convention of the time. But until the 1960s Macmillan's tales were the only examples of Indian legends with child appeal.

It remained for Archibald Stansfeld Belaney—an Englishman living in Canada who posed as a full-blooded Indian under the name of Grey Owl—to present a portrait of an Indian child as emotional as that of Johanna Spyri's Swiss child in *Heidi* (1884) or of Anne in Montgomery's *Anne of Green Gables. The Adventures of Sajo and Her*

Beaver People (1935) has a strong dose of realism—Grey Owl was both a naturalist and a conservationist—but it also contains a mystic quality in Sajo's love for her beaver pets, in their love for one another, and in the harmony between the natural and the human worlds. With its emotional power and an exciting plot, it is a Canadian children's classic.

In 1947 the Canadian Library Association established the Book-of-the Year for Children Award. The scarcity of first-rate writing for the young in the late 1940s and early 1950s can be deduced from the fact that no awards were given in the years 1949 and 1951 or from 1953 to 1956. Still, until the 1960s this was an era of some notable firsts. With *Starbuck Valley Winter* (1943), and its sequel *Saltwater Summer* (1948), Roderick L. Haig-Brown added depth to the survival story by producing the first outdoor tales to show a young protagonist with genuine personal problems whose character, as well as his skills and abilities, developed under his ordeals. Like Haig-Brown, Farley Mowat with *Lost in the Barrens* (1956) and James Houston with *Tikta'Liktak* (1965) and *The White Archer* (1967) also realized that strongly drawn characters remain alive in the reader's mind long after vivid descriptions and ingenious plots have been forgotten. Together they brought the survival story into the modern age.

In 1950 fantasy, animated by the mountainous terrain of the Kootenays in British Columbia and by Indian lore, at long last came stepping lightly into our literature. Catherine Anthony Clark was our first major fantasist, writing six books, from *The Golden Pine Cone* (1950) to *The Hunter and the Medicine Man* (1966). Rather than taking her models from the great English fantasies of the Victorian age or of the recent past, she found her inspiration in her own surroundings. Her books are not only uniquely Canadian but are imbued with Indian values.

Tales of pioneer life or of woodsmen, fishermen, explorers, or miners frequently offered dramatic conflict, but except for a few isolated episodes, provided very little humour. This void was filled, almost single-handedly, by Farley Mowat, whose *The Dog Who Wouldn't Be* (1957) and *Owls in the Family* (1961) added this much-needed ingredient to children's fiction. With these semi-autobiographical tales of his boyhood in Saskatchewan and the family pets—the super-canine Mutt, and the eccentric owls Wol and Weeps—Mowat proved himself a natural humorist, one who sees the wry and the incongruous (and even the sad) aspects of life in tandem with the hilarious. No later writer has matched the childlike style of this low-keyed, immensely skilled raconteur.

There were significant other 'firsts' in the 1950s. A selection of French-Canadian legends, collected by the anthropologist Marius Barbeau, were adapted by Michael Hornyansky and published as *The Golden Phoenix and Other French-Canadian Fairy Tales* (1958). Although the stories were more French than Canadian in ambience, their popularity with English-speaking children began a stream of retellings and adaptations of old tales from all cultures that proliferated into the 1980s.

Canada's historical past came to the fore with the fictionalized 'Great Stories of Canada' series and with the historical fiction of John Hayes. The series (by various authors) and Hayes' works were both laudable for clothing historical events in drama as well as historicity. Formula writing, unfortunately, eventually overwhelmed the series; and John Hayes' books, such as *Buckskin Colonist* (1947) and *Bugles in the Hills* (1955), concentrated on a recitation of events to the neglect of a strong fictional component.

By the middle of the 1960s realistic fiction for children, in particular that emanating from the United States, had undergone a dramatic and drastic change. At the root of it were the turbulent social upheavals of the decade in America, adult changes in attitudes towards children (they were to be liberated from the constrictions of childhood), and the increasing influence of television on the young. In children's literature this meant a change in themes from the convention of the adventure story to stories that dealt with children's problems involving the adult world—divorce, disappearing parents, drugs, alcoholism, teen-age pregnancy, child abuse, and other problems. Indeed 'problem novel' was the name given to this type of fiction, which was also called, more gently, the 'new realism'. Such novels featured mainly faceless urban settings—locales were given a minimum of description. The style was usually conversational, staccato, banal, and frequently arch, with touches of American TV sit-com humour. Richer novels of realism were being published, of course, but they were far outweighed by the problem novels, which subsequently affected all types of fiction for the young.

For about a decade and a half (until the late 1970s)—whether from conviction, isolation, or conservatism—Canadian writers stood aloof from the new concepts of realism. While American children, as seen through their books, were coping with ineffectual parents, no parents, one parent, being unhappy, growing up, tuning in, dropping out, or coping with drugs, alcoholism, homosexuality, or racism, Canadian children were still seeing themselves in their books of child life as having adventures in the out-of-doors. Unlike their American counterparts, they were portrayed as being singularly happy, puzzlingly cheerful, everlastingly lucky, and strongly extroverted; they had never heard of an identity crisis and did not feel alienated from the adult world. Actually, few Canadian writers even attempted books of contemporary child life and those that were published were eminently forgettable, except for Jean Little's stories of friendship and family life.

Most major Canadian writers at this time found their inspiration in quintessentially Canadian subjects—the Indians, the Inuit, and our early history. At the beginning of the 1960s a small but vigorous group of retellers demonstrated their skills of selection and interpretation of Indian material and made literature out of a large, unwieldy, diverse mass of oral lore hitherto locked within the pages of anthropological studies or in the memories of the Indians themselves. Storytellers such as Robert Ayre, Christie Harris, Dorothy Reid, Frances Fraser, Kay Hill, and William Toye brought Indian legends into our national consciousness, and in so doing broke the cultural barrier that had kept them in a separate stream of the oral tradition. The first book of legends specifically written for children by an Indian appeared in 1967. This was George Clutesi's *Son of Raven, Son of Deer: Fables of the Tse-Shaht People*, a grouping of tales that had been handed down in his family for four hundred years. The most memorable historical fiction was set in the Indian past: Edith Sharp's *Nkwala* (1958), Roderick L. Haig-Brown's *The Whale People* (1962), and Christie Harris's *Raven's Cry* (1966). Also for the first time Inuit legends were made appealing to children through Ronald Melzak's Europeanized tales in *The Day Tuk Became a Hunter and Other Eskimo Stories* (1967).

With the exception of Indian legends and the survival story, which showed itself capable of endless variations, other genres advanced only sporadically, as in the past. Still, there were a few fine individual works that, with hindsight, can now be seen as heralds of change. For example, Ruth Nichols introduced epic fantasy into Canada with *A Walk Out of the World* (1969) and *The Marrow of the World* (1972), which integrate Canadian settings with imported archetypal figures from English fantasy and the symbolic conflict between good and evil.

Distinguished colour illustration arrived in the glowing collages of Elizabeth Cleaver for *The Wind Has Wings* (1968), a collection of Canadian poetry compiled by Mary Alice Downie and Barbara Robertson. The combination of Cleaver's collages and simple retellings by William Toye in *The Mountain Goats of Temlaham* (1969) and *How Summer Came to Canada* (1969) gave us our first single illustrated legends. This picturebook format, widely used in the United States and England, quickly became popular in Canada and today a great number of single illustrated tales from a variety of countries reflect our multicultural society. The dearth of illustration for our literature had inevitably meant a lack of picturebooks. The single Indian tale in picturebook format helped to fill this lacuna until the early 1970s, when picture-storybooks (books that were similar to the picturebook but with a longer text) came along. *Mary of Mile 18* (1971), by the British Columbia author/illustrator Ann Blades, was almost an instant bestseller and soon made its way onto the international stage, along with the paintings and simple texts of the Manitoban artist William Kurelek in *A Prairie Boy's Winter* (1973) and *A Prairie Boy's Summer* (1975).

Another fresh arrival in the period came from Dennis Lee, an award-winning poet, who turned his talents to writing nonsense verse for children. In *Alligator Pie* (1974) and *Nicholas Knock and Other People* (1974), as well as in later collections, he frequently combined nursery and children's street-lore with Canadian urban images, thus bringing a joyous, sometimes rowdy tone to a hitherto bland area of our children's literature.

The greatest change since the mid-1970s has been in the almost overnight arrival of books for the pre-school child and the beginning reader. Picturebooks have moved from almost zero level to a veritable flood. These include such sub-genres as ABC books, bilingual books, board books, counting books, concept books, and the traditional storytelling ones, all of which, even in the recent past, had heretofore been known only in the form of imports. Their illustrators, taken together, have made use of almost every conceivable medium, technique, and art style, chiefly in vibrant colour.

The novel for young adults (generally so categorized by the age of its protagonists) also came into prominence and has joined its counterparts in other English-speaking countries in concentrating on adolescents in conflict with themselves and those around them, or caught in a traumatic moment in their lives. Much of the new fantasy also falls into the sphere of the young-adult novel. In general, books of fantasy have increased in numbers and show evidence of themes also used by writers in England and the United States, such as some form of extrasensory perception or possession by an alien influence. Again, in keeping with writing trends in the US and England, few novels are being written for middle-aged children between eight and eleven, for whom *The Moffats* (1941), *Charlotte's Web* (1952), and *The Borrowers* (1952) were intended. Most writers appear to need the freedom of adolescent life to propound their messages; they seem unwilling or unable to manoeuvre within the restrictions of childhood. Significant exceptions here are Cora Taylor's *Julie* (1985), Bernice Thurman Hunter's *Lamplighter* (1987), and some of Barbara Smucker's historical fiction.

Canada's multicultural society is increasingly reflected not only in retellings of the oral tradition but in picturebooks, realistic fiction, and historical fiction. Such books are understandably written by home-grown Canadians or former immigrants rather than by recent arrivals to this country. There is little doubt, however, that this segment of writing will increase to the point where the presentation of various cultures will no longer be considered ethnic but simply Canadian.

An interesting development in historical fiction has been a concentration on our recent rather than our distant past. Such books as *One Proud Summer* (1981) by Marsha Hewitt and Claire Mackay (the Valleyfield Strike of 1946) and *The Curses of Third Uncle* (1986) by Paul Yee (a glimpse into Chinese immigrant life in the early twentieth century) are more concerned with social history than with large-scale drama (such as the Riel Rebellion) and certainly should do much to make today's young interested in their past.

A strong sense of place still dominates our best realistic fiction, especially the outdoor survival story, such as Jan Truss's *Jasmin* (1982) or Monica Hughes' *Hunter in the Dark* (1982); but it is less obvious in the newer poetry, fantasy, or even picturebooks, with the great exception of the regional titles from the publishing firm of Tundra Books in Montreal. A sense of regional identity is also less obvious in the new social realism with urban or semi-urban settings.

It hardly needs to be said that Canadian children's literature has changed greatly since Catharine Parr Traill, in *Canadian Crusoes*, set the scene for three children lost in an Ontario wilderness in the nineteenth century who survive with courage, dignity, and ingenuity and who look to spiritual guidance whenever they are downcast. Today's writers are as much a part of their time as Traill was of hers, and their books reflect this, being more concerned with personal crises in the lives of their protagonists than physical ones, and with emphasizing, existentially, their determination to succeed. Such themes now appear to be universal in children's literature. Our children's books have become more sophisticated, more distinguished, and less parochial. But even though they have joined the 'republic of childhood' in spirit, many of the best are as distinctively Canadian as our earlier literature.

2

Realistic Fiction

Canadian children's literature began with realistic fiction and it continues to be the staple of juvenile literature here, as in other countries, chiefly because it encompasses such varied sub-genres: outdoor adventure stories, stories of child and family life, mystery stories, school stories, animal stories, and other less easily classifiable works that can simply be called light realism.

In spite of this range, the novels in all these categories have attributes in common: the attempt to emulate real life in some of its particular aspects by selecting and ordering the often random experiences of actual daily existence so as to give the tale credibility. This aim can be found (to a greater or lesser degree) in works as varied as Catharine Parr Traill's outdoor survival story, *Canadian Crusoes* (1852), L.M. Montgomery's picture of a Prince Edward Island girlhood, *Anne of Green Gables* (1908), Brian Doyle's almost surrealistic *Angel Square* (1984), and Kit Pearson's account of boarding-school life in *The Daring Game* (1986). But the best realistic fiction steps beyond the recording and ordering of the minutiae that provide a sense of reality to create in the reader a genuine emotional response to what is portrayed.

Because realistic fiction is based in contemporary life—that is, within the period of the author's own experience—it tends to date more quickly than any other type of fiction, becoming to later generations more-or-less period pieces. But life is a continuum, even though the reality of one generation is not that of another. Although Louisa May Alcott's *Little Women* (1868), set during the American Civil War, was written as a family story, almost a memoir of Alcott's own girlhood, its emotional heart continues to speak to modern children of their own feelings. The clothing and the customs described may be somewhat alien, but Jo's battle for independence is not. Montgomery's *Anne*, set about two decades later, has lasted for many of the same reasons: strong characterization, the heroine's sheer lovableness, and a sharp look at adults and small-town community relationships that have probably not changed all that much.

Alcott and Montgomery offered more than mere verisimilitude. By contrast, Mrs Traill's brand of realism consisted chiefly of a conscientious attention to detail. She falls into Northrop Frye's category of writers whose material did not come to them in the form of a story but 'as a consolidated chunk of experience, reflection and sensibility'. This ingredient can certainly produce a novel that interests its contemporary audience, but not one that can leap the boundaries of space and time. It is in the lack of emotional reality that *Canadian Crusoes* fails as a novel. We know a great deal about its young protagonists from the external evidence Mrs Traill provided, but she endows them with characteristics rather than character, and so we are not deeply moved by their experiences, as we are by those of Jo and Anne.

As a description of fiction of contemporary life for children, the term 'realistic' did not surface until after 1960. Earlier books tended to be referred to by their dominant characteristic: adventure, domestic, school, mystery stories, etc. They were also sharply divided between books for boys and girls. These distinctions have lessened over the years, although they still exist. Today's stories of contemporary life are generally subsumed under the rubric of realism and, more specifically, social realism.

In most modern works we see the young in turmoil—with themselves, their parents (or the lack thereof), their situations— struggling to make order out of the chaos that surrounds them, and growing up in the process. The harsh social realism that imbues so much recent fiction for the young doubtless impelled the English writer of children's books, Nina Bawden, to comment that 'Realism . . . has latterly, and rather sadly, come to mean to most people writing about the unpleasant side of life.' Bawden is basically correct in her estimation of modern realistic fiction for the young, but she neglects to mention the naïve honesty, courage, determination, and sensitivity with which most fine writers endow their young protagonists. While they tend to explore 'problems', both factual and emotional, they also write with a sense of moral responsibility, as Brian Doyle does in his humorous attack on racism in *Angel Square* and as Kit Pearson does in her quieter interpretation of personal integrity in *The Daring Game*.

All types of fiction can contribute to an understanding of the many facets of life, but more than any other, realistic fiction can provide full-bodied, unforgettable human portraits—characters with whom the young can empathize and recognize as imaginary companions.

THE OUTDOOR SURVIVAL STORY

While the boundaries of realistic fiction have broadened in the last forty years, the outdoor survival story still holds a firm position in Canadian children's literature, although it is no longer central. Still, there are many modern writers for whom a physical setting plays a traditional and important role. The Canadian landscape provides an impetus for plot, a strong sense of regionalism, a threat of physical danger, and opportunities for acts of heroism, intrepidness, and selflessness. The protagonists in such novels more truly deserve to be called heroes (heroines to a lesser degree) than those in any other type of realistic fiction. Yet heroism comes in many guises, and as an aspect of life as well as literature, it is often explored more subtly in the newer survival stories than in those of the past. So too is the role of the landscape. In the newer works it is sometimes used, symbolically and metaphorically, as a participating force in the events. But above all, the survival story has come to concentrate, as has most realistic fiction, on character development and the personal problems of the chief protagonist, rather than on adventure. This change did not come suddenly; it was heralded in a few books published after the turn of the century and before the 1940s.

Ernest Thompson Seton's *Two Little Savages: Being the Adventures of Two Boys Who Lived as Indians and What They Learned* (1903)—a semi-autobiographical account of Seton's own childhood near Lindsay, Ontario—has an intimate quality that is quite lacking in conventional outdoor stories, both those of an earlier era and those of the next few decades. There are no dangerous situations; not even wild animals are a threat. The two boys, later joined by other children, are *playing* at being Indians and learn woodlore, woodcraft, and survival skills, much of the information being imparted or demonstrated by helpful adults and made concrete by Seton's accurate marginal drawings. In treating play as a preparation for adult life, *Two Little Savages* was ahead of its time. The idea of children having fun while they learned did not really take hold until the English writer Arthur Ransome, in his *Swallows and Amazons* (1930) and its sequels, portrayed active, responsible children camping and sailing on their own. (In the Ransome books there is also a strong sense of the transmission of skills from the older to the younger generation.) Though *Two Little Savages* was available until 1970, it is no longer in print in Canada. Its demise may be due to its title. The arch use of the now-opprobrious 'savages' belongs to a time of great insensitivity to natives. The author admired them, and his intention was to praise their skills, not denigrate their character.

Norman Duncan's *The Adventures of Billy Topsail* (1906) was another indicator of change, with its strongly emotional tone that is not entirely due to its numerous cliff-hanging situations. Duncan may have been a mere visitor to Newfoundland, but he was able to convey not only the dangers but the courage, comradeship, and skills of the men who wrest a living from the sea.

Although there is a terrifying forest-fire scene in Grey Owl's *Sajo and Her Beaver People* (1935), from which the children escape while still caring for their pet beaver, it is not basically a story of the challenges of the wilderness. The Indian family are at one with their environment. Sajo is a lonely, motherless, sensitive child who pours all her love into caring for the two beaver kittens given to her by her father on her birthday. Lively Chilawee and his quieter, more loving brother Chikanee, become the centre of Sajo's life. When the father sells Chikanee to a zoo to provide food for his children, Sajo is inconsolable. Then, in a foreshadowing of Indian spirit guides who play a major role in several modern books, of both realism and fantasy, she seems to hear her dead mother's voice:

'Sajo, Sajo,
You must go.
To the city
You must go.'

The rescue of Chikanee is accomplished through the courage, skills, and determination of Sajo and her brother, but also through the help of kindly and understanding adults. When the beavers are eventually restored to their natural habitat, Sajo, who has come to understand the rhythm of the natural world, is content. *Sajo and Her Beaver People* has a mystical quality in its linking of the human, animal, and natural worlds, a characteristic that does not appear again until the survival stories of the 1980s.

Roderick L. Haig-Brown, with *Starbuck Valley Winter* (1943) and *Saltwater Summer* (1948), can now be seen as a trend-setter in his break with earlier stories that were simply adventurous—such as C. Phillipps-Wolley's *Gold, Gold in Cariboo!* (1894)—and those that came to be more concerned with the inner feelings of their characters than with external events. His hero, Don Morgan, has personal problems that will affect the eventual development of his life. He is an orphan, living with his aunt and uncle on a farm on Vancouver Island. At age sixteen he wishes to leave school and spend a winter trapping in order to make enough money to buy his own fishing boat. This is contrary to the wishes of his aunt, who feels that any man without a steady job (preferably in the local mill) will become a drifter. Don proves capable in his chosen venture, but his winter's trapping comes into jeopardy when he has to leave his traplines, in a race against time, to canoe and portage his injured friend and partner, Tubby, to the hospital. His winter's work is saved, thanks to an old prospector whom Don had befriended against Tubby's advice.

The complexities of Don's character are clarified in *Saltwater Summer* as he quarrels with Tubby, falls into bad company, and even breaks the law. He also has to consider if he might be better suited to life as a trapper than as a fisherman, and even if he should return to school. Here Haig-Brown approaches the theme of survival more subtly than in *Starbuck Valley Winter*. Don basically succeeds as a fisherman, but more because of the help of his friends than through his own skills; and his path to maturity is shown as a process of development, not as a melodramatic change of heart, as is so often the case in modern realistic novels. There is a sense of real time passing in both books. Haig-Brown's talents were not confined to the portrayal of his two main teenage heroes, Don and Tubby. The adults are also given depth of character, even in their cameo appearances. In *Saltwater Summer* the fishermen are strongly differentiated and given motivations for their actions. They are not the shadowy adults found in most children's books of the period.

Both *Starbuck Valley Winter* and *Saltwater Summer* were obviously inspired by a feeling for particular places—British Columbia's forest lands and the ocean that washes its coastline. Knowledge and skills are necessary for survival in the occupations that are a part of such environments, and Haig-Brown could impart the niceties of trapping, skinning a buck, making a water-wheel, canoeing, trolling, and seining, without veering into pedagogy. Haig-Brown more than sees; he feels and understands as well. He says of Don Morgan that 'He looked at everything, trying to use it and make it his own.' In their details of survival, *Starbuck Valley Winter* and *Saltwater Summer* are *real* books, as Defoe's *Robinson Crusoe* is real.

Farley Mowat's adventure stories—like those of Seton, Grey Owl, and Haig-Brown—appear to be an inevitable outcome of a passion for the world of nature. But Mowat's are at once more conventionally adventurous than those of Haig-Brown and less thoroughly realistic. *Lost in the Barrens* (1956) recounts the experiences of a white boy, Jamie, and an Indian boy, Awasin, who become 'lost in the barrens' of northern Canada. Encountering every test the North can impose upon them, they suffer near-starvation and snow-blindness; they fight to the death with a grizzly bear, and with almost unbearable suspense they miss by a hair's-breadth the Indian band they were supposed to join for the return journey to camp. They survive it all by learning from one another.

Mowat's chief strength lies in the breathless suspense he gives to his tale. The boys almost reel from crisis to crisis. But he is far too good a writer, and knows the North too well, to strain credibility completely in the interests of narrative (though he did so in the sequel, *The Curse of the Viking Grave*, 1966). Beneath the overlay of adventure there is always the solid substance of the North itself, and the character it imposes on those who live there. The crux of the story lies in an idea, rather than in an event: one must conform to the laws of the North rather than fight them.

The harsh economic facts of life in the Newfoundland outports in the 1930s give a strong sense of reality to Mowat's *The Black Joke* (1962). Once these are established, Mowat's imagination takes off, producing a rollicking tale of the sea with satisfactory villains, brave seamen, courageous, prank-loving boys, and a fine schooner (*The Black Joke*) rescued and returned to its rightful owner. Survival here is played out with gusto and melodrama, with livelihood at stake rather than life.

Of all the landscapes in which survival is a fact of life, none is more starkly realistic than the Arctic. The basic needs of Inuit life—food, shelter, and clothing—that are often dependent on combats with animals and the environment are almost too basic and austere for fictionalization. For many years Wilfred Grenfell's *Adrift on an Ice-Pan* (first published as *A Voyage on a Pan of Ice*, 1908), based on his own experiences and observations as a medical missionary in Labrador, was considered the apotheosis of the Arctic survival story. But it was more than matched by James Houston's *Tikta'Liktak* (1965). The story of the young Inuit who escaped from his floating prison of ice to equal danger and hardship on a barren island and who then, by courageous and ingenious means, made his way back to the mainland, was well known in the Arctic when Houston first heard it. With consummate skill he invested it with the quality of a literary legend without losing the kind of immediacy of storytelling that derives from actual events.

Both *Tikta'Liktak* and Houston's second book, *The White Archer* (1967), are appropriately sub-titled *An Eskimo Legend*, although the latter has a more mythical quality. An Inuit family is murdered by Indians in retaliation for sheltering strangers guilty of violating Indian territory and laws. Only twelve-year-old Kungo escapes while his sister is carried off by the Indians. Kungo devotes all his time, energy, and abilities in training himself for revenge, acquiring most of his skills from an old, wise, nearly blind archer. Four years later Kungo, dressed all in white, sets out on his odyssey of hatred and vengeance. Ending in understanding and forgiveness, the story becomes a journey of moral development and spiritual growth, symbolized by the whiteness of the snow as well as of Kungo's attire.

Houston's writing career for children has spanned twenty-five years, and with the exception of a few tales that are based on west-coast Indian lore, all are imbued with his deep knowledge of the Canadian North and a love and concern for its native inhabitants. Houston was the first civil administrator of Baffin Island and is generally credited with bringing Eskimo art to the attention of world markets. His own illustrations, in many of his books, resemble the Eskimo sculpture he has so assiduously promoted.

In his more recent works, such as his trilogy—*Frozen Fire* (1977), *Black Diamonds* (1982), and *Ice Swords* (1985)—Houston has moved from narratives that have a legendary, timeless quality to those that dramatize the modern clash of cultures in the North: the inevitable conflict between the traditional life-style and values of the Inuit and those of the south. To this end he frequently contrasts a pair of young teenagers: a white boy from southern Canada and an Inuit youth. As in Mowat's *Lost in the Barrens*, the boys learn from one another, and it is the Arctic itself that acts as a third protagonist. In Houston's stories of modern northern life, such as *River Runners* (1975), as well as in his trilogy, his style is factual, journalistic, often verging on the mundane. His boys speak in the conversational tone of ordinary young teenagers. In his stories for younger children—*Wolf-Run* (1971) and *Long Claws* (1981)—the language is both more polished and consciously economical, befitting the animistic tone of tales about children who are guided by benign animals that help to ensure their survival and the achievement of their goals. Houston's sub-titles—*A Tale of Courage; A Tale of Hardship and Bravery; A Search for Arctic Treasure*—show his link with the survival story of the past in terms of plot, action, and his knowledge and appreciation of survival skills, but his major theme is very contemporary. He is today our most prolific and articulate spokesman for the Arctic, for its people in crisis, and for a way of life that has still much to offer other cultures.

All stories of survival set in the Far North inevitably convince by their realistic details, because only those who have experienced it dare to write about it. Douglas Wilkinson was a film-maker who spent over a year as the adopted son of an Inuit family on Baffin Island. His *Sons of the Arctic* (1965) is a well-crafted, exciting adventure tale of three Inuit boys who outwit and slay a bear that appears to have more than animal instincts. But it has not lasted beyond its time—perhaps because of its lack of characterization, or because conflict and tension are superficial and quickly resolved, or because it portrays a people who are always content with what they have.

It is more difficult to explain the demise of Markoosie's *Harpoon of the Hunter* (1970), the first fiction in English to be written by an Inuit. In essence it is the apotheosis of the survival story, in that no one survives. The word 'survive' occurs frequently:

> Maybe they would be lucky and get a polar bear. But Kamik knew that hunting bear is not easy. He knew that many times hunters come back empty handed after many sunrises of chase, sweat, and exhausting work. Bear hunting is the hardest thing in the north. The bear, if cornered, can kill many good dogs or men, if he gets the chance. But that is life. To survive in this wild land, man and beast kill for food. This is the land where the strong survive. The weak do not survive.

The artless style, almost devoid of adjectives and adverbs, matches the landscape, which is empty of all but threats to life—except for the people who live in it and love and help one another. But while the writing is simple, the form of this novelette is cinematic as it moves, in brief episodes, from the hunters who go in search of a rabid bear, to events at the base camp, to the people who go for help, to the wounded bear itself. As in many other stories of the Arctic, the bear becomes almost a symbol of the struggle against odds.

In nineteenth-century boys' adventures stories Eskimos are generally pictured as faceless figures moving against a white landscape, acting as guides for the white explorers and hunters, or they are described in some detail, somewhat as a curiosity, as in R.M. Ballantyne's *Ungava* (1858). Vilhjalmur Stefansson's *Kak the Copper Eskimo* (1924) broke this pattern with his portrayal of warm family life and a young boy, Kak, a happy-go-lucky Tom Sawyer of the North before he goes through his rites of manhood by killing his first animal for food. More of such intimate glimpses of modern Inuit family life would be welcome; it is chiefly through the works of James Houston that we see individual Inuit faces and hear their voices.

Canadian writers of the 1980s brought new dimensions to the outdoor survival story, thus showing its extraordinary flexibility as a vehicle for reflecting current ideas about the young and their problems. They adopted, to a great extent, the introspective quality of the American Scott O'Dell's *Island of the Blue Dolphins* (1960), now considered a modern classic. Based on an actual account of an Indian girl who survived alone on an island off the coast of California for eighteen years in the early nineteenth century, it represented a dramatic advance in the survival story in its own country. Although

American children's literature of the late-nineteenth and early-twentieth centuries is replete with tales of adolescents proving their skills and manliness in the wilderness, they were unfortunately, mostly contained within the series format, which tends to inhibit individuality; for example, *The Dave Fearless Series* (1918-27), *The Motor Boys* (1906-24), and *The Saddle Boys* (1913-15), whose authors all wrote under pseudonyms. Such books show conclusively that their authors did not have the requisite knowledge and passion for the natural world to move beyond their formulaic structure. None have lasted into the present. In general, the Canadian outdoor survival story has outclassed the American, with the great exception of *Island of the Blue Dolphins* and Jean George's later *Julie of the Wolves* (1972), certainly the most exotic and emotional of all survival stories to date. The drama of the plot—Julie's inward struggle as she tries to decide whether she is an Eskimo girl named Miyax or whether, seeing the destruction of her native way of life, she should give in to the white world and become Julie—is enhanced by superior writing. One becomes passionately concerned not only for the individual but for a society—a rare feat in children's literature.

The survival skills of Karana and Julie are instinctive rather than learned. By contrast recent Canadian writers have placed non-native young people in a wilderness crisis; they discover their skill in the act of survival. However, like O'Dell and George, they are committed to showing that the interior space their protagonists inhabit is just as important, if not more so, than their exterior space. They have also tended to use the wilderness more as a haven and place of healing than as a direct challenge to survival. Although their heroes and heroines do face and overcome physical dangers, such tests of courage are not the crux of the novels. In Jan Truss's *Jasmin* (1982), Monica Hughes' *Hunter in the Dark* (1981) and *Log Jam* (1987), and Marilyn Halvorson's *Nobody Said It Would Be Easy* (1987), the young find through their experiences relief from personal pressures and a new self-confidence, and so achieve an ability to come to terms with themselves as well as with the difficult situations in their everyday life. The new survival stories curiously match J.R.R. Tolkien's theory about the purpose of fantasy: 'Recovery, Escape, Consolation'. Unlike the survival stories of the past, they could also be discussed under the all-embracing rubric of *social realism* or under *Canadian regionalism,* since their action is played out in well-defined landscapes, obviously known to their authors and imaginatively embraced by them. Often, too, the language is coloured by the idiom of the region.

The problems of Marilyn Halvorson's young teenager, Lance, begin in *Let It Go* (1985), in which his hand is seriously injured in a knife fight. In the sequel, *Nobody Said It Would Be Easy* (the doctor's words), Lance is both shocked and angered when he finds that his hand is still unusable for the things he loves most—working with horses and drawing. He is at odds with himself, behind at school, and is further dismayed at the appearance of his step-cousin Kat (short for Kathleen Annette Theresa), with whom he develops a love-hate relationship. Survival enters when an airplane, piloted by Lance's Uncle Joe, and with Kat, Lance, and his friend Red aboard, crashes in northwestern Alberta. (An unrealistic note in the story is certainly the rickety condition of the plane!) Uncle Joe is killed, Red's leg is injured, and Kat, numb with grief, takes off on her own into the forest against all the prescribed rules of search and rescue. Lance has to make a decision that could involve life or death—to follow Kat or to stay with Red. With Red's encouragement he trails Kat and is able to rescue her from an icy, swift-rushing river, and is forced to used his injured hand to do so. In this climax Halvorson combines the physical and the emotional survival story. Lance recovers the full use of his hand, proves himself a hero, and the breach is healed between himself and Kat. Further healing comes when he draws a picture of Uncle Joe, who was Kat's dearly loved stepfather. Lance and his mother—resolving a conflict in *Let It Go*—establish a better relationship with one another. As Lance says: 'I'm okay.' Halvorson's language is that of her teenage protagonist—flat, conversational, even banal. 'It was real late when Dad and Uncle Joe and Kat got home' is one of Lance's typical observations. This style, presumably deliberate, is doubtless intended to make a link with young readers who, like Lance, find it difficult to plough through *Hamlet*.

Given the pioneer origins of the survival story and the outdoor skills called for, it was inevitable that the chief characters in such stories were traditionally teenaged males. But the balance has been more than redressed by Jan Truss's *Jasmin*. Jasmin Marie Antoinette Stalke is in Grade VI in an Alberta town close to the wilderness. She is the eldest child (among seven) in a poor, kind-hearted, disorganized, noisy household of which the teachers say 'What a family!' Jasmin is like many modern protagonists in having too much responsibility for her age; she is the surrogate mother, with a special attachment to, and responsibility for, her mentally handicapped brother Leroy. When her science project is accidentally destroyed by two of her brothers, she decides that failure at school is certain. Under feelings of helplessness and inadequacy, and influenced by her favourite poem, Keats's 'Meg Merrilies', about a gypsy woman who lived in the outdoors 'as she did please', Jasmin packs a few belongings, including a sleeping bag, and runs off into the surrounding forest.

The details of survival are very well worked out (the author knows her territory intimately), and moreover are plausible for a child who has lived close to the forest and remembers things from her science classes. Freed from family cares, she begins to feel a mystical rapport with the forest animals (recalling Sajo's bonding to her beavers) and moulds animals from clay. Within a few days her Eden is destroyed by a freak storm and she becomes an unwilling rescuee. She agrees to return home only when she is told by her rescuers that Leroy is also missing.

Jasmin's peaceful time in the wilderness is well contrasted with the turmoil at home occasioned by her disappearance; so is the contrast between Jasmin's growth in solitude and Leroy's degeneration into almost animality as he searches for his sister. All ends well when Jasmin's forest sculptures are accepted as her science project, Leroy is to receive professional help, and the Stalke family promises to give Jasmin some breathing space. There are social and psychological elements in *Jasmin*, but its romantic touches make it exceptional in survival literature. Though Jasmin is sensible and practical, she also appreciates beautiful things and is inspired by poetry, responding to Keats's poem by taking flight without realizing that outdoor life in England bears no resemblance to Alberta in winter.

While *Jasmin* is basically built on heightened emotion, that of Monica Hughes' *Hunter in the Dark* is very real indeed, for 'the hunter in the dark' is death. At age sixteen Mike Rankin is dying of leukemia. His wealthy parents are over-protective, and desperately avoid any conversation with him concerning his illness. Mike has to find out the facts for himself. His parents refuse to let him go on a hunting trip, even when he is in a period of remission. With the connivance of his closest friend, Mike is able to slip away by himself for his own hunting expedition in the Alberta wilderness. His heart's desire is to shoot a whitetail deer. Although well equipped and knowledgeable, Mike finds himself in a dangerous situation—an unexpected storm and a series of disasters prevent him from returning to his camp—where only a will to live and his skills save his life. When he finally has a deer in his gun-sight for a perfect shot, he lowers his gun, putting aside his impulse to act like God. His closeness to the natural world has brought him to an understanding of life and death:

> The road he was on wasn't an either-or road, he had discovered. He wasn't going towards either life or death. That wasn't what it was all about, he'd got it all wrong this time. It was on through life towards death, which had to be there at the end, or else life itself would become as flat as bread without yeast . . .

Mike can now face death, because he feels he understands life.

Considering the main theme of each of these two books—a teenager facing certain death as opposed to the adventures of a runaway child—one might expect *Hunter in the Dark* to be more emotionally charged than *Jasmin*. However, the reverse is true. In McLuhanesque terms Hughes is a 'cool' writer and Truss a 'hot' one: nonetheless, both writers are true to the characters they have so carefully built up—the intellectual Mike and the romantic Jasmin. In its own way each novel is a *tour de force*.

Like Truss's Jasmin, Mike is alone in the Alberta wilderness. But while Truss juxtaposes the day-to-day details of Jasmin's experiences with strongly contrasted events in her home, Hughes uses flashbacks to delineate Mike's background—his life before his illness, at home and school, the onset of his disease and his medical treatment. Both techniques are skilfully employed, providing counterpoints to the survival theme. And both writers give cogent glimpses (remarkable in such short books) of lives other than those of the main characters. In *Jasmin* we meet the couple who save Jasmin's life, support her, and provide an example of people who 'live as they do please' on the borderline between self-sufficiency and community interaction. In

Hunter in the Dark there is an unstated but strong contrast between the organized lives of Mike's wealthy parents and the more casual habits that comprise the life-style of Mike's friend Doug.

In *Log Jam* Hughes continues to experiment with structure. She uses a double narrative that eventually brings together two disparate troubled teenagers. Isaac Manyfeathers, a native youth, has escaped from a detention centre into the foothills of the Alberta Rockies, where he tries to rediscover an identity that has been wrenched apart in the white world. A voice comes to him from an old Indian medicine lodge, bidding him to fast for four days and to follow his 'heart's way' to the river, where his spirit will come with the sun on the fourth day. Lenora Rydz—a fourteen-year-old white girl on a camping trip with her mother, her new stepfather, and two stepbrothers—is alienated by her mother's marriage. In a gesture of independence she and the younger stepbrother embark on a dangerous canoe trip that ends in disaster. Lenora escapes drowning and is found by Isaac, who sees her as the 'child of the sun' and therefore entwined with his spirit life. In the following two days of shared survival there are more crises, but they learn to respect, trust, and help one another to accept the lives they must return to.

Ninety per cent of Canadians live in urban areas, yet our vast wilderness and the spaces beyond cities and towns still influence the Canadian literary imagination. The long road from Catharine Parr Traill's *Canadian Crusoes* to Monica Hughes' *Hunter in the Dark* has offered new insights into outdoor survival for those who look upon it with fresh eyes. The modern survival story wisely continues some of the old conventions: the necessity for skills and experience and the excitement of physical danger. With the great exception of Jan Truss's Jasmin (and, to a lesser extent, Lenora in *Log Jam*), there is still a preponderance of teen-aged males who face physical and moral problems that bring them to maturity. But the simple ingredients of the traditional outdoor survival story have been broadened to include elements of social realism and mysticism, and the strong portrayal of character, often revealed through the convention of rites of passage. Containing some or all of these characteristics, the best examples of outdoor survival fiction today transcend its former sub-genre status to join the mainstream of realistic fiction.

STORIES OF CHILD AND FAMILY LIFE

This genre is fundamental to children's literature. Although when it was introduced in seventeenth-century England as having a religious purpose, and centred on the Puritan concept of death—the happy deaths of young children—such books were family stories, but of a restrictive kind. Once the main thrust of writing for children changed from religious indoctrination to the education and socialization of the young, other aspects of childhood entered children's stories. In the eighteenth and early nineteenth centuries the concentration was on the rearing of children. Such self-appointed educationists as Thomas Day with *Sandford and Merton* (1783-89) and Maria Edgeworth with a multitude of publications (such as her stories of the child Rosamond in her *Early Lessons,* 1801) came to be considered almost as guides to 'parenting' as well as moral tales for the young. Victorian stories of child and family life—particularly those written for the poor, emanating from religious publishing houses such as The Religious Tract Society—are notable for their portrayal of the darker side of children's lives, which could be overcome only by Christian faith. In these books we see them orphaned or starving, or forced to work long hours in factories or shops, sustained only by a belief in God's grace. Books written for middle-class children emphasized self-discipline and had a preponderance of detail showing the exemplary and orderly lives of the young, who are allowed now and again a few stolen pleasures.

Edith Nesbit's *The Story of the Treasure Seekers* (1889) defined the story of child and family life for the next half-century, and the Nesbit tradition of child life, whether presented in realism or fantasy, still lingers happily today, although the numbers of children involved have certainly lessened. Oswald Bastable, the young narrator of *The Treasure Seekers*, is the eldest of six brothers and sisters. He speaks in a heretofore unknown individualized child voice when he comments:

> Our Mother is dead, and if you think we don't care because I don't tell you much about her you only show that you do not understand people at all.

Nesbit children may be sensitive and caring, but unlike the children of contemporary realism they do not brood on sorrows, ill-luck, or misfortune; rather they initiate adventures to help themselves and others. That these do not always succeed, or succeed in unexpected ways, is all part of the fun.

The writers of the Edwardian era—among whom Edith Nesbit was supreme—in general extolled the virtues of childhood as opposed to those of adulthood. In a turnabout after the long Victorian era—in which the young, although appreciated, were still seen to be in need of guidance and discipline—Edwardian writers (themselves no doubt subject to Victorian influences) seemed determined to liberate children, at least in their books, from as much adult constraint as possible. In so doing they presented children as more perceptive than adults, more helpful and caring, more imaginative, and certainly more fun-loving.

When Nesbit conceived *The Treasure Seekers* she had no outstanding examples of contemporary-scene fiction for children from her own society to emulate or build upon. English Victorian children's literature was notable for its fantasies rather than for domestic stories. But nineteenth-century American writers had the shining example of the possibilities of family-life stories in Louisa May Alcott's *Little Women* (1868). They seized on girlhood as a theme, but seemingly chose as their model the one-dimensionally virtuous Becky Thatcher in Mark Twain's *Tom Sawyer* (1876), rather than complex, independent Jo March. Even more than their British counterparts, they revelled in the idealization of young girls. There was Phronsie of Margaret Sidney's *The Five Little Peppers* series that began in 1881, Kate Douglas Wiggins' *Rebecca of Sunnybrook Farm* (1903), and Eleanor Porter's *Pollyanna* (1913). Gene Stratton Porter's *Freckles* (1904) is about a young man, but the story really revolves around a girl aptly named Angel. Frances Hodgson Burnett (who belongs both to the United States and England) gave the world *Sara Crewe*, later reprinted as *A Little Princess* (1905), and Mary Lennox of *The Secret Garden* (1911). All these girls (and many more, with the striking exception of Mary Lennox at the beginning of her story) are presented as the acme of goodness, in prose that reaches the heights of sentimentality. In these rhapsodic narratives the angelic heroines solve not only their own problems but those of all who come in contact with them.

It was within this atmosphere of virtuous girlishness that Lucy Maud Montgomery created Anne of *Anne of Green Gables* (1908), with her red hair, grey eyes, and seven freckles. Montgomery's belief in her own creation perhaps accounted for her ability to make of Anne a character that attracts readers to this day—perhaps, along with Lewis Carroll's Alice, one of the two best-known 'story girls' in the world. Montgomery has described her feelings about Anne in her journals:

> When I am asked if Anne herself is a 'real person' I always answer 'no' with an odd reluctance and an uncomfortable feeling of not telling the truth. For she is and always has been, from the moment I first thought of her, so real to me that I feel I am doing violence to something when I deny her an existence anywhere save in Dreamland. . . . To tell that haunting elf that she is not real, because, forsooth, I never met her in the flesh! No, I cannot do it! . . .

Although Lucy Maud went to live with her grandparents after her mother's death at about the age of two, when her father moved to the Prairies, she obviously did not consider herself an orphan like Anne. The idea for her first book was suggested to her by a child from an orphan asylum who lived with her neighbours—acquiring a child from an orphanage to help with chores was a common practice of the period. But while all her characters are fictional, many of the details of the story were drawn from Montgomery's own knowledge and experience. She reports that Anne's tribulations over puffed sleeves were an echo of her old childish longing for 'bangs'. The setting, of course, is very real indeed. Avonlea is Montgomery's town of Cavendish on the north shore of Prince Edward Island. All the places described were dear to her and if some were named by Anne rather than Lucy Maud, they did exist.

Montgomery herself has stated that there was less of 'real life' in her second Anne book, *Anne of Avonlea* (1909). Yet the flaw in it, and in the succeeding *Anne* books, is due more to an increasingly sentimental tone than to a lack of realistic detail. At least some of Montgomery's teaching experiences, according to her journal, are included in *Anne of Avonlea*. But Anne simply becomes too much of an 'angel', a Sara Crewe or a Pollyanna, and by the time the series reaches Anne's children in *Rainbow Valley* (1919)—though in this book some adult situations are amusingly described—and *Rilla of*

Ingleside (1921), only the most avid young Anne fans can find pleasure in them. It is almost ironic that as Anne matures she loses most of the characteristics that made her beloved as a child—spontaneity, imagination, and a kind of iconoclasm that she always managed to turn to her own advantage, or that of others. Even Montgomery became tired of Anne: ' I am done with *Anne* forever,' she wrote in 1920: 'I swear it as a dark and deadly vow. I want to create a new heroine . . .'

Thus Emily of *Emily of New Moon* (1923), *Emily Climbs* (1925), and *Emily's Quest* (1927) came into existence. She is indeed altogether different from Anne, physically and emotionally. She has 'black hair and purplish gray eyes' and is far more introspective and creative than her more popular rival. The *Emily* books have a greater continuity than the episodic *Anne* series, for at the core of them is Emily's ambition to be a writer. In this respect they parallel much of Montgomery's own young life, but are not strictly autobiographical—although Emily too has lost her father and mother at an early age, is forced to live with relatives, and eventually keeps a journal, as did Lucy Maud. Montgomery's inventive mind provided Emily with a more complex family background than either her own or Anne's, and in *Emily's Quest* surrounded her with suitors who would not be out of place in a Gothic romance. In a move unusual in a Canadian novel of its time, Montgomery also endowed Emily with occasional 'flashes' of second sight. In *Emily of New Moon* she sees an episode in the past in a delirium, in *Emily Climbs* a moment of the present in a dream, and in *Emily's Quest* she looks into her great-aunt's 'gazing-ball', sees the man she loves in danger, and sends him a mental message that saves his life. Like her creator, Emily lives so emotionally that these episodes can also be seen as arising from the intensely creative visions of a writer's mind. Montgomery does not appear to have been a believer in the occult, although she once asked a friend to try to make her dream of him. The great difference between the *Anne* and the *Emily* books can be found in the character of Emily. Unlike Anne, she will not lose the personal qualities that made her so attractive as a child, nor will she give up her literary aspirations. At the end of *Emily's Quest* one feels that her forthcoming marriage will nuture her ambitions to be a writer rather than impede them.

In spite of her romantic cast of mind, Montgomery was a keen, even satirical, observer of the small-town life she saw around her and the dark currents that frequently seethed beneath it. Her descriptions of nature were lyrical, but could also become fulsome and obsessive, as in *Pat of Silver Bush* (1933).

Montgomery's long career of writing girls' romances (1908-37), and her success, were not emulated in Canada either during her lifetime or later. From the 1930s to the 1960s—a spare period in Canadian children's-book publishing—few books were entirely based on family life. This gap was filled by imports from the United States such as Eleanor Estes' *The Moffats* (1940), Elizabeth Enright's *The Saturdays* (1941), and Sydney Taylor's *All-of-a-Kind Family* (1951). England provided even more: Eve Garnett's *The Family from One End Street* (1937) and its sequels, the innumerable holiday and adventure stories of Enid Blyton, Arthur Ransome's continued sagas of the 'Swallows and Amazons' and their friends, and a plethora of pony and school stories. The few Canadian stories of child and family life had a distinctive Canadian quality and were set in stated locales—Mabel Dunham's *Kristli's Trees* (1948) outside of Kitchener, Ontario, Lyn Cook's *The Little Magic Fiddler* (1951) and *The Bells on Finland Street* (1962) in Winnipeg and Sudbury respectively. Both writers found their themes in a hitherto unacknowledged aspect of Canadian society (at least in children's literature)—the wave of European immigration after the First World War.

Dunham's Kristli is a Mennonite boy, and the life of the community is seen through his daily childlike experiences that culminate in a struggle with his conscience. Stylistically, and briefly, the book conveys the honesty, serenity, and simplicity that is associated with Mennonite life. *Kristli's Trees* was a charming tribute to a way of life deliberately set apart from the Canadian norm. *The Little Magic Fiddler* is loosely based on the childhood of Donna Grescoe, a child prodigy who achieved some fame as a violinist. The family background is Ukrainian. Elin, of *The Bells on Finland Street* is, of course, Finnish and her desire is to be a figure-skater; she wants to 'skate for Canada'. Money is scarce in both households. Both children have loving parents and are also supported by grandparents who tell them stories of the old country. *The Bells on Finland Street* is the more consciously multicultural. Most of Elin's schoolmates are children of central Europeans (though one child is of Irish extraction and another is French Canadian) and all are pleased to acknowledge their heritage. Lyn Cook's two books were welcomed and enjoyed. Both, however, show the dangers in writing with a narrow and specific purpose. Well-intentioned as they are, they are overly contrived, didactic, and burdened with lessons on Canadian history and details of ethnic food, costumes, and festivals. In a social sense *The Bells on Finland Street* is the more incongruous. Elin's father shows no resentment at his obviously poor wages in the Sudbury mines, and moreover the results of mining are seen as beautiful—even the slag heap. Immigrants are shown as accepting, grateful, uncomplaining, and hard-working.

Some aspects of harsh realism are certainly present in all these novels. Montgomery's Anne and Emily, as children, had severe disruptions in their lives; Dunham's very young Kristli has to cope with a heavy burden of conscience, and Cook's Donna and Elin, while in no way facing a hostile society, must work hard to find a special place in it. Yet the conflicts they contain are softened by a loving and stable family life.

Jean Little's first two books, *Mine for Keeps* (1962) and *Home from Far* (1965), stand midway between the old and the new realism. Her children have problems that cannot easily be solved. They have to learn to live not only with a particular situation, but with their own inner selves. Sal, of *Mine for Keeps*, has cerebral palsy (though she is very bright mentally) and after five years at a special school she must return to normal family life and school. Jenny, of *Home from Far*, has to face the accidental death of her twin brother Michael. Both girls have loving, sensible, and sensitive parents and both have brothers and sisters. They, and interaction with other children and pets, help in the healing and adjustment process. In her depiction of warm family life, Little belongs in the company of Lyn Cook, but in her presentation of children with severe problems (both physical and emotional) she was the Canadian forerunner of the new realism.

Farley Mowat's *Owls in the Family* (1961) is in strong contrast to Lyn Cook's and Jean Little's stories of children who are in the process of adjustment. The young narrator is Mowat himself, completely at home in his environment, recalling episodes in his Saskatchewan childhood centring on the pet owls Wol and Weeps. The events—the search for the baby owls, the pet parade that ends in disaster, the boys' animal circus, and an encounter with the toughest kids in town—are tinged with Mowat's sense of farce. But the elements of realism do exist—owls are owls, boys are boys, and there is a sharp sense of prairie sky and sun and cottonwoods. The style is simple yet evocative, colloquial but not overly so. Its combined attributes have given *Owls in the Family* a long life and a deserved popularity. It joins *Sajo and Her Beaver People* (as well as *Anne of Green Gables*) as a Canadian classic.

It was perhaps inevitable that Canadian writers for children in the 1970s would follow the trends and patterns of our neighbours to the south. First of all there was the noticeable popularity with Canadian children and young people of American problem novels. Throughout North America the Tolstoyan belief that 'All happy families resemble one another, but each unhappy family is unhappy in its own way' seemed to have taken hold. Diverse forms of unhappiness in the family—or the *lack* of a family or a member of it, especially a parent—characterize virtually all serious modern stories of child and family life.

When Canadian writers finally turned to an examination of the trials and tribulations of youth, they adopted the main thrust of American realistic fiction but without its excesses and stereotypes. Avoiding its most sensational topics, they employed a more literate style; they convinced by small, authentic details; and frequently provided a strong regional setting that helped to define the events. The novels had (and still have) a typical Canadian restraint, but offer a richer look at children's lives, one that goes beyond the chief problems.

The few novels of the late 1970s that deal with contemporary children facing difficulties have a quality of gentleness. In three novels—Frances Duncan's *Kap-Sung Ferris* (1977), Patti Stren's *There's a Rainbow in My Closet* (1979), and Helen Chetin's *The Lady of the Strawberries* (1978)—the young girls are in confusion over the absence of a mother. The Korean orphan of *Kap-Sung Ferris*, who wants to search for her mother back in her native land, has a loving adoptive family, a close school friend, and a great talent as a figure-skater. The scenes of active, noisy family life are convincing in their vitality. Vancouver plays a practical role in the story as a port city; Kap-Sung tries to stow away on a ship bound for the Orient. Yet she is so surrounded by understanding and goodwill that her search for identity appears more as a literary device than an inner and compelling necessity. *There's a Rainbow in My Closet* begins with tension as Emma resents her mother's departure for Europe (to fulfil her career expectations) and decides to dislike her 'Gramma' who is coming to look after her. In a quick wave of sentimentality, however, the two become fast friends, especially as Gramma understands and appreciates Emma as a budding artist. The strength of the book lies in its illustrations—in Emma's drawings and humorous cartoons—and in some of the schoolroom scenes that are obviously based on the author's own recollections.

Ten-year-old Jessica, of Chetin's *The Lady of the Strawberries*, lives on an Alberta farm with her father and six-year-old brother. Her mother could not adjust to rural life and has returned to Toronto. Jessica misses her and sometimes feels pressured by the responsibility of being an older sister, but she likes her new schoolteacher very much and tends her strawberry bed with devotion. The 'lady' of the title was intended as a scarecrow for the strawberries, but it becomes much more. It is made from her mother's dress form, a wig from her teacher, elegant old-fashioned clothes from the attic, and gradually becomes for Jessica a substitute mother. As she begins to comprehend and resent the growing friendship between her father and her teacher (the teacher was *her* friend first), she pours more and more of her thoughts and affection into the faceless figure. In a highly dramatic ending Jessica comes to see that she is not clinging to her 'lady' but merely to a 'scare-robin'. The story is enriched by the brief appearances of Jessica's adult native friend, John Bearspaw, and it is told in simple, spare language against the changing prairie seasons that are often lyrically described.

Some of the most emotionally charged stories of family life of the 1970s are set in the recent past and gain strength from their touches of social history and an attention to small details that bring an era vividly to life. Myra Paperny's *The Wooden People* (1976) is set in a small Alberta town of the 1920s and in Jean Little's *From Anna* (1972) and its sequel, *Listen for the Singing* (1977), the locale is Toronto before and during the Second World War. As in most domestic stories, the plots of all three works are episodic but are strongly coloured by a sense of family disruption and alienation.

The Jewish children of *The Wooden People* are in constant movement from one town to another because of their immigrant father's determination never to live as he had in Russia, in 'one little shtetl, town . . . with all us Jews jammed together in a small area . . . and I swore that when my chance came I'd keep moving until I saw the entire world.' The move to a desolate prairie town in which the father will run a grocery store devastates the children, especially the eldest son. In his misery he almost deliberately becomes ill; he wants no part of the new life. During his convalescence and freedom from family chores he creates a secret magic world of marionettes, drawing his brothers and sisters into the production. When the children are asked to perform in public, the secret activity, so carefully hidden from their authoritarian father, is exposed. The family conflict ends in reconciliation and the children's appreciation of their father's love. While the focus of the story is on the children, Paperny, like all fine writers from Montgomery on, does not neglect the adult world, which is often seen in its pettiness, selfishness, eccentricities, and compassion. The father has been generous to his customers, yet when a more modern store opens up in the town they desert him almost *en bloc*. Small-town prairie life is well conveyed, especially in winter with the snow, the cold, and ice-skating; in a scene where the tongue of one of the children is frozen to the town pump, all the villagers join in helping to release it.

Jean Little's Anna, as a first-generation immigrant child, has the normal problems of adjustment to a new way of life and a new language, but these are compounded by Anna's visual handicap, which is the chief theme of *From Anna* and of *Listen for the Singing*. Another is the Second World War—Anna and her family, as Germans, are seen by the community as enemy aliens; it makes little difference that they had fled Nazi Germany. Racial prejudice, however, is never evident in its extreme form. Anna, unlike Lyn Cook's children, does not have an innate, readily recognizable talent, but she develops powers of reconciliation and healing that enable her to become almost the mainstay of her family in their strained relationships during the war years. Because of her own visual disability, she is able to inspire her oldest brother, blinded in a naval accident, to take up his life again.

In the 1980s the number of titles of lasting merit in the many sub-genres of realistic fiction increased dramatically. The recent past continues to provide a springboard for many modern writers who have drawn on their own childhood experiences, especially during the Great Depression and the Second World War.

Bernice Thurman Hunter's *Booky* series (*That Scatterbrain Booky*, 1981, *With Love from Booky*, 1983, and *As Ever, Booky*, 1985) is an account of the life of the working (chiefly non-working) poor in Toronto during the Depression of the 1930s. If the scenes of poverty were extracted from the various episodes, they would make an urban documentary of those harsh years. We see Booky and her sister cutting out cardboard to line their shoes, the father slicing a rubber tire to fit the heel of his boot, the mother mending her one pair of stockings. There are nights when all the family go to bed hungry, and mealtimes when the father refuses food to give more to his children; there are violent quarrels between the parents caused by unemployment and the family's humiliation at having to accept food and gifts from the Santa Claus Fund. Most heart-rending of all is the mother's wish (not carried out) to give away the baby she is carrying to ensure a better life for it. Yet thanks to Booky (pronounced Boo-key), the stories are among the most light-hearted in Canadian children's literature. Like Montgomery's Anne, she takes delight in the simplest of pleasures—Eaton's Santa Claus Parade, night skating on Grenadier Pond, the occasional movie, visits to more affluent relatives. Booky tells her own story as she grows from a ten-year-old to an adolescent, but never concentrates on herself to any great extent—she is not egocentric. Through her eyes and voice we know the other members of the family as well as herself, especially the indomitable mother. The books are illustrated with what may be family or period photographs and with advertisements from Eaton's Catalogue. The series is so satisfying that one wishes for a better publishing format than the rather dowdy paperbacks. (Still, it could be argued that they have a Depression-era look.) Thurman's second series about a tubercular child—beginning with *A Place for Margaret* (1984)—is equally convincing in its details of social history and regional life of rural Ontario in the 1920s. Margaret, however, lacks the spunk and clarity of observation that mark Booky's character, who, after all, wants to be a writer, and is not even daunted by a less than successful meeting with her favourite author L.M. Montgomery.

Bess Kaplan's *The Empty Chair* (1986) has echoes of Paperny's *The Wooden People*, Hunter's *Booky* series, and Chetin's *The Lady of the Strawberries*, but it has a dimension of its own. It is set in the Jewish community of Winnipeg's North End during the Depression and the family lives on the edge of poverty. Becky has a warm, resilient mother, a difficult greengrocer father, and a typical friendly rivalry with her younger brother. Her life at home and at school is described with humorous and poignant details. The mother dies in childbirth, and the focus shifts to Becky's inner life as she not only struggles with her grief but also faces the prospect of her father's remarriage. In her despair her confused emotions create frightening apparitions of her mother that fill her with guilt and fear. Although the chief theme of the novel is isolation, it also chronicles a healing process as Becky resolves her sorrow and grows into life. *The Empty Chair* was first published as an adult novel, entitled *The Corner Store*, but was cut and adapted for a child readership.

Sarah Ellis's *Next-Door Neighbours* (1989) is also set in the past, the 1950s, and although the child Peggy has a problem (she is exceptionally shy), it is basically a warm-hearted family story as well as one of friendship. When the Davies family move to Vancouver, Peggy feels alienated at her new school, tells a lie to gain attention, and is ostracized by her schoolmates when it is discovered. Over the summer she makes two unusual friends, both 'next-door neighbours'. One is an adult Chinese gardener and house-boy for a wealthy woman who uses him as a kind of slave (at first Peggy thinks he is strange because he treats her as an adult). The other is a boy her own age, a Russian immigrant with harsh memories of the Second World War (at first Peggy thinks that he is 'weird' because he uses the English language with such precision and does not mind being an outsider). Their summer of friendship involves the creation of puppets, with tension caused by the gardener's dismissal (he has taken half an hour from work to attend the puppet show, which he had helped to create). In one of the best scenes in the story the children are stricken with a sense of injustice, and do their best to get a clue to his whereabouts. However, the love and sensibility of Peggy's family (she has the best of parents) ameliorate her pain and she faces the new school term with assurance. The story is quietly told and gains its strength from the author's recollections of her own childhood in a minister's family. *Next-Door Neighbours* continues the strong Canadian tradition of recognizing the Canadian ethnic mix.

Books by Brian Doyle and Joy Kogawa are part of this stream, but they are marked by far greater racial tension and by the effects of war. In Doyle's *Angel Square* (1984) the Second World War is entering its final days; but there is also a war going on in Ottawa's Lower Town. Young Tommy has just learned that the father of his best friend, who is Jewish, has been beaten up in the streetcar barns where he worked as a nightwatchman. Tommy is an *aficionado* of the popular radio series of the period, 'The Shadow', and determines to emulate his hero by solving the mystery and bringing the perpetrator of the crime to justice. This he accomplishes with the help of his best French-Canadian friend, CoCo Laframboise. It is rare to find a story of family life with such a strong plot, yet the family scenes are the most memorable. Tommy has no mother; but he has a fun-loving, wise father, an aunt who runs the household with a mania for cleanliness, a mentally deficient older sister whom they tend with love, and his father's eccentric friend. Tommy also has a boyish love for a schoolmate, Margot Lane, a link with 'The Shadow's' girl-friend of the same name.

The chief theme of the story is racial prejudice and it is Doyle's intent to show that it is the adults who are prejudiced, not the children. To this end he uses symbolism and the derogatory names then in common usage: Jew rather than Jewish, Dogans for Irish Catholics, and Pea Soups for French-Canadians. (Interestingly enough, there is no epithet for Protestants.) He describes the children fighting with a kind of comic-book violence as they make their way across Angel Square every day to attend their separate schools. 'All over the square, Dogans, Pea Soups and Jews were tearing the sleeves out of one another's coats and trying to rip each other limb from limb.' Tommy, in an effort to earn money for Christmas presents, almost reels from one part-time job to another. It is unlikely, however, that a non-Catholic child would be hired to serve as a Catholic altar boy or a non-Jewish one to sweep the synagogue. These are among many unrealistic details, distortions, and tall-tale caricatures that create an almost surrealistic dimension in the interests of social satire. In this particular aspect of the story, Doyle takes an unconventional risk and may confuse some readers as he attacks the follies of society, particularly racial prejudice. In spite of the scenes of child violence, however, which are not to be taken literally, the overall tone is one of joy, reconciliation, generosity, and acceptance. *Angel Square* is a very warm-hearted story and Tommy is the most lovable young hero in Canadian children's literature.

Joy Kogawa's adult, award-winning *Obasan* was simplified in plot and language to create *Naomi's Road* (1986), a memoir-novel of the author's experiences as a Japanese-Canadian child during the Second World War. It details several years in Naomi's life, beginning at age five when she and her brother and her aunt (Obasan) are sent from their home in Vancouver to an internment camp in the interior of British Columbia and later to an Alberta farm. Her father is in a different camp and her mother is in Japan tending her ailing parents. Naomi's loss is severe, but Obasan becomes a figure of love, family continuity, and cultural heritage. Because Naomi is very young and so naïve, she is uncomprehending of the reasons for the disruptions in her life and the hardships the family endure even after the war. Kogawa skilfully keeps a child's viewpoint, and so the story is free of the anger one might expect from experiences based on injustice and racism. It is rather a story of gentle warmth, with omens of healing and reconciliation in Naomi's play with her white child friend. Kogawa has a poet's instinct in her imagistic use of small objects, such as Naomi's lost doll, which symbolizes also her loss of home and happiness. The use of visual imagery in the best of *Naomi's Road* (complemented by Matt Gould's drawings) is echoed in the memorable watercolour illustrations of Shizuye Takashima's *A Child in Prison Camp* (1971), the first picture-storybook treatment of this sad event in Canadian history. Takashima, like Kogawa, shows neither childlike rancour nor adult resentment over her experience, but certainly *Naomi's Road* has the greater emotional impact, perhaps because Kogawa is an artist with words—or even more likely, because of its stronger fictional component.

Rather than personal experience, Carol Matas used family knowledge and research for *Lisa* (1987), a story of the Second World War set in Denmark. A simply told and often suspenseful tale, it resembles many European stories of children involved in underground resistance activities against the Nazis, from Mary Treadgold's *We Couldn't Leave Dinah* (1941) to Alki Zei's *Petros' War* (1972). But these war books by European authors are far more compelling than *Lisa* because Treadgold (English) and Zei (Greek) had first-hand experience of the war.

One of the most emotional aspects of the Second World War that affected England was the evacuation of children from the large cities to the countryside. Many British writers—including Nina Bawden with *Carrie's War* (1973) and Michelle Magorian's *Goodnight Mister Tom* (1981)—have, naturally enough, mined these disturbing events as themes for their novels. However, in most cases the evacuations are mere springboards for a probing into the effects of the disruption upon the protagonists, and their maturation process. Such books cannot be described as 'war stories' as can Matas's *Lisa*. Neither can three Canadian novels whose episodic plots are concerned with the experiences of English children who were sent to Canada. (About eight thousand arrived before the sinking of the *City of Benares* by a German submarine in 1940 put an end to the exodus.) This is fertile ground indeed, if only because of the potential for strongly delineated Canadian locales and the life-styles that come with them, as contrasted with the disrupted home-life of the displaced children or young people. Dorris Heffron's *Crusty Crossed* (1976) places three young teenagers, members of an intellectual Oxford family, with their Canadian relatives in a small town near Sydney, Nova Scotia. Their settling-in process is often humorously and realistically described, but despite Heffron's wit and sharp characterization, which recall the British writer Jane Gardam, the book develops into little more than a conventional teen-age novel, with an emphasis on first love and only a slight indication of the problems of the girls' readjustment to England. Less stylistically successful is Geoffrey Bilson's *Hockeybat Harris* (1984), which places an English boy in Saskatoon, where he has problems of adjustment, chiefly because of his anxiety about his family. Cricket versus hockey, from which David derives his nickname, is a leitmotif, but a natural and appealing one for a Canadian winter. Much more war news is included here than in *Crusty Crossed*, along with the subject of the then little-known policy of the Canadian government's non-acceptance of Jewish refugees. This painful aspect of the war in Canada is not at all misplaced in Bilson's work, but cannot be given adequate treatment in such a short book.

Both Heffron and Bilson weave their stories around three youthful characters, and although all are distinctive, none stand out as memorable. By contrast, Kit Pearson's evacuee Norah, in *The Sky is Falling* (1989), is always centre-stage. She has a strong personal presence:

> The war was the most exciting thing that had ever happened in Norah's ten years, and this summer was the best part of it. Other summers were a pleasant, mild blur of building sandcastles on the beach near Grandad's house in Camber. But one day at the end of last August, Norah had found herself filling sandbags instead of playing.

Also, she and her village friends have formed the 'Secret Society of Skywatchers', both to look out for enemy planes and to uncover spies in disguise. She is therefore outraged when her parents decide to send her and her five-year-old brother Gavin to safety in Canada. In Toronto they are assigned to the Ogilvies, a mother and daughter who live in affluent Rosedale. Mrs Ogilvie had wanted only a boy (her son had been killed in the Great War) and she quickly makes a pet of Gavin, while Norah feels an outsider. Everything conspires to compound her sense of alienation: the treatment in the reception centre (kindly but authoritarian), the contrast between her modest home and the luxury of Rosedale (she will not allow herself to be outfitted with new clothes), her isolation at school, her friendship with a German-Canadian boy (forbidden by Mrs Ogilvie), and above all her personality clash with Mrs Ogilvie (they are much alike in their stubbornness). In her unhappiness, she does not realize that Gavin is also suffering under his overly pampered condition. The minor crises mount until Norah makes a runaway attempt, taking Gavin with her. But all ends in reconciliation. Mrs Ogilvie makes Norah an abject apology (almost too abject), and Norah is delighted with the present of a bicycle for Christmas. (There are also happy Christmas scenes in Heffron's *Crusty Crossed* and Bilson's *Hockeybat Harris*. As in so many Canadian children's books—by Brian Doyle, Sarah Ellis, Jean Little, and Janet Lunn—Christmas, offering non-religious yet healing moments of loving and forgiving, signals a time of inner as well as outer joy and well-being.)

The Sky is Falling is a rich, but very childlike book that has a page-turning quality: one wants to know what happens next. War information is introduced naturally; minor characters (and there are many) come alive as real people, and the whole is enriched by a slight symbolic dimension. In the reception centre in Toronto, Norah hears the Russian story of 'Alenoushka and Her Brother', in which the older sister is able to release her younger brother from a spell. Norah is ultimately a modern Alenoushka. *The Sky is Falling* is the first in a welcome proposed trilogy, since Norah has indeed enough character to occasion several books.

In the tradition of Montgomery's Anne and Emily, most of the children in these books are highly imaginative, sensitive, and creative. The children of Paperny's *The Wooden People* make a special world for themselves with their marionettes and thereby gain friends; Emma, of Stren's *There's a Rainbow in My Closet*, sees life in the colours she mixes from her paint box, especially the colour purple; Jessica, of Chetin's *The Lady of the Strawberries*, and Becky, of Kaplan's *The Empty Chair*, both create fantasy mothers to serve their psychological needs. Like Emily in *Emily of New Moon*, Kaplan's Becky, Hunter's Booky, and Doyle's Tommy want to be writers. Tommy especially ponders what he sees around him and gives his musings articulate form. In spite of his boyish interests, or perhaps because of them, he (of all these young protagonists) is the most alive to his family, friends, and to the world in general. When he watches an eclipse of the moon,

> I could imagine standing there on the moon with this big smooth shadow coming over me. On the moon where nothing ever happens.

Tommy prays for a world that he would like to live in, a world without hatred and prejudice:

> A nice time.
> That's what I prayed for.
> The prayer might work, I thought.
> Or it might not.
> It was a mystery.

Although Brian Doyle's earlier two books, *Hey, Dad!* (1978) and *You Can Pick Me Up at Peggy's Cove* (1979), show evidence of originality and a fresh use of Canadian settings, they have more than a touch of the American problem novel about them. Megan, of *Hey, Dad!*, sets the tone in the first paragraph:

> We were going to drive from Ottawa, where I live, to the Pacific Ocean. Mum and Dad had been planning the trip for months. It was going to be the biggest thing that ever happened to us.
>
> There was only one problem.
>
> I didn't want to go.

As a thirteen-year-old, Megan has interests that are beginning to lie outside the family, and she is also of an age to feel embarrassed by her father's clowning. *Hey, Dad!* is basically a lighthearted long short story, replete with family jokes and the mishaps that can occur when a family is travelling by car on a low budget. It is chiefly enlivened by Doyle's gift for dialogue and given some depth by Megan's musings on the concept of time and by her realization that she loves her father dearly. For a few horrifying moments (as she returns from a brief runaway escapade) she mistakes a man who has suddenly died at a poolside for her father. 'I always end up thinking of those two together. Dying and loving.'

In *Hey, Dad!*, the physical aspects of Megan's journey are neatly, if somewhat superficially, combined with her emotional one. In *You Can Pick Me Up at Peggy's Cove* the Nova Scotian locale gives Doyle an opportunity for the creation of eccentric characters seen in contrast to the faceless tourists who throng Peggy's Cove in the summer. Here—as in the unique aspects of Ottawa seen in *Angel Square* and in the overwhelming breadth of Canada in *Hey, Dad!*—Doyle makes effective use of the environment, both physically and spiritually. *Peggy's Cove* is not a sequel to *Hey, Dad!* but a companion to it. It has two characters from *Hey, Dad!*: the father and Megan's brother Ryan, now a young teenager. Ryan has been sent to live with his aunt in this picturesque fishing village because his father is facing a mid-life crisis and has to decide whether or not to return to his family. In trying to come to terms with his father's defection, Ryan has to learn to appreciate other people who are 'different'. These include his two adult fisherman friends: Eddie, who replies 'Isn't that nice?' to almost every remark, and his companion Wingding, who can only communicate orally by making a 'smacking' sound. In a fairly normal adolescent ploy, Ryan acts badly in order to gain his father's attention: he helps a young professional thief rob tourists—it is his form of running away. The resolution of the story is less definite than that of *Hey, Dad!* Eddie has had his thumb torn off by a shark, and Wingding, in later trying to kill the shark, is drowned. Ryan matures morally by refusing to participate in theft any longer and by accepting the finality of loss in Wingding's death. Like Megan, he learns about 'dying and loving'. With his enlarged vision of life, he also realizes that he is only a small part of the varied life of the town. His father does come to 'pick him up', and Ryan sees himself and his father against the wide panorama of Peggy's Cove, and of life itself, as if caught in a camera lens: two 'tiny still figures in the middle of it all. That was Dad and me.'

Megan and Ryan have their experiences during summer holidays, but *Hey, Dad!* and *Peggy's Cove* cannot be categorized as 'holiday stories', like Arthur Ransome's *Swallows and Amazons* series, which show children freed from the restrictions of school and rigid parental time-tables and open to opportunities for exciting adventures that allow them to mature on their own. Rather, Doyle's books are in the current tradition of mingling children and adults in a strained but ultimately liberating relationship. The adults cause the problems, but in most cases they also help to ameliorate them and participate in the healing process.

In the American problem novels of the late sixties and early seventies death is almost a common denominator. Generally an adult dies—not a family member necessarily, but an older person whom the young protagonist has come to care for. (A notable exception to this trend is Katherine Paterson's *Bridge to Terebithia* (1977), in which a child is drowned.) The chief purpose of these deaths is to enable the young to come to terms with their problems; death has the aspect of a plot device. It is to Doyle's credit that the death of Wingding in *You Can Pick Me Up at Peggy's Cove* is not used as a convenience, but has inevitability (due to plausible circumstances) and genuine drama.

Other Canadian writers—including Doyle himself in *Up to Low* (1982)—have used the occurrence of death even more movingly and powerfully in family situations. In Kevin Major's *Hold Fast* (1978),

Michael flees from the graveside of his parents, both of whom have been killed in a car accident caused by a drunken driver. He has to run away to cry—fourteen-year-olds do not cry in public. While his brother is kept at Marten with his beloved grandfather, Michael has to leave this Newfoundland outport village for a larger community to live with an authoritarian uncle, a mouse-like aunt, and a cousin who lives in fear of his father. The trials of adjustment to his traumatic situation are not only compounded by his new family life but by his difficulties at school. Michael runs again, this time *to* something rather than *from* something. He wants to get home to Marten, to his grandfather and young brother. His flight, in which he is joined by his cousin Curtis, is carefully planned and executed. At first they head away from Marten and spend a few days camping in a deserted National Park campsite (it is close to winter) and live by trapping rabbits. When Michael finally gets home, it is to face another shock—his grandfather is dying. Michael survives it all—he will 'hold fast', like the kelp that clings to the shores of Newfoundland. He will live with his aunt and be a father and even a grandfather to his brother.

Of all first-person narrators, Michael conveys the most emotion over his distress. This is partly achieved by Major's use (not overuse) of the dialect of the Newfoundland outports. When Michael is jeered at by his fellow students in the town, he says: 'What bloody odds do it make anyway, as long as people understands what you got to say?' (a question that will endear him to many a student). Michael's use of profanity (again not overused) is to be taken as a sign of stress and adolescent rebellion—his anger at his loss demands an outlet in expletives and wrongdoing. It is made clear that he does well in his English classes.

Newfoundland itself is omnipresent in the story. It is described in the contrast between outport life and town life. In the former, traditional skills—such as fishing, hunting, and trapping—still hold pride of place. St Albert, where Michael is forced to live, could be many a town in Canada. It has 'a newsprint mill, an airport, shopping malls, two arenas . . . a Dairy Queen, and two Kentucky Fried Chicken joints.' It is only three hundred miles from Michael's home—where the natural world, especially the ocean, is dominant—but to him it could be light years away. Eventually Michael finds a panacea for his loss in an environment that demands active involvement, rather than in a passive, artificial one.

While Puritan and Victorian children's literature was filled with actual death-scenes, modern writers keep death off-stage. (Car accidents, for example, are convenient and statistically realistic.) Nor, as in the past, are religious beliefs presented to comfort and sustain the living. Modern writers appear to be existentialists. In their books (as in *Hold Fast*) the young are angry—with the natural egotism of the young—that they should be so badly treated and deprived through no fault of their own. So the emphasis is on the healing process; emotional strength must be found through family and friends.

Jeremy Talbot, in Jean Little's *Mamma's Going to Buy You a Mocking Bird* (1984), knows that his father is dying of cancer, but as an eleven-year-old he cannot entirely comprehend 'how it was going to be' without his father. He can only admit that 'Dad was dead' when he hears his mother singing the old lullaby—a sign that now only his 'mamma' would be doing things for him. But Jeremy's father, a kind and compassionate teacher, left his son his own acute perception of, and sensitivity towards, people and nature; he had encouraged Jeremy's friendship with one of his favourite pupils and he gave him a stone owl, a symbol of their shared love of bird-watching. In this book—the style of which has matured greatly from Little's early works, such as *Home From Far*, with its simple, competent, descriptive phraseology—the language has a cadence that reminds one of the flight of the birds that are integral to her simple symbolism. Little also shows the ability to leave words unsaid, conveying meanings through the glances and silences that are so much a part of everyday family interaction.

In combining humour and pathos, comedy and tragedy, Sarah Ellis's *The Baby Project* (1986) is unique in Canadian children's literature. Ellis achieves these antitheses by dividing her short work into two separate parts. The first is a picture of a modern family, just quirky enough to be interesting: there is a working professional engineer mother, a father who is a taxi-driver *cum* house-husband (his meals are excellent), a fourteen-year-old son who is beginning to show the strains of adolescence, an older one who lives away from home, and an eccentric tenant who writes parodies of country-and-western songs. Above all there is eleven-year-old Jessica, who is sensitively alive to the small world around her. She notes, for example, that her mother is too concerned about PARENTING. All the early scenes are episodic and humorous: those of the schoolroom (the teacher tries *so* hard to be perfect), mealtimes (hilarious), and a larger-than-life sleep-over party. When the mother, at age forty-one, announces that she is to have a baby, all are delighted. Jessica and her best friend Margaret, who is feistier even than Jessica, decide to change their school project. Having picked the duck-billed platypus, they now choose to research babies. When the baby is born the project continues. Jessica and Margaret tape-record the waves of the ocean as a lullaby for Baby Lucie and take an interest in what is read to her—it can be anything from excerpts from an encyclopedia to Mother Goose to *Motor Trends*.

Then a swift and stunning blow occurs: Baby Lucie dies of crib death. The second part of the book concerns the effect on the family of this mysterious medical tragedy. It is here that Ellis shows her gift for quick, sure strokes delineating character. In particular the mother's reaction is completely believable (and psychologically understandable). Part of Jessica's healing comes from Margaret, who has already suffered through her parent's divorce and abandonment by her father and has survived. When Jessica questions Margaret on the future sadnesses life may provide, she answers:

> 'I don't think it gets worse and worse. I think it just gets to be more of a . . . sort of mixture, with different kinds of happy and sad.'

'Happy and sad' is an apt description of the story, but happiness does win out. In a night bike-ride through the city that has a magical quality, Jessica and her brother experience a renewal of their family intimacy and enter into a surge of exuberance. They are children after all. As Ellis's portrayal of children rings true, so does her dialogue, whether between child and child, child and parent, or child and teacher. It is natural and colloquial, but rendered with an art that conceals art; and it is given further depth by Jessica's inward musings on what has happened to herself and her family.

The Baby Project is a sensitive probing of a childhood crisis with an equally sensitive resolution. Marilyn Halvorson's *Cowboys Don't Cry* (1984) and *Let It Go* (1985), and Mary-Ellen Lang Collura's *Winners*

(1984)—with their older male protagonists, and situations caused chiefly by either the death of parents or their desertion—have a quality of raw anger rather than the quieter struggle for acceptance that marks the novels of Ellis and Little. The Alberta settings of Halvorson and Collura, with an emphasis on outdoor life (the rodeo, the ranch, horse-raising, and the skills such occupations call for), give their novels the feel of a western movie. Their roughness of emotion is also matched by their unpolished style.

Shane Morgan of *Cowboys Don't Cry*, and Red and Lance of *Let It Go*, all have some kind of parental problem. Shane's mother has been killed in a car accident and Shane believes that it was caused by his father's drunken driving. After a childhood spent on the rodeo circuits, where his father has been demoted from champion bull-rider to rodeo clown, Shane inherits a very small ranch and a rundown house. For the first time in his life it offers him a sense of permanency, an education and a normal high-school life, with friends, sports, and school dances. But the call of the rodeo is too much for his father (he has become a champion again), and in an explosion of anger Shane tears away on his motorcycle (a gift from his father) and has a serious accident. His father disappears; as in all difficult situations, he has run away. In a climactic rodeo scene, his father, now again a rodeo clown, saves Shane's life from a raging bull. As a coda, his father gives Shane his mother's horse; the rift between father and son is healed.

Lance's mother in Halvorson's *Let It Go* has left her native husband and son to pursue her career as a country-and-western singer in Nashville. His friend Red's father and mother appear to care more for their elder son, who is hospitalized in an incurable coma (as a result of drugs), than they do for Red. Lance gets involved with the teenage drug scene and has a knife-fight with the young wealthy 'pusher', in which his hand is seriously injured. Both boys experience their father's love for them, and Lance has some communication with his mother; their relationship is further developed in the sequel, *Nobody Said It Would Be Easy* (1987).

Jordy Threebears of Collura's *Winners* is fifteen years old,

... but already he'd seen enough of Alberta to last a lifetime. Eleven foster homes in eight years, and moving again. It was enough to make him sick.

Now Jordy's social-worker has arranged for him to be placed with his grandfather (whom he has never seen) on a reservation. He finds it difficult to communicate with the old man, and at school he is unjustly accused of starting a fight. His life changes for the better through a seeming disaster. He is lost in a blizzard, but in a fantasy episode he is guided to the home of an elderly Indian by a spirit horse and rider who utters the word 'Siksika' (Blackfoot). He finds out that his father was a famed rodeo star, killed in an accident, and that his mother was later raped and killed by a white man whom his grandfather has killed in retribution and was imprisoned for his crime. Jordy gets a horse through the efforts of his grandfather and his elderly friend. The horse turns out to be a 'winner', as does Jordy. After helping a blind girl race her horse (she wins), he is in turn helped to train his own horse for an important and lucrative race. He wins it—in competition with some of the best horses, riders, and trainers in the country—in spite of losing time by stopping to rescue his avowed enemy, the brother of the man his grandfather killed.

This ending is of course highly melodramatic. The thrust of the story seems to be that Jordy will now always be a 'winner'. In its concept of winning, *Winners* begs comparison with *Banner in the Sky* (1954) by the American writer James Ullman, in which a Swiss boy does *not* reach the top of an Alpine mountain in a competition because he has stopped to help a rival. Here, as in most stories of its period, virtue is its own reward. The double theme of *Winners*—that of a lonely, embittered boy gathering together the skein of a life that had been tragically unravelled, and finding his native heritage—is strong enough to overcome often pedestrian writing.

Collura changes locale in her second book, *Sunny* (1988), set in the 'Flatlands' of Vancouver, British Columbia. The plot is in two parts. First there is Sophie's family life, with its usual scenario of a modern broken home, here compounded by the mother's abandonment of a retarded child. The second part concerns Sunny the horse, who becomes the focus of Sophie's life and, more importantly, that of the child Mike, who develops a soothing power over the highly strung animal. Collura's concept of 'winning' is as important here as in her first book. Sunny wins an important race, against all odds, with the help of the children (indeed, Sophie is the rider); his leg is broken, but the children receive him as a gift from the owner and he will be well again. The background setting, a preserve of the 'horse crowd', gives a strong sense of credibility to the story, which also offers a glimpse into lives other than those of the young protagonists. The elderly woman Olga—who has survived the Nazi holocaust and who becomes a mentor and even a surrogate mother for Sophie and Mike—relates some of her experiences to Sophie. Although her past tragic life has no effect on the plot, her strong personality does in its effect on the children's lives (somewhat like that of the grandfather in Collura's *Winners*).

Horses also play a large role in Jan Truss's *Summer Goes Riding* (1987) as four young people, on the verge of adolescence, work, play, help one another, and experience a tornado during one hot summer in Nebraska. Charlotte Mauney is obsessed with horses; she draws them, dreams about them, longs for a horse, but has never even ridden one. Her friend Red's father has been commissioned to provide and raise a foal for a wealthy English schoolboy, Sidney Topham, and this is the horse that Charlotte cares for beyond all others.

Much English fiction for children from about the 1930s to the 1960s concern horses or ponies. In these years 'horse stories' could almost be considered a separate genre. The classic of the period is Enid Bagnold's *National Velvet* (1935), the exhilarating story of a child who rides the winning horse in the Grand National but who is disbarred because she is a girl. Most books, however, were simple tales of children wanting a pony, getting one, caring for it, riding in gymkhanas, leaping fences, and winning races. Halvorson, Collura, and especially Jan Truss in *Summer Goes Riding*, show that there is a real bond between each young protagonist and the animal, but their books cannot simply be described as 'horse stories'. *Summer Goes Riding* is mainly about the family lives and the emotional development of the young people. Charlotte does not attain her heart's desire, but is hired by Red's father to help in the stables and especially to look after the foal 'All Gold'. There is a feeling of enchantment that makes the children slightly pixilated for one summer. When their activities are swept away by a tornado, Charlotte's family suffers the greatest loss and harm (her father is almost killed) and the young people take on adult roles as they help in search and rescue operations. *Summer Goes Riding* is an unusual book in the depth of its portrayal of Charlotte's obsession with owning a horse and winning races and her yearning for the best English riding boots; this obsession persists even in spite of the family's disaster. As the story ends, she appears to be farther from her goal than ever, except for her determination.

As a sequel, Truss's *Red* (1988) is a disappointment. Although there is some tension in Red's interest in a mentally handicapped girl, the drama created through the obsession with horses in the first book is here dissipated through several sub-plots. It also lacks the rich style and in-depth characterization of *Summer Goes Riding*.

As Collura and Truss have almost resurrected the 'horse story' and given it a modern psychological dimension, so Kit Pearson has remodelled and energized the 'boarding-school story'. For obvious reasons, boarding-school life has not played the strong part in Canadian children's literature that it has played in British books, especially since the days of *The Boy's Own Paper* (beginning in 1879) and *The Girl's Own Paper* (beginning in 1880). Both these magazines survived into the 1960s and relied heavily for their appeal on the school story (often combined with mysteries), as did many other British serial publications. Boarding-school stories can be considered an adjunct to family-life novels, since the young, separated from their parents and siblings, form ties and friendships, thus creating new families. In Canada there was a long gap between the *B.O.W.C.* school adventures by James De Mille in the 1860s and Veronica Tennant's story of a ballet school in *On Stage, Please* (1977). Like *Ballet Shoes* (1936), by the British writer Noel Streatfield, it is an accurate rendering of both the drudgery and romance not only of mastering a physical skill, but of achieving artistry. The lack of characterization is unimportant; young balletomanes will quickly identify themselves with the characters.

No English writer of the girl's school story—such as L.T. Meade or Angela Brazil, or a host of others—has produced one with the depth of Kit Pearson in *The Daring Game* (1986). The title, indicating a school prank that forms the chief narrative thread of the novel, is secondary to the theme of boarding-school life and to the character of twelve-year-old Eliza. She has insisted on attending a boarding-school in Vancouver out of a somewhat vague fear of the pressures and complexities of adolescence that she was beginning to face in a public school. She finds, however, that Ashdown Academy is not an escape from the real world but an entry to it. The view of boarding-school life is that of an insider: school work and school traditions, the hierarchical grouping of teachers and students, the friendships, loyalties, and rivalries among classmates, the breaking and testing of rules and regulations are all convincingly described. Eliza is forced to choose between duty and the traditions of the school and her love for her friend Helen, who has been a problem in the school and is in danger of expulsion. When the headmistress asks Eliza to tell her whether Helen has been lying and stealing, Eliza chooses friendship over the principles of the school (recalling E.M. Forster's remark: '. . . if I had to choose between betraying my country and betraying my friend, I hope I should have the guts to betray my country.') Eliza matures, changing from a shy, self-conscious child to a stronger, empathic individual capable of making moral decisions. Pearson's style is straightforward, but it has subtle nuances and a strong sense of place. Eliza, who has come from Edmonton, revels in Vancouver's scented flowering spring and its ocean breezes. Although set in the 1960s, *The Daring Game* is timeless in its emotional strength and quiet drama.

Stories of child and family life for younger readers that have a serious tone are extremely rare. Two exceptions are Jean Little's *Lost and Found* (1985) and Barbara Smucker's *Jacob's Little Giant* (1987). Little uses the pet-and-child relationship as a metaphor for a child's loneliness. Simply written, with an economy that conveys much psychological nuance, the narrative concerns young Lucy's adjustment to a new neighbourhood, her grief for lost friends, and her vulnerable love for a runaway stray dog. The small events that loom poignantly large in a young life are given the dignity they deserve and are never sentimentalized. Both Lucy and her dog are 'lost', and both are found—the dog by his original master, and Lucy by acquiring a sense of belonging in her new home. The unfolding of Lucy's intense feelings and maturing perceptions make this a rare and comforting book.

Barbara Smucker's Jacob of *Jacob's Little Giant*, is seven years old and small for his age. He is the youngest member of a Mennonite family in Ontario, the smallest child in his class and always the last to be chosen for any game. He longs to be treated as more grown-up and to take a more responsible part beside his adult brothers in the chores on his father's potato farm. His sense of inferiority, and his mother's loving admonitions to be careful when he is given a task, place an emotional stress on him, much as Kristli's conscience did in Mabel Dunham's earlier Mennonite story, *Kristli's Trees*. Then Jacob's father entrusts him with a very important summer task: he is made responsible for tending a family of giant Canada geese nesting on a pond on the farm property. Jacob falls in love with their wild beauty; but he is especially drawn to the 'little giant' of the title—the tiniest gosling, a runt like himself. Like Lucy with her stray dog, Jacob cares devotedly for his charges and in two dramatic scenes saves them from predators—both animal and human. He wins the approval of his family and the expert from the Provincial Natural Resources office. Migration time comes and the giant geese rise upward.

> Little Giant was far behind.
> Jacob called softly, 'Try harder, Little Giant. You can make it.'
> Little Giant did stroke his wings harder and faster, and he roared by Jacob's window. He honked and honked, high and shrill.
> 'I'll be back in the spring . . .' he seemed to be saying to Jacob.

Smucker does not portray a conservative Mennonite family. Unlike the traditional Amish in her *Amish Adventure* (1983), Jacob's sisters wear blue jeans or pretty clothes, work outside the home, and there is a strong sense of the family's involvement with the surrounding community. Still, there is a feeling of traditional family life, and exchanges with the father reveal him as very much the kindly patriarch. Jacob is an endearing young hero whose imagination gives him an affinity for the natural world, and we rejoice in his quiet growth in perseverance, courage, and acceptance of responsibility. Smucker tells the story in a gentle, poetic style, with some touches of family humour.

LIGHT REALISM

Not all modern realistic fiction deals with problems. A few writers— Ellen Schwartz, Betty Waterton, and Ken Roberts, among others—are interested in the light-hearted aspects of child and family life.

They see what is comic rather than serious. Such writers speak more of a generic child and childhood that could apply to most children, rather than focusing on a highly specific set of circumstances, as the majority of realistic writers do. The chief successes in this area from the United States have been Beverly Cleary's *Ramona* series, beginning in 1968, and Lois Lowry's *Anastasia Krupnik* (1979) and its sequels. The Canadian offerings are as yet too new to have reached *Ramona*'s popularity, but the present candidates are promising, like Betty Waterton's *Quincy Rumple* series, beginning in 1984. Quincy's exuberant and disastrous escapades form the skeleton of the various episodes. (In one such Quincy, as the Minotaur in her school play, startlingly reappears after her death-scene, accidentally bouncing on a trampoline, and steals the show.) However, the heart of the stories is found in Quincy's relationships with her family and friends, as recounted in *Quincy Rumple* (1984), *Starring Quincy Rumple* (1986), and *Quincy Rumple P.I.* (1988), in which she investigates haunted houses. Like *Quincy Rumple*, and indeed like most light realistic fiction, Ellen Schwartz's *Starshine!* (1987) moves from one comic episode to another. Starshine Bliss Shapiro is the child of parents who lived through the euphoria of the 1960s. Her now-mellowed eccentric parents are drawn with generous comic flair—her mother, who moulds pottery, gives birth to her creations with dramatic whoops, and her father whistles his way through stained-glass creations while giving advice on life. Starshine has her own well-decided character—she is a confirmed vegetarian and a collector of spiders.

The light touches of slapstick and farce in both Waterton and Schwartz are even further exaggerated in Ken Roberts' *Pop Bottles* (1987) and *Hiccup Champion of the World* (1988). Both stories have a cumulative tall-tale effect reminiscent of the American writer Robert McCloskey in *Homer Price* (1943) and *Centerburg Tales* (1951). *Pop Bottles* is set in the Depression of the 1930s, when the average child's desire for extra money was very real and unattainable. Young Will thinks he will become rich if only he can recover the huge cache of pop bottles set in the walkway of his new home. Maynard Chan of *Hiccup Champion of the World* is a contemporary boy whose hiccups will not go away despite the remedies (often bizarre) offered by family and friends. The mothers in both books are comically idiosyncratic contrasts to the ordinariness of their sons. The close-knit multicultural neighbourhood of *Hiccup Champion* links it to many of our earlier stories of child and family life.

Family warmth, sliding in and out of wacky satire, is even more pronounced in *Left Behind in Squabble Bay* (1988), by Jack Hodgins, who is better known as a writer of fiction for adults and the winner of a Governor General's Award. It tells of a 'Back East' boy who reluctantly finds he's stranded in the drizzly Vancouver Island world of pulp mills and larger-than-life people. Alex is a chronic worrier, a lonely amateur comic-strip artist whose acerbic cartoons of the gloomy townspeople get him into considerable trouble. Hodgins reaches below the comic surface of his bizarre characters—from the Garbo-like duchess in exile to the outcast Big Jim, once a bathtub racing champion—to explore the concept of humour. Through amusing misadventures, Alex and Big Jim restore a sense of joy to the town.

Farce is an element in all these tales of light realism. Gordon Korman's school and camp stories of young adolescents, beginning with *This Can't Be Happening at McDonald Hall!* (1978)—written as a grade-seven English assignment—are examples of pure farce, dependent on formula and slapstick. In contrast to most stories of light realism, in which adults are important members of the play, here they are stock enemies, authority figures to be outwitted. Korman's writing, with its comic-book predictability and stereotypical antics, is almost a parody of the school story.

Florence McNeil's *Miss P. and Me* (1982) is also primarily set in the school world of the young adolescent, but it stretches the borders of light realism, pushing it beyond farce to serious insight into character and childhood. The theme of self-discovery is here combined with light humour and the conventional episodic format. Narrated in a dryly witty first-person voice, the story chronicles Jane's grade-eight year in a Catholic school. The religious-school atmosphere, the deft characterization of teachers and students, and gentle social satire form a background to Jane's perceptions of an eccentric dance teacher—shifting from hero worship to intolerance, and finally to compassion. Jane's diary entries and poems, which reveal her growth as a writer, provide comic and poignant relief to the stormy plot-line of her growth into maturity as her lack of co-ordination destroys her dream of becoming a dancer.

The forms of humour and styles of writing in light realism vary widely. Betty Waterton and Ellen Schwartz write domestic comedies with simple clarity, sharing a breezy, naïve tone in describing farcical events and characters. The family is at the centre of these stories; parents and siblings carry as much emotional weight as Quincy and Starshine. The tall tales of Ken Roberts and Jack Hodgins are less episodic, built as they are around inventive comic premises that are much like cumulative jokes. Their comic tone is quite varied. While their slightly older characters display a sophisticated sense of irony, there are also elements of slapstick, caricature, and verbal wit. Florence McNeil is more fully realistic, maintaining a tension between irony and emotional subtlety. With the exception of Korman's vague eastern-Canadian settings—which have become vaguely American in his recent works, such as *Don't Care High* (1985)—these books are all set in the slightly eccentric West Coast atmosphere of Vancouver and Vancouver Island.

MYSTERY AND DETECTIVE STORIES

Detection and mystery in children's literature appears to begin with the sensational boys' magazines of the late-nineteenth century, especially those published by the newspaper baron Alfred Harmsworth (Viscount Northcliffe). As opposed to the quality literature of the Victorian age directed at the children of the well-to-do middle class, these cheap, serialized publications were intended for working-class boys to capitalize on the popularity of the pulp literature known as 'penny dreadfuls'. One of the earliest detectives, Sexton Blake, appeared first in Harmsworth's *Marvel* (1893); though an adult, he was juvenile in his perceptions and became known as 'the office-boy's Sherlock Holmes'. Youthful detectives appeared and disappeared in the pages of these magazines, surfacing in the American commercialized series such as *The Bobbsey Twins*, *The Hardy Boys*, and *Nancy Drew*, published by the Stratemeyer Syndicate between 1904 and 1930 (they are still in print). These books are about super young people or children. Sixteen-year-old Nancy Drew (age eighteen in the revised editions) can win a golf match with an injured hand, and the Bobbsey twins succeed where the whole Japanese police force has failed. Enid Blyton continued this tradition of the invincible young with her 'Famous Five' series, begun in 1942, in which four cousins (and a dog!), who meet for the summer holidays, consistently unmask and outwit smugglers and thieves, and even a gang of Nazis on a submarine off England's shores.

For a while it appeared as if the detective story for children could be a piece of quality literature—well-written, exciting, consistent in plot development, and above all childlike—when Erich Kästner's *Emil and the Detectives* was translated from the German in 1929. Emil, and the other children he meets in Berlin, organize themselves into a team to track down the thief who has stolen Emil's money. Without the help of adults, the children follow police procedures and retrieve the money chiefly by embarrassing the villain. This pattern of poor but happy, resourceful, independent children, acting in concert, continued with Paul Berna's *A Hundred Million Francs* (1957) and its sequel *The Street Musician* (1960), both translated from the French. The convention of the armchair boy-detective who solved problems by deduction alone was made popular by the Swedish author Astrid Lindgren with her 'Masterdetective Blomquivst', translated into English as *Bill Bergson, The Masterdetective* (1952), and by the American Donald J. Sobol, with his series beginning with *Encyclopedia Brown, Boy Detective* (1963).

Most Canadian mysteries for children have been published since 1980 and are the products of only a few publishing houses. They are produced in paperback editions, or with board covers, and give the impression that six new ones must be ready each month for the mass market. Most are also immediately recognizable by their titles. The formula demands the word 'mystery', or an indication of murder or suspense—*The Mystery at the Wildcat Well*, *Payment in Death*, or *The Ghost of Pirate Walk*—and the youthful detective ('Susan George', 'Tom Austen', 'Liz Austen', 'Julie Dare') is often featured on the cover, as in adult works. The writers associated with this type of novel are Eric Wilson, Marion Crook, Robert Sutherland, and Sarah Gordon, among others.

The great majority are set in Canada within specific locales, mostly rural, and with some information imparted about the district or the topical background of the mystery, or a combination of the two. Marion Crook's *The Hidden Gold Mystery* (1987), set outside of Williams Lake, British Columbia, has some insights into panning for gold and into nature lore. The lake, in Robert Sutherland's *The Loon*

Lake Murders (1987), is in Algonquin Park, and one discovers that it is an asset to know the Ojibway language. Eric Wilson's *The Kootenay Kidnapper* (1983) includes a section on spelunking; Elfreida Read's *Race Against the Dark* (1983) takes place on an island near Vancouver, and the children appropriately engage in sailing; the Hamilton setting of Lynn Manuel's *The Mystery of the Ghostly Riders* (1982) plays only a small part in the story, but William Lyon Mackenzie plays a large part as the children discover that a member of a Tory family helped him to escape. All the children and young people in these formula mysteries are of course omniscient. In Marion Crook's *Stone Dead* (1987), for example, it is the sixteen-year-old Susan George who devises the trap for a dangerous killer, while the summoned police hover in the background. In a mystery novel for the young, the young have to be centre-stage, and in spite of their authors' attempts at verisimilitude, there is an element of fantasizing that links them to the 'derring-do' of the Hardy Boys and Nancy Drew.

Only about a dozen mystery stories (those declared in the title as mystery stories) were published before 1980, and all have deservedly disappeared, as probably will most of the 1980s formula books. The few published in the 1960s and early 1970s did not include extreme violence or murder. There were, of course, dangers and hunts and chases. In Lucy Berton Woodward's *Kidnapped in the Yukon* (1968) the young hero is kidnapped by a mad prospector and is forced to elude the people who are trying to rescue him. In Robert Collins' *The Mystery at the Wildcat Well* (1965), young Rory and two Dogrib children unmask the spy who is selling information about an oil find at Fort Mackenzie. Some stories, however, are quite gentle, with a simple mystery at the heart of them. Christie Harris's *Mystery at the Edge of Two Worlds* (1978) is still the most interesting of these earlier works, and certainly the richest in background. Set around the northwest coast of British Columbia, it bears believable marks of Harris's usual meticulous research: the flora and fauna of the region, native life and artifacts, and details of sailing. It also has a lively and imaginative heroine, hints of ghosts and native spirit power, and a touch of tension in family life (the widowed mother is falling in love). But as with so many children's mystery stories, it promises more than it delivers; the dénouement involves simple theft.

On the whole there is more violence in the recent books. Marion

Crook's *Payment in Death* (1987) begins with the discovery of a body in a grocery-store's garbage bin and another in its freezer-room. In her *Stone Dead* (1987) there are two murders and a teen-age boy attempts suicide. Robert Sutherland's *Mystery at Black Rock Island* (1983) ends with a shoot-out, and the smugglers' submarine destroyed. The smugglers have not been involved with gold or even drugs, but with a much more threatening anthrax bacillus.

Eric Wilson may be credited (if, indeed, it is a credit) with introducing murder into a children's mystery story with his premier effort, *Murder on the Canadian* (1976), the first of his 'Tom Austen' mysteries. He makes use of modern themes—drug smuggling in *Vancouver Nightmare* (1978) and terrorism, demonstrations, and the dangers to human life and the environment from industrial complexes (including a nuclear plant) in *Terror in Winnipeg* (1979). Terrorism and hostage-taking are also part of *Disneyland Hostage* (1983). Wilson's books run to a little over a hundred pages of large type, so only a resolution of the plot can be accommodated—any significance suggested by the theme is entirely neglected. Books about the young detective Tom Austen (and another series about his sister Liz) are on the order of the Hardy Boys and Nancy Drew books—these sleuths are all successful—but Tom especially has a naïve and clumsy method of investigation that makes the earlier detectives seem like professionals. The same applies to his sister. It is hard to believe that even the most avid young Wilson fan (of which there are said to be many) could swallow *Vampires of Ottawa* (1985). Liz Austen has been selected, as one of a group of young people, to engage in a speech contest at the home of the Governor General. The one note of reality in the whole book is that Liz does not win the competition; her speech (on vampires!) could have been derived from an encyclopedia, or perhaps more interestingly from a reading of Bram Stoker's *Dracula*. Her interest in vampires (does she believe in them or does she not?) leads her into a gothic adventure with a wealthy reclusive Romanian Baron, and his valet, in a ruined chapel on the Baron's estate, and a fake vampire in a coffin. In the non-credible ending, one longs for a real vampire!

The recent 'Julie Dare' series by Sarah Gordon proves at least two old adages: 'There is nothing new under the sun' and, *Plus ça change, plus c'est la même chose*. Julie Dare is the reincarnation of Nancy Drew, but firmly installed in Canada. Admittedly, her hair is different from Nancy's, which is 'reddish-blond' while Julie's is either raven black that 'glints dark golden brown' or dark-brown, 'which in softer light seems raven-black'. Like Nancy, Julie is motherless and has a handsome father and a devoted aunt who runs the household. Her father is a famous doctor (Nancy's is a lawyer), and before he became a doctor he was an artist, still considered by many 'to be the greatest Canadian painter of his time'. There is no room for failures in the Dare family. Julie had a French-Canadian mother, so she is perfectly bilingual. She is also talented musically, being able immediately to recognize musical notations from a Mozart opera. Most of all, Julie is famous as a detective, more so than Nancy, because Julie has received media coverage and is therefore well known outside Canada. She has excellent connections in the police world (her uncle is a detective in the RCMP), and is able to assist the French Sureté. Gordon's *The Dangerous Dollhouse* (1988) and *Eyes of the Lion* (1988) have rather involved plots; not difficult to understand, they are more intricately patterned than those of the Nancy Drew mysteries and contemporary in their use of electronic equipment. There is one great difference between the two eighteen-year-old detectives. The various syndicated writers of the American mysteries kept assuring the reader how modest Nancy was. Gordon makes no such claim for Julie Dare, who is so obnoxiously superior that one longs to return to Tom and Liz Austen—or Nancy Drew.

Often the simpler stories that involve children, rather than teenagers, are more fun to read and show more originality in plot. Mary Howarth's *Could Dracula Live in Woodford?* (1983) involves two overly imaginative children and Sam (short for Samantha), a dog who has a penchant for mystery and adventure and who can mentally communicate with her 'dogsitter' Jennie. Jennie and her friend Beth (abetted by Sam) decide that an elderly recluse is a vampire and take steps to prove it for the sake of the town. Feeling very foolish at the end, Jennie and Beth vow to keep a tighter rein on their imaginations, but not Sam. Being thwarted over her vampire, Sam discovers that Frankenstein is indeed living in Woodford! While mysteries for older readers are cluttered with somewhat mysterious clues, part of the charm and cleverness of Howarth's humorous tale lies in the probability that young readers will keep ahead of the two sleuths.

Armchair detection, practised by Astrid Lindgren's Bill Bergson and Donald J. Sobol's Encyclopedia Brown, has been given a new and even more interesting lease of life through Joan Weir's 'Mystery Club' series—*Ski Lodge Mystery and Other Stories* (1988) and *Balloon Race Mystery and Other Stories* (1988). These have some Canadian content, along with the old-fashioned but pleasurable idea of children acting co-operatively. But it is the reader who is asked to be a super-sleuth. The linked short stories concern a group of grade-five students who have formed a mystery club and set detection problems—trying to stump each other, a rival grade-five class, and even adults on Parents' Night. The clues are meticulously given and the solutions, not all that easy, are provided at the end of the book. Perhaps only adults will have to refer to them!

While such formula novels are in the ascendancy by virtue of numbers, there are some very good Canadian mystery stories that are not labelled as such, and in most cases could fit into several other categories of fiction. Claire Mackay's *The Minerva Program* (1984) has the classic pattern of Kästner's *Emil and the Detectives*, of children acting together to right an injustice. Minerva is a bright grade-seven student who has been chosen as one of the very few to participate in a computer course. Her love of, and intense preoccupation with, the machine and its programs lead her to neglect even her best friend and to be impatient with her mother, a cashier in a supermarket, who is unhappy with the computerization of sales and feels dehumanized. Minerva is so competent that she is asked to keep the school records on the computer. In the course of updating these records she gains access to the school-district's salary list. Soon after she is accused of upgrading her physical-education mark and is banned from the computer room. In her disgrace, Minerva is supported by her friend Sophy, by another computer buff, Angelo, and by her young brother, who can climb almost like 'Spiderman'. A plan is worked out to gain access to the computer room at night and to find out who of three people found it necessary to alter Minerva's mark. The chief clue is provided by Sophy, a compulsive reader of Dickens, who spots a name from *Oliver Twist* (obviously an alias) on the key print-out. In the final scene the children act in concert, following their plan with almost mathematical precision, and unmask the villain. The writing is clear and crisp, the computer details are a necessary adjunct to the plot, and Minerva and Sophy are flesh-and-blood girls. Worked into the background are the details of an urban elementary school and Minerva's warm working-class family, with only a hint in the description of Minerva's attractive mother that the family is black.

Monica Hughes' *The Ghost Dance Caper* (1978) also has a dimension beyond the 'caper' itself. Tom Lightfoot is half-Blackfoot and half-white, and finds himself torn between the two cultures. His native father is a successful lawyer and his mother is not happy about Tom's regular Sunday visits to his great-grandfather on the reservation. When hearing of his dilemma, his great-grandfather tells him that in earlier days Tom, at his age of thirteen, would have been sent into the mountains to find his spirit. The ritual would have involved fasting and a ghost dance, which could not be held without a 'ghost bundle'. But ghost bundles had all disappeared; the last known one had been sold to the city's museum. Thus begins the first caper. Tom, and his friend Pete, spot the ghost bundle almost hidden among other Blackfoot artifacts in the museum, and with great planning and cunning (chiefly Pete's), they steal it and the dance is held. But when Tom confesses to his great-grandfather that the ghost-bundle has been stolen, he is ordered to return it by himself. After two nights trying to break into the museum, Tom finds a back door open. He also finds the guards tied up and injured and a robbery in progress: thieves are stealing valuable gold objects from a pre-Columbian Mexican exhibit. Escaping the thieves, Tom is able to reach a pay-telephone and call the police. Then, avoiding the police as well as the thieves, he manages to reach the roof of the museum where, in the darkness, he finds his spirit. *The Ghost Dance Caper* has the pace, and seemingly effortless style, of Monica Hughes' science-fiction novels and their insights into youth.

Many outstanding children's books are also good mysteries in the broad sense—from Stevenson's *Treasure Island* (1883) to Leon Garfield's *Smith* (1967). In Canadian children's literature there are others. David Walker's *Pirate Rock* (1969), set on the Bay of Fundy, is a story of international intrigue, with two teenagers causing the death of a spy, Mr Becker, and as a result pleasing the local residents, who have resented Becker's high-style life and his fenced-in estate. The plot has the pace of a John Buchan spy story, and the moral dimension of a Le Carré novel, since the two boys, having accepted a summer job from Mr Becker, feel that they have betrayed a trust and caused sorrow to Becker's wife, who loved him.

Two other good novels for children have earned a place in this genre. Joan Clark's *The Hand of Robin Squires* (see page 115), involving pirates and buried treasure on Nova Scotia's Oak Island in the eighteenth century, has enough suspense to be classified as a mystery, as well as historical fiction. And Brian Doyle's *Angel Square* is an excellent detective story, even though it deals with the serious theme of racial conflict. *The Minerva Program, The Ghost Dance Caper, Pirate Rock, The Hand of Robin Squires,* and *Angel Square* all satisfy the requirements of a good mystery story, but because they are not formula books, and do not have 'mystery' in the title, they tend to be overlooked—to be considered rather as mainstream fiction. As a result, young readers in search of a good mystery or detective novel are likely to be prevented from finding out how much depth and satisfaction this genre can provide.

NOVELS FOR YOUNG ADULTS

If the young-adult novel were to be defined only by the ages of its protagonists, then most Canadian fiction for the young (especially the early works) would fall into this category. The outdoor adventure story called for skills of survival far beyond those of children, and so most of the protagonists are teen-aged males. The trend continued. Haig-Brown's Don Morgan in *Starbuck Valley Winter* is sixteen; Farley Mowat's Jamie and Awasin, in *Lost in the Barrens,* are about fourteen; and Houston's Inuit hero in *Tikta'Liktak* is a young man. All three books were winners of the Book-of-the-Year for Children Award given by the Canadian Association of Children's Librarians. Paralleling the traditionally male protagonists of the outdoor adventure story are the heroines of the early family stories. In Montgomery's Anne and Emily books the heroine moves from childhood through adolescence to maturity, with the adolescent years (especially Emily's) forming the core of each series. Yet it is their child readership that has kept them alive.

The state of life called adolescence has been a key part of many classic adult novels—for example, Dickens' *David Copperfield,*

Brontë's *Jane Eyre*, Lawrence's *Sons and Lovers*, and Alice Munro's *Lives of Girls and Women*. The abrupt change that can end adolescence is one of the staples of fiction. Mark Twain, in *The Adventures of Huckleberry Finn* (1884), first used an adolescent as the sole narrator. An observer and a critic of the life he saw around him, Huck is also a person in crisis; he has to make a moral decision. He knows the religious and social conventions of his time, and he feels that he is committing a sin in not reporting the whereabouts of the escaped Negro slave, Jim, who has become his friend. Huck says to himself: 'All right then, I'll go to hell.' After making probably the most courageous decision recorded in literature, Huck also decides to take charge of his own destiny and 'light out for the territory'. Twain did not write *Huckleberry Finn* for a specific audience (although he reassured a worried mother that it was *not* intended for children), but it can be considered as a novel for young adults, since it has been both used in, and banned from, high-school English courses. Equally, J.D. Salinger in no way anticipated (and neither did his publisher) that *The Catcher in the Rye* (1951) would become a cult book with high-school and college students. But for more than a generation Salinger's Holden Caulfield was a symbol of rebellion against a 'phoney' adult society, and the Salinger style—the first-person narrative of a precocious, cynical teenager—became the prototype of the flood of teenage novels emanating from the United States in the late 1960s, and it is still in use.

While in a literary sense the young-adult novel of today has its roots in *Huckleberry Finn* and *The Catcher in the Rye*, its appearance in the 1960s as a publishing phenomenon had more to do with changes in society than with literary antecedents. By then the children of the post-war baby boom were a well-defined group of adolescents, targeted by commercial enterprise as having common needs and desires. They had cars, jobs, money, and many of them were being confronted by the difficulties arising from drugs, liquor, and sex. Whatever their interests were, a sense of alienation from adult society was paramount. Nevertheless adolescence, rather than childhood, was the best of all possible worlds, in contrast to earlier times. The separation of the adolescent from both childhood (children yearned to be teenagers) and adulthood was signified by distinctive styles of clothing, music, films, and eventually books, written by people who had served no apprenticeship to the art of writing but who knew the market. Publishers began to issue lists for young adults separate from those for children or adults.

In imitating Salinger, however, the American writers Judy Blume, Paul Zindel, Richard Peck, and a host of others overlooked the qualities that made Holden Caulfield such a memorable character: his sensitivity, his bewilderment, his tender love for the innocent and the underdog, and indeed his basic purity (in spite of his use of four-letter words). Salinger created a new adolescent voice, while providing authentic motives for Holden's behaviour and experimenting with a poignant open-ended resolution. But his followers all too often settled for slick dialogue (chiefly monologue), and an exploration of sexuality, and of grievances with the adult (mainly parental) world. As varied as the problems were in the American teenage novel of the 1960s, they shared a commonality in their resolutions. Their authors appeared to be intent on bringing the young to terms with themselves and their situations—but in an egotistical sense. Many books in this period had 'I' or 'Me' in the title.

Although these books were advertised and marketed as being for the 'young adult', their simplicity of style and equally simple look at the problems involved also made them as available to children as to teenagers; the lines between the two audiences became blurred. In a publishing sense the rewards were great, because the young-adult novel had two markets. This publishing trend, which continues today, helps to explain the relative dearth of novels with child characters.

In Canada, the young-adult novel as a genre defined by age, either of protagonist or readership, hardly made an appearance until the 1980s. In John Craig's *No Word for Good-bye* (1969) the problem is societal rather than personal. Two fifteen-year-olds—Ken, a white boy, and Paul, an Ojibway—meet during a summer at Ken's family cottage in Manitoba and become friends. The townspeople object to the natives' camping outside the village (they are on their traditional summer trek). Ken's father tries to intervene on behalf of the tribe, but to no avail. Ken and Paul have agreed to meet for Thanksgiving, but when Ken arrives, the tribe has disappeared. Ken is at first hurt, because Paul has not even left him a message, but then he remembers that Paul has told him that 'in Ojibway there is no word for good-bye'.

Peter Davies' *Fly Away Paul* (1974) is based on its author's experiences as a teacher in a Boys' Home in Montreal. It is an exposé of harsh and cruel treatment meted out to boys, most of whom had no criminal record but were there because, for various reasons, they were deprived of family life. The totally masculine atmosphere of the Home, with its cruelty and brutal sexuality, brings to mind documentaries of prison life. Paul, at age fourteen, is good-looking and has an air of self-sufficiency that makes him attractive to other boys and to his headmaster. He wants to be an astronomer, but is taken out of school and forced to work for the Home. Somehow he survives the death of his closest friend, drug-taking, beatings, and the loss of a girl-friend. Then, like Huck Finn, he makes a decision and escapes to Toronto to start a new life. There is a bit of Holden Caulfield in Paul. He delights in hearing a young woman in the park singing the old rhyme to children, 'Fly away, Peter,/ Fly away, Paul./ Come back, Peter,/ Come back, Paul' (Holden was delighted by 'Comin' Through the Rye'), and he cares for the child Wolf, as Holden cared for his little sister. In general Canadian writers of young-adult novels are more optimistic, and provide their characters with a broader view of life than their American counterparts, whose protagonists are very self-absorbed. The young Canadians may experience crises on their way to adulthood, but they will enter it with a *persona* of their own making.

While Kevin Major's *Hold Fast* (1978), and Marilyn Halvorson's books, such as *Cowboys Don't Cry* (1984), have young teenagers as central characters, the writing, the themes, the events, and the overall tone are simple enough to appeal to children. In fact Shane of *Cowboys Don't Cry* is reading S.E. Hinton's *The Outsiders* (1967)—the popular American work that straddles a young-adult and child readership. But whether the protagonists are childlike teenagers or adolescents on the brink of adulthood, they are more like Huck Finn, in their ability to control their destiny, rather than the emotionally lost Holden Caulfield.

Kevin Major's *Far from Shore* (1980), *Thirty-six Exposures* (1984), and *Dear Bruce Springsteen* (1987) are far more in the young-adult mould than his *Hold Fast*. Christopher Slade of *Far from Shore* is fifteen and life is difficult for him. Work is not easy to find in Marten, Newfoundland (the government has not yet built the promised fish plant), and Chris's alcoholic father has to leave for Alberta to earn money. Chris is failing at school, keeping bad company, drinking too much, and getting in trouble with the law. He is at odds with his mother and his clever sister and cannot communicate with the girl he likes. The crisis comes at summer camp when he breaks camp rules, over-estimates his skills, and almost causes a young boy's death. But he takes responsibility for his actions, and his family supports him during his court appearance.

The story is told through the multiple narratives of Chris, his mother, sister, and father, who relate their views of the family situation and their own feelings separately. The device is interesting, but the passages are too short for any real delineation of character, and the voices have a sameness to them, except perhaps for Chris's constant use of the word 'frig' and other mild profanities. This, of course, is to be taken as an aspect of Major's honest realism—it is the way many young Newfoundlanders speak. Still, it becomes tedious. One thinks of the boy in Karl Bjarnhof's adolescent novel *The Good Light* (1959), translated from the Danish, who remarks: 'I don't mind people swearing, but in a book!' Newfoundland English warrants, and has, its own dictionary, but it is in *Hold Fast*, rather than in *Far From Shore*, that such words as *scravelling*, *squid-jigging*, and *boughwiffen* give a sense of a place that has its own distinctive vocabulary and colloquial poetry. *Hold Fast* also conveys the rhythm and pattern of Newfoundland speech more effectively than in Major's more recent works. As Michael in *Hold Fast* runs from his parent's grave, he silently admonishes himself with the following words:

> Run. Run, you crazy fool of a son. Run through the paths. Jump outa the way or them thoughts'll grab ya! Bring ya up all-standing. Choke ya. Take away your last livin' breath, clean and holy.

In Major's short novel, *Thirty-six Exposures*, the title refers to the film in Lorne's camera, which captures important moments during the final weeks before his high-school graduation. His camera not only provides a record of a brief time that will change his life, but it is also a metaphor of his experience, his growing perceptions of his inner life and his Newfoundland background. The pictures he takes will remain on film, even as they are etched in his memory. Lorne fights against what he perceives to be his school's authoritarianism; he is alienated from his father and mother; he writes poetry; he and his group are undeservedly given a 'D' in their class project; he fumbles with sex; and after a reckless prank, his best friend is killed. But at the end:

> He's gone to make his picture too
> It's his own life
> to do with what he must do . . .

Canadian writers for the adolescent may be regional in their backgrounds, but they all depict the young as being in charge of their own destinies, courageously and sensibly. Rebels or misfits or the order of Holden Caulfield are absent. Typical Canadian restraint prevails.

Newfoundland is an integral part of all Major's books—its people, its customs, its economic problems, its landscape, and most of all its people's roots. None of Major's later books, however, have the passion and energy and affirmation of life of *Hold Fast*. In *Dear Bruce Springsteen* the setting is not central. Its focus is on a teenager's imaginary relationship with the American rock star. In his misery the boy pours out all his problems to his idol, especially his unhappiness about his father, who has left home and is living in another town. When his relationship with his father begins to improve, he has less and less need of his letter-writing outlet. Without Major's usual strong background, the story is little more than another problem novel.

In Major's *Thirty-Six Exposures* there is a strong emphasis on the sexual attitudes of male teenagers as they swing from the raw tenderness of personal desire to coarse 'locker-room' talk about sex. Diana Wieler also explores the pain of emerging male identity and sexuality in *Bad Boy* (1989). The third-person point of view shifts between two complex sixteen-year-olds: insecure A.J. Brandiosa and his best friend Tully Brown, a 'golden boy' who charms all who know him. Both are marginally talented junior-league hockey players who share a love for the sport and emotionally support each other through school and family conflict. Upon discovering that Tully is 'gay', A.J. rejects him in desperate fear of homosexuality and certain social ostracization. The themes of peer pressure and homosexuality are treated with a psychological subtlety missing from the majority of American young-adult novels on these topics and found in only a few exceptions, such as *Dance on My Grave* (1982) by the British writer Aidan Chambers. In *Bad Boy*, for example, the grim teenage hostility towards what is considered a sexual deviation is ironically juxtaposed with socially acceptable violence in hockey. As A.J. struggles with his emotions his inner turmoil explodes into violent acts as a hockey 'goon' and an attempted rape. Nonetheless the conflict is primarily internal and is resolved when A.J. recognizes that his friend must be free to follow his own instincts. Their friendship has not ended. *Bad Bay* is reminiscent of the American John Knowles' memorable *A Separate Peace* (1960) in its treatment of physical ability as a testing ground and in depicting the ambivalent relationship between two youths who are opposites in prowess and personality. Like Major, Wieler writes prose that is brash and staccato, charged with youthful profanity, but sprinkles her narrative with tender moments:

> She smelled of sweat, salty but not sharp, and of outside. Grass. She smelled like the last day in August when you played football on the lawn.

While teenage male sexuality is now a fairly common theme in Canadian young-adult fiction, the honest and sensitive depiction of young female sexuality is found in only a few works. The best of these is Mary Razzell's *Snow Apples* (1984), set in a small British Columbia coastal town. Sheila Brary, age sixteen, is prey to all the dissatisfactions and physical and emotional stirrings of the typical adolescent. Her father has not yet returned from the war, her mother favours her brothers, and there are tense family problems. After experiencing some sexual harassment and her own slow sexual awakening, she finds herself pregnant and alone. Throughout all of this she wishes to pursue her education to become a nurse. Her solution is a self-induced abortion (explicitly described, but given a surrealistic dimension) so that she can have a chance to make a better life for herself. Though the period is the end of the Second World War, the problems of teenagers (especially in a low-income family), their frustrations and desires, do not change with either time or geography.

The sequel, *Salmonberry Wine* (1987), shows the results of Sheila's decision to enter nurse's training at a Catholic hospital in Vancouver. The difficulties here are chiefly ones of submission to hospital discipline. Sheila questions medical ethics, but eventually adjusts to the larger world she has entered. Razzell's writing is highly descriptive, though lacking in nuances and subtleties: the West Coast town where Sheila lives is vividly portrayed, as is the daily routine of the city hospital. The minor characters, from the enigmatic mother to the rather predictable hospital administrator, Sister Maria, all have personality. In *Snow Apples* Sheila is given intense emotions, but in *Salmonberry Wine*, except for her passionate feeling for justice, she is rather a cardboard character.

Florence McNeil's *Catriona's Island* (1988), set in the Depression, is a coming-of-age-story similar to *Snow Apples* in setting but strikingly different in tone. Catriona McLeod is returning from a year of high school in Vancouver (a year she disliked) to the paradise of isolated Heron Island, where her grandparents have lived as lighthouse keepers since their arrival from Scotland some years before. Catriona's summer on the island is one of conflict as she develops phobic fears of the sea and of the lighthouse, which she once loved to climb. These phobias are accompanied by a paralysis of spirit as she avoids telling her grandparents about her desire to train as an artist rather than a teacher. The summer is dominated by a romantic infatuation with an alcoholic ex-surgeon, apeing Gaugin in his island paradise of Tahiti, who encourages Catriona in her artistic skills. In an overly melodramatic dénouement his character failings are dramatically revealed when he refuses to operate on the grandfather and so endangers his life. Catriona saves her grandfather and in so doing conquers her fears. McNeil is good at conveying by delicate imagery the sharpening vision of the budding artist, but her depiction of character rarely strikes an intense emotional chord.

By contrast Elizabeth Brochmann's *What's the Matter, Girl?* (1980) seethes with emotion. Fourteen-year-old Anna's Uncle Arion is finally coming home from the Second World War, two years after it is over. Anna expects that he will not only still be the glorious, fun-loving young man she had adored as a child but will now see her as an attractive young woman. For a week she keeps vigil on the front steps of his parents' house, close to her own, as the countdown (reflected in the chapter headings) begins. Around her swirls a complicated family—a French grandmother, a German grandfather, twin sixteen-year-old aunts and an assortment of other relatives, along with a loving brother, an affectionate dog, and a supportive father and mother who are hardly seen. Anna has written to her uncle with a child's questioning of war, and he has responded in inappropriate adult terms that show its horrors and its effects on him. (The letters echo the anti-war feelings expressed in the adult classic, Erich Remarque's *All Quiet on the Western Front*, and in its Canadian equivalent, Charles Yale Harrison's *Generals Die in Bed*.) Anna is about thirteen when the letters stop, but with a child's lack of understanding of emotional distress she clings to her faith in a dream. The events move to Arion's arrival with the inevitability of a Greek tragedy. Instead of a fair-haired prince on a white charger, she sees a white-haired shell of a man who does not recognize her. Anna flees from his presence.

Anna herself relates her childhood fixation with Arion. Brochmann is one of those relatively rare writers who can make a youthful voice totally convincing, allowing Anna to report things that she clearly does not understand. The background is rich with family life, its love and complexities, its odd ways and old histories; and the physical setting, a farm in the Alberni Valley of Vancouver Island, is shown as a childhood paradise. The structure of the book is intricate—successfully so—encompassing Anna's memories, Arion's letters, and the daily activities of a family who are prepared to cope with a tragedy of which Anna is unaware. Anna's love for her uncle has been given a kind of fairy-tale quality, but the book's end is shockingly realistic. Anna will visit her shattered uncle—'But not yet. I can't go there. Yet.' Razzell's Sheila could help to distance herself from her problems by taking a journey to Vancouver. Anna (who can see her uncle on his front porch every day) must distance herself mentally to survive. *What's the Matter, Girl?* is a book that remains with you—an impressive achievement.

Brian Doyle's *Up to Low* (1982) bears a resemblance to it in having a youthful narrator who can show his feelings—he does not have to describe them; in its major theme, which ranges far beyond a problem; and in having a more sophisticated style than most young-adult novels. The narrator is Tommy, seen in childhood in Doyle's later *Angel Square* (1984). Now a young teenager, he and his father are on their way to Low, in the Gatineau Hills, to visit their relatives. They are in a 'brand new 1950 Buick Special' driven by their friend Frank, who is usually drunk and who is the worst driver in the country. Frank, also a character from *Angel Square* (he knocked over the Christmas tree), is only the first of the eccentrics we meet on this picaresque voyage. All are described in broad shorthand strokes: Mean Hughie is the meanest man in the county; Crazy Mickey (Tommy's hundred-year-old great-grandfather) goes out into the shed every day and cries when his ninety-nine-year-old wife takes a nap; Hummer always hums to the sound of the canal's generator; Tommy's five aunts are always busy with household chores and his five uncles are always smoking. Tommy appreciates his extended family, but all he can really think about is Baby Bridget, the daughter of Mean Hughie.

Tommy remembers her from childhood—a girl with one arm and eyes that were 'the deep green of the Gatineau Hills . . . And their shape was the shape of the petals of the trillium.' On the journey Tommy learns what happened to Baby Bridget. Her arm was accidentally cut off by her father's binder machine; before he saved her life by making a tourniquet out of binder twine, which took incredible strength to break, he hit her. Now the word is out around the countryside that the legendary Mean Hughie is dying of cancer and that he has disappeared.

In his tender and burgeoning love for Baby Bridget, Tommy recognizes her need to seek out her father and to tell him that she forgives him. In a macabre scene they find him dying in the coffin he has made for himself, just alive enough to tell Baby Bridget that he was sorry he had hit her. Tommy understands:

> Healing. There was healing. But it wasn't her arm that got the healing. No. Not the arm.
> It was the heart.
> The heart got healed.
> Baby Bridget's heart!

As a whole the story has the strength of Mean Hughie's binder twine;

it is strong enough in its love and pathos to carry the comical scenes. Frank has taken a solemn pledge (before a priest) not to drink beer, liquor or wine—but this does not prevent him from getting drunk on a *liqueur!* In describing the extraordinary events of sailing Mean Hughie's coffin home in the storm-tossed canal, with Tommy's father and uncles coming to the rescue, wet cigarettes dangling from their mouths, Tommy sums up the book:

> It wasn't funny. I wouldn't say it was funny. But it wasn't sad or horrible either.

Like Doyle's *Hey, Dad!* (1978) and *You Can Pick Me Up at Peggy's Cove* (1979), *Up to Low* is basically a story of loving, healing, and dying, but it is far more memorable because it is deeper in conception.

Doyle's *Easy Avenue* (1988) falls between the simplicity of *Hey, Dad!* and the emotional power of *Up To Low*, and it has Doyle's warmth, humour, and cast of eccentrics. Hubbo (short for Hulbert) O'Driscoll lives in low-income housing (very low) in Ottawa, close to the homes of the wealthy, with his distant cousin and guardian, Mrs O'Driscoll, who is the cleaning-lady at Hubbo's High School—where for a time he goes to great trouble to avoid meeting her. Hubbo's part-time jobs give him ample opportunity to observe the lives of the wealthy. He has caddied for the worst golfer in the world at the Ottawa Hunt and Golf Club, and now two nights a week he sleeps over at the home of the ailing and elderly Miss Collar-Cuff, who lives on Easy Street, to keep her company. He also has a secret benefactor who gives him fifty dollars a month, and he is chiefly noted for his ability to do handstands. This is the least plotted of Doyle's books and has something of the feeling of an old-fashioned moral tale as Hubbo decides not to join the exclusive Hi-Y Club at school and shows his love and appreciation of Mrs O'Driscoll by hugging her in the school hallway. Although entertaining, and at times intriguingly reminiscent of Dickens's *Great Expectations, Easy Avenue* does not have the power of *Up To Low*'s tragic-comic version of life or its oral-storytelling voice.

From all accounts Doyle draws on childhood memories for the backgrounds of his books, especially in *Up To Low.* Other writers have drawn even more directly from personal experiences and have written books that may be described as autobiographical fiction. This type is best described by Jean Little in her autobiography, *Little by Little* (1987). In the author's note she writes:

> Although everything that happens in these pages has truth in it, not every word is based on fact. I took my memories and rearranged them, filling in details as I went along. I do not remember every word that I or others said so long ago. I do, however, know exactly how it felt . . .

The details in the Métis writer Beatrice Culleton's *In Search of April Raintree* (1983) do not exactly match those of the brief biography of the author given on the last page, but the autobiographical element is clear, and one is aware of the intense feelings that must have prompted this story of a young Métis in modern Canada. As children, April and her younger sister Cheryl are taken away from their alcoholic parents by the Children's Aid Society and placed in several separate foster homes. These vary from good to terrible, but since none are even remotely sympathetic to Indian values the sisters have to search for their roots. They love one another deeply, but their paths diverge. Cheryl returns to her Indian background, is disillusioned, and commits suicide; April tries to find acceptance in the white world with an upwardly mobile marriage that fails. She is also raped, faces the indignities that a court trial brings, but finally assumes responsibility for her dead sister's son and works for her people. Culleton's style is often awkward, but the details of the abuse, and her fury, are deeply moving. The book has been cut and republished as *April Raintree* (1984) for use in the Manitoba school system. All the major episodes have been retained; the language is unaltered and its authenticity is undiminished. Still, the feeling of a whole life story, leisurely told in a documentary fashion, is missing from this shortened version.

In Search of April Raintree arouses both pity and anger at the treatment of children in our so-called caring and affluent society, and at the obvious prejudice that exists towards those of mixed blood. Sandra Richmond's *Wheels for Walking* (1983), a semi-autobiographical account of an eighteen-year-old quadriplegic (injured in a car accident), arouses feelings of compassion and admiration. The emotional, physical, and sexual strains experienced by a wheelchair-bound victim are clearly delineated. Sally, like April, faces her difficulties and makes a new and courageous life for herself, as both their creators have done in real life.

Jean Little's *Little by Little* is a memoir of her childhood, but young readers, whether children or adolescents, will find in it the pace and drama of a novel. It is an account of a handicapped childhood—she had nystagmus, which her young friend correctly interprets as 'bad eyes'. Her disability left her open to childhood teasing to the extent that, at the age of seven, she realized that 'if you were different, nothing good about you mattered'. The sub-title, *A Writer's Education*, reveals her method of escape through 'story'—her dawning recognition of the power of words to comfort, protect, and sustain her during difficult times in her education. *Little By Little* is a heartening and impressive book about childhood, growing up, making decisions—and, above all, determination. It is also written with considerable dry wit.

The Cripples' Club (1988) by William Bell, while realistically based on the problems of the handicapped, has a large component of fiction and a strong plot element. Fifteen-year-old George Ma can be considered handicapped because he has lost his memory and is in a class with slow learners. Owing to the new policy of mainstreaming the handicapped, three other young people are admitted to the school: 'Hook', who is confined to a wheelchair and is so named because one hand has been replaced by a hook; Amy, who is blind; and Heather, who is deaf. Hook becomes the leader who bands them together to help one another, to guard against the school bullies (George and Hook and Amy have suffered their taunts and attacks), and in particular to draw out of George an account of his terrible experiences in a war-torn country in Southeast Asia that are blocking his memory. As 'one for all and all for one' they accomplish the goals they set for themselves—even, through blind Amy's computer skills, getting rid of the school bully. In an inner sense each one becomes a whole person. Bell's writing is simple and direct, as it must be because George is telling the story. The facts of being handicapped are not dwelt on, as they are in *Wheels for Walking*. *The Cripples' Club* is chiefly a story about friendship, one that has much of the tenderness, healing, courage, and humour of the American adult novel *Tell Me That You Love Me, Junie Moon*, by Marjorie Kellogg, about a group of the mentally handicapped who set up house together free from institutional supervision. Bell's children also gain freedom.

Fifteen-year-old Deirdre, in Mitzi Dale's *Round the Bend* (1988), is emotionally rather than physically handicapped. This first-person account of mental breakdown documents her attempted suicide and slow return to a balanced state of mind. The plot is a common one in American young-adult fiction, but is here given an intriguing tone because of Deirdre's cynical and sarcastic voice, her rapier-like perceptions, and deadpan comic lines. (Humour masking pain is also an element of Jean Little's *Little by Little*.) As in *The Language of Goldfish* (1980), by the American Zibby O'Neal, Deirdre's suicide attempt arises from her terror of growing up within her dysfunctional family. The basic plot is familiar enough terrain as Deirdre runs the therapeutic gamut until she accepts the complexities of human behaviour. Less conventional is the narrative structure, which plays with levels of perception. Incorporated into Deirdre's narrative are her daydreams of life as a female rancher (parodies of Western movies) and hints that she is telling the reader less than she knows, that she is unconscious of many of her actions in the real world. The novel is a process by which Deirdre and the reader together uncover the truth of her complex nature.

Kim, of Jim Heneghan's *Promises to Come* (1988), is also emotionally disturbed, but unfortunately for a far more universal and horrifying reason. Adopted by a Vancouver family, she tells her psychiatrist the story of her life in South Vietnam, from her childhood with her parents and baby brother to her escape as a boat-person. Scenes of shocking brutality are described, as Kim's memories of loss, violation, rage, and despair surface almost against her will, much like George Ma's did in Bell's *Cripples' Club*. To the deaths of Kim's family and companions are added horrors of starvation, beatings, and gang rape. Kim's slow return to mental health and acceptance of her survival are sensitively drawn. She must choose life and release her sense of guilt and her belief that she is cursed, bringing destruction to those who love her. Heneghan well describes the exotically beautiful landscape of Vietnam, which he sees having been raped and mutilated—as Kim's person and feelings were. Contrasted to this, and in a separate narrative, is the peaceful world of West Vancouver, with its mountains and beaches, and the initial dismay and antagonism teenage Becky feels when Kim joins her family. Kim's return to health and her painful assimilation into Canadian culture are meshed with Becky's slow acceptance of Kim, her adopted sister.

Another dramatic contrast of two ways of life is present in Barbara Smucker's *Amish Adventure* (1983), which gives a picture of a religious group in southern Ontario that sets itself apart from the mainstream of contemporary society, choosing to remain locked within its own special culture and beliefs. Unlike the physically and emotionally handicapped, who through courage and determination strive to become part of the mainstream, the Amish are determined to be separate. This condition is not maintained without cost. There are conflicts within the Bender family over the younger generation's desire to live outside the Amish community, and with their neighbours. The Benders are revealed through the experiences of Ian McDonald, a self-centred urban teenager, who is taken in by the Amish family after an accident. Ian is at first startled by a way of life that does not include electricity, plumbing, or modern machinery; but he stays with the Benders for the summer, finding a warmth in their way of life that has been missing from his own and that gives him a sense of values he didn't have before. This is a message book—but one that is palatable. It is strongly ecological—Amish-style farming does not abuse the land—and it gives a lesson in tolerance: the Benders do not press charges against the known person who burned down their barn. The last scene, in which the barn is being rebuilt, is one of harmony and reconciliation. The elder son, John, has returned home (somewhat like the prodigal son) and becomes a symbol of the strength of the Amish way of life. As he swings his hammer from the highest rafter at the barn raising, 'he seemed to be holding the whole structure together'. This novel can be valued as a celebration of the Amish way of life, even though the characters are wooden and the style pedestrian.

James Houston's *Whiteout* (1988) also depicts an outsider absorbing the shock of a different culture; the contrast here is between Inuit and non-Inuit. Eighteen-year-old Jonathan Aird has been convicted of a drug felony and has been sent for a year of community service to Nanuvik, a settlement on Baffin Island where he will live with his uncle, manager of a Hudson's Bay Company trading post. It becomes a year of challenge and transformation as Jon responds to the awesome beauty of the stark land and to the Inuit people, who accept him warmly as he tutors students in music. It is also a year of new relationships: Jon discovers the inner strength of his seemingly dour uncle and the love of Panee, an Inuit girl. There are elements familiar from Houston's children's stories of the wilderness—especially survival and culture clash. But *Whiteout* has an added dimension of enchanted realism, evident in the figure of the shaman, who haunts Jon throughout his stay, and in allusions, in carvings and storytelling, to the mythological figure of Sedna, the vengeful sea-goddess. These figures presage a disastrous storm, Panee's near-death, and Jon's rite of passage into manhood as he takes responsibility for their survival. Houston's style in *Whiteout* is more textured than in his earlier works. He creates an unforgettable vision of a double world: one of human closeness to the land and one more alien, touched by a weather condition known as 'whiteout': 'A strange white world of nothing-ness. . . . An edgeless world, where animals and humans never quite belong.' Houston eschews a romantic ending for his story. Panee decides to remain in the Arctic, while Jon returns south to pursue his musical career.

Short-story collections are rare in writing for young adults, and those that exist are usually on themes of romance and personal relationships, such as the American Norma Fox Mazer's *Dear Bill, Remember Me? and Other Stories* (1976). Several collections of Canadian short stories on multicultural themes have been published for a younger audience. Paul Yee's *Teach Me to Fly, Skyfighter* (1983) conveys a collage impression of Vancouver's Chinatown and Strathcona district, and Nazneen Sadiq's *Camels Can Make You Homesick and Other Stories* (1985) dramatizes the tensions experienced by New Canadian children and young people caught in the contrasting worlds of Canada and South Asia. Both collections have moments of grace, but are uneven in their storytelling qualities.

Martha Brooks' *Paradise Café & Other Stories* (1988) is the only collection to date that is specifically aimed at the young adult. The first-person narrators are male and female Manitoba teenagers, contemporary or from the recent past, both English and French-Canadian. All speak with slightly different voices: hesitant, witty, angry, brave, often challenging injustices and inequities. For the most part they are observers, watching patterns forming and breaking in the adult and youthful relationships they see around them—each story is a miniature study of human behaviour, a loosely plotted slice of life. When these qualities are joined to the self-awareness of the characters, and the occasional nostalgic tone, the stories enter into adult literature. *Paradise Café* raises the question: just what constitutes young-adult fiction?

According to educational psychologists the chief task of the adolescent is to achieve a sense of identity, to answer the questions 'Who am I now'? and 'Who will I become'? These themes are at the heart of most young-adult literature, at least in Western society. In an interesting and regrettable contrast, many young-adult books emanating from South Africa are concerned chiefly with racial, political, and economic survival. Yet *Go Well, Stay Well* (1979) by Toeckey Jones, a South African, is a personal story of young people set in a particular place—and there are others in this mould. They simply prove that, although finding a sense of self, psychologically, may compose the fabric of the adolescent novel, each country weaves differently coloured threads into it.

The most noticeable themes in Canadian fiction for adolescents are basically similar to the American ones: alienation, a quest for independence, burgeoning sexuality, rebellion against authority, and, latterly, the more painful and controversial subjects of suicide, rape, abortion, and homosexuality. (The themes of intellectual growth and class conflict that are common in British young-adult fiction are far from major concerns.) Within this general North American ambience, Canadian books emphasize region, which is strongly coloured, and in the case of Kevin Major's works incorporate a particular diction. Firmly placed in their own background, our young protagonists are therefore more individual-ized than those in American novels for adolescents. Kevin Major's Michael, Brian Doyle's Tommy, Mary Razzell's Sheila, and Beatrice Culleton's April speak out of their experience of place and community as they relate the pain and poignancy of growing up.

If it is to have any meaning or emotional appeal at all, fiction that addresses the complex subject of maturation must have depth and resonance—qualities that perforce align it with the adult novel. The young-adult novel is (or should be) more than a mere bridge between the children's story and adult fiction. The British writer Jill Paton Walsh in *Goldengrove* (1972) and *Unleaving* (1976), and the American writer Katherine Paterson in *Jacob Have I Loved* (1980), have proved that this is so. In Canada, Doyle's *Up To Low* is, as yet, the only work that shapes the diverse realities of adolescence into a work of art that transcends the category of young-adult fiction.

Nevertheless, Major, Razzell, Hughes, and Brochmann, among others, have also created moving and realistic stories that offer authentic patterns of behaviour and sharp insights about life. From such books our teenagers may not only share the feelings of their peers, but learn what it is like to be human in this country and this world.

3

The Realistic Animal Story

In the late-nineteenth and early-twentieth centuries, when most writers of fiction were slavishly following the accepted English literary tradition, the realistic animal story appeared in Canada as a genuine native product and spread outward to influence the animal story around the world. It was the creation of two Canadians, Ernest Thompson Seton and Charles G.D. Roberts, and it was their works that gave it both its definition and its highest form.

The realistic animal story can best be described as animal biography in fictional form. Although it can vary greatly in the amount of fiction purposefully used, it is founded upon scientific observation and a profound knowledge of animals. Using knowledge, and with affection and respect, the writer brings an animal alive in its own world and in complete harmony with its own nature. The realistic animal story is not concerned with talking-animal fantasies and fables or with satires based on animals, such as George Orwell's *Animal Farm*: these genres do not really contain works about animals but about human actions and aspirations. Neither should it be confused with the kind of modern story in which a horse or a dog plays an auxiliary role in helping the young to resolve their problems, as in Jean Little's *Lost and Found* (1985) and *Different Dragons* (1986). The realistic animal story under discussion here has its closest link with the writings of naturalists like Jean Henri Fabre, Raymond L. Ditmars, and Gerald Durrell.

It is obvious that the naturalist would not indulge in anthropomorphism—the endowment of animals with human traits. It is not so clear that the writers of even the best animal stories should not or do not do so. Some transference of human intelligence and emotion to the animal character can, in good hands, heighten the emotional impact of a story and strengthen the rapport between writer and reader. Animal lovers, both children and adults, often ascribe super-animal qualities to their pets, and it should be no surprise that some of this feeling has worked its way into animal literature. But it takes a sure sense of the limits of credibility to keep the realistic animal story from being maudlin or, worse, so confused as to be neither animal story nor outright fantasy.

That the realistic animal story should first have appeared and developed in Canada is not entirely the result of chance. When Seton and Roberts wrote, knowledge of animals, especially wild animals, was still a necessity for natives, who depended upon them for food, for those who hunted for profit, and for those concerned with conservation; and of course protection and interest have always made some knowledge essential. In a sparsely populated country the forces of nature still played a major role, as indeed they do today in many parts of Canada. Probably in no other part of the world were the cities so close to the forests. In Canadian art, in Canadian novels, in Canadian poetry there was still an intense concentration on descriptions of nature. Seton and Roberts maintained this emphasis, but added to it a new dimension—a genuine insight into the habits of the animals that roam our woods and forests.

The novelty and scope of their achievement may best be seen in relation to the general pattern of the animal story that had been established earlier. It is easy to imagine that the first animal stories ever told must have been highly realistic: a primitive hunter relates his escape or his kill to an admiring group of friends—colouring his account a bit, perhaps, but telling the truth nonetheless. Later, the primeval relationship between man and animal became encased in mythology and legend, and the denizens of forest and field, sky and water, were used mainly to point a moral for the benefit of mankind. From this outlook came the medieval bestiaries (very shaky nature lore indeed) and fables—those of Aesop and La Fontaine and the anonymous *Reynard the Fox*. Writers for children in eighteenth- and nineteenth-century England produced highly moralistic animal stories, on the assumption that faults and virtues would be made clearer to children if they were attributed to animals. For example, in a charming book by Dorothy Kilner, *The Rational Brutes; or, Talking Animals* (1799), an ass is made to remark: 'Well, I think it would be the happiest thing for this nation that ever yet was thought of, if some plan could be contrived to destroy every boy upon this island.' The theme, of course, is cruelty to animals. The moralistic animal story and 'talking animals' (though not the kind used in fantasies) reached a culmination in 1877 with Anna Sewell's *Black Beauty*. Written in the heavily sentimental style of the Victorian era, this book became the first of the tear-jerking 'hanky' animal stories. In 1894 the Canadian writer, Marshall Saunders, duplicated Sewell's effects and phenomenal success with *Beautiful Joe*. In short, whatever the variety of purposes and techniques, the animal stories before Seton and Roberts had one trait in common: animals were employed and not described.

For the moralizing and sentimentality of their predecessors, Seton and Roberts substituted a rigorous naturalism. They were interested in their animal subjects as animals, not as devices. They assumed that their animal heroes were as intrinsically worthy of interest as any human being might be and they created, in effect, 'animal biographies'. Like the biographer, then, they undertook an analysis of character that was based on the influence of environment, youthful training, and education, with a selection of facts and events to make the portrait emerge clearly. Their animals are not mere automatons, led by blind instinct; they are creatures that possess the faculty of reason—but not human reason. The plots are chiefly life-and-death struggles in the wilderness. Most of the animals fall to the laws of nature, and usually if man is pitted against them, man is the victor. As Seton put it, 'The fact that these stories are true is the reason why all are tragic. The life of a wild animal always has a tragic end.' (*Wild Animals I Have Known*, 1898.) Roberts, with his greater poetic skill, put it thus: 'And death stalks joy forever among the kindred of the wild.' (*The Kindred of the Wild*, 1902.)

Both Seton and Roberts frequently used composite animal characters. That is, although the incidents related happened to an animal, they would not all have happened to the same animal or in the sequence presented. Both writers wisely used the short-story form and the novella. Lengthy animal stories, especially those about wild animals, can easily become repetitious, and a preponderance of gory detail can surfeit the reader and break the dramatic impact.

The first collections of stories were by Roberts in 1896 (*Earth's Enigmas: A Book of Animal and Nature Life*—though Roberts' first animal story, 'Do Seek Their Meat From God', was published in December 1892) and by Seton in 1898 (*Wild Animals I Have Known*). The two men had much in common. They were born in the same year, 1860; each respected the other's work; each succeeded at his chosen occupation and regarded his animal stories as something of a sideline. Seton was a naturalist and a hunter; his scientific work, the four-volume *Lives of Game Animals* (1925-7), is still useful. Roberts came to be considered the dean of Canadian letters because of his poetry and his novels. It is somewhat ironic that the enduring fame of both men now rests on their animal stories, which have largely been kept alive by the young.

Many of Seton's best attributes as a writer can be seen in *The Biography of a Grizzly* (1900): his straightforward, still-modern style, his humour, and especially his ability to create an intimate picture of animal life. It also shows that Seton gave in occasionally to sentimentality and archness, but in general these qualities do not destroy the overall clarity of his vision of wild-animal life. The sentimental touch is sometimes quaint—an attempt on Seton's part to link animals to human behaviour without complete anthropomorphism:

> They [the bear cubs] were well acquainted with the common little brown ants that harbour under the logs in the uplands, but now they came for the first time on one of the hills of the great, fat, luscious Wood-ant, and they all crowded around to lick up those that ran out. But they soon found that they were licking up more cactus-prickles and sand than ants, till their Mother said in Grizzly, 'Let me show you how.' (*The Biography of a Grizzly*)

Neither in Seton nor in Roberts does an animal actually talk, but they communicate in such a way that a kind of conversation is frequently suggested. Seton explained his theory about this in 'Raggylug, the Story of a Cottontail Rabbit':

> Truly rabbits have no speech as we understand it, but they have a way of conveying ideas by a system of sounds, signs, scents, whisker-touches, movements and example that answers the purpose of speech: and it must be remembered that though in telling this story I frequently translate from rabbit into English, I repeat nothing that they did not say.

He also repeats nothing that an animal could not do. For example, his greatest story, 'Lobo, the King of Currumpaw', about the white wolf Blanca and her mate Lobo, is based on personal observation. Seton actually trailed the great wolf in New Mexico. He tells us there is almost no deviation from the truth and that Blanca's death happened precisely as related. Lobo is finally captured because of his love for his mate. Forgetting his usual, almost super-animal cunning, he trails her body to the ranch, is captured, and although offered food and water, steadfastly refuses it and dies (who can say otherwise?) of a broken heart.

Though the incidents of Lobo's life did actually happen, the emotions with which they are invested are anything but naturalistic. The death of a wolf is made to evoke from the reader feelings of pity and terror that are akin to the moving quality of *Wuthering Heights*. There is no doubt that Seton here strove deliberately for the effects of tragedy and in so doing came very close to justifying the charge of anthropomorphism that was frequently laid against him. But he delicately questions rather than states—and so the believers have as much evidence as the skeptics.

Seton often came just as close to the borderline in his comic effects. In a humorous episode in the otherwise moving and tragic story of Wahb, in *The Biography of a Grizzly*, a smaller bear craftily conducts planned manoeuvres against Wahb. He climbs on logs and stones to rub his head upon a tree and thus shows his height as greater than that of eight-foot Wahb.

It is difficult, and probably pointless, to try to decide which of his stories Seton particularly intended for children, for of all types of writing the realistic animal story makes perhaps the least distinction in the age of its readers. Who could say—certainly their authors gave no clue to the answer—whether *The Call of the Wild* (Jack London), *Tarka the Otter* (Henry Williamson), or *Rascal* (Sterling North) were meant for children or adults? The one instance in which we can be certain of Seton's intended audience suggests that he would have done better not to try to pinpoint his target. In straining for what he thought would appeal to children in *Bannertail* (1922), Seton produced his poorest story. Although it is an accurate picture of squirrel life, he indulged excessively in cuteness, even to the extent of personifying nature as 'Mother Carey'. *Bannertail* is his closest approach to the pathetic fallacy. In writing down for children to the extent of distorting animal nature, Seton almost emerges in *Bannertail* as the forerunner of those concoctors of animal travesties, Thornton Burgess and Walt Disney.

Seton was a professional naturalist and his stories were based on the scientific observations of an adult. The stories of Charles G.D. Roberts derived from recollections of his boyhood in the forests of New Brunswick. This association gives Roberts' work a romantic cast, in contrast with Seton's more matter-of-fact approach to the wilderness. Here, in two sentences, Roberts sets the stage and mood of 'The Boy and Hushwing' in *The Kindred of the Wild*:

> A hollow, booming, ominous cry, a great voice of shadowy doom rang out suddenly and startled the dark edges of the forest. It sounded across the glimmering pastures, vibrating the brown-velvet dusk, and made the lame old woman in the cabin on the other side of the clearing shiver with vague fears.

Roberts can write with equal excitement of the largest animal (and his favourite), the bear, in a group of stories brought together in 1947, *Thirteen Bears*, and of the tiny ant in 'The Prisoners of the Pitcher Plant' (*The Haunters of the Silences*, 1907). It is understandable that Roberts, a poet and man of letters, often became intoxicated with words. Phrases such as the 'intense sapphire of the zenith thrilled and melted' ('In the Deep of the Silences', *The Haunters of the Silences*) and 'his baby face of tenderest cream and pink . . . the hair . . . like a fleece all over his head, enmeshing the sunlight in its silken tangle' (*Jim, the Story of a Backwoods Police Dog*, 1919) suggest nineteenth-century floridity. But in many stories, and in books such as *Red Fox* (1905), *The Feet of the Furtive* (1912), and in the posthumous collection *Thirteen Bears* (1947), Roberts' poetic descriptions add beauty and richness and give the works individuality and distinction.

Roberts' animal stories have been criticized more harshly than those of Seton. His book-length *Red Fox*, for example, is not as scientifically presented as are most of the works of Seton. In his attempts to bring drama to his stories and to emphasize the personality and cunning of his hero, he often strains credulity. That animals are instinctively on guard against man-made traps is a fact of hunting. But when Roberts had Red Fox and his mate deliberately leave the trap uncovered 'so that no other of the forest dwellers might be betrayed by it', and then go off to find out what other treasons man had plotted against the 'wild folk', he leaves reality for fantasy. However, as Frank Underhill once pointed out, 'biography only becomes interesting and alive when the biographer is partisan', and perhaps this is Roberts' way of being partisan to his hero. The story of Red Fox is spellbinding. He is shown as the strongest and most intelligent of the litter and is the only one to survive, even outwitting his human captors twice by playing 'dead'. At the end of the story he has triumphed over the hunters and the hounds and finds a home in a new wilderness. This represented to Roberts the triumph of the wild animal and a glorification of its freedom and strength.

Not all of Roberts' animals are endowed with the intelligence of Red Fox. Sometimes a beast's limitations are treated humorously: a young muskrat belonging to a litter of nine is killed by a duck. 'The attention of the little mother was just then occupied, and never having learned to count up to nine, she, apparently, never realized her loss.' ('The Calling of the Lop-Horned Bull' in *The Secret Trails*, 1916).

The first heir of Seton and Roberts was certainly Roderick L. Haig-Brown. Indeed, *Silver: The Life of an Atlantic Salmon* (1931) recalls Roberts' biography of a salmon, 'The Last Barrier'. *Silver* describes the life-cycle of a salmon from the time he is spawned until he is finally caught in his own stream by the 'Good Fisherman' in true sportsmanlike fashion. Completely authentic in its details of salmon life, it is lightened by an intimate, at times almost lyrical, style. Haig-Brown addresses his readers as if he were telling the story in person and is quite explicit about 'making things up', such as what Silver might have said or thought. Fishing skills, sportsmanship, and conservation are skilfully woven into a story. It takes a craftsman to make something as narrowly special as salmon interesting to the general reader, but Haig-Brown managed to do it.

Ki-Yu: A Story of Panthers (1934) is Seton and Roberts brought to complete realism. Ki-Yu is by no means an attractive character. (Even the most predatory animals of the earlier writers are appealing.) The wilderness is presented in all its starkness, and there is little to show 'the kindred of the wild'. *Ki-Yu* is perhaps more a documentary of wild-animal life than a sympathetic animal biography. The drama of the story appears in the deliberate stalking of Ki-Yu by a professional panther hunter; when his dogs are killed by the panther, the sympathy is with the dogs and the hunter rather than with the hunted animal. Here we are made to feel much more the depredations of wild animals upon domestic animal life.

Haig-Brown, like Roberts and Seton, also shows the inevitability of death in the wilderness. In the end, when Ki-yu is old and wounded and caught between two enemies, man and wolves, it is his own wild kind that tear him apart.

Ki-Yu is over-long and sometimes wearying, particularly in the description of the constant killing and feeding of the wild animals. Even so, all the details in the story are so realistically presented that they have a considerable holding power. Haig-Brown convinces by realism, not by invention.

Grey Owl—the name the Englishman Archibald Stansfeld Belaney wrote under, and was known by, until he died in Canada in 1938, thirty-two years after his arrival—was a naturalist and conservationist. As the author of *Sajo and Her Beaver People* (1935) he comes close to being considered a writer of the realistic animal story. But his emphasis is on the child Sajo, and the beaver kits are chiefly seen in her home surroundings. When they are returned to their own habitat the story has ended. Still, with or without the inclusion of *Sajo* in this genre, there was a gap of thirty years before another naturalist and conservationist applied writing skills to the revelations of wild-animal life.

Farley Mowat was known as a passionate defender of the Arctic environment when he was asked by government officials to investigate the charge that wolves were decimating the caribou herds. No doubt he put in an official report, but *Never Cry Wolf* (1963) is his personal account of his observations and experiences with a specific family of wolves. Like his *The Dog Who Wouldn't Be* (1959), it was not written for children, but its subject matter, its humorous incidents, its vivid images, and most importantly Mowat's natural storytelling ability make it more than accessible to them. He becomes so fascinated with the wolves (as does the reader) that he finds himself adapting to their rhythm of existence—even to the point of learning to 'wolf-nap' so that he can observe them as closely as possible. He also takes some time out from wolf-watching (and almost wolf-living) to satirize government departments, officialese, and red tape, but the strength of the book is in its picture of wild-animal life. It is rather ironic that most of the points made about the hunting habits of wolves were made earlier by both Seton and Roberts. However, if the members of the government department concerned in Mowat's personal expedition had read and understood the animal lore of these experts (particularly Seton), Mowat might not have had his adventure and the literature of the Canadian realistic animal story would have been all the poorer.

Although Mowat's rapier wit gave the animal biography (or here a documentary) a new dimension, *Never Cry Wolf* is very much in the strong realistic tradition of Seton. Roberts' more poetic voice is heard in Fred Bodsworth's novella about birds, *The Last of the Curlews* (1954). The Eskimo curlew, on its long migrations from the Arctic to the grasslands of South America, always returns to the Arctic to mate. Through the years and the depredations of hunters the breed has become almost extinct. Bodsworth tells of one curlew who returned to the North several times and always found himself alone. At last a mate comes and loneliness disappears. On a flight north the female is killed, leaving the male to fly on alone; we know that he will now be alone until he dies.

Although the author could not have observed all the details, the reader is not conscious of fiction among the facts. All is so well blended that there is never a jarring or obtrusive note.

> Behind them now the Arctic's aurora borealis was flashing vividly above the Labrador sky-line, but when they came to earth again, with flight feathers frayed and their breast muscles numbed by fatigue, it would be in dank jungle river-bottom of the Guianas or Venezuela. Yet there was no fear or hesitation now with the takeoff, no recognition of the drama of the moment. There was only a vague relief to be off. For it was a blessing of their rudimentary brains that they couldn't see themselves in the stark perspective of reality—minute specks of earthbound flesh challenging an eternity of sea and sky.

Last of the Curlews strikes a haunting tone of loneliness and sadness; it is also a protest against the wanton destruction of wild life. In beauty of writing and in its perception of nature and universal values, it matches in many ways not only Roberts, but the writings of the great naturalist W.H. Hudson. A single sentence may sum up Bodsworth's spare and restrained approach to animal portrayal: 'It was a blessing of their rudimentary brains that they couldn't see themselves in the stark perspective of reality.' For Bodsworth, honesty of depiction is the paramount virtue, and only such dramatic values as are wholly justified by the actual circumstances of the natural environment are allowed to colour his narrative.

This faithfulness to reality, of course, is not necessarily the road to popularity. *Last of the Curlews*, highly esteemed but not all that well known, thus forms an interesting contrast with Sheila Burnford's *The Incredible Journey* (1960), which had a great success in its time. It was made into a motion picture almost immediately after publication, and for good reason. The book represents almost all the virtues and failings characteristic of popular films: a simple plot, a strong emphasis on characterization, a large measure of sentimentality, and a compelling vividness, pace, and charm.

The plot parallels at many points British-born Eric Knight's *Lassie Come-Home* (1940), the story of a collie dog of unusual intelligence, courage, and determination who makes a 400-mile journey from Scotland to Yorkshire to be with her original master. Three animals make an almost similar trek in Canada in *The Incredible Journey*. Two dogs and a cat, beloved household pets, have been left with a friend while their owners are in Europe. The younger dog, a Labrador retriever, determines to make his way back home and leads his companions on a 250-mile trek through the Northern Ontario wilderness to do so. En route they face every hazard, including starvation, wild animals, cold, weariness, and near-drowning. And still, of course, they succeed.

The journey is imaginary, but the animals are modelled after the author's own pets and are given all the human attributes that pet-lovers are apt to ascribe to their charges. Thus the Labrador is represented as following not instinct but consistent, logical thought:

> Only one thing was clear and certain—that at all costs he was going home, home to his own beloved master. Home lay to the west, his instinct told him; but he could not leave the other two—so somehow he must take them with him, all the way.

Indeed, when the dog sees a 'temporary master' leaving, so firmly does he know that this is a time for departure that he presents his paw to the master in a gesture of farewell.

So, too, the cat exhibits such motivations as selflessness (it attacks a bear cub and even a bear on behalf of the bulldog) and generosity (continually hunting food to give to the older dog). And there is not a moment's altercation among the three animals; they treat each other with complete sweetness throughout a long and difficult journey when their own survival was hourly at stake. All this Burnford relates so graphically and even poetically that it very nearly convinces. But not quite. The journey remains incredible and, despite its undoubted emotional impact, the book is not entirely honest in the sense that the stories of Seton, Roberts, Haig-Brown, and Bodsworth are basically honest in their treatment of animals. *The Incredible Journey* will be read and remembered, but not as a true exemplar of the realistic animal story. It should be considered rather as the heir of *Black Beauty* and *Beautiful Joe*, in which there is a deliberate attempt to use animals as vehicles for human emotions.

That there can be emotion in the animal story without arrant emotionalism is triumphantly seen in *The Black Wolf of River Bend* (1971) by Helene Widell and *The Winter of the Fisher* (1971) by Cameron Langford. *The Black Wolf* begins, as do most animal biographies, with the birth and survival of the best and luckiest of the litter and his normal adventures as a creature of the wild. But the scene shifts dramatically when a forest fire drives Blackie from the Cariboo Mountains into new territory, Robson Valley. Here he gradually adopts an immigrant ranch family, driving in game, playing tag, calf-sitting, guarding the youngest child, but never allowing himself to be petted or even touched. Human cruelty brings the idyll to an end when Blackie is shot by a pair of drunken hunters in front of a busload of school children. Helene Widell can generate the kind of moral outrage displayed by Farley Mowat in *A Whale for the Killing*, but she also cushions the shock with the attitude of the sensitive and sensible parents. In this story the natural caution and instincts of a wild animal are not betrayed; it is logically surmised that the wolf, having once escaped from a steel trap, could never take the one step necessary for escape from the valley—the crossing of the steel railway tracks. The story is told very simply, without frills or flourishes—much as it might be told to children around a campfire with the song of wolves echoing from a distance.

Cameron Langford's *The Winter of the Fisher* is at once a full-length animal biography and a well-crafted novel. It begs immediate comparison with Roberts' *Red Fox*, not only because of its length—it is 222 pages of close type without illustration—but because of the sustaining of interest within that length. But in literary power, and in the delight it arouses, it is closer to two classics by the English naturalist Henry Williamson: *Tarka the Otter* (1928) and *Salar the Salmon* (1935). Langford's narrative, which is without dialogue, has neither Seton's sometimes coy and often didactic manner of addressing the reader directly, nor the almost intrusive chatter of Roberts' human characters:

> In the gray dark of a hunter's moon, the mother fisher led her brood along the eastern shore of the lake. Occasionally, she glanced behind to see if they were keeping their proper stations. They had come far in the eight weeks since their first wild and hilarious hunting foray. Now they slipped in disciplined quiet through the classroom of the night. Yet, for all their stealth, the hushed night sounds died at the moment of their passing, to whisper forth again when they had gone. They moved as in a soft cocoon of tiny silences.

The protagonists are never named; they are identified only as 'fisher', 'trapper', and 'Ojibway'. The landscape is never made explicit; it is the vast wilderness of Northern Ontario, which becomes apparent only through internal evidence. The slight delineation of character needed for the dramatic action is handled so skilfully that both men and animal are raised to archetypal proportions—the humans becoming symbols of their kind and the fisher the symbol of all wild animals. In the same way locations are never specifically identified other than by 'the cabin on the shore', 'the head of the lake', 'the den beneath the old spruce', which each of us knows or can imagine. By establishing an aesthetic distance between the reader and the background of his story, Langford requires that we reach into our own memories to participate in the creation of a setting that is much more familiar and intimate than word-pictures would make possible.

Much of the conflict, and the climax, come from the contrasting characters and attitudes of the two humans in the story: the old Ojibway, who hunts only for sustenance and befriends and protects the fisher, and the white commercial trapper, who is at first annoyed with the fisher for robbing his traps and then pursues him with a relentless, almost mindless fury. The author analyses the struggle in reasoned terms and keeps it always within the bounds of possibility:

> The trapper had his human brain, experience and skill in his trade. Against these, the fisher pitted his natural intelligence and wiliness, both highly developed qualities in his kind, plus his exceptional agility and incredibly delicate senses. In truth, it was the trapper who held the edge. But the fisher had luck, and a silent ally in the Old Ojibway.

Like Roberts' Red Fox, the fisher escapes in the end, scarred but wiser and still independent.

With David Allenby Smith's *Sharptooth: A Year of the Beaver* (1974) and *Andy Russell's Adventures With Wild Animals* (1977), by the conservationist and animal photographer Andy Russell, there can be seen a return to the rigid realism of Haig-Brown in *Ki-Yu*. Their animals are not composites, as are those of Seton and Roberts, and so the stories are less shaped by fiction. *Sharptooth* is a meticulous résumé of the cycle of beaver life for younger children without a hint of anthropomorphism—or excitement or emotion. Smith's concern is to emphasize the instinctive cycle of animal life. In describing the female beaver's preparations for birth, he writes:

> And the pattern, as it is with all the patterns of all the varieties of life in the world, was designed to lead to the repetition of life—the production of new life. . . . and so, to the survival of beaver.

Andy Russell describes the lives of six animals (and an owl) of the Rocky Mountains. His accounts are generally presented from the point of view of an observer, but he has a noticeable ability to empathize with the feelings of animals (and to detail them) when they are on their own. In this sense his stories are true animal biographies rather than simply descriptions. The liveliest one relates the adventures of 'Kleo' the cougar, who is captured, rather than killed, to be made into a movie star. He is to have a part in 'nature pictures that were in many ways anything but natural'. The director has had a high compound built to contain him, and a 'mule deer doe' (a camp pet) is provided for his kill. However, the script is ruined when the deer, in a frenzy, attacks Kleo and he, in a desperate effort to escape her, leaps the high wire fence and finds his freedom.

Great Canadian Animal Stories (1978), edited by Muriel Whitaker, is an amalgam of Indian animal legends, excerpts from quasi-realistic animal stories such as Farley Mowat's *The Dog Who Wouldn't Be* and Sheila Burnford's *The Incredible Journey*, and tales drawn from the realistic animal tradition—a short story each from Seton and Roberts, and excerpts from Haig-Brown, Bodsworth, and Langford, among others. The collection is attractively illustrated in colour by Vlasta van Kampen. Anthologies, especially those for the young, and especially those dependent on excerpts, are intended to encourage the reader to seek out the full work or other stories by the same author.

The most significant point to make about the realistic animal story in the 1980s is that its numbers have declined to almost zero. The cause may well lie in the genre itself. Considering the limited characteristics of animals, it is not surprising that there is a certain sameness, and even repetition of particular incidents, in most animal biographies. Roberts' Red Fox reacts to the horrors of the trapline much as Langford's Fisher. Seton's wolves behave as Mowat's do. All the outstanding writers of the realistic animal story have been conservationists and protectionists; they have treated animals with respect and honesty in their natural habitats. Their themes are timeless and therefore timely—and similar. They either state or imply that we must respect and ultimately love nature for what it is, and that we must see it for what it is in order to understand man's place in the scheme of things. Following the example of Seton and Roberts, they have wished to spare the reader emotionalism and sentimentalism (indeed, they encourage neither); and they have all chosen the same method—the placing of an aesthetic distance between their readers and their animal characters. We know their animals but we do not identify ourselves completely with them.

All of this is to say that realistic animal stories, taken as a group, present a rather static composite picture. Canadian writers seem to eschew the kind of mystical rapport between man and animal that can be found in the writings of the French René Guillot in such books as *The Elephants of Sargabal* (1966) and *Fodai and the Leopard-Men* (1969). Nor, with the exception of Grey Owl's *Sajo and Her Beaver People*, and Roberts' short story 'The Boy and Hushwing', do they capitalize on children's affection for wild animals, as the American writer Sterling North did in the international bestseller *Rascal*, about a lonely boy's love for his pet racoon. These particular books are still part of the realistic animal stream because the habits of the tamed creatures of the wild they describe are so well delineated. Most books about children and their pets—horses, dogs, etc.—are usually a branch of the adventure novel; the child's involvement and emotions are more pronounced than the study of the animal. But even with these slightly differing approaches, it is difficult to see how there can be any dramatic changes or developments in the genre.

A great many books about animals have been written and published in Canada. Most of them, however, are not concerned to tell about animals in a narrative or literary form but constitute a branch of popular science. However, pre-school and primary schoolchildren have been provided with realistic animal picture-books—spin-offs from the highly popular nature magazine *Owl*: *Slip the Otter Finds a Home* (1984) and *Flip the Dolphin Saves the Day* (1984) both written and illustrated by Olena Kassian, and *Snow Babies* (1985) by Eric Rosser, illustrated by Olena Kassian. *Slip* and *Snow Babies* are simply descriptive of animals, while *Flip* has more than a touch of anthropomorphism: Flip is left out of dolphin games because he is so small, but then his size proves to be an asset. Here he resembles the young human protagonists of many a picturebook. In its minor way *Flip* again raises the question of how much fiction is appropriate to a basically realistic animal story. The answer is surely that a touch of fictional shaping makes animal realism more interesting.

In the larger issue of the decline of the realistic animal story, one can hope that within the broad increase of writing and publishing a new star will rise. The animal story has an in-built margin for success because it can command, as in the past, both a child and an adult audience. And after all, the animals are still here for the seeing and the telling, and their appeal is perennial and universal.

4

Historical Fiction

Historical fiction is surely nothing less than the imaginative re-creation of the past. The good historical novel involves the reader in a bygone era, dramatically and emotionally. It makes readers, and especially young readers, identify themselves with the past and live it in their minds rather than study it as they would a work of history.

'Living the past' depends squarely and solely on the writer's evocative skill. The parcelling out of so much history and so much fiction cannot create the conviction and atmosphere that a successful historical novel must have. Both Rosemary Sutcliff and Leon Garfield are successful writers of historical fiction, but their approach to it varies greatly. In *Song for a Dark Queen* (1978), Sutcliff focuses on the known events surrounding the life of an early figure in British history—the warrior Queen Boudicca and her tribe's stand against the Roman legions in AD 60. Here Sutcliff basically fictionalizes fact, providing the historical characters with motivations, both psychological and emotional, for their actions. She fleshes out the bare bones of history. Garfield in *Smith* (1976) weaves in details of eighteenth-century social life to the completely fictional account of a young pickpocket and his adventures with the notorious highwayman, Dick Turpin, who is the only historical figure in the story. Garfield's carefully researched descriptions of London slum life, the horrors of Newgate prison, and the contrasting life of a wealthy gentleman bring the past to life, as do Sutcliff's invented conversations between Queen Boudicca and the Roman procurator, Catus Decianus. Both writers are skilled at evoking the aura of a specific time and place;

nevertheless, one never forgets that no matter what the design of the framework—firm as in *Song for a Dark Queen* or loose as in *Smith*—Garfield and Sutcliff are primarily writing fiction. The adjective merely particularizes the noun, as does 'science' in science fiction and 'detective' in detective fiction.

This scale of priorities allows the creators of historical fiction considerable freedom in the treatment of their material. They may expand events or telescope them; interpret a fact or ignore it as not pertinent to an artistic aim. They may even enjoy the liberty, denied the historian, of going beyond the bounds of historical evidence. But this must be done warily. The adjectival novel depends in part for its effectiveness on the facts that it embodies and the writer must respect them. Put vegetation on the moon and the credibility of science fiction is destroyed. Costume drama must get the costumes right and the detective story should not cheat on clues. Accuracy is an asset; plausibility is essential.

Between the contending pulls of imagination and authenticity the historical novelist must take a firm stand. It is all too easy to lean in one direction and be drawn to the most readily attainable goal. Authenticity, which costs hours of work, is within the reach of almost any writer with a flair for research, but imagination is something that effort alone cannot purchase. The dual nature of historical fiction, then, often lends itself to a misinterpretation of goals. Many writers rely on the supposition that all one needs is a historical period with plot attached. Or, one step higher but not high enough, they become so embroiled in maintaining historical accuracy that the imaginative content of the story is submerged in an accumulation of detail. The best writers of historical fiction are the masters of their material, so steeped in their period that they can choose unerringly just the right details to make both their settings and their characters concrete and alive.

The artistic problems inherent in the historical novel are increased in books for children. Here events must be more closely winnowed and sifted; character more clearly delineated, but without condescension or over-simplification. Child readers must be moved rather quickly into the consciousness of another time and their imagination immediately stirred by it. Because the child has greater need than the adult for self-identification, the hero or heroine of the past must have some immediacy for the young reader of the present. Perhaps the greatest contribution the historical novelist can make to children's reading is to show them that an event in the past did not happen in isolation but was part of a continuous series of events that have influenced and given meaning to the present time.

Writers for children have at their disposal one convention that has been tried frequently and successfully: the introduction of an invented boy or girl character who represents the reader in the past. A variation of this approach, now less commonly used, makes the hero or heroine an actual historical figure, but at an age level close enough to the reader's to make identification possible—young Richard the Fearless in Charlotte Yonge's *The Little Duke* (1854) or seven-year-old Queen Isabella in Hilda Lewis's *The Gentle Falcon* (1952). But whatever the plot device, the finest novels are those in which child calls to child across the years (as with Garfield's *Smith*), or in which the characters and events are so vividly brought to life and dramatized (as in Sutcliff's *Song for a Dark Queen*) that they leave an indelible impression.

Historical fiction of a romantic cast was a strong and popular part of Canadian adult literature in the nineteenth century, as exemplified by John Richardson's *Wacousta* (1832), William Kirby's *The Golden Dog* (1877), Gilbert Parker's *The Seats of the Mighty* (1896), and Charles G. D. Roberts' *A Sister to Evangeline* (1898). Historical fiction for the young developed surprisingly slowly; the contemporary outdoor adventure story held sway almost to the exclusion of all other genres. The prolific writer James Macdonald Oxley did turn to the past among his thirty-one books for boys. His *Fife and Drum at Louisbourg* (1890) is quite lively historical fiction, with interesting details about the siege of Louisbourg. The twin boys who accompany the American army under General Pepperell are effectively contrasted, and, unlike the boys in much historical English and American fiction of the 1940s and 1950s (Geoffrey Trease's *Cue for Treason*, 1940, and Esther Forbes' *Johnny Tremain*, 1943), they are not credited with changing the course of history. Neither are the young people in Emily Weaver's *The Only Girl* (1925), in which the Rebellion of 1837 in Upper Canada is seen through the eyes of the sister of a young rebel.

The general paucity of children's books during the early years of the twentieth century is doubtless the explanation for a lack of historical fiction. An unusual book, by virtue of its child heroine (rather than a male teenager), was Muriel Denison's *Susannah: A Little Girl With the Mounties* (1936) set in and around the barracks of the Royal Canadian Mounted Police at the end of the nineteenth century in Saskatchewan. It provided a vehicle for Shirley Temple in 1939, sure proof of its popularity and sentimental tone. Still, as usual, the book is more realistic than the movie. Susannah is a displaced child; she has been sent to live with her RCMP uncle while her parents are delayed in India. Denison only lightly indicates that her loneliness and lack of supervision lead her into mischief. But Susannah longs to be a member of the Force and to wear its uniform. In an act of both sense and bravery she accomplishes her goal. The great moral of the story is: 'The Mounties always get their man.' From the late 1940s to the early 1960s the bulk of children's fiction was based in Canada's past: Indian life, explorers, settlement, and wars. But it was more history than fiction, on the whole—almost in direct opposition to *Susannah of the Mounties* (the title of the film). Its virtues lay in the reporting—not the recreating—of history, its failings were literary. Writers could claim full marks for the conscientious and accurate assemblage of dates, names, and events; but on the whole the plots were manipulated and the characters made of papier-mâché. Even the historical personages had a rubbed-out appearance. In paraphrasing Canada's history our writers liked to fill their pages with irrelevancies and snippets of lore. They would parcel out so much narrative and so much history, favouring the latter. And how they loved to teach! Gratuitous dates and place-names abounded, along with 'how-to-do-it' information: how to prepare pemmican, to make candles, to tan a deer hide, to construct a Red River cart—all interesting in themselves but misplaced in the pages of a novel.

Olive Knox's *The Young Surveyor* (1956) is typical of this pedagogical approach. It is based on the Jarvis survey for the Canadian Pacific Railway in British Columbia in 1874 and 1875. A seventeen-year-old boy accompanies E. W. Jarvis and learns surveying from him. The reader perforce learns it too, since the first two chapters consist of little more than questions and answers on the subject. Christie Harris's *Forbidden Frontier* (1968) has more of a story-line but she too fell into the didactic trap:

Alison was excited about going to Kamloops. Once it had been the connecting link between the Company's two vast areas of operation west of the Rockies: New Caledonia that reached north to Alaska, and the Columbia District that stretched south to California. It had maintained two thousand horses for the Brigades that wound south to the Columbia River through the easy, open Okanagan Valley.

Alison is nine years old, hardly of an age to grasp the full significance of going to Kamloops from Fort Alexandria, even in the 1860s. Imparting information while pretending to tell a story was a literary device regularly perpetrated in eighteenth- and nineteenth-century England. Children responded by ignoring such stories in favour of real stories when they came along—a warning to all writers of didactic fiction.

Any market is best exploited by a standardized product. Understandably, then, many an attempt has been made to apply the theory to writing, especially writing for children. Such books are commissioned by a publisher, written to a formula, and designed to form part of a series. Not that the series link is in itself necessarily damaging. Arthur Ransome's 'Swallows and Amazons', Edith Nesbit's 'The Bastable Children', the 'Narnia' books of C. S. Lewis, the 'Eagle of the Ninth' group by Rosemary Sutcliff—all these author series show that their creators had so much to say that their joy in their subjects and characters could not be contained in one book. Publisher-series books, however, are dependent upon a formula—both in the writing and in physical appearance. Each book may be by a different writer, but they are all marked by a similarity of approach. Of the two early Canadian series, the 'Buckskin Books' and the 'Frontier Books', the publisher of the former had admittedly the more difficult task because 'Buckskin Books' were intended for younger children. As a genre, historical fiction almost demands some built-in interest from its readers, and certainly some background knowledge. Each book consisted of no more than 122 small pages of large type bound uniformly. The vocabulary was strictly limited, except for proper names, and the story-line lay on a bed of a few historical facts: in Adelaide Leitch's *The Great Canoe* (1962), for example, a little Huron boy attaches himself to Champlain. The best of the series were the least pointedly historical. Catherine Anthony Clark's *The Man With Yellow Eyes* (1963) is a dramatic little story of a boy on horseback racing a stagecoach to record his father's mine.

The 'Frontier Books' exemplified the deficiencies of the formula story at the older age level. Described by the publisher as historical novels, they were completely based on history and no fictional characters of any consequence appeared in them. Typical of the series was *John Rowand, Fur-Trader* (1963) by Iris Allan. Rowand was an actual fur-trader who left his home in Montreal as a boy of fourteen to spend his days with the North West Company. We follow his rather uneventful life until he dies at the age of sixty-two. The outstanding happening is the amalgamation of the North West Company with the Hudson's Bay Company. John W. Chalmers' *Horseman in Scarlet* (1961), which recounts the career of the famous Sam Steele of the North West Mounted Police, is a mere refurbishing of facts.

John Hayes for almost twenty years virtually captured the historical-fiction market with his entries into Canada's past, as far apart as the seventeenth century when the English 'Fishing Admirals' dominated Newfoundland (*The Dangerous Cove*, 1957) to the completion of the Canadian Pacific Railway (*The Steel Ribbon*, 1967). Hayes' historicity is impeccable, but it is, unfortunately, matched by blandness. Historical fiction, much more than history, allows the writer, and so the reader, the opportunity to 'take sides'. Geoffrey Trease in *The Grey Adventurer* (1942) can turn our sympathies from the gay cavaliers to the more prosaic Roundheads, as can Rosemary Sutcliff in *Simon* (1953). But Hayes never exploited the conflicts inherent in his well-chosen subjects. His *A Land Divided* (1951) is about the Acadians, tragic victims of a war that settled the fate of empires. But emotion or the taking of sides was shunned. Give the young hero a father who is an English army officer and a mother who is Acadian. Have Michael's Acadian cousin Pierre help in the search for Michael's father when the latter is captured by the French. In turn, of course, Michael's father will kindly and courteously help his Acadian relatives to settle in the foreign town to which they have been banished; this succeeds so well that the impression is given that they will be far better off there anyway. Michael's mother presents no dramatic problem either; she takes the oath of loyalty to King George. Why did Longfellow become so emotional about Evangeline?

Even in Hayes' *Treason at York* (1949), blandness and impartiality set the prevailing tone. The issues would seem to force a choice—after all, Canada was invaded in the War of 1812—but Hayes somehow enables hero and reader to escape involvement. Various circumstances ensure that the hero shall bear little or no sense of enmity towards the American adversary. In many ways the book is a plea against fighting with one's neighbour. This is admirable morality but does not satisfy the claims of either entertainment or historical truth.

Hayes does come round to committing a hero in *Rebels Ride at Night* (1953), on the Rebellion of 1837 in Upper Canada. The protagonist takes sides with Mackenzie, though more for personal than political reasons. This definite identification makes it perhaps the most satisfactory of Hayes' books and certainly far better than the other two novels on the same subject, Emily Weaver's *The Only Girl* (1925) and Lyn Cook's *Rebel on the Trail* (1953), in which the Rebellion is seen from the periphery by young heroines. While both their families are alarmed by the mild attachment of the elder son for Mackenzie's cause, the Rebellion itself is treated as a pointless scheme of a foolish few. It is implied that a little more patience and equanimity would have obviated the whole incident. Although this is the view of current historians, there seems to be considerable evidence that the Rebellion followed and indeed was caused by a period of strong tension. This is well shown in James Reaney's *The Boy with an R in His Hand* (1965). The year is 1826 and two orphan boys come to 'muddy York' to be under the protection of a proud and greedy uncle, who seems to have stepped out of an old fairy tale. He represents the arrogance and ritualistic attitude of the ruling class that came to be known as the Family Compact. A picture of the society of the time emerges clearly, even though the book is short (101 pages); we read about a hanging for cow-stealing, a girl who has been branded a thief without evidence, an apprentice system that secures a boy from childhood to twenty, how a man's livelihood is destroyed while the authorities look on, and a fight for a free press. It is difficult to say whether Reaney deliberately chose to tell the story in the stereotyped convention of Victorian children's books—that is, with the characters either all bad or all good. If he did, the manner doesn't quite succeed, but the book has undoubted impact. It comes as a surprise at the end of the story to realize that the Rebellion is still ten years off.

D. Harold Turner's *To Hang a Rebel* (1977) is the most thorough fictional examination to date of the causes of the Rebellion of 1837. Although filled with eccentric characters, both fictional and real (including William Lyon Mackenzie himself), the book has the major flaw of earlier historical fiction—too much history and too little plot. The rebel to be hanged is not Mackenzie but young Doug Lachlan, who has been a spy for the rebel leader—but he escapes his captors. The actual events of the Rebellion are dealt with summarily, and somewhat chaotically; it is Upper Canada's social and political life of the period that really has the major role.

In concentrating on political and social injustices, *To Hang a Rebel* is rather a cold story. Barbara Greenwood's *A Question of Loyalty* (1984) deals with the emotions the Rebellion aroused, those that so often must have been aroused in real life for personal and humanitarian reasons. While Deborah Wallbridge's father and brother are in Toronto to do their share in stopping the rebels, Deborah finds one—wounded and starving—in the family barn. By her first act of giving him a drink of milk she commits herself to him, although not yet to his cause. When the truth has to be told to her family, the rebel Dan is taken in, nursed, hidden from antagonistic neighbours, and plans are made for his escape across the border. The actions of the Wallbridges—and of another family—are dictated by feelings of humanity rather than by political alignment. Deborah, of course, falls in love with the young rebel. *A Question of Loyalty* is in no way marked by a memorable style, but it is a warmly personal look—and often a suspenseful one—at 1837, a significant year in Canada's past.

It is strange that Canadian historical fiction gingerly sidesteps the greatest issue in Canadian history: the conflict between French and English. The few books available to children dealing with the events culminating in the Battle of the Plains of Abraham are all by British or American authors: G. A. Henty's *With Wolfe in Canada* (British—1886), Ronald Welch's *Mohawk Valley* (British—1958), Virginia Watson's *Flags Over Quebec* (American—1941), Allan Dwight's *Guns at Quebec* (American—1962), Wilma Pitchford Hays' *Drummer Boy for Montcalm* (American—1959). It seems as though the emotional implications of this theme for Canadians can hardly be toned down, and hence had best be avoided altogether. However, the scarcity of material on the age of exploration and the French and Indian wars seems beyond explanation. Only a few writers (Fred Swayze in *Tonty of the Iron Hand*, 1957, and *Iroquois War Trail*, 1965, Adelaide Leitch in *The Great Canoe*, and Beulah Garland Swayze in *Father Gabriel's Cloak*, 1962) have dealt with this earlier period. Even the story of that heroine beloved by the textbook writers, Madeleine de Verchères, has been left to our American compatriots—*Madeleine Takes Command* (1946) by Ethel C. Brill and *Outpost of Peril* (1961) by Alida Malkus.

Both Edith Sharp with *Nkwala* (1958) and Roderick Haig-Brown with *The Whale People* (1962) turned to the far-distant past. They dealt not with recorded events nor with personages from history but with a social setting no more specifically defined in time and place than British Columbia 'before the white man came'. This is not to say that the narratives are not based on solid historical research: the historicity is evident but never obtrusive; fact underlies every fictional event but never dictates its design. Both authors had a firm belief in the truth of their stories and the power to engage the belief of their readers.

Nkwala is a Salish Indian boy of the Spokane tribe. At twelve years of age, as prescribed by Salish law, he seeks a dream, a song, or any spiritual happening that will reveal to him his protecting guardian spirit and give him a man's name:

> Ahead were days and nights of trial, when the boy went alone into the mountains to search for his guardian spirit, his song and his name. This was as his father, his father's father and father's father before him, had done. He went alone, but always and forever with him went the law.

But Nkwala's dream is withheld from him. Then, forced by hunger, the Spokanes enter the land of the Okanagan tribe. The Spokane chief remembers that Spokane and Okanagan were once the same blood and hopes to establish the Spokane's 'blood right' to the Okanagans' root-digging grounds before battle is joined. The story, quietly begun and quietly told, moves to a swift and dramatic climax as Nkwala risks his life for a moment of speech between Spokane and Okanagan and so receives his name.

The Hotsath tribe of the west coast of Vancouver Island are 'the whale people'. They hunt the whale from dugout canoes with weapons of wood and bone and horn. Atlin, a boy of the tribe and the son of its chief, receives both practical and spiritual training to prepare him to take his father's place as the whale chief. Upon his father's death he subjects himself to severe discipline in order to receive the spiritual insight—the appearance of his 'tumanos' or particular spirit—that will confirm his leadership. As a chief he is able to lead his tribe back to prosperity, wisely avoiding war with the neighbouring Tsitidat tribe and winning the chief's daughter for his wife. The greatest drama in the story derives from the whale hunt—puny man pitting his skills and primitive weapons against the largest mammal on earth:

> The whale was travelling very slowly now, tail flukes sweeping wearily from side to side in a narrow arc, his body heaved and rolling on the following swells. . . . Then the canoe lifted on a swell and, through a moment of terror, seemed to hover over the whale's back. In that moment Nit-gass jumped and the ready paddles backed and swung the canoe clear of danger. Atlin saw his father slip once, recover his balance and run forward along the whale's back as far as the little flipper that showed when he rolled. There Nit-gass made two swift and fearful thrusts. The whale shuddered, drove with his tail and forced his body half out of the water.

While there is a similarity in the emphasis on initiation rites and a peaceful settlement of tribal disputes, the styles of Sharp and Haig-Brown in these books vary considerably, although each is successful in its own way. Haig-Brown's is simple, almost unadorned by descriptive adjectives in its starkness, akin to the Inuit Markoosie's *Harpoon of the Hunter* (1970). Sharp's has a softer, more romantic feeling in keeping with Nkwala's mystical experience, one more spiritual than that of Haig-Brown's Atlin. Both authors have obviously researched their basic material, but it is through the characters of the two boys that the past speaks to the present. Their rites of initiation, although surrounded by tribal ritual, are carried out in loneliness and isolation and match to a considerable degree the more random but enforced rites of passage of modern protagonists.

While *Nkwala* and *The Whale People* are fully contained within native culture and life, Christie Harris's *Raven's Cry* (1966) relates the history of the white man's impact upon the Haida from 1791 to the present. But on this broad canvas the effect of the central theme—the white man's cruelty, stupidity, and indifference towards the native people—is dissipated. In presenting the Haida as noble (although also weak, mistaken, and indecisive), the author ignores their own brand of sophistication: the slave society, the dark side of the potlatches, and their own divisive wars. A less partisan look at this particular era would have revealed more clearly the internal forces that destroyed the Haida, as well as the external ones: the organization of the European political and commercial empires and their technology. In its presentation of history *Raven's Cry* falls somewhere between fictionalized history and historical fiction, and although it works well as a *cri de coeur* on behalf of the Haida, its lack of youthful fictional characters central to the story and the long time-span it covers reduce its emotional impact as a story for children.

The escape of the United Empire Loyalists to Canada after the American War of Independence has built-in drama, but the events were used differently by John Hayes in *On Loyalist Trails* (1971) and by Mary Alice and John Downie in *Honor Bound* (1971), not least because the Canadian setting for Hayes' book is New Brunswick while that of the Downies' is Ontario. Both stories take place just after the war. Davey Hunter's family in *On Loyalist Trails* planned to join the Loyalist evacuees in New York and sail on British ships (under a treaty) to the Maritimes. But they are pursued because of a personal vendetta, and once in New Brunswick the settlers are harassed by the American 'Sons of Freedom' who invade Canadian soil. The action is fast-paced, but as usual Hayes' characters have no personality.

Honor Bound (the title neatly refers both to the name of the young heroine and to the loyalty of those who remained true to the British cause) is rather predictable in its beginning—like the Hunters, Honor's family must leave their home by stealth in the middle of the night, taking only a few cherished possessions. The background of the war and the hardships endured (always without complaint) are as authentically described as in *On Loyalist Trails*. However, once the children are in Kingston, the Downies engage them in an adventure and a mystery that add an appealing and childlike dimension to historical events and personages.

The basis of historical fiction broadened in the late 1970s with Barbara Smucker's *Underground to Canada* (1977) and *Days of Terror* (1979), although certainly the theme of 'escape to Canada' links them to the United Empire Loyalists. Before *Underground to Canada* the only children's book that disclosed the 'Canadian connection' to the 'Underground Railway', the escape route for American slaves, was *Railroad to Freedom* (1932) by the American author Hildegarde Swift, a fictional biography of the famous black freedom-fighter Harriet Tubman. Smucker also introduces a real character in the person of Alexander Ross, a Canadian abolitionist. No account of slavery, whether in documentary or fictional form, can be less than moving and important and *Underground to Canada* has these built-in components. But young Julilly and Liza, who are central, are portrayed in a strangely wooden manner; they come alive only once in a while—as when, momentarily safe in an Underground 'station', they have a hot bath and revel in being clean all over for the first time in their lives. The book's ending combines coincidence and reality: Julilly is reunited with her mother, but she is warned that Canada is not the promised land. There will still be prejudice, but there will be hope.

The hardships and horrors imposed on the Mennonites during the Russian Revolution are far more graphically and emotionally described in *Days of Terror* than slavery is in *Underground to Canada*. *Days of Terror* is a story of contrast—the Neufeld family is happy and secure before the 'days of terror' that finally drive them into exile in Canada, where they are able to start a new life. All the events are seen through the eyes and feelings of the young boy Peter as he observes his old world being torn apart and a new life rebuilt in a new one. Exodus and arrival, a flight from hardship and injustice and a journey to freedom in the New World, is the great North American theme. Although concerned with blacks and Mennonites in the nineteenth century, these stories have an emotional link to the immigrant experience today. Smucker's research went deep and her details are authentic. Except for a somewhat gratuitous elaboration of Mennonite history, culture, and politics in *Days of Terror*, she can present historical facts naturally, in simple language, letting them speak for themselves.

Barbara Smucker's works deal with highly emotional events. Other books are perhaps best classified as historical adventures. The term appears to suit both Tony German's *Tom Penny* (1977) and its sequels, and Joan Clark's *The Hand of Robin Squires* (1977). Both begin in England and involve journeys to Canada that are fraught with danger and excitement. Tom Penny's family are to leave for Canada in 1829 when the father and his cousin are offered four hundred acres of land in the Chaudière District of Quebec for their services in the War of 1812. But before they sail. Father is murdered, and on the voyage the ship is wrecked and Tom's mother and young brother are drowned. Only Tom and his uncle are left to farm their land. The plot is action-packed, with Tom's near-drowning in the Chaudière Falls, a boisterous time with the shantymen of the district, and a fight to the death with the villain of the piece.

The Hand of Robin Squires has more than a whiff of the sea about it in the larger-than-life tradition of Robert Louis Stevenson's *Treasure Island* (1883), with its pirates, stolen plunder, and the plans for hiding it. The villain is truly villainous, unlike Stevenson's Long John Silver, who becomes the most memorable character in Stevenson's romance. The tale was inspired by Nova Scotia's famed Oak Island and the legends of its buried treasure.

In the early eighteenth century Robin Squires sails with his uncle from England to America to assist him in assembling a pump that Robin's father (now dead) has invented. He finds himself in a pirate maze of treachery, horror, and murder on Oak Island, as his uncle and his nefarious crew set about burying their treasure in a huge shaft. The treasure is eventually to be salvaged by means of the pump, the work accomplished by slave labour—imported chained blacks—and by Robin and a captured Micmac, Actaudin, who has become Robin's friend. The title of the story becomes clear when, at the end, Actaudin has to cut off Robin's hand to save him from being murdered. Robin recounts his adventures over five years later in the measured words that befit an educated youth, while in no way destroying the immediacy of the events.

The concept of 'high adventure', so ably conveyed in *The Hand of*

Robin Squires, is not a popular one in modern children's literature in general; most writers opt for realistic problems in modern life rather than for adventures in the past. The great proponent of the larger-than-life approach (although with authentically described details) is still the British writer Leon Garfield. However, the tradition of adventure at sea, which allows for heightened drama—established by Norman Duncan in *The Adventures of Billy Topsail* (1906) —is continued in two novels by Bill Freeman. His *The Last Voyage of the Scotian* (1976) and *First Spring on the Grand Banks* (1978) are rousing tales that take place chiefly on mid-nineteenth-century sailing ships, with land locales of Quebec City, Nova Scotia, and Newfoundland.

To date Freeman has used the same young teenagers in all his books—John and Meg Bains, or their younger brother Jamie. In *The Last Voyage of the Scotian* Meg and John are in Quebec City and John is shanghaied aboard *The Scotian*; in going to his rescue, Meg is also forced to stay aboard. John and Meg face the typical situations of the times—bad food and sleeping quarters, harsh discipline (they are locked in irons for a night and almost witness a flogging and a near mutiny). However, they stand up to their troubles, learn the ways of the sea, and make a friend among the crew. *First Spring on the Grand Banks* is a sequel in which John and Meg help their friend Canso recover his ship. The plot and the Newfoundland setting are reminiscent of Farley Mowat's *The Black Joke* (1962). Freeman includes in all his books (see also pp. 119-20, 123-4) contemporary photographs or drawings that indicate his attention to detail. He has in no way the literary command of either Farley Mowat or Joan Clark, but his adventure stories can be appreciated for their page-turning quality.

T.H. Smith's *Cry to the Night Wind* (1986) is an even more compelling tale of high adventure than any of the books of Freeman (it is more of a companion to Clark's *The Hand of Robin Squires*), but like them it is based in historical reality. At age eleven David Spencer sails with his captain father on the HMS *Langley* to continue charting the inlets of the northwest coast of North America begun by Captain George Vancouver. The time is 1779. On board ship David has his tasks and his studies; he also earns the enmity of three rebellious sailors and—most importantly—makes friends with a seal pup. In a believable series of events (almost a sequel to the first chapters of Christie Harris's *Raven's Cry*), David is kidnapped by natives and is saved from either death or slavery only by the shaman who sees him as 'Spirit Child' because of his golden hair. He (accidentally) adds to the myth by his acrobatics with the seal pup and his seeming power over it. David's weeks with the unnamed tribe (possibly the Haida) provide a rich description of native life with growing tension between the shaman and the chief over David's role in their lives. David's escape with a Nootka slave girl, to be reunited with the *Langley* and his father, is filled with suspense and genuine terror. Smith expertly ties up all the threads of the plot, and even the fate of the mutinous sailors is dealt with in a sly epilogue.

Major changes in Canada's history—those recorded in history books—have attracted only a few recent writers as themes for a story. Mary Beacock Fryer's *Escape: Adventures of a Loyalist Family* (1982) adds to an understanding of the Loyalist experience. The American War of Independence has been over for five years, yet old hostilities are very much alive. Mr Seaman is accosted by a former enemy and is to be charged as a British spy. Twelve-year-old Ned recounts the events as he and his seven brothers and sisters and his parents slip away from Schenectady and make their way to Johnstown across the Canadian border. Their flight is marked by a jail escape, the breaking up of the family, disguises, assumed names, tussles with American militiamen, and an arduous trek of fording rivers, rafting, climbing mountains, and being plagued by mosquitoes. However, most of the tension is in the first part of this short novel and it becomes a record of physical difficulties rather than a story.

Janet Lunn's *Shadow in Hawthorn Bay* (1986) has a strong historical fiction component that gives strength to its fantastic elements (see pp. 259-61). The year is 1815 and fifteen-year-old Mary Urquhart has made her way alone from Scotland to Upper Canada to join her betrothed, who has summoned her as he lies drowned beneath the waters of Hawthorn Bay. The people of the community on Lake Ontario who succor Mary have adjusted to the hard pioneer conditions after leaving their homes either during or after the American War of Independence. Practical, hard-working, and friendly, they have put the past behind them and are determined to make the best of their situation. They are shown in their daily round of work and play, of neighbourliness and family difficulties, always struggling to make better lives for themselves, such as by seeing to the education of their children. They welcome Mary, and her own hard-working ethos and caring nature endear her to them. However, Mary's Scottish belief in ghosts and boggles disturbs the community. Her patroness, Mrs Colliver, speaks her mind bluntly: 'Seems to me God's got plenty on his hands taking care of us living, without sending us the dead to deal with.' Even more alien to her neighbours are Mary's second-sight warnings of ills to come—especially when they prove to be true. The mythic sense of the novel dominates at the end, but still Lunn's picture of a sturdy, independent society with strongly drawn minor characters makes *Shadow in Hawthorn Bay* a novel of social history as well as of fantasy.

The War of 1812 provides the background for Gregory Sass's very brief novel *Redcoat* (1985). In what can be considered a coming-of-age story, young Shadrach Byfield flees his problems at school and home (chiefly because of poverty), enlists in a regiment bound for Canada, and finds himself in the army of General Brock. The details of the war, seen by those fighting in it, who have little or no idea of what it is all about, make this the harshest book in Canadian children's fiction. In the midst of the cruelty, fighting, desertions, and floggings, Shadrach's determination not to return home until he 'had lived to be a man' seems almost irrelevant.

Far-away events impinge on the life of some Canadian-Chinese in Paul Yee's *The Curses of Third Uncle* (1986). The year is 1909, and in China the ruling Manchu Empire is under attack by the dissident larger Chinese population. In Vancouver's Chinatown there are supporters of the overthrow of the Manchus and there are supporters of the Empire. Fourteen-year-old Ah-Lai (her Canadian name is Lillian) is unaware of all this as, on her fourteenth birthday, her father goes off on another of his mysterious trips over the protests of his pregnant wife. He disappears for months and the family, never well off, sink into abject poverty and are under the control of 'Third Uncle', the father's cruel, drunken youngest brother, who plans to send the family, composed of girls, back to China. Girls, in his words, are 'seet bon foh'—no-profit goods. Lillian finds out that her father has been collecting money to send weapons to China to fight the Manchus and has been murdered for his notebook, which lists the names of all who have contributed. She also discovers that 'Third Uncle' is involved and she moves to save her father's work. In Vancouver's Chinatown the Empire is routed, as it soon was in China.

Much of the interest of the story lies in Lillian's daily life—the pictures of the extended family, the storytelling, the girls' education, Lillian's trip to Revelstoke in search of her father, and the contrast between her home and the Canadian family for whom she works for a short time as a servant. The father's concern for, and involvement in, events in China are rather lightly explained. He has felt that a more modern China would give the Chinese in Canada more prestige and so a better life for his children. The other side of the coin, that immigrants should leave their quarrels at home and not make their new country a battleground, is ignored. Yee's somewhat pedestrian writing is often compensated for by his unusual plot and his knowledge of the times he wrote about.

Rooted as they are in historical events, the books of Sass and Yee exemplify the changes that have taken place in Canadian historical fiction since the days of John Hayes. A historical event does not merely provide a stage for the characters; it moulds their lives. The historical events do not move to a climax but end with a formative period in the protagonists' lives; they have changed and matured and that is the point of the story. Even Sass's Shadrach briefly muses on what he has experienced. The British writer of historical novels, Hester Burton, perhaps expressed the feelings of most modern writers when she wrote: 'As a novelist, I am primarily interested in one kind of story; it is the story of young people thrown into some terrible predicament or danger, and scrambling out of it, unaided.' The youthful protagonists of much recent Canadian fiction are caught briefly in the net of history, become entangled in the mesh of the adult world, and like their counterparts in modern realistic fiction, cut themselves free to begin their lives anew.

Among the increasingly varied topics chosen by social historians are unions and strike action. These form the core of Bill Freeman's *Shantymen of Cache Lake* (1975) and *Trouble at Lachine Mill* (1983), Marsha Hewitt's and Claire Mackay's *One Proud Summer* (1981), and Geoffrey Bilson's *Goodbye Sarah* (1982). *Shantymen of Cache Lake* was Freeman's first book and introduced John and Meg Bains, who are very much children of pre-1960s historical fiction: spunky, courageous, self-reliant, and strong defenders of justice—Meg even more than her brothers. Here they are employed in a lumber camp after the death of their father in 1873 (they are now the breadwinners of their family) and discover that their father was trying to organize a union and was probably murdered. The incidents, in which the children play a decisive part, are realistically violent, but the details of lumbering are too instrusive. The shantymen of Cache Lake strike, win their union, and although the company they worked for failed the next season (as the notes in an Epilogue relate), the spirit of unionism survives.

The two strikes in *Trouble at Lachine Mill* have a more emotional force than the one in *Shantymen at Cache Lake*, chiefly because the workers are largely women and young people, such as Meg and her younger brother Jamie, who is only twelve. They are much more helpless under the cruel foreman (a veritable Simon Legree) than are the burly lumbermen of the Ottawa Valley. The conditions in the shirt factory in Montreal in the 1870s are appalling. Meg and Jamie work twelve hours a day for $1.50 a week and, like all the workers, are subject to punishments, threats, and verbal abuse. When the second strike comes (the first one fails), it succeeds, thanks to Meg's planning; a new foreman is appointed and the strikers are rehired.

In *One Proud Summer*, Lucie Laplante's father has also been killed on the job, like Freeman's Mr Bains, and with no pension or compensation available the mother has to work in the one mill in the town, as does Lucie at age thirteen. The conditions at the mill are those of nineteenth-century England, although the year is 1946. Though the workers are French-speaking, the degrading epithets of the English bosses are well understood. For the young working girls another hazard is sexual harassment. It all leads to the famous Valleyfield strike. The authors manage to bring the strike to a high level of emotional tension while quickly inserting authentic strike details that read like fiction—they did not have to embroider. Lucie matures during the long hot summer of the strike, playing a role that befits her age. Yet as the authors suggest in a poignant image, her childhood has ended too soon. After an especially hard day at the mill, with her week's wages docked, Lucie jumps on the swing her father had made for her as a child:

Higher she went, and higher still, all her tiredness gone now, her body light and free in the pliant air, floating, flying, swooping up, and back, up, till she saw the shingles glinting black on the roof for a single motionless instant, then down, her stomach plunging with delight, back through the leaf-dark shadows, her breath coming fast through her open mouth, while the old tree creaked and groaned, and she didn't care.

There is a strong familial and feminine element in the story, one that emerges in nuances—provided by Lucie's feisty grandmother who had taken part in a strike some years before, Lucie's mother who joins the strike after some doubts, and by the healing of a strained relationship between Lucie and her mother.

The Winnipeg General Strike of 1919 was marked by violence and blood and police action. In the late Geoffrey Bilson's *Goodbye Sarah* the events are seen through the eyes of young Mary Jarrett, whose father is a member of the Strike Committee. When the strike ends in failure it is not the poverty the family has endured that hurts Mary, nor the open resentment of her teacher and her schoolmates—not even the family's enforced move to Ontario. It is the loss of her friend and next-door neighbour, Sarah, whose father has been violently opposed to the strikers. Mary goes to say goodbye, but Sarah has found another 'closest' friend. In very simple prose Bilson conveys the strong bond between Mary and Sarah, which survives the strike until almost the end, the social situation that caused this major strike, and, in small touches (such as the delivery of milk), shows a city divided against itself. However, the essence of the story is a young child's personal tragedy.

The horrors of the cholera epidemic in Montreal in the early nineteenth century, as described in Bilson's *Death Over Montreal* (1982), should have a greater impact than the effects of a strike but somehow they do not. In contrast to *Goodbye Sarah*, too many threads are put on the loom of this short book. There is the immigrant experience of the Douglas family as they arrive from Scotland, the irresponsibility of the father and his death from cholera, the mother's tribulations and illness, and young Jamie's new-found gifts as a 'healer', in addition to several other incidents. Bilson's chief strength here lay in his ability to create a social milieu in quick, deft strokes, not in plot or characterization.

Native life of over a hundred and fifty years ago, based on records, inspired one of our finest historical novels, Jan Hudson's *Sweetgrass* (1984). Sweetgrass is a fifteen-year-old Blackfoot girl who chafes against the restricted role of women in her tribe. She is in love with her childhood friend, but her parents may have other marriage plans for her. She sees that her life has been circumscribed by changes brought about through contact with the white man. Compared to her grandmother, who enjoyed relative freedom in her youth, Sweetgrass finds her activities severely limited. Then tragedy strikes with a raid from another tribe, winter starvation, and smallpox. Her youthful dreams of the husband she wants are consumed in the need to save her family. This she does with self-reliance, ingenuity, courage and—most importantly—the breaking of tribal taboos. In all these aspects, particularly the latter, she resembles in her fight for survival the American Indian girl Karana of Scott O'Dell's *Island of the Blue Dolphins*. With all its taut drama, Hudson's story is also told in quiet, rhythmic prose and spare, sensuous imagery. Framed within a single year, it reflects the changing prairie seasons and the women's endless cycle of physical labour. Like Karana, Sweetgrass tells her own story. At the beginning all is happiness:

> I sighed with happiness as we picked the small fragrant berries. We must be careful or else the strawberry blood would stain this perfect day. Sun, sand, sage and small red berries—a bird sang to us from a rosebush clump, joyfully—the pattern of our lives.
>
> All things moved as they should. Our lives seemed fixed as in a beaded design or the roundness of an old tale told on winter nights. Time would soon make women of us in marriage.

While Sweetgrass is steeped in her own culture, Isobel Macpherson of Brenda Bellingham's *Storm Child* (1985) feels that she has to choose between her father's white heritage and that of her Peigan mother. The crisis comes when her father deserts Isobel and her mother and returns to his native Scotland. When her mother marries another white factor, Isobel determines to go and live with her Peigan grandparents and adopt her native name, Storm Child. Although the plot involves the trading practices of the natives and Canadians and Americans, and a battle between the Peigans and the Crees, the key to the story is Isobel's choice. She has models before her of two ways of life. Jamey Jock Bird, a handsome, dashing halfbreed, has been educated in England but has preferred to adopt his native background; Henry Rowand, the son of the chief factor, is half Cree and intends to study to be a doctor in England, although he will return to practise in his prairie home. Isobel makes her decision:

> Her mother had said she must one day choose which trail she wanted to follow—the way of her father's people or the way of her mother's. But maybe she would blaze a new trail, somewhere between the two. She was neither all white nor all Indian. She was part Isobel, part Storm Child—a country-born girl.
> Her excitement grew. Her way would be different, probably difficult, but it would be her way, no matter what.

As the above paragraphs indicate, *Storm Child* is simply and directly told. It reveals the unfortunate realities of social history that are still very much a part of modern Métis life, as Beatrice Culleton shows in *In Search of April Raintree* (see page 81). However, in writing style this book lacks the emotional impact of either Culleton's work or Hudson's *Sweetgrass*.

Bill Freeman continued his miniature pictures of social life in Ontario in the 1870s with *Harbour Thieves* (1984) and *Danger on the Tracks* (1987). Both have his spirited sister-and-brother team of Meg and Jamie Bains, with Jamie given the central role and Meg that of the sensible older sister. Toronto is the harbour of *Harbour Thieves* and much of the action is played out on its waters. The main theme is the street life of homeless boys whose only source of income is selling newspapers, and who are led into participating in major thefts. Jamie's one chance of avoiding the reformatory is to find the hidden loot, a feat he accomplishes with Meg's help. In *Danger on the Tracks* Meg and Jamie have left Toronto and find work as the cook's helpers in a railway camp outside of London, Ontario. Jamie chafes under the cook's bullying and finds work as a stable boy for the major stage-coach line for the district. This puts Meg and Jamie on opposite sides of the rivalry that has developed between the Ryan brothers who run the stage coach, and who see their livelihood threatened, and the men of the railway who herald the future of transportation. While

Harbour Thieves ends in a chase between the police and the thief, *Danger on the Tracks* ends with a race between the stage coach and the train. The mystery of sabotage is solved, the Ryans yield to progress, and Jamie receives the reward money, which means a reunion of the whole Bains family. As in all Freeman's books the style is competent, but lacking in grace; unfortunately all suffer considerably from an unattractive physical format.

A few novels are set in the past simply because their authors want to use the physical and social environment of an era for studies of character and family life. Books such as Marianne Brandis's *The Tinderbox* (1982), and its sequel *The Quarter-Pie Window* (1985), and Bernice Thurman Hunter's *Lamplighter* (1987) do not contain the slightest mention of a historical event (a war or a rebellion) or a social situation (the plight of homeless boys or labour disputes). These are individual life stories that could take place today but are set in the past.

Emma, aged thirteen, and her younger brother John of *The Tinderbox* are the only survivors of a fire that destroys their log cabin and with it their father, mother, and younger sisters. Emma and John are taken in by kindly neighbours and are able to earn their keep with farm and household chores. Then a Mrs McPhail appears from York claiming to be Emma's and John's aunt and guardian, and also part-heir to their estate. She wants to take the children to York where John will become a stable boy and Emma will serve in her aunt's hotel. Emma is suspicious of her aunt and her male companion, who is interested in buying the farm, and she has to undertake investigations by herself (including a difficult trip to York to consult a lawyer), with only the help and support of her neighbours' aged and dying grandmother. Then Emma has an offer of marriage from a young man who is still clearing his land. If she stays with the neighbours, he will wait a year for her. Her choice is between life on a bush farm and a venture into the unknown. Emma feels that she has 'to turn her life in a different direction, have it shaped by a different prevailing wind.'

The orphaned heroine and her young brother who are heirs to their parents' property, the manipulative relative, and in *The Quarter-Pie Window* a move to a questionable new life give more than a touch of old-fashioned romance to Brandis's two books. Historical authenticity is achieved through the daily round of bush and farm life in Ontario in the 1830s, the seasonal and household tasks, the bustling life of Toronto, and the routine of a hotel of the period. Although not first-person narratives, all the events, sights, sounds, routines, and people are sifted through Emma's perceptions of them. Like Jo of Louisa May Alcott's *Little Women* (1868), Emma is an acute and sensitive observer of life. Like Jo, too, she struggles against the restrictions placed on women at the time, and while in no way defying conventions, she seeks ways to make a more ample life for herself and her brother. Brandis is one of our few writers for the young who can truly be called a stylist. She is not as obvious a one as Brian Doyle in *Up To Low* (1982) or Elizabeth Brochmann in *What's the Matter, Girl?* (1980). Brandis's style has a cumulative effect, only gradually revealing its quiet elegance.

The woodcuts by G. Brender à Brandis that adorn both books serve more than an aesthetic purpose—although they do this very well. They both complement and extend the text; there is part of a parlour of the 1830s, a butter churn, a morning cup, harvest tools and much more. They provide the concrete details of the past and allow Marianne Brandis to concentrate on human emotions rather than on descriptive details.

Bernice Thurman Hunter's *Lamplighter* is also loosely set in place and time—the pioneer country of Muskoka, Ontario, in the 1880s. Although *Lamplighter* has the same quality of emotional sensitivity as *The Tinderbox*, and its concrete details of social life, it has been written for much younger children. Wee Willie Adams is only six years old when the novelette begins, and almost eight when it ends. Thus *Lamplighter* is a story of childhood (in contrast to Emma's girlhood), but one that is also based on the small details of daily living. Incidents such as removing warts, choosing a Christmas tree, making presents, listening to stories and details such as homemade comforts and remedies are balanced against tensions and child tragedies—a confrontation with a dangerous mother bear, a terrible winter storm, the death of the grandmother and the drowning of kittens. Like Jacob, of Barbara Smucker's *Jacob's Little Giant*, Willie is worried about his slow growth and his role as the youngest child in the family and has a need to prove himself by taking his share in the family chores. He does not have a chance to prove himself as modern Jacob does with the wild geese, but at the end his father realizes his need to be called 'William' rather than 'boy'. The title of the book comes from Willie's desire to become a lamplighter when he grows up—he is fascinated by the one he meets while visiting relatives in Toronto. Hunter does not link images of lamps and lights to her tale, but one feels that Willie will always light up the lives of those around him.

Hunter's Willie is an unusual protagonist in historical fiction because of his age. Most are young teenagers as befits their involvement in large events (Lucie of Hewitt and Mackay's *One Proud Summer*), or are of an age to live independently (Bill Freeman's Meg, John and Jamie Bains). The readers of such books can be presumed—unlike younger children—to have a deeper sense of memory and time. Younger children have not yet developed a subtle understanding of personal and social history. Writers for the seven-to-ten age-group generally represent the past in a reversal of scale so that a small detail can loom large and significant. As D.H. Lawrence put it, in his poem 'Humming-bird', 'We look at him through the wrong end of the long telescope of time'. The end-of-the-telescope technique is the one most used in this special sub-genre, along with the packing of drama into a short time-period and the presence of child rather than teenage protagonists. These short books are usually contained within a publisher's formula series, such as the earlier 'Buckskin Books', although they are not always given a series title.

Geoffrey Bilson's *Goodbye Sarah*, an example of younger historical fiction, works very well owing to its simple plot about the effects of a strike on a young child, while his *Death Over Montreal*, although given a short time-span, is too overladen with details to make anyone at all memorable. Mary Hamilton's *The Tin-Lined Trunk* (1980), and *A Proper Acadian* (1980) by Mary Alice Downie and George Rawlyk, are also publisher's companion pieces. Homeless eleven-year-old Polly and her older brother Jack of *The Tin-Lined Trunk* become wards of the great British social reformer Dr Barnardo in 1877 (his homes for neglected children are still in existence), and, like so many children of the time, are sent to the colonies as domestic and farm workers. Polly is quite well treated on a Canadian farm, but Jack is mistreated. However, he is eventually taken in with Polly and she unpacks the 'tin-lined trunk' that Dr Barnardo had sent her for her voyage. The scenes in England are particularly effective—Polly has been a 'little match girl' on the order of Hans Christian Andersen's famous creation, and when sent to a Barnardo home she does *not* like baths and new, clean clothes.

Mary Alice Downie's *The King's Loon* (1979) offers a pleasing glimpse of Count Frontenac as seen through the adventures of a young orphan boy who stows away on Frontenac's expedition to build a fort on Lake Ontario. Downie's fictional element is composed of both humour (Louis's aunt can be described as a 'character') and pathos (as a captured loon pines in captivity), and is meshed with the history in a lively style. Far less successful is *A Proper Acadian* which, also in 62 pages, attempts to provide the history, background, and culture of the Acadians and an account of their expulsion. This large and tragic sweep of history does not mesh with the fictional plot-line of an American boy who, within one year, rejects his American Protestant background to become 'a proper Acadian'. Unfortunately, here Lawrence's hummingbird is observed through the large end of the telescope.

There are few examples of memorable historical fiction for younger children. In Canada, pride of place can certainly be offered to Hunter's *Lamplighter*, and in the United States to Patricia MacLachlan's *Sarah, Plain and Tall* (1985), and to Laura Ingalls Wilder's earlier (and still popular) *Little House* series that began in 1932, all of which are endearing stories of child and family life as well as of pioneer experiences. For many years Howard Pyle's *Otto of the Silver Hand* (1888)—the violent, yet tender story of a young boy caught between the warring feudal barons of the Holy Roman Empire—was considered the classic piece of writing for younger children. Its disappearance from their reading may be partly accounted for by its length, nearly 200 pages. Today it is almost axiomatic that such fiction be contained within about 60 pages!

Historical fiction presented within a picture-storybook format is quite rare. The Northern Lights series (six titles to date, all published in 1980) offers vignettes of early Canadian life as experienced by young children. These books are small in format, each made up of 32 pages, are on the whole attractively illustrated, and are certainly accurate in their historical details. Those with a narrow focus are the most successful. Shelley Tanaka's *Michi's New Year*, illustrated by

Ron Berg, is the poignant story of a Japanese immigrant child in 1912 who misses the New Year's festivities in her homeland but finds comfort in the friendly greeting of a neighbourhood boy and a gathering of friends and family. Mary Hamilton's *The Sky Caribou*, illustrated by Debi Perna, and Donald and Eleanor Swainson's *The Buffalo Hunt*, illustrated by James Tughan, portray (as their titles suggest) aspects of early native life. In the former, Little Partridge relates how his father, the chief of the Chipewyans, helps Samuel Hearne explore the Coppermine River. Here the author's historicity is impeccable. She does not say that Hearne discovered the Coppermine—after all, the Indians knew where it was! The fictional component (with a touch of legend) is a plausible story of friendship between two native boys. However, all the remaining titles, Susanne McSweeney's *The Yellow Flag*, illustrated by Brenda Clark (the cholera epidemic in Montreal), George Rawlyk's *Streets of Gold*, illustrated by Leoung O'Young (an American boy at the siege of Louisbourg), and Mary Alice Downie's *The Last Ship*, illustrated by Lissa Colvert (preparation in Quebec for the last ship leaving for France before winter sets in) are too diffuse, lacking one major incident to make them memorable.

Few writers of historical fiction have drawn completely on events outside Canada, although those that deal with the immigrant experience or high adventure have their origins in other countries, especially Britain and the United States. In earlier decades Donald J. Goodspeed and Herbert F. Wood (under the pseudonym of John Redmayne) wrote well-constructed, exciting spy tales of the Napoleonic era, beginning with *Redcoat Spy* (1964), and Herbert Tait, in *Redwulf the Outlander* (1972), recounts the adventures of a young Viking with a rather heavy historical hand. Karleen Bradford's *The Nine Days Queen* (1986) is a compelling novel about the unfortunate Lady Jane Grey who ruled England for nine days on the death of Edward VI and was beheaded at age sixteen. It is unusual in modern historical fiction for children in having a historical figure at its core. Bradford suggests the complex factors and intrigues that surrounded Lady Jane's sad life and the education and religious beliefs that helped form her nature, providing the historical tragedy with a selection of details comprehensible to a young reader with no knowledge of the period. But even with all this background *The Nine Days Queen* has the pace and suspense of an adventure story. Unfortunately its quality is obscured by its shoddy paperback format.

In discussing novels that deal with the past the question must arise: what *is* the past? As Alfred T. Sheppard points out in *The Art & Practice of Historical Fiction*: '. . . two minutes ago is, strictly speaking, as much the Past as two generations or two thousand years; and in that sense it is . . . difficult to draw any exact line . . .' In another sense, all contemporary-scene novels become historical novels with the passage of time. Lyn Cook's *The Bells on Finland Street* (1950) is now very much a book of a time past, not in its ice-skating theme but certainly in its picture of immigrant life. There are also the many stories that look back on only a recent past—to the Depression years, to the Second World War, or to a childhood in the 1920s. Many of these books, such as Bernice Thurman Hunter's 'Booky' series, are based on the writers' own memories of their childhood. Past-time fantasies—from John Buchan's *Lake of Gold* (1941), which describes specific eras and events in Canada's history, to Kit Pearson's *A Handful of Time* (1987), which looks back to a social milieu of only about thirty years ago—also have a right to be described as historical, as well as stories of the supernatural. And certainly what is in the personal memory of an adult can be considered historical for modern children.

This chapter has been confined to those novels in which writers have re-created a period in which they did not live, or, to a lesser extent, have written about a situation of which they had no personal experience—for example, *One Proud Summer* by Marsha Hewitt and Claire McKay, about the 1939 Valleyfield strike.

As with all other genres, Canadian historical fiction has increased and improved. Modern Canadian children now have a wealth of historical narratives to choose from, all of them disproving the old cry that 'Canadian history is dull.' Our new writers strive mightily for relevance to the present and often succeed in showing that the past is indeed the present. In our emotions and behaviour, we of the present are little different from those who have trodden the road before us. In their various ways the new writers share the conviction of the Danish writer Erik Christian Haugaard about historical fiction:

> The man without a past is a fiction; even wilful ignorance cannot erase our history. Only in eternal night will man be shadowless, and the past not follow the present into the future.... Knowledge of the past—of history—gives perspective to our world. Without that knowledge our loneliness would be harder to bear and sorrow would easily crush us.

5
Picturebooks and Picture-Storybooks

Collections of early English children's books, dating from the seventeenth century, generally include ABC and counting books, little pictorial Bibles, and eight- or twelve-page booklets with pictures of animals or artifacts, matched by a few descriptive words, all printed in black-and-white or coloured by hand. The book with simple text and accompanying mechanically coloured pictures, designed as much for the child's pleasure in looking as in reading, came late in the development of children's literature—the 1860s. The new technology of printing in colour was of course responsible for the change, but much credit for initiating the 'golden age' of children's picturebooks was due to the engraver and printer Edmund Evans, who was interested in producing quality colour work and inspired the three leading illustrators of the day—Walter Crane, Randolph Caldecott, and Kate Greenaway—to devote themselves to books for children. In their earliest books these artists displayed their particular genius: Crane his brilliant colours and fine design (*The House That Jack Built*, c. 1865), Caldecott his energetic wit and his ability to extend the text with his pictures (*The Diverting History of John Gilpin*, 1878), and Greenaway her vision of childhood as romantic and pretty (*Under the Window*, 1879), with 'babies in baskets of roses', to paraphrase John Ruskin. The books of Crane and Caldecott, published in inexpensive soft covers, were advertised as 'Toy Books' (not at all the modern concept of a toy book), while Greenaway appeared only in hardcover. Hundreds of thousands of their works were sold in their own time. These three 'Victorian greats' introduced the concept of books for young children that made pictures and text

131

equally important, that eventually became refined and defined as the picturebook we know today.

The picturebook may be the creation of an author-illustrator, such as Maurice Sendak, or it may represent the combined talents of an author and an illustrator, as in Margaret Wise Brown's *Goodnight Moon* (1947), illustrated by Clement Hurd. But whether crafted by one or by two, the picturebook at its best reflects an interdependence of words and pictures, neither being complete without the other. Together the very basic text and the complementary illustrations form a perfect whole.

Not a step up from the picturebook, but rather a step to the side, is the picture-storybook. It is generally recognized by its longer text and by its more formal arrangement of text and pictures—usually one page of text with a matching picture—and so lacks the fluidity of the picturebook. The picture-storybook has a longer history than the picturebook—hundreds of examples of chapbooks in early children's literature preceded Walter Crane's illustrated folktales of the 1870s (e.g. *Beauty and the Beast*) and Beatrix Potter in 1902 (*The Tale of Peter Rabbit*). Because the picture-storybook was (and sometimes still is) intended for beginning readers, its vocabulary is often restrained—not controlled, as in school readers, but usually lacking the word-magic of the later picturebook stylists: 'There were hundreds of cats, thousands of cats, millions and billions and trillions of cats' (Wanda Gag, *Millions of Cats*, 1928)—though many of the works of Beatrix Potter achieve this kind of textual memorability.

Until well into the twentieth century, England held the ascendancy in the picturebook field. One thinks of L. Leslie Brooke (*Johnny Crow's Garden*, 1903), William Nicholson (*Clever Bill*, 1927), and Edward Ardizzone (*Little Tim and the Brave Sea Captain*, 1936). After the First World War the American picturebook sprang into prominence, owing largely to an influx of European immigrant artists and to cheaper and more efficient colour-processing. Edgar and Ingri D'Aulaire produced books with a background of Mrs D'Aulaire's country of birth, Norway, in such books as *Ola* (1932), and also saluted the childhood of famous Americans in brilliant colour with *Abraham Lincoln* (1939) and *George Washington* (1936). Maud and Miska Petersham at first turned to their native Poland for inspiration in *Miki* (1929), but also created picturebooks on American topics.

Wanda Gag, whose *Millions of Cats* was translated into countless languages, retold and illustrated some of the Grimms' fairy tales in the tradition of her Czech grandmother. H.A. Rey, the author/illustrator of the still-popular *Curious George* (1941), came to the United States from Germany. American-born illustrators in this period also created picturebooks that are considered classics: Robert McCloskey's *Make Way for Ducklings* (1941) and Virginia Lee Burton's *The Little House* (1942).

All these books, and hundreds of others, were widely distributed in Canada, so that young Canadians grew up on the picturebook art and lore of other countries. The story of the Canadian child coming home from school and announcing that 'George Washington is the father of my country' is not necessarily apocryphal. Today, in both the United States and Great Britain, the number of picturebooks that writers, illustrators, and publishers collaborate on seems to increase annually to produce a flood—a veritable industry. (As we shall discuss below, Canada has added significantly to this flood in the 1980s.) Fortunately quantity has not ruled out quality, for among the huge output of the last quarter-century, we have Maurice Sendak's *Where the Wild Things Are* (1963), John Burningham's *Mr Gumpy's Outing* (1970), and Arnold Lobel's *Frog and Toad* stories (the 1970s), to name only a few outstanding titles.

In Canada the picturebook was the last genre to develop; a Canadian example was almost unknown until the 1960s. The reasons mainly had to do with problems of high cost of production and small population—which in the post-war years plagued the publishing industry generally and the publishing of children's books in particular—and the paucity of creative talent. Four-colour printing was prohibitively expensive, and a pool of excellent book illustrators (such as we have today) simply did not exist. Furthermore, children's-book publishing as a whole was sporadic and unfocused, since editorial expertise was lacking: there were no professional children's-book editors.

What has been called the first Canadian picturebook is somewhat of an anomaly because it was made by an Englishwoman, a visitor to Canada. Amelia Frances Howard-Gibbon drew and lettered *An Illustrated Comic Alphabet* in 1859, probably for the teaching of her little pupils in Sarnia, Ontario; but it was not published until 1966, somewhat as a historical curiosity. The text, even when Miss Howard-Gibbon illustrated it, was old in English children's literature—'A was an Archer and shot at a Frog,/B was a Butcher who kept a great Dog'—and her drawings (she was a gifted amateur) are of English scenes and figures. Canadian content arrived with *A Canadian Child's ABC* (1931), with verses by R.K. Gordon and drawings by the then well-known artist Thoreau MacDonald. The verses are doggerel, although what is written about has an amusing modern ring, almost of parody:

> To Ottawa from coast to coast
> The chosen come to make the laws.
> For weeks they talk about a lot
> Of different things with scarce a pause:
> The railway line to Hudson Bay,
> Taxes and tariff, immigration,
> The great St Lawrence waterway,
> And whether we are yet a nation.

On the whole the drawings have more charm than the verses, even though they are baldly realistic. 'O for Ottawa' is accompanied by a sketch of the Parliament Buildings. 'M' has a blackly inked Mountie with a suggestion of prairie and sky behind him. With simplicity and factualness, though with no artistic flair, the drawings manage to convey scenes that are recognizably Canadian.

A Canadian Child's ABC is essentially an illustrated book (not by any means a picturebook), and so is a relatively more lavish book that appeared a few years later: Hazel Boswell's *French Canada: Pictures and Stories* (1938), which has a charming watercolour opposite each page of short, non-continuous text. *The Princess of Tomboso* (1960), a fairy tale selected and adapted from a popular collection, *The Golden Phoenix and Other French-Canadian Fairy Tales* (1958), collected by Marius Barbeau and retold by Michael Hornyansky, can be considered our first picture-storybook—or, if not the first, at least the first one of quality. The amusing illustrations by Frank Newfeld, in four colours and black-and-white, are well integrated with the text.

Elizabeth Cleaver was Canada's pioneer picturebook illustrator and, before her death in 1985, was internationally recognized as a major artist in this field. She made her début as the illustrator of *The Wind Has Wings: Poems from Canada* (1968), in which she burst on the scene as a highly professional collage and linocut artist. (She added illustrations for *The New Wind Has Wings* in 1984.) With her first two picturebooks the next year, *The Mountain Goats of Temlaham* (1969) and *How Summer Came to Canada* (1969), retellings of native legends by William Toye, she carried her abilities as a collage artist even further, demonstrating a striking sense of design, blazing colour, rich textures, and a sensitivity to the milieu of the text. Her materials were coloured monoprints (handprinted colour papers) torn and cut and integrated with coloured linoprints and often real objects, such as pieces of fur, pine, and birchbark. Her technique became even more confident and rich in two subsequent books of native legends, *The Loon's Necklace* (1977) and *The Fire Stealer* (1979). She captured, in semi-abstract form, their archetypal imagery while being faithful to authentic details. In general Cleaver's collage technique has greater richness and variety than that of the acclaimed American collage picturebook artists Ezra Jack Keats, Leo Lionni, and Eric Carle.

Cleaver drew on her Hungarian background for *The Miraculous Hind* (1973), in which she narrated and illustrated the legend of Hunor and Magyar, who helped to form the Hungarian nation. But in this book—which pays fine and decorative attention to details of landscape, custom, and dress—she allowed her interest in typographical effect to disrupt the flow of the story by introducing lines of the text in bold cut-out letters on a brightly coloured ground, making it difficult to read. Cleaver's growth and mastery of the collage technique can be seen in her *Petrouchka* (1980), inspired by the ballet created by Igor Stravinsky and Alexander Benois. The tragic story of the clown-puppet Petrouchka, his love for a ballerina-puppet, and his death and spiritual rebirth, are illustrated with linocuts. When viewed separately the puppets, appropriately, have the stilted awkwardness of toy dolls, but when viewed as a unity they become fluid, as in a dance or an animated film. Each image is formally framed above the separately framed text, a device that gives the illusion of viewing a puppet-show, or a ballet through the proscenium arch of a stage. The radiant colours of the Russian folk-art patterns add a lavish winter-carnival atmosphere to the book.

Following this series of brilliantly colourful books and a clever, small-format *ABC* (1984), Cleaver's last work was a dramatic departure. *The Enchanted Caribou* (1985), an Inuit legend, is a beautiful example of how black-and-white illustrations, endowed with the utmost simplicity, can achieve a certain power. Each illustration is an arrangement of shadow puppets, cut with scissors out of black paper, placed behind a lighted screen and photographed from in front. The scenes evoke the barren tundra, but the shadowy figures create the illusion of magical transformation, which is the basis of the story.

The 1970s were also enriched by the work of two author-illustrators: Ann Blades, who still continues to produce quality work, and William Kurelek, who died in 1977. Blades and Kurelek share a style of consciously naïve art, with primitively rendered child figures set against recognizable Canadian landscapes.

Blades' *Mary of Mile 18* (1971) portrays the daily life of a little Mennonite girl in northern British Columbia (north on the Alaska highway for 73 miles, then right for 18). It is a monotonous, hard-working existence whose pattern is broken only when Mary acquires a wolf-pup for a pet. She is an earnest miniature adult going about the serious business of living—all work and little play. The simple text has an inner rhythm that supports full-page watercolours, which are warm, unsentimental evocations of a bleak, yet glowing, northern scene.

> One clear night in February the temperature drops to forty degrees below zero and the northern lights flash across the sky. Mary Fehr gets out of bed and goes to the window to watch and listen. She hears a crackling sound and smiles, excited. Mary likes to pretend that if she hears the music of the lights, the next day will bring something special.

The illustrations have a dream-like calm. There is poignancy in Blades' asymmetrical compositions—as if life has been caught and held in the primitive toy-world of childhood art: houses look like toy boxes, children like wooden dolls. The subtle texture of layered washes, the wet- and dry-brush techniques, the pebbly watercolour paper, the skilful blending of colours, and the tonal variations all convey a remarkable impression of weather, seasons, night and day in the lonely northern landscape. Blades' *A Boy of Taché* (1973) strives for the same quality in the text but it lacks the polish of *Mary of Mile 18*. On an Indian reserve in northern British Columbia a young boy is preparing to accompany his grandfather on the annual hunt to trap beaver. The grandfather falls ill with pneumonia and Charlie goes for the help that will summon a rescue plane. The illustrations show Blades' great talent as a landscape artist and as an interpreter of Indian life. From the beginning of her career she set a standard in her depiction of children of different ethnic backgrounds living in a real Canadian setting.

William Kurelek exhibited a more sophisticated primitivism than Ann Blades. His reputation as a gallery artist was extended by the acclaim he received as an illustrator of his first picture-storybooks, *A Prairie Boy's Winter* (1973) and *A Prairie Boy's Summer* (1975). In the former, Kurelek's minutely rendered illustrations of a Ukrainian-Canadian childhood, spent on a Manitoba dairy-farm in the 1930s, form a set of striking paintings in coloured pencil and ink loosely linked by a straightforward descriptive text. There is a glowing nostalgia in the naïvely styled pictures of the boy William against the changing seasonal backdrop of farm chores, children's games, and animal life dwarfed by the endless prairie and sky. Overpowering all other elements in the art and text is the sense of place—the farms of Manitoba—and of human life in relation to the land and climate. In his companion books, and in *Lumberjack* (1974), the texts are also brief and unpretentious autobiographical accompaniments to each picture. The authentic drama of personal experience is present, but not the extra dimensions of fiction.

In *A Northern Nativity: Christmas Dreams of a Prairie Boy* (1976) Kurelek moves from memoir to dream and legend. He sets one of the most resonant of narratives, the Nativity, against a kaleidoscope of Canadian scenes. Based on a series of Kurelek's childhood dreams, the paintings place the Nativity in a modern social context—the Depression era of Kurelek's childhood—and relocate it in a cinematic journey across the country. The Holy Family, depicted as representing all Canadians, is placed in settings from the foothills of the Rocky Mountains to Ottawa, and appears in many changing cultural identities, including Inuit, black, and Indian. The images allude to the classic motifs of nativity paintings, but have their own atmosphere of calm, magical mystery.

The late 1970s and 1980s brought a veritable explosion in the picturebook field—in numbers, diversity, and quality. From a complete dependence on imports, the publishing scene changed to include our own ABC books, counting books, board books, concept books, and bilingual books. The traditional realistic and fantasy picturebooks that tell a story—apart from native legends—are now outnumbered by others that treat aspects of contemporary child life, immigration, and multiculturalism. These new picturebooks also display an impressive range of illustrative styles, techniques, and media. Although decidedly individual in vision, and drawing on diverse backgrounds of gallery and commercial art, their illustrators are not wholly resistant to classification. They reflect certain shared visual sensibilities and stylistic traditions. While a picturebook must be viewed as an entity, the deluge of books in the 1980s calls for some separation of text and art in appraising them, in order to cast light upon trends, themes, formats, and illustration styles. Many of the works are therefore discussed twice: first by category within the genre, beginning with stories of child and family life, and secondly by artistic styles that link the illustrators beyond specific works. This latter division is especially necessary today because Canadian illustrators have joined the international world of the picturebook; many are now commissioned by non-Canadian publishers.

Since the publishing spate is of such recent origin (barely encompassing ten years), time has had little chance to play a part in the winnowing-out process. It is as yet too soon to speculate about which books will win the hearts of young children and have lasting appeal. Many can be seen simply as vehicles for gifted illustrators; others can be deemed useful for a specific purpose, or have a special relevance, but will not necessarily endure. Those chosen for some discussion here seem to be strong contenders in the endurance sweepstakes and represent the picturebook of the late 1970s and 1980s at its best. Unfortunately the competitive outpouring of a multitude of titles may work against some worthy books, preventing them from achieving the popularity they deserve.

THE REALISTIC PICTUREBOOK

A large group focuses with simplicity and warm humour on the minutiae of everyday experiences and small domestic dramas of pre-schoolers. One of the earliest and best of these is Sue Ann Alderson's *Bonnie McSmithers, You're Driving Me Dithers* (1974). It describes a daughter's antics and a mother's irritation, with a final gentle reconciliation between the two. The rattling repetition of the title and its following line, 'And blithery blathery out of my mind', has made the title a pre-school household catchphrase. The illustrations, by Fiona Garrick, are not artistically outstanding, but her stylized line-drawings express the creative energy of the small child.

A somewhat similar tale of a tussle between mother and daughter is Kathy Stinson's *Red is Best* (1982). A little girl's love for the colour red and her defence of the colour against her mother's pragmatic suggestions for objects in other colours is told in the first person as a miniature, intimate character study. The repetitive text flows rhythmically, with unpretentious grace, and there are some memorable lines: the child says 'Red paint puts singing in my head.' The drawings by Robin Baird Lewis exploit red to its utmost, transmitting the child's emotional attachment to the colour. Stinson's *Big or Little?* (1983), also illustrated by Lewis, warm-heartedly portrays a pre-schooler's feelings about his size—sometimes he is little and vulnerable and at other times he is growing into strength and competence. The illustrations have the same warmth as those in *Red is Best* but lack their graphic unity with the text. Paulette Bourgeois's *Big Sarah's Little Boots* (1987) also treats the theme of childhood growth as Sarah laments the loss of her now too-small yellow boots. The simple representational art by Brenda Clark catches the emotional attachment of small children to their belongings.

Many of these books look at the pre-schooler's relationship to parents, as is quite natural. In Gail Chislett's *The Rude Visitors* (1984) Bram uses his vivid imagination to avoid confrontations with his mother. A host of rude animal visitors take the blame for Bram's general messy toddlerhood. The language is pared to simple nouns and verbs as befits a child who is still young enough to eat his meals in a high-chair. In its simple way it is as much a charming story of parenting as it is of young childhood. Mother calmly accepts Bram's explanations, such as an elephant sitting on his potty. 'Darn elephant,' she says. Barbara Di Lella makes Bram's imaginary animals both concrete and funny. The elephant—embarrassedly glancing over his shoulder while sitting on Bram's potty—is an unforgettable image. *Simon's Surprise* (1986) by Ted Staunton is about the idea of size and mastery. To Simon's request that he be allowed to wash the family car, his parents reply, 'When you're bigger.' Simon doesn't wait, but goes ahead with his plan while his parents are sleeping. The text is simple and descriptive, with one outstanding paragraph as Simon scrubs the tires:

> He used the pot scrubber, the vegetable scrubber, the back scrubber, a scrub brush, a shoe brush, a hair brush, and his tooth brush. 'Nothing to it,' he said.

Colourful representational art by Sylvie Daigneault vivaciously chronicles Simon's ingenious escapade. Priscilla Galloway's *When You Were Little and I Was Big* (1984), illustrated by Heather Collins, is about a mother-daughter role reversal. The daughter's thoughts are visualized in pictures that show the little girl playing the adult, with her mother as the dependent child.

The above writers see the comic side of the daily struggles and achievements of young children. Another group addresses more serious concerns in works often used as bibliotherapy and as tools in education and parenting. The focus ranges over a wide spectrum of problems—from parental separation and divorce, as in Kathy Stinson's *Mom and Dad Don't Live Together Any More* (1984), illustrated by Nancy Lou Reynolds, to the disabled child, as in Emily Hearn's *Good Morning Franny, Good Night Franny* (1984), illustrated by Mark Thurman, and child abuse, as in *Tom Doesn't Visit Us Any More* (1987) by Maryleah Otto and illustrated by Jude Waples. Most such books are published by small presses that are committed to child advocacy and social issues. It would appear that the quieter and subtler the treatment of a problem, the more effective the message. *Granny Is a Darling* (1988), written and illustrated by Kady MacDonald Denton, is about a small boy's relationship with his grandmother and his fear of the dark. Billy overcomes his fears by defending his grandmother against the night monsters—his weapon an imitation of Granny's long and mellifluous snores. The text is so simple that it almost defies any kind of comment, but it is animated by the illustrator. Denton's quiet watercolours mute the terror of the monsters, while the letters that make up the word 'snore' dance boldly across two double-page spreads.

A child's fear is also the theme of the picture-storybook *Teddy Rabbit* (1988) by Kathy Stinson, illustrated by Stéphane Poulin. Pre-schooler Toby is afraid that his stuffed toy Rabbit will not be accepted at a 'Teddy Bears' Picnic' to be held at Toronto's Centre Island. The tension is increased on the subway ride to the ferry when Teddy Rabbit falls on the tracks. Rabbit is rescued and happily welcomed on the Island at the multi-animal and multicultural picnic. Stinson's sympathy for the emotional life of young children is augmented by acerbic observations of adult behaviour:

> 'He looks a bit big to me to be worrying about a teddy,' said a sharp woman with long red fingernails. She turned her pinched face away . . .

Poulin's sombre-toned artwork strongly evokes Toronto's summer street life, outdoor markets, subway, and harbour. Small vignettes cunningly amplify details found in the full-page illustrations.

Urban life is also the background for *Have You Seen Josephine?* (1986), by Stéphane Poulin, and its sequels. Daniel tells the story of his Saturday detective adventure as he tracks his cat Josephine through the colourful streets and back alleys of east-end Montreal. The full-page illustrations alternate with black-and-white sketches and provide narrative flow and humour as the runaway Josephine has to be spotted on every page. Like Poulin's illustrations for *Teddy Rabbit*, those for his *Josephine* series incorporate images of Canada's urban ethnic mix. In his latest Josephine book, *Could You Stop Josephine?* (1988), the setting shifts to the countryside. The pictures here are as true to rural Quebec as the earlier books are to Montreal. A passing train bearing the CN logo demonstrates how faithfully Poulin incorporates details of Canadian life.

Ted Harrison is also a visual chronicler of a region—the Yukon. His *Children of the Yukon* (1977), as its title indicates, has a large geographical sweep. A spare text and panoramic paintings evoke the daily life of Arctic peoples—Inuit, Indian, and white. The human figures are small, dwarfed by the vastness and drama of the landscape, and their ethnic identity is secondary to their activities in this Northern world.

The small native presses also place Indian children and adults within their daily round, most often set against a domestic, rather than a spectacular, or particularly regional, background. These publishing houses, which have increased in number since the mid-1970s, have produced, along with folklore and novels, a substantial number of picturebooks of native pre-school life. Like the storybooks originating with small alternative presses, these works, by native and non-native authors and illustrators, have matured in quality and universality over the past decade.

Bernelda Wheeler uses rural, school, and home environments in *A Friend Called "Chum"* (1984, illustrated by Andy Stout), *Where Did You Get Your Moccasins?* (1986, illustrated by Herman Bekkering), and *I Can't Have Bannock, But the Beaver Has a Dam* (1984, also illustrated by Bekkering). In the latter, a playful dialogue between a native child and his mother, in a cumulative folk pattern, recounts the boy's desire for bannock bread. Similarly, the theme of a native child seen within a warm family context is treated by Peter Eyvindson in *Kyle's Bath* (1984). Eyvindson's *Old Enough* (1986) presents a common adult anomaly where a father who had been too busy to play with his son lavishes attention on his grandson. Both are illustrated in expressive black-and-white line drawings by Wendy Wolsak. Wolsak also illustrated Meguido Zola's *My Kind of Pup* (1985) and *Nobody* (1983), written by Zola and Angela Dereume. *Nobody* has an extra dimension in the children's invention of 'Nobody', an imaginative child-surrogate reminiscent of trickster figures from native folklore. The title character in Iris Loewen's *My Mom Is So Unusual* (1986), illustrated in line by Alan Pakarnyk, is an unconventional single mother in a native family who provides a glimpse of modern social realism in an urban setting, in contrast to the conventional family life pictured in Peter Eyvindson's *Chester Bear, Where Are You?* (1988), with its well-worn theme of a family's search for the child's missing teddy bear; the colour illustrations are by Wendy Wolsak-Frith.

Mainstream presses also have published picturebooks on native child life, written and illustrated by non-natives who have a sensitivity towards native culture and who see it within the universality of childhood. *A Salmon for Simon* (1978) by Betty

Waterton is about a West Coast native child's desire to catch a salmon. When he does so, he is impelled to release it, but in an ingenious manner. The story is quietly and rhythmically told and the text is complemented by Ann Blades' scenes of seashore and native village, and by her rendering of Simon's earnest face. Blades also illustrated Jean Speare's *A Candle for Christmas* (1986), set in a rural reservation. Cast in picture-storybook narrative style, it tells of Tomas, on Christmas Eve, as he waits for his parents' return from a crisis visit to his uncle's farm. The child's yearning for them is symbolized in his dream of the candle on the windowsill, lighting his parents' homeward path. After the journey home in a storm, his mother tells Tomas that the more she thought of him, 'the brighter and clearer the way became.' This touch of Christmas magic is set against the warm reality of community life and family feeling. Speare's text has a simple but evocative imagery:

> A snow road took them down a long hill between many small houses whose yellow windows were little more than dim smudges in the evening light and whose ribbons of smoke tapered straight up into the sky.

Blades' washes of the rural village, softened by snow and under changing skies, are a perfect accompaniment to the story.

An interesting addition to the picture-storybook field has been the appearance of two sophisticated works that tell the adventures of adolescent natives in long texts, while still using the technique of picturebook illustration. Donald Gale's *Sooshewan: Child of the Beothuk* (1988) and Ted Harrison's *The Blue Raven* (1989) go beyond the contemporary domestic drama to create coming-of-age survival sagas of native children. Gale does not attempt to provide an overview of the extinction of the Newfoundland Beothuk in the nineteenth century, but rather presents a dramatic story in the classic survival mode as Sooshewan seeks her father through a terrible winter, saves his life, and gains recognition as a young woman. The stylized artwork in flat blocks of colour by Shawn Steffler incorporates decorative and authentic elements of native art. The simplicity of Gale's text is in contrast to Ted Harrison's overly detailed account of a Yukon Athabaskan Indian youth's search for the Great Shaman. Nik's dangerous journey leads to gifts, and hunting knowledge, that he shares with his starving tribe. Harrison's luminous paintings give his quasi-legendary tale a contemporary-feeling.

Jan Andrews' *Very Last First Time* (1985), illustrated by Ian Wallace, is a much simpler Arctic survival tale. The plot is highly dramatic for a book for young children. Eva, a contemporary Inuit child, walks alone on the ocean floor under the ice, gathering mussels while the tide is out. The details of Eva's preparation for this regular occurrence in Inuit life, and the exact descriptions of the seabed, precede a suspenseful dénouement when the tide returns. The dreamlike underworld evoked by the illustrations is memorable.

With unusual versatility Ian Wallace has also created an unnamed urban Chinatown in his *Chin Chiang and the Dragon's Dance* (1984), and his illustrations here are as powerful as those that unfold an Arctic world, and just as convincing. The story tells of a young boy who is afraid of joining his grandfather in the Chinese New Year's dragon dance because he feels inadequate. In a flight through Chinatown he meets an elderly woman, Pu Yee, who teaches him the steps. Chin Chiang overcomes his fears, joins his grandfather, and in an exuberant moment also draws Pu Yee into the dance. The exploration of a child's emotional crisis and growth into maturity are seen more clearly in the pictures than in the words, as is the major theme of the story that life is motion and change. There are choreographic images of flying pigeons and sweeping dragon costumes and vistas of changing skies. Despite the recognizable buildings, street signs, and architectural details of Vancouver and Victoria, Wallace's Chinatown is meant to stand for every Chinatown in North America. There has been criticism from the Chinese community that Wallace's text is not authentic—women do not participate in the dragon dance, nor do they know the steps. Nevertheless this is acceptable poetic licence in a very effective book.

Chin Chiang is not concerned with ethnic tensions. But in Ian Wallace's *The Sandwich* (1975), written with Angela Wood, and in *Stone Soup* (1974), by Carol Pasternak and Allen Sutterfield, the message of tolerance is concretely expressed and symbolized by the communal sharing of ethnic food. Both are set in a multicultural urban classroom. The title of *Stone Soup* is taken from the French folktale in which three soldiers show the villagers that they do indeed have enough food for all by the ruse of using a stone as the basis of soup, tricking the villagers into adding their hidden stores.

Pasternak's version has the original's cumulative pattern, but certainly not its humour and vigour.

In Warabé Aska's *Who Goes To the Park* (1984) and *Who Hides in the Park/Les Mystères du Parc* (1986) multiculturalism is conveyed only through the illustrations. In essence both are paeans of praise for urban pastoral refuges: Toronto's High Park and Vancouver's Stanley Park respectively. *Who Goes to the Park* has a highly sentimental text, with some elements of free-verse describing the seasons from winter to winter. It is fortunately overwhelmed by the originality and colour of the artwork. Naïvely styled figures drawn from the cultural mosaic of Toronto fill the foreground in scenes of realistic play and festivities. These are juxtaposed with sky scenes of dream imagery. *Who Hides in the Park* continues the portrayal of a multi-ethnic society, with the illustrations including some of the magical figures of native West Coast mythology.

Ethnic identity and cultural heritage are also major themes in two of the picturebooks and picture-storybooks by Dayal Kaur Khalsa: *Tales of a Gambling Grandmother* (1986) and *How Pizza Came to Our Town* (1989). Together with Khalsa's *I Want a Dog* (1987) and *My Family Vacation* (1988), all four form an ongoing family saga set in the 1950s in New York and its environs, unobtrusively linked by the spirited child May. *Tales of a Gambling Grandmother* is a first-person narrative in which a child (presumably May) tells of her Russian, and presumably Jewish, grandmother's unusual and dramatic experiences and relates her grandmother's 'Laws of Life': 'Law Two: Just in case the Cossacks come to Queens, learn to say 'Da' and always keep plenty of borscht in the refrigerator.' Grandma takes May to interesting places (Coney Island, a Chinese restaurant, a vaudeville show), gives her advice, teaches her to play cards, nurses her when ill, and sometimes enjoys a peaceful afternoon. Eccentric and independent Grandma is a gambler, and on one California poker-playing expedition she wins a gold-and-diamond ring, which becomes the child's remembrance of her when she dies. The hilarious episodes in Grandma's life, combined with tender moments, and the poignant tone of the ending, make this a very special book. Khalsa's illustrations should be scanned very closely to uncover their minor delights. For example, Grandma has a cameo appearance in one picture in *How Pizza Came to Our Town*. In this book we are told that May's town was once far from being a child's paradise for, as the opening sentence states, 'Long ago, before there were pizza stands and pizzerias and frozen pizza and pizza mixes, there was hardly anything good to eat.' When Mrs Pelligrino arrives from Italy for a visit, she does not appear to enjoy herself. May and her friends attempt to cheer her up with special attention, and they finally discover that the key to her happiness is in the word 'pizza'. They visit the library, consult a cookbook, shop for ingredients, and Mrs Pelligrino makes the town's first pizza, with the aid of the rolling pin she has brought from Italy. The children are delighted:

> It smelled as good as toast and french fries and ketchup and grilled cheese sandwiches and spaghetti all rolled into one. They sniffed long and deep.

Amidst the fun and the humour there is, as in *Tales of a Gambling Grandmother*, a very clear sense of the emotional link that can develop between the young and the old.

May has two books to herself in *I Want a Dog* and *My Family Vacation*. 'May wanted a dog more than anything else in the world', and her efforts and ploys to convince her parents to give her one lead her to extremes of imagination, bordering on fantasy, as she adopts a rollerskate substitute for a dog. *My Family Vacation* takes May, her Mom, Dad, and big brother Richie, from the snows of New York State to sunny Florida. The cramped car journey, the motels and souvenir shops, and the exotic sights are seen through May's eyes. The pictures, rather than the text, make this book a gentle satire on tourism.

Khalsa's texts are plain, but her dialogue and descriptions have an ease and selectivity that are believable; May's behaviour and feelings are completely childlike. In *My Family Vacation*:

> When they got to the motel that night May was so excited she couldn't fall asleep. She had never slept away from home before. She loved everything about the place—from the big bouncy beds to the paper covers on the drinking glasses to the writing paper and envelopes in the night-table drawer. The miniature bars of soap, though, were her favourites. She took them all as souvenirs.

May is a three-dimensional character. In Khalsa's four books about May, she explores a child's inner life to a degree that is not always possible in one picturebook. The naïvely styled illustrations, like the texts, meld humour, tenderness, and concrete reality.

The books by Khalsa—who, sadly, died in 1989—were obviously based on her own childhood experiences. Other writers are more deliberately autobiographical, offering a set of nostalgic reminiscences of childhood at a definite time and place, as William Kurelek did in *A Prairie Boy's Winter*. Sing Lim's *West Coast Chinese Boy* (1979) stresses the conflict between Canadian culture and the ethnic culture of the parents, but the boy's anger at being forced to choose between them is tempered by the universality of art, for the child grows up to be an artist. Sing Lim comments:

> The struggle between being Chinese and being Canadian, between Chinese culture that was so important to my parents' generation and Canadian culture, I resolved in my own way. I found in art a more universal culture.

Lim's illustrations brim with frenzied activity. Sophisticated monotype glass paintings, numerous line-drawings, and dancing, childlike scrawls overflow the margins, giving life to a visit to a traditional Chinese herbalist, to an opera, and to a native bear-paw feast.

John Lim's memories of Singapore in the 1930s are put into picturebook format in *At Grandmother's House* (1977) and *Merchants of the Mysterious East* (1981). The texts are simple journeys through a tropical countryside and an alluring city, rich in astrologers, storytellers, and fortune-tellers. The folk-art serigraphs have a surreal quality: human figures are columnar, resembling glazed pottery dolls, their identical faces on oddly angled heads.

The title of Shizuye Takashima's memoir, *A Child in Prison Camp* (1971), refers to the internment camp for Japanese-Canadians during the Second World War in the mountainous Kootenay region of British Columbia. Despite the injustice of the experience, Takashma—like Joy Kogawa in *Naomi's Road* (1986)—tells her story from a child's viewpoint, without resentment or rancour, in a series of fragmentary vignettes. The muted, impressionistic watercolour paintings—haunting landscapes and blurred figures—are washed in a haze of emotion and memory.

As well as this group of childhood memoirs, there are a number of more traditional child-life stories set in the past that offer fictional vignettes of social history, as do the picturebooks of Fiona French in Britain. Adele Wiseman's *Kenji and the Cricket* (1988) gives a glimpse of the homeless children of Japan after the Second World War. But there is a happy ending as Kenji's love for a cricket brings him a home. Crickets and their bringing of good luck are a strong part of Japanese folklore. The legend-like quality of the story is enhanced by Shizuye Takashima's soft, semi-abstract watercolours.

Shelley Tanaka's *Michi's New Year* (1980), illustrated by Ron Berg, describes a young Japanese child's perceptions of Canadian life in the Vancouver of 1912. Michi longs for the traditional Japanese New Year celebrations, but her spirit is lifted when a Canadian boy wishes her 'Happy New Year'. Then family friends arrive to join in the customary homeland festivities. Berg's meticulous illustrations contrast the active social life of Japan with the emptiness of the wintry-brown Vancouver street bleached of colour and emotion. The last scene, where friends and family gather, brings vivacity and colour into the book as well as into Michi's new life in Canada.

A different kind of immigration experience is presented in Betty Waterton's *Pettranella* (1980), illustrated by Ann Blades. A family arrives from an unspecified country in nineteenth-century Europe to homestead in Manitoba. Pettranella's grandmother has given her flower seeds to plant in the new world, but Pettranella loses them as the family nears the end of their journey. Then they are discovered in the spring, flourishing beside the rough road where they had been lost, a glowing symbol of new life. Blades' paintings move from dark, cramped images of European city streets and immigration depots to those of open spaces under fresh skies.

These stories of discovering a sense of belonging in a new country are also about children's emotional growth. Responsibility is the theme of Sue Ann Alderson's *Ida and the Wool Smugglers* (1987), illustrated by Ann Blades. Ida, a child of turn-of-the-century settlers on an unnamed Gulf Island of British Columbia, wants to be useful to her family. When smugglers come to steal the family's sheep for their wool, Ida senses their presence and rescues her sheep. Blades' old-fashioned adult and child figures, and her use of traditional fabric patterns and artifacts, provide a warmly nostalgic sense of the past, while her green landscapes are true to a lush island setting.

The early twentieth century is also the period of *The Sparrow's Song* (1986), written and illustrated by Ian Wallace. Set in the Niagara peninsula, this picture-storybook is given a specific landscape by beautiful, detailed watercolours that are as evocative of a place as Blades' washes of a Gulf Island. The simple story-line—the rescue of a sparrow by the child, Katie—is overwhelmed by illustrations that are rich with images of nature lore and children at wild play, imaginatively transformed through costumes and face paint.

May's dog, Kenji's cricket, Ida's sheep, and Katie's sparrow are children's pets and these stories show the children's emotional attachment to them. The domestic farm animals of Lindee Climo's *Chester's Barn* (1982) belong to a faceless, anonymous Prince Edward Island farmer of the more recent past, though the farm is decidedly old-fashioned in operation and atmosphere. The barn and their occupants take on a life of their own in the daily round. The narrative is completely descriptive; the energy of this picture-storybook comes from the animal portraits.

The new breadth and sophistication of Canadian publishing for children are well exemplified by the appearance of fictionalized picturebook biographies of three famous artists—two painters and a great classical composer: Emily Carr, Edgar Degas, and Joseph Haydn. Susan Gaitskell in *Emily* (1986), about Carr's childhood, correctly (according to adult biographies) portrays the British Columbian artist as an outsider and the black sheep of her family. Emily is misunderstood and unappreciated by her older sister and her art teacher, who advised her to pray and to paint still-lifes. Her individualistic creative spirit impels her to paint the wild hills and dark forests (which she at first fears) in the company of her tame crow. Kellie Jobson's sombre, dark sketches are meant to portray the life of an unhappy child, not her adult success as an artist. Despite a certain clumsiness, they are more appropriate to this slight biography than to Carr's artistic sensibility.

The emotional atmosphere of the artist at work is more successfully portrayed in *Meet Edgar Degas* (1988) by Anne Newlands. Written to accompany a retrospective exhibit of the nineteenth-century impressionist by a curator of the National Gallery of Canada, it has an imaginative, ingenious text that is accompanied by reproductions of Degas's paintings, or details of them. The voice of the artist is heard in a warm first-person narrative that illuminates his art. Joseph Haydn is a background figure in David Lasker's *The Boy Who Loved Music* (1979), with artwork by the American Joe Lasker.

Karl, a young horn-player in Haydn's chamber orchestra at the court of Prince Nicolaus Esterhazy, provides insight into the life of an eighteenth-century court musician. The translucent watercolour paintings have a gentle period character.

FANTASY

Most of the early picturebooks from both the United States and Britain were lightly touched with a tall-tale fantasy element, whether the protagonists were animated machines (Virginia Lee Burton's *Mike Mulligan and His Steam Shovel*, 1939), anthropomorphized animals (H.A. Rey's *Curious George*, 1941), or children engaged in activities slightly larger than life (Edward Ardizzone's *Little Tim and the Brave Sea Captain*, 1936). Many recent Canadian picturebook creators follow this tradition.

The most prolific exponent of the tall tale is Robert Munsch. His tongue-in-cheek child-satires show brave and plucky kids surviving absurd adventures, ingeniously extending the limits of their freedom while thwarting authority figures such as arrogant dragons, pompous mayors, curmudgeonly teachers and principals, and cold technology. Munsch's style is comfortably colloquial, fast-paced, and rich in sound patterns—rhythm, onomatopoeia, refrains, and nonsense sounds that invite the child to participate in the telling. His cumulative or shaggy-dog stories were developed, like folktales, orally as he told them to groups of pre-schoolers. Consequently they have a theatrical style that is intensified when they are told or read aloud. This oral genesis pares away any non-essentials of plot or background and makes them internationally enjoyable.

Munsch's first book, and probably his most memorable, is *The Paper Bag Princess* (1980), a feminist parody and reversal of the standard fairy tale of the prince who rescues the princess. The princess's denunciation of the prince, 'Ronald . . . you are a bum', sets the tone for the rude vigour and iconoclasm of much of Munsch's later works. In *Jonathan Cleaned Up—Then He Heard a Sound, Or Blackberry Subway Jam* (1981), *Mortimer* (1983), and *Thomas' Snowsuit* (1985), the young children exuberantly test authority. Munsch's use of cumulative repetition and catchy refrains is seen at its best in

Mortimer, about a conflict between a pre-schooler and his family, rooted in domestic realism, but exaggerated into farce as Mortimer-refuses to fall asleep and chants loudly,

> Clang, clang, rattle bing-bang.
> Gonna make my noise all day.

And he does, into the night! *I Have to Go!* (1987) is a similar story of conflict as, naturally enough, the child has 'to go' as soon as he is in his snowsuit or in bed. The simple repetition of 'I have to go' is not Munsch at his best. The liveliest Munsch farce is *Pigs* (1989) as pigs stampede into the schoolhouse and the school bus. All these books are illustrated by Michael Martchenko in playful, spirited cartoons that accentuate the stories' engaging silliness and light satire. Martchenko's illustrations in *Pigs*—of rebel anthropomorphized pigs—are among his most outrageously funny drawings, and make the story completely fantastical.

Munsch's theatricality is toned down in *Love You Forever* (1986), illustrated by Sheila McGraw. Its sentimentality is somewhat of a surprise after Munsch's pre-school dramas, until one remembers that he has the ability to draw the utmost from emotions that most families take for granted—here a mother's love for her son is shown at all stages of his life, even into manhood, as she cradles him in her arms and croons:

> I'll love you forever,
> I'll like you for always,
> As long as I'm living
> My baby you'll be.

The positions are reversed when the elderly mother is ill and the son cradles *her* in *his* arms, singing the same awkward, cloying song, but substituting 'Mommy' for 'baby'. A very natural family bond here is reduced to almost neurotic emotionalism, and the technique of repetition that works so well in humour is here drowned in bathos. The insignificant illustrations are as banal as the text.

Allen Morgan's *Matthew* series—*Matthew and the Midnight Tow Truck* (1984), *Matthew and the Midnight Turkeys* (1985), and *Matthew and the Midnight Money Van* (1987)—are humorous and highly successful dream fantasies, also lightly touched by the tall-tale factor. In *Matthew and the Midnight Tow Truck* the pre-schooler's interest in toy trucks and love of red licorice become the matter of his dream. The rough but child-like midnight truck-driver who commandeers Matthew in his night-time escapade appropriately has a lunch-box full of red licorice. He offers Matthew a child's delight:

'Take some,' said the midnight tow-truck driver. 'Take as much as you need. You can never get enough red licorice you know. It's good for you and it gives you big muscles.'

Most of the perfection of Morgan's stories comes from his unobtrusive linking of Matthew's dreams with his ordinary life. Also, the texts give the illustrator, Michael Martchenko, ample opportunity to exploit his sly humour.

Marie-Louise Gay, in *Angel and the Polar Bear* (1988), also created a tall-tale dream fantasy, more bizarre than the *Matthew* series. The decidedly unangelic Angel combats nightmare figures as her parents sleep on. Threatened in the apartment by a flood, a polar freeze, and a polar bear, she conquers all and protects her sleeping parents. The surrealism is balanced by touches of real family life:

Angel is almost six years old.
She has a very loud voice.
And every single morning Angel's mother says,
'It's too early. Go back to sleep.'
Angel's mother has a very tired voice.
Angel's father sleeps like a log.

Angel's insouciant 'Pippi Longstocking' character is conveyed in Gay's dynamic, sophisticated cartoons.

Like Angel, Leanna in *Leanna Builds a Genie Trap* (1986), by Hazel J. Hutchins, takes on the role of family saviour, trying to create traps for the genie she believes is stealing small household items. The combination of child inventiveness and adult reaction rings true:

'Please may I saw a hole in the floor to make a trap door to catch the genie?' asked Leanna.

Leanna's mother was kind, intelligent, and multi-talented but she was sometimes not as imaginative as Leanna would have liked her to be.

'No,' said Leanna's Mother.

Catharine O'Neill's whimsical cartoons, with oddly tilting dream-like perspectives, provide an atmosphere both cosy and fantastic as Leanna finds out that the genie is the sofa and learns to trade with it.

Like Angel and Leanna, David Finebloom of Tim Wynne-Jones's *Architect of the Moon* (1988) is also a 'fixer', a surrogate adult, but on a cosmic rather than a domestic scale. Responding to a message from outer space, 'Help! I'm falling apart! Yours, the Moon', David gathers his blocks, and 'Whoosh' he is off to the moon. His blocks rebuild the planet in a charming allegory of lunar cycles. The comforting ending (David returns home in time for breakfast) is akin to that of Maurice Sendak's *Where the Wild Things Are*. The minimal text has a modern and jaunty ring, and the illustrations by Ian Wallace successfully capture the spirit of a child's imaginative play.

A stronger patina of realism marks *Morgan the Magnificent* (1987) by Ian Wallace. Morgan fantasizes being a high-wire circus artist and practises her balancing skills on the barn roof, until her father says: 'We'll have no more of that stunt.' The narrative slides into fantasy when the circus comes to town (or does Morgan imagine the circus visit?) and Morgan dazzles all with her trapeze artistry, but only with the help of a star trapezist. The romantic, yet concrete, pictures of the barnyard animals and an old-fashioned early-twentieth-century circus combine to make Morgan's fantasy very real indeed.

Maryann Kovalski's *The Wheels on the Bus* (1987) and *Jingle Bells* (1988), although based on traditional songs, take a leap into exaggeration through the imaginary feats of the characters as they project themselves into details of the songs. Grandma, out with her two granddaughters in *The Wheels on the Bus*, introduces them to songs when they miss the bus and, with a slight shift into fantasy, find themselves on a London doubledecker. In *Jingle Bells* they adventurously take a sleigh-ride in wintry Central Park in New York. The boisterous humour of the songs is extended by the lively, even

By ANN BLADES for *Ida and the Wool Smugglers* by Sue Ann Alderson

By LASZLO GAL for *A Flask of Sea Water* by P.K. Page
Illustrations © Laszlo Gal 1989.
Oxford University Press Canada.

 s she sat in school daydreaming about dogs, May had a great idea. If she could show her parents how much dogs were attracted to *her,* maybe they would get her one.

When she got home that afternoon she ran right to the refrigerator and grabbed a thick slice of salami. She went outside and began strolling slowly down the street. Every dog on the block jumped up as May walked by.

By DAYAL KAUR KHALAS for *I Want a Dog*
Crown Publishers.

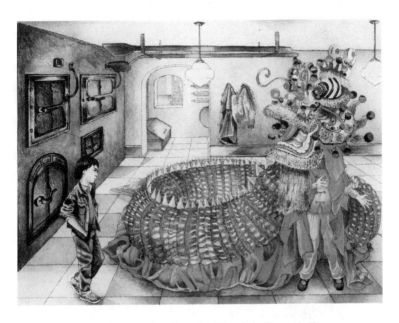

By IAN WALLACE for *Chin Chiang and the Dragon's Dance*

Text and illustrations © copyright 1984 by Ian Wallace.
A Groundwood Book/Douglas & McIntyre.

By KEN NUTT for *Zoom Away* by Tim Wynne-Jones
Illustration © copyright by Ken Nutt.
A Groundwood Book/Douglas & McIntyre.

By BARBARA REID for *Have You Seen Birds?* by Joanne Oppenheim
© 1986 by Barbara Reid.
Reprinted by permission of Scholastic-TAB Publications Ltd.,
123 Newkirk Road, Richmond Hill, Ontario.

By STÉPHANE POULIN for *Have You Seen Josephine?*
© 1986 Stéphane Poulin.
Published by Tundra Books.

frenzied, drawings of the grandmother with her two endearing charges.

An international trend in the picturebook world since the 1960s can be seen in many works that have more adult themes, symbolic allusions, and social and political commentary. These more sophisticated picturebooks call for an audience of older children, teenagers, and even adults. Among them are Maurice Sendak's combination of traditional folklore and psychological problems in *Outside Over There* (1981), and *When the Wind Blows* (1982), by the English picturebook writer and illustrator Raymond Briggs, which relates, in comic-book format, the last days of an elderly couple dying of atomic fall-out. Such sophisticated texts or stern warnings are not yet a feature of the Canadian picturebook scene, but there are two Canadian books that both break the sunny tradition of childhood usually revealed in picturebooks and venture into surrealism: Tim Wynne-Jones's *I'll Make You Small* (1986), illustrated by Maryann Kovalski, and Joan Clark's *The Leopard and the Lily* (1984), illustrated by Velma Foster.

Roland, of *I'll Make You Small*, lives next door to an eccentric recluse, Mr Swanskin, who threatens children by saying, 'You get away from here . . . or I'll make you small!' When Mr Swanskin has not been seen for a few days and Roland's mother is worried, Roland offers to take him a pie. In the crumbling mansion filled with garbage and broken toys, he is then made small. He is about to be dropped into the garbage when Mr Swanskin smells the pie. The combination of threatening magic (reminiscent of E.T.A. Hoffman's *The Nutcracker*), along with the portrayal of a disturbed adult with a child-like mind who feels compelled to fix his childhood toys, is an uneasy one, despite the reassuring ending. Maryann Kovalski's cartoon-like artwork in colour interprets both the normal and abnormal aspects of the story. Joan Clark's *The Leopard and the Lily* is a complex allegory of death in which a dying child and an old leopard, caged in a zoo, are united by a dream-image of a white lily. The surrealistic text explores the inner musings and fantasies of both the child and the leopard. The attempts at symbolism, however, are ultimately pretentious, and Velma Foster's drawings in colour and black-and-white are as confusing as the text. Although *I'll Make You Small* has more coherence in its threatening atmosphere than *The*

Leopard and the Lily, both have themes that are too overwhelming for the picturebook format.

Anthropomorphized animals have dominated picturebooks from the now-classic works of Beatrix Potter to Arnold Lobel's recent *Frog and Toad* series. Children's natural affection for animals, and their sympathetic identification with them, make animal fantasy a rich terrain for story and illustration. In the modern child-oriented picturebook world, however, there are fewer animal fantasies than in the past, when the animals were made to act as child surrogates, as in H.A. Rey's *Curious George* (1941) and Roger Duvoisin's *Petunia* (1950). The device of animals taking on human roles still attracts Canadian storytellers, but the newer tales are far more sophisticated than those of the past, and the animals are frequently given adult characteristics, leading to satire, even caricature.

Two earlier simple animal fantasies with considerable charm are Jack Richards' *Johann's Gift to Christmas* (1972) and Dorothy Joan Harris's *The House Mouse* (1973). Johann is a Swiss mouse who lives in a church because he loves to hear beautiful music. In a time of hunger he nibbles away the bellows on the church organ and it cannot be played on Christmas Eve. In the face of this disaster the organist is inspired to compose a new hymn and have it played on a guitar. Thus came 'Silent Night', first sung in the Tyrol over 150 years ago—Johann's 'gift to Christmas'. The pictures are by the well-known cartoonist Len Norris, who keeps a slight touch of caricature in his mice and human figures. The story is a successful combination of humour and sentiment and deserves a place, if a modest one, beside such lasting Christmas picturebooks as Ezra Jack Keats's *The Little Drummer Boy* (1968) and Ruth Robbins' *Baboushka and the Three Kings* (1960).

Dorothy Joan Harris's *The House Mouse* is best described as a long picture-storybook. Four-year-old Jonathan befriends a mouse who lives in his sister's doll's house. One season later Jonathan's new interest in the world beyond his window leads him to neglect the mouse and lose his understanding of the mouse's speech. In this simple, well-told tale there is a subtle suggestion that the mouse has been a fantasy friend. The charm of the miniature, found in Beatrix Potter's *The Tale of Two Bad Mice* (1904), is here blended with humour by the American illustrator Barbara Cooney, and ultimately with pathos.

Patti Stren's *Hug Me* (1977) and *Sloan and Philamina; or, How to Make Friends with Your Lunch* (1979), and Maryann Kovalski's *Brenda and Edward* (1984), emphasize a search for friendship and love in a light, humorous style, with the animals standing as surrogate adults. After an absurd quest, Stren's porcupine in *Hug Me* slowly, gently, and carefully hugs his new-found mate who is just like himself—but a female. Entirely different are the unlikely couple of the anteater and the ant, in *Sloan and Philamina*, who fight familial disapproval and find companionship together. Stren's texts have elements of comedy routines, jokes, and adult throwaway lines, some of which have no meaning for children, though they might be amusing to adults, such as the reference to the ant's famous Uncle Lou: 'He's spent the last seventeen years as a stand-up comic on the Borscht Belt.' Both books are integrated with comic-strip dialogue balloons and minimal, witty line-drawings.

Maryann Kovalski's *Brenda and Edward*, also a fable of animal friendship, has a gentler humour and a more delicate sensibility than Stren's works. In a quiet parody of adult romance, Brenda and Edward are dogs who love and lose each other, but who are reunited in old age. Kovalski's pastel tones add to the sentiment (never sentimentality) of the tale, and to its understated poignancy. Shifts from larger perspectives to a dog's-eye view perhaps signify the helplessness of an animal in a human world. The last scene is completely human as Brenda and Edward, embracing, view the outside world from the window.

In Catharine O'Neill's *Mrs Dunphy's Dog* (1987), adults become the target of picturebook humour. Mrs Dunphy's 'James' lives a cosy life with his mistress, who is an avid newspaper reader. His life is changed forever when he learns to read sensational headlines:

James studied Mrs Dunphy. She must be awfully intelligent. After all, she'd been reading papers for as many years as he's been tearing them up. Soon James was intelligent, too. He took easily to reading and learned many fine things:

WOMAN BECOMES HUMAN MOUSE TRAP
BOY TRADES SISTER FOR BIKE
DOOMED MAN TAKES MAIL TO WORLD BEYOND

Beginning to doubt the authenticity of such stories, James finds greater satisfaction by sinking his teeth into books that have dog characters: *Peter Pan*, *The Wizard of Oz*, and *Lassie Come-Home*. The humour works perfectly on two levels, child and adult, as it has done in the past only rarely. The sly wit and endearing portrayal of the affectionate dog and his mistress are also present in the illustrations of rounded figures and comic caricatures.

Some writers use animals more allegorically, sending them on quests—for adventure, for self-discovery, or for a resolution of problems and mysteries. Tim Wynne-Jones's cat Zoom, in *Zoom at Sea* (1983) and *Zoom Away* (1985), is on a quest for adventure. Zoom is an unusual cat who likes to play in water. His explorer uncle's diary, with instructions on how to reach the sea, leads him to the gypsy-like woman Maria who, through her magical Victorian house, grants his desire. She releases from within a single room an endless expanse of sea for Zoom to explore:

> He danced around on his driftwood deck and occasionally cupped his paws and shouted very loudly back to shore. 'More waves,' or 'More sun,' or 'More fish.'

In *Zoom Away* the questing cat goes with the enigmatic Maria to the North Pole in search of Uncle Roy. Here the house of infinite size appears to stand for limitless imagination as Maria and Zoom climb the winding frozen staircase and wander along snow-driven corridors into rooms that open onto the endless space of the North. The existence of the Arctic, always at the back of the Canadian imagination, is here made both threatening and liberating. Zoom's dance at the North Pole (like his dance at sea) is a celebration of inner freedom as well as of the completed quest. Both texts are rich with imagery and the concrete detail that befits an allegory and they are superbly complemented by Ken Nutt's pencil drawings. His characters are unforgettable: Maria is subtly goddess-like and Zoom is entirely endearing, changing from a home-loving bourgeois gentleman to a courageous adventurer—much like Tolkien's Bilbo Baggins in *The Hobbit* (1937).

Goldie and the Sea (1987) by Judith Saltman is also a fable-like quest for the sea, mixing animal and human characters. Goldie lives alone (somewhat like Astrid Lindgren's Pippi Longstocking) with her cat

Foss and parrot Jake. As an artist she yearns to paint the sea and sets off with her two companions to find it. A folk-like convention is present in the structure of three friends, three days, and meetings with three strangers who both challenge and aid her. A parable of an artist's growth, the story ends with Goldie beginning to paint the sea:

> Jake flew down to her shoulder and Foss curled up in her lap. Together they watched as a magical picture flowed from Goldie's hands.
> Deep within his throat, Foss began to purr.

Kim LaFave's illustrations enliven the story with humorous touches—Goldie is a Charlie Chaplinesque figure.

The workhorse Clyde in Lindee Climo's *Clyde* (1986) changes his self-image in his imagination like Wynne-Jones's Zoom. When he is replaced by a tractor, his fantasies move him through a kaleidoscope of transformations, from a tractor horse to an amalgam of horse, fish, and duck. Climo's vibrant, painterly pictures of the multi-Clydes bring an absurdist humour to the conceit.

While Clyde is on an internal quest for a new identity, the young turtle in Dorothy Joan Harris's *Four Seasons for Toby* (1987) wants to find the seasons that have been so marvellously described by his grandmother. Impatient and curious, Toby leaves his rock in the pond and sets off to find spring. Following the farmyard fence, he travels slowly, in true turtle fashion, through the four seasons, discovering the magic of change until the fence leads him back to his own pond. The message that seasonal change also comes to those who stay quietly at home is very clear. The warmth of Harris's feeling for nature is well expressed in Vlasta van Kampen's representational art—though her detailed nature studies are marred by her jarring cartoon portrayals of Toby, who in the text remains true to his turtle nature.

Paulette Bourgeois's anthropomorphized turtle Franklin, in *Franklin in the Dark* (1986), behaves like a pre-schooler who is afraid of the dark; he will not go into his shell. When he discovers that all animals have a special fear, he bravely enters his shell—and turns on his night-light! Brenda Clark's primary-coloured cartoon art is as cosily reassuring as the text.

Franklin overcomes his problem with courage and ingenuity, and so does Rusty of Tom Harpur's *The Mouse That Couldn't Squeak* (1988). As the title suggests, Rusty is a mute; his handicap makes him an outsider in the mousery. (This picture-storybook is highly eclectic, with echoes of E.B. White's mute swan in *The Trumpet of the Swan*, 1970, and the 'wild woods' of Kenneth Grahame's *The Wind in the Willows*, 1908.) Rusty's handicap becomes a virtue when, at Christmastime, he is the only mouse who can bring stores for the Christmas feast, tricking the owls who overlook him because of his silence. This parable of an unlikely saviour is rather fulsomely written, but the drama of the tale is paralleled in Dawn Lee's paintings, which are redolent with atmosphere and suspense.

A few books move easily between a realistic animal picturebook and one of fantasy. *Jill and the Big Cat* (1984) by Etho Rothstein and *Amos's Sweater* (1988) by Janet Lunn are slightly exaggerated tales, but the animals are not anthropomorphized. Jill lives a very comfortable dog's life in North Vancouver, but her innate resourcefulness is challenged by a direct confrontation with a cat that arches its back, raises its tail, and spits. Jill uses the same trick on the biggest cat she has ever seen and so, unknowingly, trees a cougar. Maureen Paxton's line drawings in colour and black-and-white give added humour to the tale. The ram Amos in *Amos's Sweater* is rather crotchety: 'Amos was old and Amos was cold and Amos was tired of giving away all his wool.' Amos rebels against shearing and stubbornly attempts to recover his wool. He is placated only when Aunt Hattie returns it in the form of a sweater. This quietly witty tale has the quality of an animal fable that is successfully given a slapstick flavour by Kim LaFave's blithely playful line- and wash-drawings.

LITERARY FAIRY TALES

Folk motifs and patterns have been cleverly used in many picture-storybooks, in the past as well as the present. Such works are by no means versions of tales from the oral tradition but are rather transmutations of them that form a new and imaginative entity. In thus straddling the line between folklore and fantasy, they are referred to as literary fairy tales. Hans Christian Andersen was the true originator of the genre and Oscar Wilde contributed to it with

'The Happy Prince' and 'The Selfish Giant'. More recently we have Maurice Sendak's *Outside Over There*, which uses images from folklore and mythology to create a psychological drama.

As a kind of hybrid, the literary fairy tale calls for very special skills, and there are not many examples that are completely successful. The few Canadian writers who have invented plots in a fairy-tale or literary convention have produced books that are interesting only because the genre was attempted at all—or because of their illustrations. These include Jennifer Garrett's *The Queen Who Stole the Sky* (1986), David Birch's *The King's Chessboard* (1988), Meguido Zola's *Only the Best* (1981), and *A Promise Is a Promise* (1988), co-authored by Robert Munsch and Michael Kusugak, an Inuit. *The Queen Who Stole the Sky* is a moral tale about a selfish, vain queen who asks her tailor to make a dress from the sky, which she has stolen. The lack of a sky causes a drought and the queen's people are starving. Their saviour is an ingenious little girl who outwits the queen and restores the sky. Linda Hendry's quaint cartoons imbue the tale with an eighteenth-century court atmosphere. *The King's Chessboard* is an interpretation of the classic folktale confrontation between a foolish king and a wise man, here set in India. The means by which the sage cleverly outwits the king is amusing, but not surprising to one who understands the convention of the folktale, in which the wise man always wins. The illustrations—by a non-Canadian, Devis Grebu—provide a flavour of ancient Indian culture.

Details of Jewish festivals and traditional Jewish life are linked to a folktale-style narrative in Meguido Zola's *Only the Best*, illustrated by a British artist, Valerie Littlewood. The folktale quality is evident in the cumulative structure and in the father's repetitive phrase as he seeks a gift for his first-born child: 'Yes, yes, but is it the *best*? I want *only* the best. *Nothing* but the best.' The richly detailed illustrations mix contemporary and historical clothing and artifacts to give this picture-storybook a timeless quality.

Contemporary Inuit culture lends substance to *A Promise Is a Promise*, in which the universal folk-structure of parents outwitting a mythological creature's claim on their beloved children provides the plot. Allashua, a modern Inuit child, fishes in the ocean despite her parents' warnings about the Qallupilluit, mythical troll-like beings who live under the ice and prey on children, much like the West

Coast native cannibal Tsononqua. Before she meets the Qallupilluit, Allashua muses:

> On TV I have seen Santa Claus, Fairy Godmothers and the Tooth Fairy, but never any Qallupilluit. I think my mother is wrong.

The illustrations by Vladyana Krykorka, although true to Inuit features and dress, have an anomalous European quality.

Two lighter works that also juxtapose the contemporary and folklore worlds in both art and text are Phoebe Gilman's *The Balloon Tree* (1984) and Richard Thompson's *Jenny's Neighbours* (1987). In *The Balloon Tree*, the tongue-in-cheek story of a princess who foils her wicked uncle is enlivened by deliberate anachronisms. The parody of a medieval atmosphere is reinforced by the illustrations, which meld illuminated manuscript conventions, allusions to Flemish Renaissance painting, and contemporary details such as balloons. *Jenny's Neighbours* is a fairy-tale romp. Jenny and her friend are invaded in their play by characters from fairy tales and nursery rhymes, including the Big Bad Wolf and Little Bo-Peep. The cumulative arrivals crowd the room until the father ends their play. Kathryn E. Shoemaker's representational drawings avoid the pitfall of cuteness inherent in such a parade and bring liveliness and humour to the situation.

A Flask of Sea Water (1989), by the renowned Canadian poet P.K. Page, is an over-long and complicated tale about a young peasant who succeeds in winning the King's daughter against all odds. It is disappointing to find that Page draws heavily on the conventions of the folk-tale, *The Arabian Nights*, medieval romance, and Ruskin's *King of the Golden River*, among other sources, without employing any fresh creativity or originality. Laszlo Gal's illustrations, which interpret the narrative as an *Arabian Nights* tale, are beautiful in themselves but merely decorate the narrative.

Margaret Crawford Maloney has retold Hans Christian Andersen's famous literary fairy tale in *The Little Mermaid* (1983). Andersen individualized what had originally been an anonymous collective voice. In her version Maloney has not deviated significantly from the definitive translation by Erik Christian Haugaard (a Dane, like Andersen), except for the ending, where she has excised Andersen's

Christian mysticism and substituted one that is secular. Laszlo Gal's romantic gouache and watercolour paintings are theatrically framed in turn-of-the-century style, giving the story the poignant dignity it demands.

CONCEPT PICTUREBOOKS

Concept picturebooks are designed for the very young as first learning experiences, and are developments from the earliest of educational tools such as horn books, battledores, and primers. ABC books and counting books, which are most numerous, and books introducing such concepts as shapes and noise, most of them splendidly illustrated, have appeared chiefly in the 1980s.

Almost all our ABC books, beginning with *A Canadian Child's ABC* (1931), are strongly Canadian in content, often celebrating a specific region, city, or culture. In the regional context there are Ted Harrison's *A Northern Alphabet* (1982), Ann Blades' West Coast-oriented *By the Sea: An Alphabet Book* (1985), and Nicola Morgan's *The Great B.C. Alphabet Book* (1985). Combining regionalism and the environment of native children are *Alphabet Book* (1968), in which 'Y' is for 'Lesser Yellow Bird', and *James Bay Cree ABC in Song and Picture* (1983) by Jane Pachano and J. Rabbitt Ozores. The earlier book is illustrated with considerable verve by native children in black-and-white line drawings that in their simplicity are more appealing than much of the artwork in the newer, lavishly illustrated ABC books. The text of the latter is based on letters of the alphabet, but is extended into verse that reflects the environment: 'trappers/ trek/ through/ swamp/ and/ snow,/ Setting/ snares/ where/ rabbits/ go.' Coloured photographs of the landscape and native children are juxtaposed with line-drawings and paintings by three artists.

Young children have been offered views of three cities as they learn or practise the alphabet: Allan Moak reduces Toronto to child-size in *A Big City ABC* (1984); Stéphane Poulin is highly lyrical about Montreal in *Ah! Belle Cité!/A Beautiful City ABC* (1985); and Gordon Roache, in *A Halifax ABC* (1987), illustrates the influence of the sea on the city and features activities common to childhood. All three illustrators include the ethnic mix of their cities, interpreted in a naïve style.

Jan Thornhill's large-format, beautifully illustrated *The Wildlife ABC: A Nature Alphabet* (1988) focuses on the fauna of North America. The somewhat stylized framed pictures use shifting perspectives, moving from long-shots of cavorting whales to microscopic closeups, such as that of a 'Queen Bee' (for Q), with decorative borders showing the development of an embryo. (The text, however, is marred by clumsy rhymes.) Elizabeth Cleaver's *ABC* (1984) is also an alphabetical nature book—a treasure-box of numerous images for each letter that discloses the first mysteries of a young child's world. Its small square shape fits comfortably into a child's hand.

In the first Canadian counting book, *The One to Fifty Book* (1973), native children in southwestern Ontario chose objects in their environment to count and illustrated it with the same childlike drawings as were made in black-and-white for the *Alphabet Book*, but this time with a few in colour. It is a most satisfactory childlike introduction to numbers. Most of the newer books strain for originality and depend heavily on illustrations for their appeal. *One Watermelon Seed* (1986) by Celia Barker Lottridge chronicles the growth of a garden, its planting and harvesting, with tactile collages of fruits and vegetables by Karen Patkau. Franklin Hammond's *Ten Little Ducks* (1987) features the activities of an ever-increasing number of playful ducks. The fuzzy pastel illustrations have a nursey-art quality. Sophisticated cats grace the rhyming text of Ebbitt Cutler's *If I Were a Cat I Would Sit in a Tree* (1985), illustrated by Rist Arnold with framed and stylized comic tableaux. The most original counting book is one that eschews factual numbers. Simon of *Simon and the Snowflakes* (1988), by Gilles Tibo, admits on the first page that he loves to count. But then he realizes:

> I cannot count the lights in a city,
> the stars in the sky,
> the flakes in a snowfall.

This concept of the immeasurable is also transmitted through the stylized line and wash illustrations in hazy, muted tones, with toy-like figures set against a background of winter.

Alphabet and counting books in English and French reflect

Canada's cultural identity and will probably increase in number. Both Barbara Wilson's *ABC et/and 123* (1980), illustrated by Gisèle Daigle, and Stéphane Poulin's *Ah! Belle Cité!/A Beautiful City ABC*, humorously illustrated, contain words chosen for oral and visual similarities between the two languages, as does Sheldon Oberman's *The Lion in the Lake/Le Lion dans le Lac* (1988), handsomely illustrated by Scott Barham. David May's text for *Byron and His Balloon: An English-Chipewyan Counting Book* (1984) was created to provide a context for the ingenuous watercolours, by native children, of life in the Saskatchewan community of LaLoche. Angela Wood's *Kids Can Count* (1976) combines black-and-white photographs in the urban style of the American Tana Hoban with words in English, French, Chinese, Italian, and Greek.

A few books with simple text in English and French go beyond the basic bilingual concept book. Among the earliest were Jacques de Roussan's clever, minimal science-fiction picturebooks, *Beyond the Sun/Au-delà du Soleil* (1972) and *If I Came from Mars/Si j'étais Martien* (1977). Warabé Aska employed his magic-realist style in illustrating *Who Hides in the Park* (1986), a trilingual exploration of Vancouver's Stanley Park, with text in English, French, and Japanese. The pedagogical value of these bilingual or multilingual books is debatable. It would appear to lie primarily in their striking artwork rather than in their effectiveness as methods of language acquisition. Most teachers and librarians seem to use them for the illustrations, and as a single-language track, rather than for their bilingual or multilingual content.

Other concept books for the pre-schoolers explore perception, the senses, and language. Joan Bodger's *Belinda's Ball* (1981), illustrated by Mark Thurman, is based on Jean Piaget's psychological theories of object constancy and representation. Some of the text is printed in red to encourage language development and child involvement in the story of a little girl's search for her ball. A quest is also the theme of Michèle Lemieux's *What Is That Noise?* (1984), a fable of a bear's fascination with sounds. The bear, a child-surrogate, searches for the source of the regular thumping sound that is always with him, finally discovering that it is the beat of his own heart. Lemieux's paintings of an anthropomorphized bear in a peasant setting give the story a folk-tale quality. Other such animal characters are engaged in absurd activities in Nicola Morgan's *Pride of Lions* (1987), a picturebook of collective nouns. The idea of illustrating a compendium of animal group nouns (e.g. a murder of crows) has been used by other illustrators (as in *Birds*, 1967, by the famous English artist Brian Wildsmith), but seldom with such dry wit: 'When/Lordly and/Loving/Lions/Get together/They become a/Pride.' The alliterative word-play on each noun is given concrete form in satirical images, from wealthy executive parrots to a black-leather-jacketed delinquent elk. Morgan's dynamic colours and visual puns make *Pride of Lions* a memorable picturebook in this genre.

Though the literary content of concept books is minimal or non-existent (where only the letters of the alphabet appear), they provide scope for ingenuity, wit, information, fine illustration, and design, and deserve not to be ignored in considering a child's first books.

ILLUSTRATORS AND THEIR STYLES

Certain traditional art styles can be identified in the visual statements of Canadian illustrators—though many have developed a stylistic signature that is immediately recognizable. While individual variations within styles are to be expected and welcomed, specific and consistent categories help in classifying the modes of expression, such as magic realism, naïve art, cartoon art, and romanticism as well as particular mediums, such as collage and plasticine.

Stylists. A handful of illustrators may be categorized primarily as stylists because they use a specific medium for the transmission of idea and story. So far, in Canada, these are collage and plasticine. Collage emphasizes surface texture and structure. Images are formed by cutting and tearing different materials, applying these shapes to a flat plane, and often adding line-drawings or paintings. Elizabeth Cleaver's collages initiated the development of Canadian picturebook illustration of an international calibre. A new star has emerged with Karen Patkau. Her art is less abstract and stylized than that of Cleaver, more representational and three-dimensional. Her collages for Robert Heidbreder's collection of verses, *Don't Eat Spiders* (1985), first revealed her skill in dealing amusingly with a wide variety of subjects. In *One Watermelon Seed* (1986) by Celia Barker Lottridge, she manages to convey the energy of growth in a garden. Her *Ringtail* (1987), however, illustrating a lively verse-story by Patricia Sillers, is perhaps the richest and most amusingly detailed collage-work one can find. The tactile quality of the racoon—whose search for food in a Toronto ravine leads him to a kitchen—and of other animals is remarkable. A quieter nursery atmosphere of imaginative child-play and fantasy is evoked by Patkau in *Seal is Lost* (1988) written by Priscilla Galloway. In this tale of a lost toy, multi-layered images have the quality of soft toy sculptures.

Barbara Reid's plasticine technique is even more familiar to children in kindergarten than collage. She controls (or perhaps one should say releases) plasticine with such dexterity that she is able to suggest the movement of birds in *Have You Seen Birds?* (1986), with verses by the American Joanne Oppenheim. In *The New Baby Calf* (1984), with text by the American Edith Chase, one wants to reach out and touch the modelled animals. In her miniature lattice-work pictures for *Sing a Song of Mother Goose* (1987), Reid employs subtle visual wit in expressing the humour and caricature of the nursery rhymes. In all her art the bright colours and intricate detail are captivating.

Magic Realism. This art-form is basically realistic, but with a slight intrusion of something unreal—a magical element or overtone that can create a supernatural atmosphere. Its images can be drawn from dream and the unconscious, with symbolic allusions and luminous or psychedelic coloration. Magic realism is a strong component in the artwork of Warabé Aska, Ian Wallace, Ken Nutt, Ted Harrison, and Lindee Climo. Aska offers the most definite example of this style in *Who Goes to the Park* (1984) and *Who Hides in the Park* (1986) in which his sophisticated oil paintings have a surrealistic dimension. Ordinary human activities in *Who Hides in the Park* are bathed in an effulgent, eerily radiant light: the sky and forest are playgrounds of half-hidden animals and native mythic images.

Ian Wallace's magical artwork in *Chin Chiang and the Dragon's Dance* (1984), *Morgan the Magnificent* (1987), and *The Sparrow's Song* (1986) has a dreamlike quality. The iridescent paintings in *Chin Chiang* change dynamically in perspective and size—paralleling the boy's emotional growth—and in tonal intensity, climaxing in a dominance of bright Chinese red, signifying resolution and joy. In *Morgan the*

Magnificent pictures in watercolour, pen-and-ink, and crayon are basically realistic, but the magic edge of eerie colour and the dramatic manipulation of scale and perspective propel the story into fantasy. Wallace has also successfully illustrated the works of other authors—Jan Andrews' *Very Last First Time* (1985) and Tim Wynne-Jones's *Architect of the Moon* (1988). The elemental reality of Inuit life and the harsh, unearthly beauty of the North inform his paintings in *Very Last First Time*. They are laden with half-hidden images drawn from Inuit mythology, which dramatize the strange descent to the bottom of the sea by an Inuit girl. In *Architect of the Moon* Wallace's usual representational style becomes appropriately geometric and abstract in this fantasy of a boy who rebuilds the crumbling moon with his child's blocks.

Whereas the magic realism in Wallace's illustrations tends to inject fantasy into the realism of a story, Ken Nutt's exquisitely detailed and realistically conceived black-and-white pencil drawings work in the opposite direction—they inject realism into the outrageous fantasy of the quest stories about Zoom the cat by Tim Wynne-Jones, *Zoom at Sea* (1983) and *Zoom Away* (1985). Unlike the magic-realism of Aska and Wallace, Nutt's realism conveys a more subtle magic; he does not exploit the emotional power of colour, or exaggerate perspective and figure, but juxtaposes ordinary images with the fabulous and supernatural, both rendered with the same meticulous detail. His work is close to that of the American illustrator Chris Van Allsburg. Ken Nutt has used the pseudonym Eric Beddows to illustrate *Night Cars* (1988), written by Teddy Jam, in an entirely different style and medium—full-colour paintings featuring rich hues and vibrant brush-strokes. Magic realism is evident in the mysterious quality of the night-life seen through a window by a baby and his father.

Another form of magic realism appears in Ted Harrison's acrylic paintings of the Yukon in *Children of the Yukon* (1977) and *A Northern Alphabet* (1982). Faceless, anonymous, generic figures enact their daily round against a wild Arctic background, made fantastical by psychedelic shapes and neon colours. The swirling, curvilinear style heavily outlines the flat shapes of figures and buildings, which are like pieces of stained glass. Piercing, vertiginous streaks of colour light up the bleak landscape and endless sky, turning the North into an abstract state of mind as much as an actual place. Harrison's illustrations for the two most famous poems by Robert W. Service, *The Cremation of Sam McGee* (1986) and *The Shooting of Dan McGrew* (1988), are influenced by commercial and poster art, as well as folk art. *Sam McGee*, with its emphasis on a mythological landscape, is more successful than the portraiture and interior scenes of *Dan McGrew*. Magic realism is most apparent in Harrison's *The Blue Raven* (1989), which combines realistic details of contemporary native life with images of legendary power.

Lindee Climo's brand of magic realism is more strongly touched with folk-art than that of Harrison. Her oil paintings for *Chester's Barn* (1982) have a curvilinear quality reminiscent of early Canadian folk carvings. Her farm animals exude a radiant and compelling spirit, while the farmer is faceless and anonymous. The variety of shapes and contour-lines displays Climo's dramatic sense of design. Her *Clyde* (1986) is more fluid in style, and more colourful, moving from the folk quality of *Chester's Barn* to a freer and more expressionist imagery that depicts the changing fantasies of the horse. In both Climo's and Harrison's works there is more than a touch of naïve art.

Naïve Art. In its truest sense this style refers to the work of self-taught artists, such as Grandma Moses, and is recognized by such characteristics as doll-like or distorted figures, tentative draughtsmanship, absence of perspective, brilliant colour, and intricate patterns—elements that trained artists also consciously make use of. William Kurelek and Ann Blades were our first illustrators in this style. They have been joined by Dayal Kaur Khalsa and Stéphane Poulin. From her first books, *Mary of Mile 18* (1971) and *A Boy of Taché* (1973), Blades has grown as an artist in her abilities to depict character and convey atmosphere as well as landscape. In *Pettranella* (1980), written by Betty Waterton, Blades' characteristically quiet watercolour style and subtle modulations of colour convey the emotional transition from old country to new, and from harsh winter to soft spring. In Sue Ann Alderson's *Ida and the Wool Smugglers* (1987), Blades' paintings demonstrate a conscious naïveté in the simplified compositions in floating space, and in the repetitive decorative details that fill the page.

Blades usually illustrates picture-storybooks, in which her illustrations are primarily narrative, with full-page pictures facing a page of text. For *By the Sea: An Alphabet Book* (1985) she worked within the format of a picturebook: letter and scene are combined. The paintings are small, showing soft, sweeping lines of sand, ocean, and mountains, with an even smaller scale of children's seaside play, all bathed in the translucence of ocean light. Her children, as always, are sturdy figures within a magical landscape.

Dayal Kaur Khalsa used such elements of naïve art as doll-like figures, flat blocks of intensely brilliant colour, and pages massed with intricate detail drawn from life in the 1950s, especially evident in *My Family Vacation* (1988). The conscious naïveté of her pictures is matched by the gentle humour, simplicity, and child-like naturalness of her texts. In *I Want a Dog* (1987) her gouache and coloured-pencil artwork includes direct allusions to historical art-styles and masterworks, from Seurat's 'A Sunday Afternoon on the Island of La Grand Jatte' to late twentieth-century photo-realism. Many of her individual pictures are highly memorable—even outrageous, as in *Tales of a Gambling Grandmother* (1986), when grandmother is seen soaking in a large bathtub full of orange juice on a train surrounded by attendants, or when Cossacks are shown eating borscht in a 1950s kitchen in Queen's. Her style is simplified in the rhymed lullaby *Sleepers* (1988), with less detail evident in the rounded shapes appropriate to the miniature format.

Stéphane Poulin has contributed his own style of naïve art to Kathy Stinson's *Teddy Rabbit* (1988), which features his clean, humorous, and crisply rendered oil-paintings of Toronto's streets, subway, and harbour. Like so many modern illustrators, Poulin depicts his children as 'unpretty', distorted in face, squat in figure, and comically endearing.

Cartoon Art. This is not a derogatory term, despite the predominance of banal cartoon illustration in the picturebook field. It is represented by the largest group of illustrators, who tend to be visual narrators, storytellers, and humorists, in contrast to the more restrained artists of magic realism or naïve art. Fine cartoon art is considered a branch of expressionism in its distortion and juxtaposition of figures, objects, and situations, and the implicit exaggeration lends a lightness of spirit and a playful incongruity to the pictures. Many such illustrators are strong line artists. The works of Robin Baird Lewis, Michael Martchenko, Catharine O'Neill, John Bianchi, Maryann Kovalski, Kim LaFave, Brenda Clark, and Kady MacDonald Denton all demonstrate, in different ways, the light wit and freedom of the quick sketch rather than the finished painting. Victor Gad and Marie-Louise Gay, on the other hand, are more surrealistic.

Within this group, Lewis, Clark, Denton, and Martchenko illustrate picturebooks for toddlers and pre-schoolers that focus, with simple clarity, on their everyday experiences. Robin Baird Lewis's casual and minimalist sketches for Kathy Stinson's *Red Is Best* (1982) give an atmosphere of emotional reassurance to the story of a little girl's obsessive love for the colour red. The ingenuous line-drawings with red overlays capture the pre-school child's energy. Lewis's illustrations for *Big or Little?* (1983), also written by Stinson, possess the same simplicity and warmth as *Red Is Best*, but lack its simple strength.

Brenda Clark's style of cartoon art, touched with representational realism, is similar to that of Lewis in its simple line drawings that capture the generic child-figure, whether a small girl, as in *Big Sarah's Little Boots* (1987), or a young turtle, as in *Franklin in the Dark* (1986)—both written by Paulette Bourgeois. Clark's understated images are invigorated by bright primary colours.

Kady MacDonald Denton, in *Granny Is a Darling* (1988), shows herself to be a subtler cartoonist and draughtsman than either Lewis or Clark. In contrast to the many Canadian cartoon illustrators whose styles share a provenance with American artists, Denton seems very British. Her light, airy pastel sketches are reminiscent of Edward Ardizzone's classic images of childhood in such books as *Little Tim and the Brave Sea Captain*.

Michael Martchenko is a more outrageous caricaturist than Lewis, Clark, or Denton, as we can see in his supremely silly illustrations for Robert Munsch's *Mortimer* (1983), *Thomas' Snowsuit* (1985), *I Have to Go!* (1987), and *Murmel, Murmel, Murmel* (1982). His sketches, in water-colour and pencil—which employ a loose, exuberant line and a spontaneous application of colour to build detail and caricature—match Munsch's tall-tale texts with exaggerated comic play. In Allen Morgan's *Matthew* series (1984, 1985, 1987), the visual background is contemporary urban: the child is shown as rumpled and spunky, dressed in cowboy boots and a baseball cap. In such details as the red-licorice-chomping trucker, Martchenko indulges a fascination with contemporary social images and a wry delight in political and social satire.

The cartoonist's propensity for social satire is evident also in Catharine O'Neill's pen-and-ink and pencil sketches for *Mrs Dunphy's Dog* (1987). The droll text is extended through whimsical drawings that are marked by lively curvilinear line and impressionist dabbings of warm colour. O'Neill's drawings for *Leanna Builds a Genie Trap* (1986), by Hazel Hutchins, are less satirical (as befits the story), although they are marked by her usual swirling style. Maryann Kovalski is an equally gentle cartoonist, with an eye for human foibles. In *Brenda and Edward* (1984) her loose cartoon images gently parody the human world from a dog's perspective. The sketchiness and pastel tones of her gouache and watercolour drawings add to the tale's delicate blend of sentiment and understated humour. The family warmth of *Brenda and Edward* is continued in Kovalski's *The Wheels on the Bus* (1987), *Jingle Bells* (1988), and *The Cake That Mack Ate* (1986) by Rose Robart. In these picturebooks the illustrations have a cumulative effect, with a vast range of characters drawn into the expansive spirit of the texts. The flexibility of cartoon art is shown in Kovalski's drawings for Tim Wynne-Jones's *I'll Make You Small* (1986), where her usual blithe tone becomes appropriately sombre. Dramatic perspectives and cinematic close-ups create a threatening atmosphere for a threatening story.

The cartoonist's quick insight into the foibles of character and behaviour—which marks the work of Kovalski and O'Neill—is also evident in John Bianchi's illustrations for Helen Levchuk's *The Dingles* (1985). Bianchi's absurdist and exaggerated drawings of a nonsensical woman and her comical cats recall the wild images of the classic British nonsense artist Edward Lear. In Bianchi's other picturebooks featuring his own texts, such as *The Bungalo Boys: Last of the Tree Ranchers* (1986), his sketchy watercolours are more wryly adult, alluding to social concerns and attitudes. (Michael Martchenko's similar play with social imagery is more accessible to children.)

The cartoon art of Victor Gad and Marie-Louise Gay shows a strong element of grotesquerie. Both have illustrated poetry; Gad a collection of verse, *Mischief City* (1986), by Tim Wynne-Jones, and Gay a single poem, *Lizzy's Lion* (1984), by Dennis Lee. The concentrated form of poetry (or rather verse in these cases) lends itself well to being extended by picturebook illustration—as Randolph Caldecott first demonstrated in his illustrations for *John Gilpin* (1878). Gad shows himself a striking draughtsman in his gouache and coloured-ink illustrations for *Mischief City*. His satirical imagery—as in his many-mouthed faces—pushes the artwork into the realm of symbolism. For Dennis Lee's *Lizzy's Lion*, Gay's cartoons in pencil, watercolour, and dyes on gesso—combining caricature and grotesquerie in the tradition of sophisticated cartoon art—are a perfectly appropriate accompaniment to such episodes in Lee's extravaganza as the watch-dog lion devouring a wicked robber; perhaps fortunately, however, they tend to distance the viewer from the literary violence.

Both Gay and Gad combine cartoon art with an intense, emotional expressionism—their bizarre characters live in the realm of imagination and psychological power. Marie-Louise Gay's own texts for *Moonbeam on a Cat's Ear* (1986) and *Rainy Day Magic* (1987) are simple narrative verses about children in imaginative play, with typical Gay illustrations featuring angular, ungainly child figures and a manic, frenzied atmosphere. *Angel and the Polar Bear* (1988) carries Gay's original vision to the ultimate in eccentricity of character, as seen in the child Angel, with her brillo-pad hair and anarchic energy.

Moving to a gentler, more romantic cartoon tradition, Kim La Fave's soft watercolour illustrations, combined with line drawings, for Judith Saltman's *Goldie and the Sea* (1987) show him to be an expert visual storyteller. The details of home, pets, and a journey to the sea set the fantasy quest in a very real world. In LaFave's pictures for Janet Lunn's *Amos's Sweater* (1988), frothy watercolours spill across double-page spreads, depicting with great exuberance Amos the sheep's recapturing his woollen coat in the form of a knitted sweater. Humour is also the dominant tone of LaFave's earlier satirical, and crisply hard-edged, oil paintings for Carole Spray's *The Mare's Egg: A New World Folk Tale* (1981). His illustrations perfectly match this often-told tale of a noodlehead—here transported to the New World as a pioneer simpleton; they reveal aspects of pioneer life while maintaining a folk atmosphere.

Romanticism. As a style and approach to art, romanticism uses literary, historically remote, and exotic subject matter and treats it in an emotional and dramatic manner. The heightened atmosphere created is appropriate to the legendary content of folklore and is most strikingly found in the visual interpretations of fairy tales from the turn-of-the-century—the high point of children's-book illustration. The romantic style of Arthur Rackham and Edmund Dulac has appeared in Canada in the work of Laszlo Gal and Robin Muller, illustrating a single folktale or legend. Both work within this general style in different ways: Gal is closer to representational art while Muller verges on cartoon stylization. Gal's first Canadian book was *Cartier Discovers the St Lawrence* (1970), with text by William Toye, where his illustrations are dramatically visualized but static depictions of place, time, landscape, and native life. His pictures for Janet Lunn's version of *The Twelve Dancing Princesses* (1979) and for Andersen's *The Little Mermaid* (1983), retold by Margaret Crawford Maloney, feature grave and sculptured figures, pastel tones, and decoratively framed compositions. His illustrations in gouache, watercolour, and pencil crayon do not extend the stories in the manner of typical picturebook illustrations; rather they stand separate from the text, often formally framed, offering windows into a world of faerie, where figures are forever frozen in graceful gestures. Gal has also illustrated folktales and myths from various cultures retold by Americans. These include the Norse myth *Iduna and the Magic Apples* (1988), retold by Marianna Mayer, and *The Enchanted Tapestry: A Chinese Folktale* (1987), retold by Robert D. San Souci. These later illustrations have become more polished, but also more stylized, with the result that the universality of the tales is emphasized at the expense of their individuality. History and legend are combined by Margaret Crawford Maloney in *The Goodman of Ballengiech* (1987), a picture-storybook about James V of Scotland, for which Gal's realistic images of peasants and lords in sixteenth-century Scotland have a darker, more lowering tone, and more specificity of place, than his work for the folk and fairy tales.

Robin Muller combines some aspects of romanticism with those of cartoon art, shifting from images of representational realism to highly stylized caricature. He has retold and illustrated traditional tales—*Mollie Whuppie and the Giant* (1982), *Tatterhood* (1984), *The Sorcerer's Apprentice* (1985), *The Lucky Old Woman* (1987), and *Little Kay* (1988)—with boldly coloured pencil-crayon and ink illustrations that reveal fine draughtsmanship and a crisp clarity of image. The romantic-gothic atmosphere of *The Sorcerer's Apprentice* is heightened by his use of irregular composition and perspective. In other tales the strong heroines are depicted with humour and verve, their child-like features animated by a mischievous expression. From the black-and-white line drawings in *Mollie Whuppie* to the full-colour paintings, alternating with black silhouettes, in *Little Kay*, Muller's comic, often sentimental touches demonstrate an artistic affinity with, perhaps even a debt to, the earlier American illustrator Maxfield Parrish.

The classic picturebook is a miniature novel; it tells a story with a beginning, a middle, and an end. Picturebooks are also a microcosm of the larger world of children's books; they portray, although in miniature, the themes of the parent literature. In Tim Wynne-Jones's *Zoom at Sea*, for example, the traditional fantasy quest story, with its multi-levelled meanings, is distilled into one kernel of experience. Equally, picturebooks are a macrocosm of a child's world; small is made big and given importance. In such books as Kathy Stinson's *Red Is Best* the feelings of a pre-schooler are given emotional weight.

In addition, many picturebooks, while having wide child appeal, reveal aspects of the culture from which they originated. Two such examples from the past are Jean de Brunhoff's *Babar* books and the works of Beatrix Potter, which have been translated into innumerable languages from the original French and English. Babar wittily represents the French bourgeoisie and Potter's *The Tale of Mr Tod* (1912) the English county gentry. Other picturebook creators eschew a cultural background and draw on a very personal view of child-hood, treating it with some psychological depth. The supreme example here is Maurice Sendak's *Where the Wild Things Are*. But in all these books the story is for the child; the interpretations are for adults.

Our ground-breaking picture-storybooks and picturebooks of the late 1960s and early 1970s were marked by a strong Canadian content. Ann Blades and William Kurelek rooted their works in a particular region, while showing children (in words and pictures) engaged in typical Canadian activities that implied a particular set of values and lifestyles. Elizabeth Cleaver's illustrations for William Toye's retellings of native legends have familiar back-grounds—mountains, snow, lakes and rivers. Tundra Books of

Montreal has deliberately sought out and published works with a strong Canadian flavour (including Blades and Kurelek) that have more recently ranged from Sing Lim's *West Coast Chinese Boy* to a series of alphabet books—Ted Harrison's *A Northern Alphabet* and Gordon Roache's *A Halifax ABC*. Indeed most of the creators of alphabet books draw their words and images from what they see around them. There is rarely a 'Z for zebra'. Recent Canadian picturebooks with a strong story component and a Canadian setting are generally those that deal with native life (Jan Andrews' *Very Last First Time*, illustrated by Ian Wallace), or the past (Betty Waterton's *Pettranella*, illustrated by Ann Blades)—though they are outnumbered by those that concentrate on the home life of small children and their delights or problems. Still, there is now a relative plenitude of books that can give Canadian children a sense of their cultural background. These have been supplemented by those that reflect, in illustration only, our multi-ethnic population. The few books about native-child domestic life are also in the new mode—only the illustrations show that the families are Indian or Inuit. It is to be expected, and welcomed, that differences in culture will be subsumed into childhood experiences that take precedence over a specific culture. There is, after all, a 'republic of childhood'.

Fantasy picturebooks also constitute 'a new wave' in the sense that they now form a considerable and varied group. By definition they claim their provenance from the imagination and rarely have a specific regional or local background. However, like their counterparts from European and other English-speaking countries, the Canadian offerings have a strong storytelling component while achieving, to a greater degree, a simple, childlike, exaggerated, humorous tone. We do not yet have a Chris Van Allsburg, whose conceptual play with reality and illusion, and a surrealistic atmosphere, are central to his *Jumanji* (1981). Here young children face the magic of a sinister board-game that transforms their home into a truly threatening jungle. Canadian picturebook heroes and heroines are more apt to meet imaginative threats with humorous aplomb, as does Angel in Marie-Louise Gay's *Angel and the Polar Bear* or Leanna in Hazel Hutchins' *Leanna Builds a Genie Trap*.

Whatever the genesis of a picturebook, or its cultural background, it is the originality of the story, and the freshness, artistry, and complementary quality of the illustrations that give it its lasting power. But, as in the novel, it is the characters that children remember. Peter Rabbit, Babar, Curious George, Max, and dozens of others are very much alive because of their three-dimensional reality, remarkably conveyed in both story and pictures. In Canada, Ann Blades' Mary and Sue Ann Alderson's Bonnie McSmithers still hold a place in children's imaginations, and may be joined (in a few years) by Tim Wynne-Jones's Zoom, Maryann Kovalski's Brenda and Edward, Robert Munsch's Mortimer, Janet Lunn's Amos, Allen Morgan's Matthew, Dennis Lee's Lizzy (and others) as entries in a 'Who's Who' of memorable characters in Canadian children's literature. And their adventures are sure to elicit that perennial child demand for a favourable story, 'Read it again!'

While time will winnow out many of the books discussed in this chapter, one thing is very clear. On the threshold of the 1990s—in all aspects of books for the pre-school and young child, from the emergence of new talents in illustration to the originality of the storylines—one can now speak with assurance and pride of 'the lively art of the picturebook' in Canada.

6

Native Legends

To the French who sailed across the Atlantic in the sixteenth and seventeenth centuries, the land that was entered by the great Rivière du Canada appeared to hold limitless possibilities of fulfilling their imaginings and desires—gold for the taking, spices for the picking, and the Great Western Ocean and the Indies, which beckoned them forever onward in their travels like a mirage. There were wonderful tales to be heard too. Marc Lescarbot in 1609 recounts the following:

> There is another strange thing worthy of record. . . . It is that to southward, near Chaleur Bay, lies an isle where lives a dreadful monster called by the savages Gougou, which they told me, had a woman's shape, but very terrible, and so tall, said they, that the top of the masts of our vessel would not have reached her waist . . . and that she has often devoured, and still devours, many savages, whom she puts in a great pouch when she can catch them, and then eats them; and those who had escaped the peril of this unchancy beast said that this pouch was so large that she could have put our vessel in it.

Seventeenth-century Europeans found it difficult to separate fact from fiction in a land inhabited by 'savages', where anything could happen. Such stories were not recognized for what they were—indigenous myths, which in fact resembled the tales from Greek and Norse mythology to a remarkable degree. The titans who could move mountains, the one-eyed Cyclops, Polyphemus who could swallow a man whole, the god Thor swinging his gigantic hammer, the goddess Artemis who demanded the sacrifice of a young girl—all these larger-than-life figures of myth could easily have fitted into the native material that Lescarbot recorded with such wonder. Only the names and cultural context were different.

Such a close correspondence of themes strongly suggests that the motivations and intentions involved in the creation of myths must have been roughly similar for all primitive peoples. Just what those motivations and intentions were remains unknown, although there are theories aplenty to account for them. Plato, Vico, Frazer, Freud, Jung, and in our own time Lévi-Strauss, Mircea Eliade, Joseph Campbell, Northrop Frye, and Susanne Langer are only a few thinkers who have tried to explain the radical differences in world view between pre-literate and literate man. In most parts of the world mythologies have been analysed and separated out into various branches: myth proper (gods and heroes), folktale (stories about ordinary people whose lives are touched by magic—e.g. Cinderella, Rumpelstiltskin), and historical legend (Arthur, Roland). Whatever term is used to describe the various branches of myth, it is all material from the collective imagination of the race, passed down from generation to generation by word of mouth, given new life by each reteller and often interpreted anew by each generation.

Although the making of myths undoubtedly preceded the development of graphic symbols, myths became widely known and available only in written form. In the case of European myths, centuries of rewriting undoubtedly smoothed away the shapes and textures of the original narratives. Even more important, the development of writing froze or locked in ideas and traditions that were originally fluid and variable. Once the theme had been written down, few variations were possible.

There has been as yet no classification of native myths and we refer to them, often improperly, as legend. One fascinating feature of Canadian Indian and Inuit myths is that they are the product of a *living* oral tradition that is still being transmitted and transmuted. In a sense, however, the opportunity to witness myth-making in process may cloud rather than clarify interpretation. For example, the knowledge most of us have of native tales is based on versions we have read in children's books. It is possible that these retellings, effective though many of them are, do not begin to suggest the significance and hidden meanings the stories hold for native peoples—the legends may be far richer than the versions we know. It is well to recall the classic warning of the famous anthropologist Claude Lévi-Strauss: 'A primitive people is not a backward or retarded people; indeed it may possess a genius for invention or action that leaves the achievements of civilized peoples far behind.'

Another frequent mistake is to remove myths from their original and still-living context as ritual. Among the West Coast Indians, for example, tales would be told and danced out for several evenings as part of the potlatch ceremony. Sometimes a tale would be deliberately shortened to a sentence or two, in which case it would more nearly represent the white man's equivalent of an anecdote or a joke and be told in a series. Many Indian legends were almost the property of a particular family. They became highly stylized and could be distinguished from other families' stock of tales by a sense of individuality and inheritance.

INDIAN LEGENDS

The term Indian legend, like many other generalizations used for convenience, is misleading, for it suggests a greater degree of homogeneity than is actually the case. The word 'Indian' itself is much disliked by the native peoples—they called themselves by whatever word each group had for 'the people'; the various tribes were highly differentiated in many ways, including language. And many of the stories—such as those accounting for the creation of the world—are not legends but myths, and somewhat resemble the myths of other lands. Prometheus stole fire for the Greeks; Raven stole it for the West Coast Indians; Nanabozho for the Ojibway or Chippewas; and Glooscap for the Micmacs. The Canadian rabbit lost his tail as did rabbits around the world; and whereas Noah built an ark to escape a flood, the Indians built a raft or canoe. Still 'Indian' continues to be sparingly used—with apologies—and the word 'legend' is justified too by common usage.

On the whole the characteristics peculiar to these legends considerably outweigh the similarities that unite them to the mainstream of the primitive tale. These characteristics stem from the unique culture evolved by North American Indians in response to their environment. The Indians did not make the distinction between god and hero that is found in the Greek and Norse mythologies. They created a being whom the anthropologist describes as the 'culture-hero or transformer'. This being (who has various names in various parts of the country) bent the natural phenomena to his will and generally conferred favours on his people, often forcing benefits on them. The motivation of these heroes was not always purposeful, however. Much of the work they accomplished for mankind was through trickery and even mischief. Therefore Indian legends often lack the dignity that is found in other mythologies. The image of the Greek Titan, Prometheus, chained to a rock by Zeus as punishment for bringing fire to mankind, has the awesome and direct qualities of sacrifice and perpetual punishment. Indian versions of the same story lack both impact and simplicity because the theft has either a suggestion of futility or an air of the ridiculous. In one retelling, Raven goes to great efforts to get fire, finally stealing the baby of the Chief of the Fire People and holding him for ransom. When the Chief learns that all Raven wants is fire, he says: 'Why did you not say so at first and save us all this trouble and anxiety? Fire is the most plentiful thing in our kingdom and we hold it in no value.' (Cyrus Macmillan, 'How Raven Brought Fire to the Indians', *Canadian Fairy Tales*.) In another version, Raven, in the form of a deer, steals fire from the Snowy Owl and manages to set the woods on fire while carrying it. His people at first think little of his gift. (Robert Ayre, 'How Raven Brought the Fire', *Sketco the Raven*.)

Unlike the basically consistent characterizations of the gods, goddesses, and heroes in European mythology, Indian trickster heroes are subject to sudden alterations of mood, and change themselves seemingly at random from demi-god to human to animal. Many times there is indeed some uncertainty about whether the hero is appearing in his semi-divine, human, or animal nature.

The same elusive, quicksilver quality applies to the plots of the stories. Whereas European tradition has trained the reader to expect a tale with a beginning, a middle, and an end, with all parts neatly tied together, the Indian legend is full of loose ends. It is a mélange of anecdotes rather than a single unified narrative, patterned after dreams rather than following a conscious development. Professor

Penny Petrone, in *The Oxford Companion to Canadian Literature*, puts this in a different way:

> Viewed in the context of English literary standards—rather than as a non-literate people, who have developed in a different cultural framework, might perceive them—Indian myths offer little or no narrative appeal. They lack dramatic emphasis and highlights, subtlety, characterization, and plot motivation. Anecdotal and episodic, they tend to be a pot-pourri of unrelated and incomplete fragments, often very brief and almost incoherent; some are merely summaries of reports or events. To people schooled in the English literary tradition (including many Indians who understand little of the language of their ancestors), the rambling conversational manner and exaggerated action of Indian myths can be tedious, their arcane subject matter and hermetic meanings frustrating.
>
> According to Indians themselves, much of the dramatic power and fun of their mythology and folklore emerges only when their stories are told in performance in the native language.

Two paragraphs from the raw material of the anthropologist may illustrate the point:

The Origin of the Canoe

Gluskap made the first canoe. He took as his model the breastbone of a bird. He procured a bird by killing it with a stone. From its flesh he had a good dinner. While he was picking the meat off the bird's breast, he thought, 'If something of this shape were made, it would float on the water.' He went into the woods to procure some bark. 'If I should kill anything in the water, I could go out for it in this, and would not have to swim.'

Gluskap was a Micmac. At Middle River, Cape Breton, he procured a beaver. About a hundred and fifty years ago the Indians found there the bone of a year-old beaver, one end of which bone fitted the hat of the finder. One end of the bone of the beaver's leg was as large as the man's head.

The rough-hewn quality of the above example reflects the fact that such accounts are the product of a stone-age unlettered people. The stories of the European oral tradition must originally have been equally crude in form. But over many centuries of literacy, the European myths and folktales were polished and refined. The Indian groups, though valuing eloquence, never had the opportunity to subject themselves to the discipline in communication imposed by the written word, and so their materials remain essentially unsifted.

A modern example of the formlessness of the Indian material can be found in Norval Morriseau's *Legends of My People: The Great Ojibway* (1968). As the editor points out in his preface, the stories were 'poured out of Morriseau's mind and memory without regard for sequence, so that in their original form they comprised a fascinating but often confusing *potpourri* of legends, anecdotes, observations, reports and personal comments.' However, this source book is also notable for its poetic flavour as well as its authenticity. As Fraser Symington points out in *The Canadian Indian*: 'Indians used words in normal talk as poets of the literate societies used them in writing.'

Almost twenty years later, a retelling for adults of the Raven legends—*The Raven Steals the Light* (1984) by poet Robert Bringhurst and native artist Bill Reid—still shows aspects of native legends that would be considered inappropriate for children. The tales (unlike Morriseaus's) are elegantly, even poetically retold through a narrator who, in asides, laments the losing of his native heritage. Present, however, are the bawdy elements of trickery, scatology, and sexuality that have been somewhat pruned away in modern retellings (as they are from the Greek myths for children like *The Golden Shadow*, 1973, by the British authors Leon Garfield and Edward Blishen).

The same artlessness that makes the Indian legend so loose in structure also makes for baldness in presentation. The embellishments and devices that have kept the stories from the European oral tradition alive and flourishing are quite lacking in their Indian counterparts. For example, the repetitive quality of an English folktale 'Mr Fox' subtly builds the narrative to a climax. 'Be bold, be bold; be bold, be bold, but not too bold; be bold, be bold, but not too bold lest that your heart's blood should run cold'—and the tale gains in suspense and memorability with each restatement of the refrain. The Indian legends employ repetition too, but they express it in a highly monotonous manner; incidents and sentences are reiterated with a simple exactitude conducive to boredom, unless one is steeped in the conventions of native lore. The cyclic pattern that binds together the incidents of a European hero story is seldom found in an Indian legend. Subordinate tales do not reinforce each other and an Indian story is thus not only difficult for a non-native to tell orally but is almost impossible to recall.

To these intrinsic deficiencies of artistry must be added the difficulty arising out of simple unfamiliarity. Indigenous though they are to Canada, Indian legends are no more native to most Canadian children than an Ashanti lullaby—they are culturally 'imported'. Hiawatha apart (though his familiarity is due only to Longfellow's anglicization of him), the Indian heroes are wholly remote figures. Tom Thumb and Robin Hood are part of the literary heritage of Canadian children and are effortlessly absorbed into their consciousness. Na-pe and Wisakedjak become known only by purposeful discovery.

All this is to suggest that the making of a fine collection of native legends is no mere anthologizing labour. Scholarship is required to make them both intelligible and reasonably faithful to the originals, craftsmanship to give them shape, and most of all creative artistry to communicate the freshness, spontaneity, sense of wonder, directness, and humour that represent their greatest appeal to children. It is not easy to meet such demands, whether the tales are retold by natives or non-natives.

Three early collections reflect these difficulties. Pauline Johnson's *Legends of Vancouver* (1911) was not created for children, but for many years it stood alone as a readable entrance for them to an unfamiliar world and was used extensively in children's library collections. The tales are unique in that Johnson heard them directly from Chief Joe Capilano of Vancouver. Not understanding his language (she was half Mohawk), she listened to his halting English and put them into literary form. While complete authenticity can therefore be in doubt, through the polished phrases one can hear the nostalgic voice of the old 'tyee' as he speaks of a time when 'Indian law ruled the land. Indian customs prevailed. Indian beliefs were regarded.' The titles of Cyrus Macmillan's *Canadian Wonder Tales* (1918) and *Canadian Fairy Tales* (1922) are significant. Macmillan, a professor of English at McGill and a polished writer, saw the Indian legends as an extension of the European folktale tradition and, although he actually heard the tales (according to his prefaces), and had studied the originals, he clothed them in the form of the European fairy tale with magic coats and wands, ogres, giants, and mermaids—put somewhat into a Canadian setting. Significantly, one story is called 'An Indian Cinderella', and a fair inference is that some of the stories are actually white men's tales that have been adapted by the Indians. But with all the dated literary conventions of Macmillan's writing, it must be said that he was a great storyteller; many of his tales still give enjoyment and are in their own way generally faithful to the spirit of Indian lore. The best stories are about the Micmac hero Glooscap and these were brought together and published as *Glooskap's Country and Other Indian Tales* in 1955—the most significant collection of Indian tales published before the 1960s. All the stories in Macmillan's two books were reissued in one volume under the title *Canadian Wonder Tales* (1974).

Hilda Mary Hooke's *Thunder in the Mountains* (1947) also has considerable charm. It is divided into three parts—Indian tales, stories about the coming of the white man, and stories with a French-Canadian background. In the Indian tales Thunderbird swaggers across the sky, causing a storm on Lake Superior; Whale puffs on the pipe that Glooscap gave him; and Nana Bijou 'lies on Thunder Cape, his face turned to the sky, waiting for Gitchi Manitou to wake him up'.

Macmillan and Hooke can be credited with bringing completely unknown tales to a child audience. Despite the romantic cast of their retellings, these were sympathetic interpretations of a then-inaccessible culture. To their credit, neither lapsed into the stereotyping of natives so often found in adventure stories and historical fiction of the period.

Retellings sprang into new life in the early 1960s with a group of white retellers who demonstrated the skills of selection as well as a knowledge of native life, and successfully made literature out of a large, unwieldy, diverse mass of oral tradition. These were Robert Ayre (*Sketco the Raven*, 1961), Christie Harris (*Once Upon a Totem*, 1963), Dorothy Reid (*Tales of Nanabozho*, 1963), and Kay Hill (*Glooscap and His Magic*, 1963).

The most adept use of such material is found in Robert Ayre's *Sketco the Raven*, which provides a pattern for the great Raven cycle of legends. These were known and told among many Indian groups of the Northwest Coast—the Tlingit, Haida, Tsimshian, and Kwakiutl—although they knew Raven under various names.

'Beyond the rim of the world, in the high North, in the North beyond the North, Sketco the Raven was born.' Ayre sometimes has a powerful eloquence suited to the native style. He gives unity to the cycle by consistently emphasizing Raven as the friend and benefactor of mankind, and chose the stories in which Raven uses his wits and his magic to bring comfort and hope to the Indians living in a darkened world. Raven steals fire from the great Snowy Owl, so that men may be warm; he releases the Sun that they may have light; and he brings game and moves the ocean to provide food from both the land and the sea. In these stories Raven is not only a magical being with power to transform himself into a Raven as well as other animals; he is also a small boy who grows to manhood determined to avenge the murder of his three brothers. Collectively the legends are a tale of high adventure as well as of mythic power.

Ayre retains much of the sly fun of the original stories while avoiding their characteristic earthiness. Sketco jabs 'The Man who Sat on the Tide' with his harpoon, first in the knees and then in the buttocks, and, as the giant yells and lunges at his tormentor, the sea pours down into a hole like the gurgling of the water going down the bathtub drain. There is also a capricious Poseidon called Fog Man, who makes fog by pulling his hat down over his head and provides comic relief in Sketco's odyssey of revenge.

Harris's *Once Upon a Totem* contains five legends relating to the natives of the North Pacific Coast, a people unusually rich in myth and legend. In their days of lordship the abundance of the sea and forest gave them leisure to organize a highly complex social structure, to raise handsome cedar lodges, fronted by majestic totem poles, and to decorate them with totemic symbols of their past and present greatness. Living above the level of the mere struggle for survival, they held sumptuous potlatches that became the heart of their tribal, social, and commercial life. They had time for song, time to dance—and time for the telling of tales.

The first story, 'The One-Horned Mountain Goat', is a version of one of the most famous West Coast legends, not only because it has been the most frequently retold but also because it reveals so dramatically the native concept of respect for animals. The people in the village had grown wasteful and careless, oblivious to the old laws that stated they should be kind to animals and kill only those they needed for food. When the hunters went to the mountain, Stekyawden, and killed goats wastefully and, as a final insult, brought home a kid for the village children to play with, the goats grew angry. Later, the people of the village were invited to a feast by a new tribe that lived on Stekyawden. The tribe, which was made up of mountain goats, fêted the villagers lavishly and then sent them tumbling down the mountain to their death. The only villager saved was the man who had been kind to the kid and protected it from the children. To this man the kid lent his coat and shoes to help him climb safely down the mountain.

This story has been retold for adults by Diamond Jenness in *The Corn Goddess* (1956), by Marius Barbeau in *The Downfall of Temlaham* (1928), and is the first story in *Men of Medeek* (1962) by Will Robinson. It has been retold for children by Hugh Weatherby in *Tales the Totems Tell* (1944), by Olive Fisher and Clara Tyner in *Totem, Tipi and Tumpline* (1955), and by an American, Fran Martin, in *Nine Tales of Raven* (1951). William Toye's version, *The Mountain Goats of Temlaham* (1969), in picturebook format, is by far the best for younger children.

Although the legend loses nothing in a simple retelling—such is its innate power—Christie Harris has enhanced it with detail and in so doing has added a new dimension, much as Walter de la Mare re-clothed the old folktales in his *Tales Told Again* (1927). The hero, Du'as, is a boy rather than a young man or a chief. Harris has added a stern old grandfather, the proud chief Wi-ho-om, and the gay little sister, Katla. Du'as is torn between inner compulsion and training to honour the tribal taboos and his hero-worship of one who violates them. The author's style is simple and vivid; when she is describing the vengeance of the goats, one feels the rhythm of the archetypal legend:

> He felt the hard earth quake, he heard it rumble deep in the rocks beneath him; he saw the feast house collapse, with its giant timbers. People and poles and flames moved out before him. They dropped in a hideous rock slide. Screams tore the air. Boulders tumbled and crashed and bounced off, thundering down toward the river valley.

Many Indian legends have a quality of anonymity. In their original form, characters may not even be identified, or their traits may be so little individualized as to make them types rather than people. But

Harris, in her first sentence, brings her hero close to the reader:

> Long, long ago there lived an Indian boy, Du'as, who found one northern summer almost endless. It seemed to him that the golden tints of autumn would never brighten the aspen trees along the lower slopes of Stek-yaw-den.

At the same time Harris does not sacrifice authenticity to literary values. The stories in *Once Upon a Totem* are based on ethnological reports and on the author's direct experience of mingling with natives, as much as possible in their homes and in their villages, listening to the stories being told. Three have overtones of European folktales but stand sturdily on their own feet as indigenous products. The author tells us that the last tale—'Fly Again Proud Eagle'—is a historical adventure, based on actual happenings. Be that as it may, it is also a portrayal of the longing, as old and as new as human experience, to recapture a lost homeland.

Most stories from the oral tradition are improved by pruning, honing, polishing, and refining until not a word seems out of place and the basic concept emerges with clarity, but with enough depth and mystery to allow readers to make their own interpretation. In Harris's second collection, *Once More Upon a Totem* (1973), the considerable risk inherent in the embellishment of myth and legend is all too apparent. The first story, 'The Prince Who was Taken Away by the Salmon', is a famous Tsimshian tale, which, as recorded in Franz Boas's *Tsimshian Mythology*, has a definite mythological shape. In transferring it to the short-story or novelette form, Harris destroyed its legend quality and, indeed, its basic pattern. Length becomes even more of a hazard in the second story, 'Raven Travelling', which is long and repetitious; while the third one, 'Ghost Story', is so long and involved that it cheats the reader of the shivers promised by the title.

No one has done more than Christie Harris to bring an understanding of the native spirit world to the non-native reader. This she accomplishes not only through her research and her knowledge, but also through her own belief in that world. In her novel *Secret in the Stlalakum Wild* (1972), for example, the spirits, the 'stlalakum', are not described as totally supernatural, but rather as something 'real'—perceptible to all who are sensitive to the natives' concern for nature: 'Insensitive men who crash through the fragile, living wilderness would never understand about stlalakums. So the Indians keep their silence.' The same believability surrounds the character of 'Mouse Woman' (a tiny being, half-grandmother and half-mouse), even though she lived 'in the time of very long ago, when things were different.' Harris has plucked Mouse Woman from a mass of West Coast native oral lore and has refined and animated her character. This shapeshifting 'narnauk' (a supernatural being like Raven) is at the heart of her trilogy: *Mouse Woman and the Vanished Princesses* (1976), *Mouse Woman and the Mischief-Makers* (1977), and *Mouse Woman and the Muddleheads* (1979). Mouse Woman is not only the link among the stories, but acts as a spirit-guide, bringing balance, order, and justice to a world that is going awry. The outstanding quality of the trilogy is its humour. In *Mouse Woman and the Mischief-Makers* the giantess, Snee-nee-iq, carries off children and eats them. A child, who howls for everything she wants and does not believe the story, seeks her out. Mouse Woman helps the girl to defeat the giantess—but at a cost. Although Snee-nee-iq is consumed by fire, every ash is turned into a mosquito; they follow the girl home. Mouse Woman is satisfied:

> The small had vanquished the big. And the big had turned into a very small. A girl who had wanted too much had got more than she ever wanted—a horde of mosquitoes. The two who had been upsetting the order of the world had dealt with each other to bring back the order of the world.

Although Mouse Woman sets the world aright, she has mouse characteristics—'she had developed the habit of tearing woollen tassels into a lovely, loose, nesty pile of wool with her ravelly little fingers.' Most of Harris's collections have been evocatively illustrated in meticulous pen-and-ink drawings by Douglas Tait, who has taken great care to base them on authentic details.

Harris's *The Trouble with Princesses* (1980) deals chiefly with adolescents of long ago in crisis. Short introductions link the spirited native princesses with those of European folklore. Its strong coming-of-age-theme thrusts the princesses into rites-of-passage adventures with gently erotic undertones. *The Trouble With Adventurers* (1982) links daring West Coast native youths to the spirit of all daring adventures, whether in folklore or myth (such as that of Theseus) or in history. The last story in the collection is an account of the young Englishman, John Jewitt, captured by the Nootka chief Maquinna, and his adventures that were stranger than fiction.

One of Harris's great strengths lies in her evocation of the Northwest Coast landscape. Joan Skogan's *Princess and the Sea-Bear and Other Tsimshian Stories* (1983) shares the same sense of setting and atmosphere. Without bowdlerizing the originals, Skogan gives a sense of dramatic conflict and romance to the primal violence and sexuality of the stories.

The great Ojibway counterpart to Raven is the subject of Dorothy Reid's *Tales of Nanabozho*, and the Micmac hero dominates Kay Hill's *Glooscap and His Magic*. Both collections emphasize the trickster qualities of their heroes, who, however, gradually change from buffoons to characters of dignity. Dorothy Reid keeps to the spirit of the originals by showing Nanabozho as foolish, capricious, and often cruel. In one story, when Nanabozho discovers that his secret hoard of silver is known to the white men, he and Thunder Bird cause a great storm. This in turn prevents his wife, Minnehaha, from getting fish for his supper. When the Great Man finds that his food is not ready, he explodes in a rage and turns his beloved wife into a stone. He himself is turned into stone for causing a storm to harm the white people, against the orders of the great spirit, Gitche Manitou—a quick ending. While deliberately conveying the unpatterned quality of the Indian tale in *Tales of Nanabozho*, Reid has organized the material into an authentic-sounding, coherent life story—made of self-contained tales. Her achievement is all the more noticeable in comparison with an American publication, Thomas B. Leekley's *The World of Nanabozho* (1965). The number and diversity of these tales, and the resulting lack of cyclic continuity, make Leekley's Nanabozho a far less memorable hero than Reid's.

Like Macmillan, Kay Hill in *Glooscap and His Magic* presents Glooscap as eternally benevolent. His tricks are good-natured and always serve to help someone in distress. However, here the similarities end. Macmillan's version tends to present Glooscap as almost a fairy-tale character. When Glooscap is making the birds, Macmillan has him wave a wand to achieve their transformation. Hill, more effectively, concentrates on the comic effect of the birds' vying for Glooscap's attention. Another great difference is in the style. Macmillan's is almost completely narrative, while Hill makes effective use of dialogue. She is also able to characterize the animals who were Glooscap's friends. Her telling of how Ableegumooch, Glooscap's messenger, lost his tail is the most memorable of all the versions of this story. The book begins with the tales of organization and creation—Glooscap creates the world, then the animals, and then men; there is even a Cain and Abel theme—and ends with Glooscap's giving the game of lacrosse to his people.

Glooscap and His Magic has a robust and full-blooded tone reminiscent of the heroic European tradition. Many of the tales have in fact their almost exact counterpart in the oral literature of the world. There is the tale of the poor boy, Tabulech, who wins the chief's daughter by making her laugh—aided, of course, by a magic flute donated by Glooscap. The story of Oochigeas is the Micmac's answer to Cinderella. Maltreated and abused by her older sisters, Oochigeas nevertheless triumphs over them in winning Team, the invisible brave, who will appear only to the truthful. However, in spite of such parallelisms, the writer has successfully maintained in her retellings a flavour and a spirit that are distinctly native.

More Glooscap Stories (1970) shows a greater assurance with the material of legend than does Hill's first book. Everything is slightly sharpened—the style, the humour, the conciseness, and above all a sense of conviction that does not even need the precise use of Nova Scotian place-names to give the tales credibility.

As the Canadian poet Alden Nowlan points out in his introduction to his retellings of *Nine Micmac Legends* (1983), all surviving Micmac (or Ellenu, as the tribes called themselves) legends owe their existence to Silas T. Rand (1810-89), a Baptist minister to the natives of Nova Scotia who learned their language and compiled a 40,000-word Micmac dictionary. This no doubt explains why the plots of some of Nowlan's tales resemble some of those retold by Macmillan—Nowlan's 'The Invisible Boy' is a version of Macmillan's 'An Indian Cinderella', while 'The Star Brides', an echo of the Eros and Psyche myth, appears to be common to a variety of tribes. Only one Glooscap story is included in *Nine Micmac Legends*. All the stories are told briefly and crisply and, with slight pruning, would be admirable for storytelling, especially 'Three Boys and the Giants', a lively companion to 'Jack the Giant-killer'.

For the Blackfoot Indians the 'Big Man' was Na-pe, the Old Man, and his story is told in Frances Fraser's simple and skilful *The Bear Who Stole the Chinook and Other Stories* (1959). Of all the Indian 'Big Men', Na-pe is the most consistently irascible. He alternately tricks the animals into helping him and then turns on them, or is tricked by the animals. The stories about Na-pe himself are more anecdotal than the other tales in the book, and have a light-hearted humour. All the stories, however, have dignity and charm as well as a genuine native quality. The book proves that it is possible to write native tales for younger children without over-simplification. Fraser gets her effect from the selection of her incidents rather than from condensing a mass of material. Again, even in these simply told tales, the resemblance to other folk literature is noticeable. 'The Ghost Pipe' is the Indian Orpheus and Eurydice; 'The Girl who Married the Morning Star' has echoes of the flood stories.

Diamond Jenness tells us in *The Indians of Canada* that the Blackfoot Indians were 'the strongest and most aggressive nation on the Canadian prairies in the middle of the eighteenth century . . .' They fought with their neighbours, treated their women harshly, and certainly knew privation and starvation. These harsh realities are reflected in Fraser's second book of Blackfoot tales, *The Wind Along the River* (1968), making it considerably different from the more humorous and lyrical *The Bear Who Stole the Chinook*. Four Na-pe stories apart, the remainder are obviously based on historical incidents from the not-so-distant past—stories of tribal wars, kidnapping, torture, and revenge. They display many characteristics of the native legend that trouble the non-native reader. They are anecdotal in character rather than full tales; they are unfinished and unpolished; they convey a sense of reportage rather than story. They were indeed reported to Fraser 'by the elders of the tribe', and although they should no doubt be read and understood within the totality of the life and customs of the Blackfoot of the time, this would not always be obvious to an uninformed reader, particularly a child reader. Some stories, for example, exhibit the concept of long-delayed justice that is cold and chilling and alien to the child mind. They are first generation in that this appears to be their first appearance in printed form. A search in anthropological and ethnological literature did not reveal any prototypes. However, one story, 'The Blue End of the World', appeared as a Blackfoot tale called 'The Story of Scar Face' in Lewis Spence's *The Myths of the North American Indians* (1914), though the older version ends happily and the newer one ends in sudden and startling revenge. *The Wind Along the River* is an important collection, but for children it will not be as persuasive an introduction to native lore as the retellings by Ayre, Harris, Hill, and Reid, who have presented the legends in a familiar rather than a distinctive pattern.

It is quite possible, of course, that in many cases the Indian legend's echoes of, and resemblances to, European folk literature are illusory. They may actually derive more from the retellers than from the tales themselves—from the fact that the non-native authors, steeped in European traditions, have unconsciously imposed the patterns and flavour of the European tale upon the native material. The test of this hypothesis is still in the making, for retellings by natives deliberately intended for children did not appear until 1967, in *Son of Raven, Son of Deer* by the Nootka chief George Clutesi.

His sub-title—*Fables of the Tse-Shaht People*—reveals the essential point of his stories. As his use of the word 'fable' implies, these are beast tales—the adventures of the foolhardy Son of Deer and the greedy and thoughtless Son of Raven—used to teach the mores and morals of a society to children. With the exception of the first story, a moving and dignified version of the 'bringing of fire', each tale has that favourite native personage, the anti-hero, who struts and boasts until, in the end, the last trick is played on him. Clutesi's stories seem closer to *Aesop's Fables* than to the main body of legend, but the author assures us that the stories were handed down in his family for at least 400 years, so there is no question of their authenticity and independent origin. The ease and polish of these fables are no doubt partly due to Clutesi's literary skill, partly to a long history of retelling.

> Ko-ishin-mit loved to copy and imitate other people—especially the clever people. He would watch them doing their tasks, then he would go home and imitate them, no matter how hard it might be. He loved to go around visiting his neighbours at meal-time, looking for free meals. He would walk for miles for a feed. Oh, how Koishin-mit loved to eat! Ko-ishin-mit would eat anything put before him, he was so greedy.

In some respects the introduction to *Son of Raven, Son of Deer* is as significant as the stories themselves. Clutesi tells us that the European nursery rhymes can be puzzling and disturbing to the Indian child. For example, he takes exception to 'Rock-a-bye Baby' on the grounds that 'The Indian child feels bewilderment with this type of nursery rhyme because there seems to be no concern or regard for a very apparent injury inflicted upon a little child.'* Similarly, he finds in 'Humpty Dumpty' evidence of 'the white man's' callous disregard of suffering. If native children in general really view the European folk tradition in this way, can it be that non-native children—or adults, for that matter—are equally guilty of misinterpreting native legends? One begins to wonder uneasily how much is really untranslatable from different cultures and literatures.

Son of Raven, Son of Deer was immediately popular, especially in British Columbia, but Clutesi's success as a storyteller both with native and non-native children was not repeated either in the 1960s or 1970s. Other native retellers seemed to see themselves as recorders of a cultural heritage rather than as artistic tellers of tales. Their introductions invariably point out that the old people can still recall 'how it was' and that the tales were lifted from their memories and passed on as the ethnic life-blood of succeeding generations. When literary intent is present, the capacity for execution may not be. As Norval Morriseau has pointedly reminded us, 'Among the Indians, as among other nations, some people are born artists, but most are not.' Publications by native writers such as Patronella Johnston's *Tales of Nokomis* (1970), Alex Grisdale's *Wild Drums: Tales and Legends of the Plains Indians* (1972), and *Tales From the Longhouse* (1973) by native children in British Columbia, should thus be seen for what they are—unpretentious and, within their aims, successful attempts to bring together important stocks of legend, lore, and even history.

For *Tales from the Longhouse* native children on Vancouver Island were asked to write their own tales and legends. Their first attempts

---

*The *Oxford Dictionary of Nursery Rhymes* by Iona and Peter Opie says that the authorship of 'Rock-a-bye Baby' has been attributed to a Pilgrim youth who, arriving on the Mayflower, noticed the way the Indians hung their birchbark cradles, with baby inside, on the branch of a tree.

were about television and movie 'Indians'. The elders stepped in to tell the children their own versions of the stories. The results, couched in spare prose, quite often project a feeling of authenticity and timelessness. As may be expected with this kind of group effort, there is considerable variation in the nature and quality of the material. Perhaps the best renderings occur with the retelling of familiar stories—'In the Beginning' (the creation of the world by Nanabozho), and 'The Legend of the Flood' (a version of the basic flood story), and 'A Legend of Spring Salmon' (a famous Tsimshian tale). Other stories are less-known local legends, while the remainder are snippets of lore and customs.

Relatively unpolished and little known as most of these publications are, they offer a fascinating view of folktales in the making, as it were. The same process of recall and assembly of tribal lore, of ordering and refining the material, and the same gradual shift in emphasis from ethnic to artistic values, must have occurred with the now-classic European stories. It is heartening to note that more recent native retellers combine literary and storytelling qualities and cultural authenticity.

The voices of the Rama Ojibway elders are heard in *The Adventures of Nanabush: Ojibway Indian Stories* (1979). The recorders and compilers, Emerson and David Coatsworth, have melded the inflections of various elders into a confiding voice that seems to belong to a single contempory storyteller. In asides and introductions the narrator looks back to the early days of the creation myths and 'how and why' stories and to the old Ojibway storytellers who shared a cosmological vision and a belief in the spiritual truth of the legends. The accompanying Eastern Woodland-style paintings by Francis Kagige are as emotionally convincing as the deft retellings.

Basil Johnston, an Ojibway and an ethnologist at the Royal Ontario Museum, has also made use of the living native oral tradition in *Tales the Elders Told: Ojibway Legends* (1981). Although his retellings do not have the emotional impact of *The Adventures of Nanabush*, they are far more than a step beyond the recording of basic material. The coloured paintings and black-and-white line drawings by the Cree artist Shirley Cheechoo do much to create a legendary atmosphere.

Johnston has also compiled a slight collection (45 pages) of retellings about Nanabush and his extensive travels in *By Canoe and Moccasin* (1986). It has a specific and interesting purpose, being designed to show the derivation of place-names used in the Great Lakes area, names that were poetically and often humorously assigned by the Ojibway (the Anishinaubaug) before the white men came and later shortened or revised by them. Lake Winnipeg was once 'Weenigeegosheeng'—'the murky watered lake' because Nanabush once fell into it and was imbedded in the mud. In cleaning him off, 'the waters of the lake were forever begrimed.' These short, short tales have considerable charm. So have those in *Giving: Ojibwa Stories and Legends from the Children of Curve Lake* (1985). These are 'how and why' stories about the length of an Aesop's fable; they are simply and imaginatively illustrated by the children themselves. In background, the tales are from the Eastern Ojibway or Mississaugas and the editor, George Elston, has provided a brief history of this particular band. In keeping with the recent trend, the editor prefers the name 'Anishinabe' (which means 'original' or 'first man') to 'Indian'.

Following the publishing pattern of folklore in general, many native legends are now produced in picturebook format. The first were the result of the happy collaboration of William Toye and the artist Elizabeth Cleaver with *The Mountain Goats of Temlaham* (1969) and *How Summer Came to Canada* (1969). These were followed by *The Loon's Necklace* (1977) and *The Fire Stealer* (1979). All four are now classic Canadian picturebooks and among the best retellings of these legends.

The newer picturebooks are chiefly the products of small native or regional publishing houses. *Murdo's Story: A Legend from Northern Manitoba* (1985)—retold by Murdo Scribe, a Cree—tells how the animals come to share summer and winter. The illustrations (a meld of realism and imagination in black and white) are as charming as the story. The fisher, who plays a courageous part in it, ends up as the Big Dipper. Perhaps in Canadian skies *Ursa Major* must give way to Fisher Major!

Two other Cree tales, translated and edited by Freda Ahenakew—*How the Birch Tree Got Its Stripes* (1988) and *How the Mouse Got Brown Teeth* (1988)—are illustrated naïvely, sometimes surrealistically by George Littlechild in full colour, one full-page illustration accompanying no more than a few lines of text (sometimes only one line). These stories were first composed by Cree youngsters who were studying their native language, and so 'the writing has been standardized to represent the sounds of a single variant of Plains Cree—the Central Saskatchewan dialect spoken on the Atahk-akohp reserve.' The text shows the power of nouns and verbs—there is not an adverb or an adjective to be found. It all works well in English.

Theytus Books of British Columbia, a native publishing house, has produced picturebook versions of three Okanagan legends without a designated reteller: *How Names Were Given* (1984), *How Food Was Given* (1984), and *How Turtle Set the Animals Free* (1984). They are illustrated with simple line drawings by Ken Edwards that show the animals in upright positions wearing native dress—for these 'how' stories take place before the 'Great Spirit' made 'New People' to live with the 'Animal People'.

The Métis writer Maria Campbell combines realism and legend in *Little Badger and the Fire Spirit* (1977), which emphasizes the continuity of legend in contemporary native life. An Alberta Indian girl leaves the city to visit her grandparents, who live in a log house and follow the old traditional hunting and trapping ways. The old people tell her a fire-quest legend, one that lives on in their tribal and personal memories.

Anne Cameron's interest in the stories she heard as a child from a native woman on Vancouver Island has led her to produce several books of legends, including *How Raven Freed the Moon* (1985), *Orca's Song* (1987), and *Lazy Boy* (1988). In style, all of them are a curious mixture of simplicity and fulsomeness. The first book is the most interesting in an ethnological sense because it presents the traditionally male figure of Raven as a female.

The dedication page of Tom Dawe's *Winter of the Black Weasel: A Tale Based on a Newfoundland Micmac Legend* (1988) states that the story was told by a native and first written down in Beothuk and Micmac in 1922. The legend tells how long ago in Newfoundland 'the Micmacs and the Red Indians lived there together in peace'. The appearance of a black weasel in winter (it should be white) signifies evil, and when killed it causes a fight between the young boys of the tribe and then war among the adults in which the Red Indians are defeated. The Red

Indians are obviously the Beothuks, so named because of their lavish use of red ochre, but this is not mentioned in the text. The white man who makes an appearance and who 'snaked his way into the heart of the Micmac community' and caused the final destruction of the Red Indians is probably meant to symbolize the evil weasel. However, in a legendary sense it is rather a wonderment that the Red Indians are destroyed when it was a Micmac who killed the animal. Of course the actual demise of the Beothuks is ascribed by historians to the encroachment of the Europeans, to disease and certainly slaughter, but not specifically to another native tribe. Dramatic as it is, the text appears to belong to an outdated view of history rather than to modern thought. One suspects that the legend was chosen as a vehicle for the artist Anne MacLeod, who has illustrated it with distorted expressionist paintings, brilliantly coloured and rich with details and patterns drawn from native art.

The 1960s, and into the 1970s, were the high point of publishing Indian legends. Few books, except the modestly produced retellings by natives, have appeared in the 1980s. Whether white retellers have backed away from this material because natives want to be its sole interpreters is unclear. One would hope that the material itself can be considered more important than who retells it, although authenticity of course is essential. As yet, native legends have not entered the consciousness of Canadian children as a whole. They need to be told and retold and told again with different interpretations and for a spread of age groups. Here anthologies of native legends from already published material would be an asset. As handsomely illustrated as many of the picturebook single tales are, they pose a critical dilemma for both reteller and reader. A single tale cannot reveal the ethos of a culture or the power of the legends as a mythological or historical entity. It takes at least several tales read in sequence for a reader to become familiar with the conventions of these legends (for example, the trickster hero and the belief in the spirits of animals) and to appreciate their depth or humour.

As yet the stories that we have, whether by native or non-native, merely open the door on the fascinations of a world that is at once alien and strangely familiar. Although the differences between native legends and their European counterparts have been noted, the native legend does take its place in the world commonality of the oral tradition. The combination of familiarity and strangeness is an aspect of all myths, hero stories, and folktales, and is their chief appeal to children. They reassure by their naïveté, enthral by their matchless story qualities, and stretch children imaginatively and emotionally as they learn the fundamental qualities of the human race. Canadian writers have shown clearly that Nanabozho of the Ojibways, Sketco of the North Pacific Coast, Glooscap of the Micmacs, Wisakedjak of the Crees, Na-pe of the Blackfoot, and the hundreds of Indian chiefs and their privileged daughters and their animal friends—Bear, Rabbit, Turtle, Badger—belong as surely to children of the world as do their counterparts from other countries. The legends about them also have a strong appeal for children because they reveal a world that is in many ways close to that of a child—a world in which 'every thunderclap came as a threat and every night as the last.' Furthermore, it is one in which imagination has free reign and society is colourful, independent, close to nature, and filled with animal lore. Many of the virtues the legends extol are universal: an affinity with the animal world, courage and strength in the face of adversity, loyalty to family and tribe, unfailing devotion even unto death. The legends have special value for Canadians because they deal with a physical environment that is familiar to us: the mountains, rivers, and animals are ours, along with the frightening wilderness, the endless prairie, the swift-moving rivers, the fruits of earth and sea. Nor is the native relationship to nature beyond our understanding: it has a special relevance when the erosion of the environment is now a universal concern.

Above all many stories have humour—a quality that is conspicuously lacking in most Canadian children's books. It is sometimes sly and subtle, and often rather unusual, but it is there, as witness this Cree tale, which was doubtless invented by some wag around the campfire after the white man came:

> When Great One made mankind, he first made an earth oven. Then he modelled a man of clay and put him in to bake. He was not baked enough and came out white. Great One tried again, but this time he baked the man too long. He came out black. The third time Great One baked the man just the correct time, and he came out red. That is why different races have different colours.

INUIT LEGENDS

The early Greeks conceived their world as arising out of a vaporous, formless mass; the Scandinavians saw theirs emerging from a chaos of fire and ice. In both mythologies man appears only after great primeval struggles with Titans and giants, with startling dramas played out in terror and trickery and battles, and in sacrifice and beauty. Such tales are the foundation of Western literature. In strong contrast, Inuit creation myths seem simple, even naïve:

> It was in the time when there were no people on the earth plain. During four days the first man lay coiled up in the pod of a beachpea. On the fifth day he stretched out his feet and burst the pod, falling to the ground, where he stood up, a full-grown man. . . . When he looked up again he saw approaching, with a waving motion, a dark object which came on until just in front of him, when it stopped, and standing on the ground, looked at him. This was a raven, and as soon as it stopped, it raised one of its wings, pushed up its beak, like a mask, to the top of its head, and changed at once into a man.

This is part of the Raven cycle of legends, which is probably not indigenous to the Inuit since Raven as creator and as bringer of light and fire was known also to the Northwest Coast Indians and the Northeast Asians. A Greenland tale, recorded by Rasmussen (in *Eskimo Folk-Tales*, 1921), is even less impressive. It simply states that the earth fell down from the sky and then, 'when the earth was made, came men'.

There is scarcely any region on earth that presents conditions more severe and inclement for humankind than the Arctic, for apart from the animal habitation it is bare of all that is elsewhere considered necessary for life. And yet the Inuit long ago came to terms with their environment and have successfully waged the struggle for existence. While doing this they have given only the most fleeting thought to the phenomenon of creation. In some stories Raven is the sole creator; he also provides by stealth the sun, the moon, and the stars. But there are other very brief stories of the spirits of a sister and a brother who, having quarrelled, become the sun and the moon. Variations in legends are, of course, accounted for by the differences among widely scattered tribes who rarely, if ever, came in contact with one another.

There is a matter-of-factness about the Inuits' idea of their origin—a modesty, even an indifference that is unmatched in the myths of any other peoples. But human achievement, in the Inuit context, forms the core of their world of legend.

The superior beings of the Inuit may outdistance ordinary people, but they are human beings through and through, rarely supported by magic and witchcraft. When the supernatural does occur it is often tossed in as an aside: a young man suddenly appears to have the powers of a shaman or an angakok; an ordinary girl can throw up a mountain and turn a stream into a river. And so the supernatural seems in every way as normal as the everyday tangible world in which the stories are set. With the exception of Raven, animals are rarely mythologized—perhaps because they were the sole source of food and clothing. Certainly there are no animal figures to match those found in the Indian tales such as Ableegumooch the rabbit. Animals are portrayed almost invariably in their natural actions and locations. (It is the animal tales that are most frequently retold for children.) Basically there is a whole-hearted reality to Inuit legend in its succession of incidents probably based on historical events, especially the meeting of Inuit and Indian. The protagonists are chiefly hunters, but the plots are liberally sprinkled with grandfathers and grandmothers and particularly orphans, a sharp reminder of the hazards of hunting.

Although it is Eskimo carvings and prints that have received the greatest popular acclaim, among the Inuit themselves their legends take pride of place. In the long Arctic nights the storytellers achieved the status of the bards and troubadours in early European culture and hold that position even today. The stories varied greatly in length. Some were mere anecdotes, while others took several nights to tell, with the storyteller feeling particularly successful if the audience fell asleep. The stories themselves seem to emerge from the environment, just as the igloos were sculpted extensions of the snow and ice upon which they lived. A young boy carves a snow bear in order to frighten a real bear; a girl flies by attaching to her arms the feathers of a snow goose; the Inuit test their strength against the Indians. The brief Arctic summer has been praised for its beauty and lamented for its brevity, but it is interesting to note that most legends take little notice of it. Winter is generally the background, whether in the vast outdoors or in the close quarters of igloo or tent.

The struggle for existence has certainly induced a certain fear of the environment—a combination of the healthy and the fatalistic. The Inuit Aua expressed this fear to Knud Rasmussen, the Danish explorer and ethnologist, in 1921:

> We fear the weather spirit of earth, that we must fight against to wrest our food from land and sea. We fear Sila.
>
> We fear death and hunger in the cold snow huts.
>
> We fear Takanakapsaluk, the great woman who down at the bottom of the sea rules over all the beasts of the sea.
>
> We fear the sickness that we meet with daily all around us; not death, but the suffering. We fear the evil spirits of life, those of the air, of the sea and earth, that can help wicked shamans to harm their fellow man.
>
> We fear the souls of dead human beings and of the animals we have killed.

The most important and terrible figure in Inuit lore is the spirit of Nuliajuk (or Takanakapsaluk, or Sedna), the mother of sea animals. She notices every little breach of a taboo, for she knows everything. Whenever people have been indifferent to her, she hides all the animals and mankind has to starve. But the Nuliajak or Sedna legend, while it is the basic taboo legend, is only one of many that deal with the theme 'thou shalt not'. A good many stories are concerned with sudden killings and long-delayed vengeance. A mother lets her blind son starve; when he regains his sight years later he has her dragged into the water by a walrus. A girl who has been mistreated by her father turns into a bear and kills him. The losing team in a ball game resorts to magic to kill the winning team; a survivor plots a punishment that takes a long time to accomplish.

Like folklore around the world, many of these tales suggest a moral code, and reflect Inuit feelings—what they admire, and what they despise and condemn. They love strength and fearlessness, helpfulness and kindliness. Cruelty not only hurts the person ill-treated, but recoils upon the doer. Nothing is more certain than Nemesis.

Inuit folklore does not lack robust fun and humour—the Inuit do not take themselves too seriously. Like much Indian folklore, their tales have an underlying earthiness that is smoothed out or omitted by the retellers for children. It is perhaps inevitable that retellings are cast in the European mould, with a strong and decisive plot line. Such is not always the Inuit way. As one Inuit has stated:

> 'It is not always that we want a point in our stories—if only they are amusing. It is only the white men that want a reason and an explanation for everything, and so our old men say that we should treat white men as children who always want their own way. If not, they become angry and scold.'

Many stories have obviously been embellished after the coming of the white man. A basic legend tells of the woman who married a dog who took on a man's shape. But her offspring were dogs. The mother set them adrift and they formed various tribes. The last of the brood stayed with the woman and became the ancestors of the Inuit. An obviously later version relates that four of the offspring were white men. 'The girl put the four white men in the sole of a boot and set it adrift in the sea. The men drifted down and produced all the white men that are now in the world.' (Helen Caswell, *Shadows from the Singing House: Eskimo Folk Tales*, 1968.)

There is a great wealth of lore locked up in anthropological and ethnological reports that have been available since the turn of the century. Even considering all the difficulties inherent in translating in one leap an oral literature into a written literature in another language, it is still somewhat surprising that Canadian publishers have ignored this material for so long. Fortunately Americans have been more aware of its imaginative qualities and it is thanks to them that we have had such substantial collections as *Alaskan Igloo Tales* (1958) by Edward L. Keithahn, *Tundra Tales* (1967) by Nola W. Zobarskas, and an earlier book, *Beyond the Clapping Mountains* (1943) by Charles E. Gillham. The reteller has two basic choices: to keep as close as possible to the original, whether it was recorded by anthropologists or taken down orally, trusting readers to make their own link with an alien culture; or to retell the story with substantial modifications, keeping the basic spirit but adding an original and compelling creative quality. In general the Keithahn and Zobarskas collections respect Inuit culture and endeavour to appeal to children through the kinds of stories selected rather than by imposing totally

European patterns on them. Gillham, however, in *Beyond the Clapping Mountains*, softened the generally rather severe and realistic animal stories into sweet animal fantasies of the white man's tradition. This misapplication probably reflects the date of the book's publication; in the 1940s retellers and publishers did not yet understand the importance of respecting and preserving the authenticity of native material—especially in books for children.

Ronald Melzack's *The Day Tuk Became a Hunter & Other Eskimo Stories* (1967) appears to be the first Canadian collection for children. It shares many of the characteristics of Helen Caswell's *Shadows from the Singing House* (1968), based on Alaskan Eskimo lore. Both retellers used standard sources for their tales—Rasmussen, Boas, and Powers, as well as more recent collections such as Keithahn's *Alaskan Igloo Tales*—and both cast their stories very much in the European mould. However, an interesting contrast develops in their retellings of the famous story of Sedna, the archetypal undersea figure who vigilantly and mercilessly takes care that all souls of both animals and man are shown the respect that ancient rules of life demand. The Caswell book includes the starker details of the original. Sedna and her father and/or brothers (depending on the version) are pursued by Sedna's husband, and in order to lighten the boat the men throw her overboard. As she clutches the edge of the boat they cut off the first joint of her fingers, then the second, then the third, then the whole hand. Sedna becomes a sea goddess while the dismembered limbs turn into the animals that inhabit the sea—whales, walrus, and seals.

The rather gory details of the Caswell version are not all that prevalent in Inuit stories. When they do occur they are no more shocking than such episodes in European folklore and have just as strong a mythic sense. In general, Inuit stories lack the European tale's strong delineation of what is good and what is evil; a moral tone, however, might have been imposed by later generations in the stories' long cultural transmission.

Many tales, of course, are neither as stark nor as distinctive as the Sedna legend. Some, such as 'Why the Raven Is Black' (Caswell) and 'How the Raven Brought Light to the World' (Melzack), are as much Indian as Inuit, while others echo the standard plots of European folklore. 'Leealura and Maleyato' (Melzack), in which the great hunter Maleyato marries the girl whose needle makes no sound while she sews, is kin to the test story—Patient Griselda, or Cinderella and her glass slipper. 'The Man and the Star' (Caswell) is a kind of 'Jack the Giant Killer' tale and the two children in 'The Witch' (Melzack) are as victorious as Hansel and Gretel.

In *Raven, Creator of the World* (1970) Melzack says frankly that 'it was necessary to retell the stories in a way that would appeal to children in our culture'. Appealing the book is, with its attractive format and large, bold, ice-blue pictures by Laszlo Gal. The rather soft writing style is calculated to make the stories palatable as an introduction to the legends for younger children. The stories have been pieced together from various anthropological sources to make a continuous cycle of the adventures of Raven. The treatment is somewhat similar to Robert Ayre's *Sketco the Raven*—about the trickster-hero of the West Coast Indians—but lacks its strength and rough humour. Indeed, the Melzack retellings fail to evoke the power and dignity of the bird itself in its own habitat.

The Melzack book begins gently: 'In the beginning there was only Raven and the falling snowflakes' and continues through Raven's rather mild adventures until he defeats a huge serpent; he then takes his leave, since '[he] knew what he had created was good'. Inuit folklore in general reveals a more pragmatic outlook on life than deciding what is good in the world and what is bad.

In *Tales from the Igloo* (1972) Father Maurice Metayer allows the stories to speak for themselves; there is little modern embellishment. They were taken directly from the oral tradition since, as the preface tells us, they were 'first recorded on tape; each story was analyzed to obtain an exact translation. This translation in turn served as the basis for French and English texts. On occasion the text as it appears here departs from the literal translation in the interests of adhering to the style of the English and French languages. Yet the smallest detail of Inuit thought has been faithfully respected.' (Father Metayer, who has lived with the Eskimos since 1939, has also written *Unipkat: Tradition esquimaude de Coppermine, Territoires-du-Nord-Ouest, Canada*, 3 vols, 1973.) Although *Tales from the Igloo* is mainly based on the culture of the Copper Eskimo, several of the stories, such as 'The Blind Boy and the Loon', are found in other Inuit groups. The majority are animal stories, but several are obviously based on historical events, especially 'Lost at Sea', which has the traditional plot of a young man adrift on floating ice. In many of the stories poetry is used as naturally and joyfully as it is used by the Inuit themselves. The illustrations are very fine—bright in colour and active in line. They are by Agnes Nanogak, whose father was with Stefansson when he lived with the Copper Eskimos in 1910.

Agnes Nanogak is both the reteller and illustrator of *More Tales from the Igloo* (1986). As the preface notes:

> The stories Nanogak tells here are not concerned with the creation of the cosmos or the religious beliefs of her people, they are concerned with problems of everyday life, they are legends that have some basis in historical facts and events.

They are also ones that Nanogak drew upon from her own vast personal knowledge of Inuit myth and legend of the Western Arctic. Nanogak divides her retellings into three parts: 'Tales of Birds and Beasts' (folklore), 'Tales of Adventure' (legend), and 'Tales of Sorrow and Revenge'.

In most of the stories the events seem to have a deeper meaning than can be understood by a non-Inuit. In 'Kopilgok (Worms)' a wife accidentally kills her brother-in-law, who has been teasing her. When the husband finds the body of his brother, he plots his revenge by preparing a pit of worms that feed off the bodies of dead caribou. He intends to throw his wife into the pit, but she has been warned by a lemming she has befriended and by magic the husband falls into his own trap. The story ends: 'The wife turned into a wolverine and went on her way.' The reason for the wife's sudden transformation is puzzling, like so many transformations in Inuit lore. By contrast 'The Wealthy Man's Daughter' is a simple, coherent version (but without a happy ending) of the numerous European tales of the proud daughter who refuses to accept a husband of her father's choice, generally a young man who outwits the princess and wins her love.

On the whole, *More Tales from the Igloo* is a more intriguing collection than *Tales from the Igloo*, chiefly because of its stronger mythic sense and its illustrations that interpret the inner power of the story surrealistically. Although based on the oral tradition as recounted by an Inuit, *More Tales from the Igloo* is still a book in translation: the tales were put into English by Nanogak's son and daughter-in-law.

Herbert T. Schwarz, in *Elik and Other Stories of the Mackenzie Eskimos* (1970), also comes close to the living oral tradition. On a four-month storytelling hunt Schwarz found exemplars of a still-vigorous tradition who told their stories in English or in their own dialect with on-the-spot translation. (Vignettes about these storytellers form an interesting appendix to the book.) As a doctor practising in the North, Schwarz joins the small group of professionals—explorers, missionaries, and administrators—who have done the most to preserve and spread the culture of the North.

Because the tales in *Elik* are rooted in one geographical location (the Mackenzie District), with an identifiable topography, and in everyday life rather than in a mysterious and primitive past, they seem more immediate and modern than most legends. Some are now standard: the story of the boy who was blinded by his stepmother (in other versions his mother), the story of Raven and the whale spirit (the spirit of the whale is always a beautiful girl). Others are less imaginative than informative: about the events that occur when Inuit and Indian meet, the preparations and the hazards of the whale hunt, etc. Present in all the stories is respect for taboos and for the power of the medicine man, revealing a people who are cautious in the face of a harsh environment rather than superstitious. The work of the Inuit illustrator Mona Ohoveluk is in the tradition of the lively, impressive graphic art that has become familiar in the last three decades through Eskimo prints and drawings.

Stories from Pangnirtung (1976) has far less of a storytelling quality than *Tales from the Igloo* and *More Tales from the Igloo* since it is more oral history than legend. Told by survivors of the nomadic way of life, these recollections include elements of folk customs and traditions. They are illustrated by an Inuit artist, Germaine Arnaktavyok.

Three books of single illustrated Inuit tales are beautifully illustrated and show the diversity of Inuit material. If it were not for the descriptive passages, James Houston's *Kiviok's Magic Journey: An Eskimo Legend* (1973) might have stepped from the pages of the Brothers Grimm, with its theme of the beautiful girls whose cloaks of goose feathers are stolen while they bathe. Here the girls are snow geese, the thief who steals the feathers of one of them is Raven in his wicked manifestation, and the hero who travels far to recover his wife and children is Kiviok the Eskimo. The axe of a friendly giant flings out bright chips of ivory and Kiviok is carried into the sea beneath the ice on the back of a sea trout. Calling the silvery fish, he chants: 'Bubbles, bubbles/End my troubles./Help me now,/Oh magic fish.' All these details, especially the incantation and the journey itself, are reminiscent of European folklore.

Houston has long been known for his authentic legend-type stories of the Inuit—spare narratives that in style, detail, and impact are honed to the essence. He has diverged from that style in *Kiviok's Magic Journey*, probably to interest quite young children for whom this picture-storybook is intended. His illustrations are softer than his usual severe, sculptured pictures based on Eskimo carvings; they swirl and dance. Like the text, they give the story a fairy-tale quality that is remarkably different from other published Inuit tales.

Kiviok's Magic Journey works well as an integrated picture-storybook; it is an interesting story well told, although deviating from the more general harsh stories of Inuit lore. By contrast, Garnet Hewitt's picture-storybook, *Ytek and the Arctic Orchid* (1981), gives evidence of research into Inuit life, but is in many ways too complex for the age-group the format invites. It tells of a rites-of-passage quest that is filled with psychological and archetypal meanings and lacks a clean narrative shape. When young Ytek finds his spirit guide (his Tornrak) he becomes a shaman and sets out to find out why the caribou (the Tuktu) were deserting the Inuit hunting grounds. Ytek is guided by his Tornrak (a gyrfalcon) and comes across some beautiful crimson flowers, seemingly untouched by the bitter wind:

> Uncertain if he was awake or dreaming, he bent his head and touched one of the velvet-soft petals with his lips. At the moment his lips met the petal, the entire ice surface trembled. . . . With a loud noise the middle of the circle splintered into a slippery funnel.

The magic orchids plunge him beneath the ice into a world of both winter and summer inhabited by the spirits of the Tuktu from whom he learns the reason for the disappearance of the caribou. He faces and defeats the evil—a 'great-bear-demon'—and saves his people from starvation. The orchid of the title, introduced as a contrived piece of magic, disappears from the plot. The story is more than a little redeemed by Heather Woodall's illustrations that in brilliant colours combine traditional Inuit motifs with contemporary graphic designs. The double-spread of the demon-bear is particularly effective.

The third single-legend book is perhaps the most distinctive and most beautiful. *The Enchanted Caribou* (1985)—sadly, Elizabeth Cleaver's last book—has as its implied theme metamorphosis and symbolic death and rebirth. Her simple, haunting text, which includes sacred chants and magical incantations, recounts the enchantment of an Inuit maiden who is transformed into a white caribou and then back into a woman. The stunning illustrations—black silhouettes, contrived for shadow puppetry—beautifully complement the text.

There is a vast pool of Inuit material still lying undisturbed in the pages of anthropological studies, and probably much more residing untapped in the memories of old people. Neither source is easily reachable. The report literature is fragmented, and imbedded within the wider framework of Inuit thought and culture. From all accounts the Inuit are shy about revealing their tales. After all, myth, legend, and folktale should be shrouded in mystery, linked as they are to religion, ritual, and taboo. And, naturally enough, the storyteller does not stop to explain things to his audience.

There are not many books of Inuit legends for children, but those we have—whether they are in the European tradition of Melzack and Caswell, or in the less-polished but more authentic tradition of Schwarz and Metayer—have revealed a rich world of fact and fantasy that has irresistible appeal. They show us not only the distinctive landscape of snow and ice, igloo and tent, walrus and polar bear, but the inner meaning of the way of life that the land imposes—the desperate struggle for survival, the kinship with animals, the reasons for Inuit fear and laughter, for revenge and kindness. The world of the Inuit and of his imagination has universal significance.

7

Folk and Fairy Tales

In a letter to her family in England, written in 1833, Catharine Parr Traill commented on the lack of faerie lore in Canada, her new home:

> As to ghosts or spirits they appear totally banished from Canada. This is too matter-of-fact country for such supernaturals to visit. Here there are no historical associations, no legendary tales of those that came before us. Fancy would starve for lack of marvelous food to keep her alive in the backwoods. We have neither fay nor fairy, ghost nor bogle, satyr nor wood-nymph; our very forests disdain to shelter dryad or hamadryad.

Of course with hindsight we realize that our forests, lakes, rivers, mountains, and plains *were* filled with supernatural beings, those of our native peoples. Still, over a hundred and fifty years later one of our modern fantasists—Janet Lunn in *Shadow in Hawthorn Bay* (1986)—makes the same assumption about the lack of 'faerie' in the new world as did Mrs Traill. Lunn's fifteen-year-old heroine, Mary Urquhart, a Scottish immigrant in the early 1830s, who is endowed with second sight, sees that she and her kind are the lone vessels through which folklore and its attendant benefits will be poured from the Old World into Canada.

There can be little doubt that the early English settlers, like the French, brought with them in their emotional baggage the tales and superstitions of their own country. But in England of the 1830s folk and fairy tales were not, in general, thought appropriate reading for children (see Chapter 1), and it is not surprising that in a pragmatic, hard-working pioneer society the folktale did not take root either by virtue of planting or of transplanting. For the early settlers the cutting down of a tree meant shelter and firewood and the clearing of the land for crops, not the disturbance of a tree fairy who would then grant the poor woodcutter three wishes. In Mrs Traill's own Ontario milieu, replete with Loyalists or their descendants, she would not have heard tales that had been carried across the border, for although the indigenous American 'tall tales' might have been in the making by the 1830s, they had not yet been written down and so were not generally known. The first major published American works of myth, legend, and folklore were all mined from British and European material—Nathaniel Hawthorne's retelling of Greek myths in *A Wonder Book* (1852) and *Tanglewood Tales* (1853), Thomas Bulfinch's *The Age of Fable* (1855) and *The Age of Chivalry* (1859), and Howard Pyle's *The Merry Adventures of Robin Hood* (1883). However, they are part of American literature by virtue of their having been retold and rewritten by Americans, and it is in such a context that the first major collection of Canadian fairy tales must be viewed. However, it comes one hundred and twenty-five years after Mrs Traill's lament.

The Golden Phoenix and Other French-Canadian Fairy Tales (1958) by Marius Barbeau and Michael Hornyansky is, as its subtitle indicates, a group of stories brought over from France by the colonists who settled along the lower St Lawrence River. They were collected by the noted French-Canadian ethnologist and anthropologist Marius Barbeau, who mentions in an end-note that their original versions are filed in the National Museum of Canada. He published in 1950-3 a large collection of his own retellings of them in French in twelve paperback volumes, *Les Contes du Grand'Père Sept Heures*, from which *The Golden Phoenix* stories were selected. Hornyansky translated and retold them so well that they will surely never be improved upon in English. Indeed, their polish gives them the sheen of well-told English folktales; but the mode of the oral storyteller, which is an essential ingredient of the French originals, is very much present. Two of the stories concern Petit-Jean, the traditional hero of the folktale in Quebec; like Jack of the English fairy tales, he is usually the youngest son—quick-witted, kind, and resourceful. The stories are excellent in themselves, for telling as well as reading, and Hornyansky has provided what can be considered touchstone versions of each of them in a tone close to the witty and urbane style of the French seventeenth-century poet and courtier Charles Perrault, who gave classic form to the stories of 'Cinderella', 'Bluebeard', and 'The Sleeping Beauty.' Those in *The Golden Phoenix* range from the traditional 'fairyish' fairy tale, 'The Fairy Quite Contrary', to a rather naughty *fabliau*, 'Jacques the Woodcutter', a plot first made famous by Boccaccio.

The first story in the collection, 'The Princess of Tomboso' has become the best known (partly because in 1960 it was published in a picture-book version with lively, humorous illustrations in colour and black and white by Frank Newfeld). It recounts the familiar theme of the vain and selfish princess who eventually gets her come-uppance. An astute mixture of the traditional and realistic, it has a refreshingly tart ending and Hornyansky has retold it in a contemporary idiom and with a rhythm and lilt that bring out all its humour:

> He took the bowl and shook it. A leather belt fell out. Written on it in letters of gold were these words:
>
> PUT ME ON AND TELL ME WHERE:
> QUICK AS LIGHTNING YOU'LL BE THERE
>
> Jacques lost no time. Clasping the belt around his waist, he wished himself into the castle. Whoosh!—and there he stood inside the castle. He wished himself back into the barn. Whoosh! There he was back again.
>
> 'Well, it works,' he said. 'Now I can travel cheap.'

The Golden Phoenix is a work of distinction and alongside of it other books from about the same period seem lifeless. James McNeill's *The Sunken City* (1959) and *The Double Knights* (1964) are collections of tales from around the world with no attempt made to give them a Canadian interpretation, and the retellings are so uniform in style as almost to deny any relationship to a country of origin except for some place-names. The value of the books lies in their selections—they are not the most familiar or standard tales of each country. *The Lucky Coin and Other Folk Tales Canadians Tell* (1972) by Leslie Quinton (pseud.) includes stories from the homelands of some of the ethnic cultures that make up the Canadian population—Norwegian, Finnish, Sikh, *et al.*—along with those of native, French, and English origin. The sources are standard, but only in one case is an acknowledgement given. Notes on the cultures represented are so oversimplified as to be condescending, if not misleading and sometimes comic. For example: 'Ukrainians crave freedom' (as if no one else does), and 'Among the twenty thousand people of Spanish descent in Canada, few are fishermen.'

Almost twenty years after *The Golden Phoenix* was published, Mary Alice Downie retold nine French-Canadian folktales in *The Witch of the North* (1975), which was illustrated by Elizabeth Cleaver. These tales of the Witch Canoe, the Loup-Garou, and other figures from French-Canadian folklore are retold with storytelling expertise in a book that deserves greater recognition. Downie's *The Wicked Fairy-Wife: A French-Canadian Folktale* (1983), illustrated by Kim Price, is a powerful treatment—unusual in picture-storybooks—of good and evil, romantic love and violent revenge. Stories of tricking the Devil appear in most Christian cultures. Downie's retelling of *How the Devil Got His Cat* (1988) is set in eighteenth-century Quebec complete with pious nuns and a mischievous black cat that had grown 'as fat as a priest'. The voice of the oral storyteller is heard as it begins: ' "You all must know," said my grandmother, "that the Devil keeps a cat." ' In this story he acquires it through the wit and cunning of the Mother Superior. The charming silhouettes by Jillian Hulme Gilliland demonstrate her sharp eye for details of landscape, architecture, and dress of the period, as well as for comic caricature. Claude Aubry's definitive retellings of legends of French Canada in *The Magic Fiddler* (1968) show how French-Canadian storytellers have been particularly adept at melding legend, history, and native life to make a unique folklore. The same amalgam is present in Joyce Barkhouse's *The Witch of Port LaJoye* (1983), a Prince Edward Island legend of a French-Canadian woman who married a Micmac and was branded a witch at Port LaJoye in 1723. Daphne Irving's shimmering watercolours add to the romance of the tale.

One of the very few lavish picture-storybooks of the 1970s was *Simon and the Golden Sword* (1976) by Frank Newfeld. About the quest of three sons for the Sword of Light, and the triumph, after misadventures, of the youngest, it is akin to many classic European tales, though the text was adapted by Newfeld and William Toye from a story told by Wilson MacDonald of Glenwood, N.B., and recorded by Helen Creighton. The formula of the story never ceases to appeal, but it is Newfeld's beautiful, witty, and elegant colour illustrations that give this book distinction.

The idea behind Eva Martin's *Canadian Fairy Tales* (1984), illustrated by Laszlo Gal, was to retell some of the stories 'collected by folklorists in the early twentieth century from the second or third generations of settlers who in their retelling of the stories retained the original theme motifs, and adapted the stories to suit their new environment.' Martin's versions are, therefore, retellings of retellings, and on the whole are disappointing. Except for the introduction of the name Ti-Jean (Petit-Jean) in three of the tales, all of them are European (stories of princesses, giants and witches—the stuff of the classic fairy tales) and have no local colouring. Indeed, in retelling Cyrus Macmillan's 'St. Nicholas and the Children' she deletes the word 'Canadian' from his first sentence and substitutes 'far to the north'. Some of the stories are simply not worth the retelling; and others are available in far better versions. 'Beauty and the Beast', for example, bears no resemblance to Mme de Beaumont's famous tale of the girl Beauty who asked her father for only a single rose, in contrast to the two elder daughters who demanded extravagant gifts. We are given instead a mishmash of several well-known European tales, with scenes of violence that are not in the convention of fine folktales. The opening story in this collection, 'The Healing Spring', is faithful in plot to its Nova Scotian source, but it is not a good story. The rivalry between the wicked brother and the good brother is a common theme in folktales, generally recounted with humour, much like that of the 'tall tale'. Rather than humour, this story has violence that is untypically disturbing. The wicked brother murders his wife for gain, but the so-called good brother is a trickster and not all that pleasant. 'The Princess of Tomboso' is more briefly told than by Michael Hornyansky in *The Golden Phoenix*, and one immediately longs for the cadence of his language and, in particular, his rhyming couplets: 'Blow one end, and your troops appear;/The other, and the field is clear'. There is an overall feeling that these retellings require the warm voice of the storyteller to bring them alive. Laszlo Gal's artwork projects two very different styles. His full-coloured paintings have a romantic quality and are akin to those that adorn many turn-of-the-century collections of European tales. The Canadian element is found in the borders surrounding them, being sketches in black-and-white of pioneer artifacts and flora and fauna, with hints of the ever-present wilderness.

The impact of New World culture and mythology on the first explorers, adventurers, and missionaries is shown very clearly in Mary Hamilton's *A New World Bestiary* (1985). These early visitors to North America, though keen observers, were far from unwilling to believe any strange stories they heard—monsters of the imagination that include the Newfoundland 'Uniped', the St Lawrence cannibal 'Gou-Gou', and the 'Sasquatch' of British Columbia. The monsters are given concrete form in Kim LaFave's swirling illustrations in sepia and full colour—the whole making an unusual picture-storybook.

Canadian pioneer literature is filled with references to settlers (especially from England) who came to this country with no experience of farm life. In *The Mare's Egg: A New World Folk Tale* (1981) a naïve immigrant who needs a horse is tricked into believing that a pumpkin will hatch a foal. Carole Spray has cleverly combined what was probably fact with the gullible character so familiar in folk literature and produced a 'noodlehead' tale that is an excellent example of the transference of an old theme to a new locale. Kim LaFave's illustrations draw every ounce of humour out of the tale and give it the appropriate pioneer setting.

Jenni Lunn's transference in *The Fisherman and His Wife* (1982) of the Grimms' tale to modern Nova Scotia is less successful, although it does have some delightful touches, such as the refrain 'Wifey-wifey, love of m'lifey'. However, the wife's wanting bathrooms, servants, and her husband to be Chief Inspector of the Fisheries Department has in no way the awesome, cumulative power of the Grimms' wife wanting to be king, emperor, and then Pope. The moral of the old tale is the simple one of the consequences of greed; Lunn unfortunately felt obliged to add a lesson about the importance of the natural environment.

Joan Finnigan is a specialist in the lore of the Ottawa Valley and in *Look! The Land Is Growing Giants: A Very Canadian Legend* (1983) she builds her knowledge of Joe Montferrand, the gentle lumber-boss whose giant size and courage became a local legend in the nineteenth century, into a witty 'tall tale'. It is very Canadian indeed, with its rollicking catalogue of Ottawa Valley place-names, the epic battle between Joe and the native evil spirit, the Windigo, and its conclusion with Joe's children becoming the first Montreal Canadiens and their children's children eventually forming all the hockey teams in North America. Finnigan adds a gentle touch of satire. When the Windigo is being burned (it is the only way to get rid of a Windigo),

For the first time in the history of the Ottawa Valley, the Ladies' Aid of Ladysmith Catholic Church and the Ladies' Aid of Shawville Methodist joined together and set up Baked Bean, Pie and Cake Booths to feed the multitude on the hillside.

And after fighting the Windigo, when Joe goes to see his 'lady-friend', 'people all along the shore in both Quebec and Ontario came out to cheer him in both French and English.' Richard Pelham's sketches are as humorously rooted in place and time as the text.

It is reasonable to suppose that the nineteenth-century Ukrainian collection of fables, *Fox Mykyta* by Ivan Franko, was chosen for re-publication in Canada in 1978 both to provide a vehicle for the artwork of the well-known Ukrainian-Canadian artist William Kurelek, and as an extension to the brief illustrated memoirs of his own Ukrainian-Canadian childhood presented in *A Prairie Boy's Winter* (1973) and *A Prairie Boy's Summer* (1975). Whatever the reason, it is a wonderfully funny collection of fables. *Fox Mykyta* is reminiscent of the medieval trickster Reynard the Fox. Kurelek's black-and-white sketches of anthropomorphized animals reveal a sharp eye for satire that is in no way present in his picturebook memoirs. Other Ukrainian folktales, translated and retold by Victoria Symchych and Olga Vesey in *The Flying Ship* (1975), are standard ones, but these are not distinguished retellings.

Children's versions of most of the world's folktale heritage are available in English, and have been so for some time—at least since the 1960s. However, it is only in recent years (indeed, since *Fox Mykyta*) that some members of our various cultural groups have retold the tales of their native land in Canadian books. *Fables and Legends from Ancient China* (1985), retold by Shiu L. Kong and Elizabeth K. Wong, is a collection of short tales, often with a humorous twist. In the first story a seven-year-old girl mathematician shows her elders how to divide seventeen peaches by three (and no fractions!), and in the last story a clever servant outwits his miserly master. In between are a few stories with universal themes, such as that of an old couple who waste their three wishes, as in the Grimms' tale of the old couple and the sausage. A companion volume is *Korean Folk Tales* (1986), 19 short tales—gentle, humorous, and moral in tone—retold by Yu Chai-Shin, Shiu L. Kong, and Ruth W. Yu. *Gonbei's Magic Kettle: A Folktale in Japanese and English* (1980), by Michiko Nakamura and illustrated by San Murata, is a classic tale here retold with wit and simplicity. It is in the Kids Can Press 'Folktale Library', a series of bilingual picture-book editions of international folklore. The parallel texts in the language of origin and the English translation suggest that cultural continuity is possible within the Canadian multicultural mosaic, and that the folklore of all ethnic groups can enrich mainstream Canadian culture while retaining its own identity.

English-language retellers have not neglected the oral tradition of other cultures. The sub-title of Gwendolyn MacEwen's *The Honey Drum* (1983) is *Seven Tales from Arab Lands*. She notes in her preface that five of them are 'as well known in the Arabic-speaking world as *Cinderella* or *Hansel and Gretel* are in the West'. The tales are certainly Arabic in tone, and 'The Honey Drum' has even become familiar through other retellings. However, none are retold in a memorable style and the two tales that MacEwen wrote herself are even less distinguished. Still, the collection is valuable as the only example of Arabic folklore to come out of Canada.

As with native legends, the retelling and publishing of a single folktale is a noticeable trend. Many are lavishly illustrated and produced and, in general, taken from the European tradition. Janet Lunn's *The Twelve Dancing Princesses* (1979) is a version of 'The Shoes That Were Danced to Pieces' by the Brothers Grimm, in which an old soldier, with little to lose, risks his life to discover the secret of the twelve princesses' worn-out slippers. As a reward for his success he is offered the hand of one of the princesses in marriage and chooses the eldest—since, as he says, 'I am no longer young.' The tale is more commonly known as 'The Twelve Dancing Princesses' and is attributed to a French source (Charles Deulin's *Contes du Roi Cambrinus*, 1874) by the American reteller Virginia Haviland, in her *Favorite Fairy Tales Told Round the World* (1959). Both French-based versions (Haviland's and Lunn's) are highly romanticized (a young peasant lad wins both the heart and the hand of the youngest princess), and both also verge toward the longer, sophisticated literary fairy tale rather than to the short, taut Grimms' folktale, with its implied peasant shrewdness. Lunn's style is much more graceful than that of Haviland and is enhanced by rhyming couplets. The romantic essence of the tale is carried out in the illustrations by Laszlo Gal, who also provided a similar style of artwork for Margaret Crawford Maloney's *The Little Mermaid* (1983), a version of Hans Christian Andersen's tale. Maloney's text does not deviate significantly from the definitive translation by Erik Christian Haugaard (a Dane, like Andersen), except in Andersen's ending, which has a Christian mysticism. Maloney's is completely secular.

Robin Muller has retold and illustrated several folktales: *Mollie Whuppie and the Giant* (1982), *Tatterhood* (1984), *The Lucky Old Woman* (1987), and *Little Kay* (1988). Of them all, 'Mollie Whuppie' is the best known through the collections of English fairy tales by Joseph Jacobs and Flora Annie Steel. Mollie is one of the many feisty heroines of folklore. She saves her own and her sisters' lives from the cruel giant, tricks him, steals his treasures, and obtains husbands for her sisters and herself. Muller extends the older versions with minor details, such as Mollie making the giant's wife promise to turn her castle into a shelter for travellers. Muller felt it necessary to change the giant's traditional salutation, '*Fee-fi-fo fum,/ I smell the blood of an Englishman*' to '*Fee, fie, grunt and groan,/ I am ready for blood and bone.*' The short, rhythmic exchanges between Mollie and the giant, given only slight variations by Jacobs and Steel, are here lengthened, and Mollie's imprecation differs each time. One such is:

> Grump, grump, you gormless lump,
> Stupid threats don't frighten me.
> Grump, grump, you gormless lump,
> I'll be back, just wait and see!

Folktale heroes and heroines are always brave and wily, but they are never rude!

The sources of Muller's tales are not indicated in any part of the book, so it is difficult to make comparisons with other versions unless one has personal knowledge of them. His title *Tatterhood* brings to mind the English folktale 'Tattercoats', but except for the duplication of tattered clothing, there is little resemblance between Muller's story and that of Joseph Jacobs in *More English Fairy Tales*. Little Kay is not Sir Kay of the Arthurian legends but a brave and cunning girl-child (Muller seems to specialize in them), who has the verve of a Mollie Whuppie and here has wandered into an Arabian Nights setting. Muller's *The Sorcerer's Apprentice* (1985) has only the title in common with the old, old tale—first told by Lucien of Samosata (about AD 200) and in verse by Goethe—about the apprentice who learns only part of his master's spells and gets into trouble when he cannot stop them. Muller's apprentice has to fight against an evil magician and is aided by a white dove, who finally turns into a beautiful princess. Wherever Muller has found his sources, he does not have the innate poetic voice of the best of the old storytellers, nor does he have an effective modern voice. As with so many single illustrated folktales, one suspects that his texts have been devised as vehicles for the illustrator—in this case himself. And he has interpreted them with a good deal of spirit (see pp. 179-80).

Frances Harber's *My King Has Donkey Ears* (1986)—the tale of a selfish, cruel, arrogant king who suddenly grows donkey's ears—has an obvious source in the Greek legend of King Midas who was given asses's ears by Apollo for preferring music other than Apollo's. Midas preserved his shame from all except his barber, who could not resist telling about it, and so whispered it into a hole in the ground. However, the reeds that grew out of the hole whispered it whenever the wind blew through them. Harber has made the king Korean and has changed the barber to a tailor who makes the king a gorgeous turban to hide his disgrace. She keeps the whispering of the reeds, but has the tailor tell his secret to his three concerned friends (he could have his head chopped off for telling it), which makes for considerable suspense and humour, and she adds a clever wife. The story, which is very well told, is delicately but humorously illustrated by Maryann Kovalski.

Variants of folktales exist in all cultures (there are about four hundred extant of 'Cinderella'), and modern retellers certainly have the privilege of change and adaptation, as did our anonymous ancestors. The Americans George and Helen Papashvily wisely tell us in their *Yes and No Stories* (1946) that 'A story is a letter that comes to us from yesterday. Each man who tells it adds his word to the message and sends it on to tomorrow.' However, licence should be used both cautiously and deftly. More importantly, the spirit of the original story should not be changed; if it is, one wonders about the admissibility of using the same title. Both the Canadian trend towards retelling stories from other cultures (particularly European) and a departure from standard texts that amount to pointless revisionism can be seen in Adele Fasick's *The Beauty Who Would Not Spin* (1989), H. Werner Zimmerman's *Henny Penny* (1989), and Tamara Lynn Thiebaux's *Goldilocks and the Three Bears* (1989), which are also obvious vehicles for the artistic interpretations of their reteller-illustrators and, in the case of Fasick's book, of Leslie Elizabeth Watts.

Fasick, in *The Beauty Who Would Not Spin*, drastically changes the girl's character from that of the standard Irish version found in Seumas MacManus's *Hiberian Nights* (1963) and from the better-known English 'Tom Tit Tot'. Fasick makes her loving, cheerful, and lively rather than shiftless and lazy. The charm of the traditional versions lies in the fact that the girl wins through anyway. Zimmerman decorously closes *Henny Penny* with a discreet reference to the barnyard fowl who followed the fox into his den and 'were never seen again'. Excised from Joseph Jacobs' 'Henny Penny' in *English Fairy Tales* (1892) is the suspense and violence of the fox snapping off each bird's head, as well as (surprisingly) Henny Penny's satisfying escape. The story of 'The Three Bears' has been attributed both to the poet Robert Southey and to Eleanor Mure (in the nineteenth century), but it can be said to have passed into folk literature. Flora Annie Steel in *English Fairy Tales* (1918) may have been the first to replace Southey's and Mure's 'little old woman' with the child 'Goldilocks'. Thiebaux's *Goldilocks and the Three Bears* is traditional enough in its title, but the repetitive and rhythmic phrases such as 'and [the porridge] was neither too hot, nor too cold, but just right' have been gracelessly replaced. The greatest change, however, is in Goldilocks herself. Rather than being presented as a curious (perhaps mischievous) child, she here repents for breaking Baby Bear's chair and makes amends by giving him a new one. In all these three retellings, the life and humour of the original stories are provided by the illustrations, not by the texts.

There is a legend that Robert I of Scotland (Robert the Bruce), when defeated by the English, learned determination and patience from watching a spider persevere in spinning its web. Margaret Crawford Maloney's *The Goodman of Ballengiech* (1987) is a similar combination of history and legend. It is taken from an episode in Sir Walter Scott's *Tales of a Grandfather* (1827) concerning James V of Scotland, generally remembered now as the father of Mary, Queen of Scots. As a young king, James wandered in disguise among his people to learn first-hand of any injustices. His life was saved by a farmer whom he suitably rewarded. Maloney does not deviate to any great extent from Scott's tale, nor does she embellish it, and her retelling is greatly enhanced by Laszlo Gal's illustrations, which capture the atmosphere of sixteenth-century Scotland. They are among the best he has ever done.

Folktales have long been available on records and cassettes, especially from the United States, and are frequently read by well-know actors and actresses. Collections of folktales on cassettes are now published in Canada with the voices of professional Canadian storytellers. Notable are Alice Kane's *Tales from an Irish Hearth* (1985), ten traditional Irish cottage tales; Sarah Ellis and Bill Richardson's *Mud & Gold* (1986) and *Pobbles & Porridge Pots* (1986), a medley of tales chiefly from the European tradition; and Nan Gregory's and Melanie Ray's Chinese *Moon Tales* (1989).

Folklore comes in many guises, from non-verbal ones like embroidery and dances to songs and games. In *The Lore and Language of School Children* the famous English collectors and interpreters of such material, Iona and Peter Opie, quote Dr Arbuthnot, the eighteenth-century physician and writer: 'Nowhere was tradition preserved pure and uncorrupt "but amongst Schoolboys whose Games and Plays are delivered down invariably from one generation to another." ' That Canadian children are still carrying on their own traditions in songs, rhymes, and games (the nursery rhymes are transmitted by adults) can be seen in Edith Fowke's *Sally Go Round the Sun: Three Hundred Songs, Rhymes and Games of Canadian Children* (1969), in which she has brought together the street-lore of Canadian children. Although her material is not exclusively Canadian, some old rhymes have acquired a Canadian reference: 'Oh, I don't want no more of army life/ Gee, Mom, I wanna go / Back to On-ta-ri-o!' As the Opies' book has shown us, children creatively invent and unselfconsciously perpetuate jokes and rhymes and games without any interference from adults. 'Roses are red, violets are green / My face is funny, but yours is a scream' may not be great literature, but it shows that the oral tradition of children's games is alive and well in Canada. Fowke's companion volume, *Ring Around the Moon: Two Hundred Songs, Tongue Twisters, Riddles and Rhymes of Canadian Children* (1977), also offers a look into the brash energy of children's demotic language as well as at the ongoing folk-life of children's verbal games. For adult interest, source notes are provided. In the last decade musical performance of this traditional poetry has increased greatly with the rise of popular Canadian singer-songwriters—such as Raffi, Fred Penner, and the trio of Sharon, Lois, and Bram. They have moved beyond performance and recording to produce books of verse, music, and song. The best of these is *Sharon, Lois and Bram's Mother Goose* (1985), a collection of traditional and contemporary verses with piano and guitar arrangements and playful illustrations by Maryann Kovalski. Thematically structured, the cycle of 153 rhymes and songs chronicles a single day in the life of an exuberant family. Its panoply of language and image resembles the richness of the now-classic *Mother Goose Treasury* (1966), a bumper collection robustly illustrated by the British artist Raymond Briggs. Plasticine art by Barbara Reid decorates a smaller but completely traditional collection of nursery rhymes in *Sing a Song of Mother Goose* (1987).

'Once upon a time there was—a king, a sultan, a princess, a poor shepherd, a poor woodcutter.' Thus, with few variations, begin the folk and fairy tales that are a part of the world's heritage of traditional literature. Their origins are unknown; they survived by word of mouth until they were captured on the printed page. However, the advent of print did not lock the stories into an immutable formula, as occurred with the myths. The tales of Psyche and Eros or Oedipus are so fundamental that their very names have become symbols larger than themselves, and their variants are literary rather than ethnic—Sophocles' classical presentation of Antigone and Creon, as opposed to the revisionist approach of Jean Anouilh. This is in contrast to folklore, in which character, plot, and cultural background have constantly changed in retelling. Every country has its store of national tales—'Tom Thumb' (England), 'Rapunzel' (Germany), 'The

Baba Yaga' (Russia), 'The Boy Who Learned to Shudder' (Japan), 'Stan Bolovan' (Romania), and the tales of Anansi the Spider (Africa and the West Indies). Yet versions of all of them (or at least echoes of them) can be found in other parts of the world. No one knows if the tales spread outward from a common stock, or if their themes were so universal—reflecting the love, fear, terror, passion, and humour that dwell in the human heart—that each country in its primitive era evolved much the same plots.

Since the folktale, by strict definition, is the product of a primitive, non-literate society, North Americans, other than the Indians and the Inuit, cannot claim an indigenous literature. However, Americans, far sooner than Canadians, adapted and recreated folktales deriving from European, Asian, or African origins. An early example is Joel Chandler Harris's *Uncle Remus: His Songs and Sayings: The Folk-lore of the Old Plantations* (1881), which has its origin in African folklore, but which made Brer Rabbit and Brer Fox American household words. Richard Chase's *The Jack Tales* (1943) transferred the stories of the English Jack ('Jack and the Beanstalk', 'Jack the Giant-killer') to an Appalachian setting and dialect. 'Tall tales' are not an American invention (consider those of Baron Munchausen), but in many ways the Americans made them their own by combining legend and fact with their own heroes—Davey Crockett, Johnny Appleseed, John Henry, and the baseball hero 'Casey at the Bat'.

French-Canadians have a store of folklore that fitted early and easily into the local atmosphere and culture—including many of the supernatural/religious tales that can now be considered Canadian classics: 'The Flying Canoe', the 'Loupe Garou', and 'Rose Latulipe', about the French-Canadian peasant-girl who was danced away by the devil, but was rescued by the local parish priest. In comparison, the folklore of English-speaking Canada appears to be small, fragmented, and regional. Still, in embracing all ethnic cultures, it may well come to be the most Canadian of all.

8

Fantasy

The sub-title of J.R.R. Tolkien's *The Hobbit; or, There and Back Again* epitomizes the tradition of fantasy for children from its beginnings in the middle of the Victorian age to the 1960s. The protagonists (and so the readers) enter, and return from, a fully created Other World: Lewis Carroll's Wonderland or C.S. Lewis's Narnia or J.M.Barrie's Never-land or Charles Kingsley's riverscape of *The Water-Babies* (1863). Such worlds, described by Tolkien as 'Secondary', are not to be considered inferior to the real or Primary world, for it takes art to create them. Many fantasies plunge us into make-believe worlds from the first line of the first page and keep us there until the story is over: we live completely in Tolkien's Middle-earth, Ursula Le Guin's Earthsea, or Lloyd Alexander's Prydain. In others the protagonists make only brief trips into another time or dimension, as does little Diamond, nestled snugly in North Wind's hair, in George MacDonald's *At the Back of the North Wind* (1871), or Will Stanton, questing in the Lost Land, in Susan Cooper's *Silver on the Tree* (1977).

Whatever type of unreality these authors contrived, the meaning and purposes of fantasy remained the same. Fantasy was used to illuminate (indeed intensify) reality, not to distort it; to propound a set of universal values, not to preach; to link the natural and supernatural worlds without denigrating either. In all such serious fantasies a journey is at the heart of the plot and embodies the heroic quest as expressed by Joseph Campbell—the departure, the initiation, and the return. This aspect of fantasy kept it close to its roots of myth, legend, and folklore. The Mesopotamian hero

Gilgamesh (*The Epic of Gilgamesh*, 3000 B.C.) goes on a quest that turns out differently from what he expected and he comes back a changed person; so do Bilbo Baggins in Tolkien's *The Hobbit* (1937) and Ged in Ursula Le Guin's *Earthsea* trilogy (1968-74). Whether used literally or symbolically by fantasists, the quest story essentially leads to a change for the better in its heroes and heroines. George MacDonald's Curdie of *The Princess and Curdie* (1883) and his Diamond of *At the Back of the North Wind* attain a higher spirituality (much like King Arthur's knights, who go in search of the Holy Grail); the children in C.S. Lewis's *Narnia* chronicles (1950-6) or in Susan Cooper's *The Dark Is Rising* quintet (1965-77) struggle to save a world from evil; and Winnie, in Natalie Babbitt's *Tuck Everlasting* (1975), comes to understand the meaning of mortality. But whatever the purpose of writers in expressing themselves through the use of the supernatural, fantasy offered (in Tolkien's words) 'Recovery, Escape and Consolation'.

Since the middle of the 1960s most fantasies have almost reversed these conventions, with writers using the supernatural as forces to break into the real world, often bringing with them violence and terror. Frequently the events are caused by the unhappiness, or the problems, of the chief protagonist, much as in the realistic problem novel. Modern writers of fantasy are more realists than fantasists. Moreover, the premises they use for their plots are rarely magical. In C.S. Lewis's *The Lion, the Witch and the Wardrobe* (1950) the children enter Narnia through a magic cupboard; Philippa Pearce's Tom of *Tom's Midnight Garden* (1958) finds the garden when the clock strikes thirteen. In strong contrast, Robert Westall's Simon of *The Scarecrows* (1981) summons up evil powers because he hates his stepfather so much, and Theresa of Virginia Hamilton's *Sweet Whispers, Brother Rush* (1982) enters her family's past because she is burdened with too much responsibility for her age.

In the fantasies of the past the children rarely had magic powers themselves, although they frequently had the use of talismans for a brief time. A modern trend is the endowment of the protagonist with special powers, such as second sight, extra-sensory perception, mind-thrust, and witchcraft, giving rise to the term 'psychic' fantasy.

It is not surprising that fantasy began in England, a land steeped in tradition and myth, where every hill and pathway had been named for hundreds of years and where one was prepared to glimpse an elf, a fairy, a goblin, or a brownie if one just turned one's head quickly enough. As well as its heritage from the oral tradition, most of which was in print by the end of the fifteenth century, England had adult works of a highly imaginative and fantastical quality from Shakespeare, Spenser, Swift, and Coleridge (with 'The Rime of the Ancient Mariner' and 'Kubla Khan'). When the Victorian Age brought a change from the Puritan view of childhood to one that allowed for the liberation of the imagination, everything combined to produce a shift from a century and a half of realistic moral tales to the great Victorian fantasies of Charles Kingsley, Lewis Carroll, George MacDonald, and many others.

For early nineteenth-century pioneers and writers the Canadian land was simply vast tracts of wilderness—unexplored, unnamed, unsettled, and where settled unloved. It was threatening. This, plus the fact that there were few writers, and virtually no writers for children, clearly demonstrates why Canada was not fallow ground for fantasy. (The lore of the native peoples was unfortunately unknown or ignored.) When in the 1880s the Confederation Poets came to terms memorably with the land, even expressing love for it, their writings were for the most part earthbound and naturalistic, as far away from fantasy as it is possible to get. (There are at least two exceptions, however: the poetry of Isabella Valancy Crawford, published in 1884 to almost no public response; and, in prose, James De Mille's science-fiction fantasy, *A Strange Manuscript Found in a Copper Cylinder* of 1888.) Since writing for children tends to follow and not lead writing for adults, it was not until 1950 that the first real Canadian fantasy for children was published—a neat example of the cliché that cultural developments in Canada lag fifty years behind those in the United States: the first major American fantasy for children, Frank Baum's *The Wizard of Oz*, was published in 1900.

In keeping with the beginnings of realistic fiction for children, the first recognized Canadian fantasy was by a visitor, John Buchan (Lord Tweedsmuir), when he was Governor General of Canada. *Lake of Gold* (1941) is a past-time fantasy in which two contemporary children learn the history of Canada. The story is so pedestrian in tone and style that it is difficult to believe that it came from the author of the fast-paced spy stories *The Thirty-nine Steps* and *Greenmantle*. *Lake of*

Gold shows most clearly that the props of history and geography, accuracy and instruction—the modest goals of unimaginative writers—are not pertinent to the writing of fantasy.

Yet fine fantasy eventually arrived—with the books of one author, the British Columbia writer Catherine Anthony Clark. In retrospect her achievement was remarkable. Her first book, *The Golden Pine Cone* (1950), was followed by *The Sun Horse* (1951), *The One-Winged Dragon* (1955), *The Silver Man* (1958), *The Diamond Feather* (1962), and *The Hunter and the Medicine Man* (1966). Not only did she make her mark in a rarely ventured genre, Canadian fantasy, but no other Canadian writer for children of her period produced such a substantial body of work. Clark was also the first writer to find her inspiration in a local setting, the mountainous land of the Kootenays. Those who know British Columbia well take delight in pinpointing some of the places she described. Moreover, she had the imagination to people the snowy peaks, the forests, and lonely lakeside paths with a peculiarly Canadian kind of spirit-folk—the Rock Puck, the Ice Folk, the Head Canada Goose, the Lake Snake—and with prospectors who live on the borderline between the real world and the world of the supernatural. Interwoven with her plots are the symbols of some of the ancient myths and legends of the native tribes of British Columbia—Raven, Thunder Bird, Killer Whale, and the Magic Woman. Even more symbolical are her Indian chiefs and princesses, often clothed in white, who rule the spirit lands with justice.

The children in these books are at one with their setting. They are not, like Alice in Wonderland, aliens in a card game or a looking-glass world; they are not swept, as are the children in C.S. Lewis's *Narnia Chronicles*, from holiday or school life into a wholly unrecognizable land. Clark's children drink sparingly from the magic potion; they are exposed to events that seem only somewhat larger than life, and to a land that remains familiar to them. Clark's concept of fantasy is best described as enchanted realism, a term that has its origin in the art style of magic realism. In such art the real, exactly rendered, is mingled with, and lent a supernatural dimension by, something other—a quality that heightens the sense of reality. In her creation of quasi-magical worlds (rather than Other Worlds), which she began with *The Golden Pine Cone*, Clark was ahead of her time. The outstanding works of enchanted realism from England and the United States came later—Lucy Boston's *The Children of Green Knowe* in 1952, Philippa Pearce's *Tom's Midnight Garden* in 1958, and Natalie Babbitt's *Tuck Everlasting* in 1975.

All six of Clark's books are based on the formula of the quest story. The children, a boy and a girl in each case, go in search of a person (as in *The Sun Horse* and *The One-Winged Dragon*), or set out to return an object they have found (as in *The Golden Pine Cone*, *The Diamond Feather* and *The Silver Man*). These journeys are always taken on behalf of others; Clark's moral philosophy is basically one of selflessness. Her children do not undergo great changes of character, nor do they need to. They are innately good, self-sufficient, patient, courageous, practical, determined, and above all caring. Early in *The Sun Horse*, Giselle is established as a child of good sense:

> Giselle was a girl who liked to listen; she was quiet and peaceful and like a little woman in some ways. She washed her blue slacks and white blouses herself and had a red ribbon always tied neatly round her black hair. She would not linger playing if there was work to be done at home.

And at the end of *The Diamond Feather*, when the children have completed their quest, they are saluted by the great and mystical chief Raven:

> 'Jon and Firelei, children from the Outer World, we have respect for you. Against your wills, you came here to help us, showing kindness, truth and courage beyond the common.'

Except for Bren and Lucy in *The Golden Pine Cone*, all the children have some reason to be unhappy; Clark deprives them of their parents, or at least one parent through death. But they do not dwell on their loss or show anger at fate, as do most protagonists in modern children's books. In her concept of childhood Clark was very much a writer of her time. In the major books of the 1950s, whether from the United States or England, whether in fantasy or realism, children, whatever the disruptions in their lives, are shown as coping with them.

Clark was in no way a stylist. Her writing varies greatly—and within one book. She could write simply and effectively, but she could also be both prosaic and overlush. While her minor characters are certainly the products of a fertile imagination, they are not always welded into the plots. Perhaps her most memorable creation is the clownish Rock Puck in *The Diamond Feather*. But his place in the events resembles his gait—he hops in and out of the story and is in no way necessary to it. Clark did not develop as a writer. With her last book, *The Hunter and the Medicine Man*, it was evident that her formula was as firmly fixed as the mountains of British Columbia. Yet her place in Canadian children's literature is just as secure. She is not only our first fantasist of note, but—with her intuitive link to the landscape, and her respect for childhood—the one most deeply rooted in a Canadian consciousness.

Clark did not set off a wave of fantasy, as did the first Victorian writers; it rather jerked along, much like her Rock Puck. The poet Anne Wilkinson used allegory, more than fantasy, and a touch of Greek mythology in her *Swann and Daphne* (1960) as a poetic and spare prose vehicle to satirize society's view of people who are 'different'. Swann, who has soft feathers for hair, and Daphne, whose hair is green leaves—after being persecuted, then admired, then exploited—are turned into a swan and a birch tree respectively. Satire also plays a strong part in Pierre Berton's *The Secret World of Og* (1962), its title indicating its Other World setting. It is characterized by liveliness and modernity (both admirable qualities), but in its attacks on the mass-media, racial discrimination, the aimlessness of an imitative society, and a fear of the unknown, it fails as a fantasy because its messages are so overt.

With Ruth Nichols' *A Walk Out of the World* (1969), epic fantasy in the tradition of J.R.R. Tolkien's *The Hobbit* and C.S. Lewis's *The Lion, the Witch and the Wardrobe* arrived in Canada. The events are played out over a wide landscape, there is a battle between good and evil, and the children go into an Other World and back again. *A Walk Out of the World* begins with the simplicity of a folktale:

> Once there were a brother and sister who lived in an apartment house in the middle of the city. It was the sort of building that is not a home and does not become one no matter how long you may live there.

Because of the neighbouring forest, the sea, and the surrounding mountains, and because of its 'newness', the city is undoubtedly Vancouver. But it is also an Everycity, an example of urban development that has pushed nature aside. For Judith (and, to a lesser degree, her brother Tobit), the apartment and the city are claustrophobic. Judith says: 'I want to run . . . but it's as if we're shut up in a box and can't breathe.'

In opposition to the city, but adjacent to it, is a wilderness that is seen as the secret enchanted wood of the fairy tale, or what D.H. Lawrence called the 'dark forest of the soul'. The children enter the wood, although it has been forbidden to them. Judith is inexpressibly drawn to its 'delicate world of wandlike trunks' and its 'pale twilight like the ghost of some forgotten day.' It is the bridge to the children's 'walk out of the world'. Once over it, they find themselves in an ancient, archetypal kingdom where the people have been enslaved for hundreds of years and awaiting a promised deliverer from the evil Hagerrak. Judith is thought to be the deliverer because she has silver hair and blue eyes, unlike the dark-haired people of the Lake House where the action begins. Judith accepts her destiny; she feels a 'deep, obscure joy' as she awakens on her first day in this magic world. Both she and Tobit gradually take their places as adults in the struggle, much as the children in C.S. Lewis's *Narnia Chronicles* ruled as kings and queens in the enchanted land but are ordinary school children in their own. At the end, Judith alone faces Hagerrak and defeats him in a battle of wills.

Nichols' second fantasy, *The Marrow of the World* (1972), has a greater sense of evil than *A Walk Out of the World*, and one that has a more personal context. As an adopted child Linda has not yet come to terms with her new life. She is haunted by troublesome dreams—Jung's race memories—that come to fruition in a fantasy world:

> A low cry broke from Linda: half animal, a wordless sound of recognition. Philip knew, for she had told him, that she had seen this creature in dreams fifty times before.

Like Judith, she has a prior link with this Other World and is summoned into it by forces beyond herself. But unlike Judith, she has to make a choice under threat and coercion from her witch half-sister Ygerna, who orders her to undertake a quest for 'the marrow of the world', a substance that will increase Ygerna's evil powers. The final struggle becomes not only the universal one between good and evil, but also a struggle between the opposing sides of Linda's own nature, for she is half-witch. The struggle that evolves is one for a person as well as a world.

Nichols' Canadian settings are more other-worldly than those of Catherine Anthony Clark, but like Clark, Nichols is not defeated by their enormity and anonymity. In *A Walk Out of the World* the scene shifts from the edge of urbanization to the Lake House that is built on pilings of weathered unpainted logs, to a more primeval world (the Red Forest, with its underground dwellers), to the Whispering Plain (open and free as the Prairies), to farmlands and villages (the beginnings of settlement again), and to the White City (built on a hill), which is the abode of Hagerrak and therefore represents a dissociation from the natural world. The Georgian Bay area in Ontario at the end of summer ('a time of autumn magic') is the real-world setting for *The Marrow of the World*. But it too becomes an imaginary landscape with the underwater domain of the Mer-people, the dark kingdom of the dwarves, a forest inhabited by a lone wise man and a noble huntsman—all part of a land that does not exist under our stars, yet is familiar.

Although the terrains described do not have the intimacy of those of Clark, Nichols' figures from European folklore and legend do find a comfortable place in them: subterranean mountain caves and passages harbour old-world dwarves rather than bears. The children are truly Canadian. Like their counterparts in the outdoor realistic adventure stories, they move through immense distances and attendant perils with an assurance born of knowledge and experience:

> Linda squinted dubiously at the swift-flowing clouds. 'Do you think it's going to rain?'
> Anxiety sharpened Philip's voice. 'With the country you grew up in, you don't know the look of a snow cloud when you see one? It won't rain.'
> 'We'd best find somewhere sheltered to camp then.'

Nichols' fantasies are eclectic. Indeed, quite a satisfactory game can be played identifying the links with English fantasies. For example, in both books the boys play a loving and protective role towards the girls, as does Sam Gangee towards Frodo in Tolkien's *The Lord of the Rings*. But Nichols is eclectic only in the sense that fantasy itself is eclectic, drawing on its roots in the oral tradition and on its primitive patterns of quest and morality that must be played out again and again. In any case she has added her own distinctiveness to the as-yet small stock of Canadian fantasies: a rather mannered style, a linking of personal unhappiness to a basically unselfish quest, a sense of the loss of the natural environment in *A Walk Out of the World*, and in *The Marrow of the World* the creation of a truly original magical artifact—the primeval substance 'the marrow of the world', which brings eternal life to its possessor. Her later two books—*Song of the Pearl* (1976) and *The Left-Handed Spirit* (1978)—move uneasily between fantasy and mysticism, and in readership between young adults and adults.

Before the 1960s all major English fantasies were set in lands, real or imagined, that were basically remote from urban areas. This pattern was broken by Alan Garner with *Elidor* (1965), in which the plot begins and ends in the slums of Manchester, and with William Mayne's *Earthfasts* (1966), in which all the events occur in a large English market town in the north. Both writers proved that there could be magic in cities. So did Janet Lunn with *Double Spell* (1968; published in the United States as *Twin Spell*). Although the Toronto background (Yonge Street and its environs, and an old lakefront house) may not be as necessary to the plot as is the natural landscape of Catherine Anthony Clark, it adds both interest and verisimilitude to a story in which the supernatural breaks into the real world.

The twins Elizabeth and Jane are strangely compelled to buy a valuable old doll in an antique shop whose proprietor, in turn, is strangely compelled to sell it to them for a pittance. Its possession seems to change the girls' lives. Their family acquires a house in which twins in the past have suffered at the hands of their cousin Hester. Hester's hatred reaches into the present and Elizabeth and Jane are saved from it only by that indefinable bond that exists between twins. This bald recital of events in no way does justice to

Lunn's skilful manipulation of the fantastic versus the real, or to her unfolding of family history. The twins' research into this, somewhat on the order of a school project, adds a realistic childlike note. Then, in a dramatic fantasy twist, one of the modern twins is sucked back into the ghostly world.

There are some flaws in Lunn's schema. The doll plays a rather tenuous part in the plot, and as a whole the story is too short and so too slight a vehicle for the dark events that erupt so suddenly at the end. Still, its virtues far outweigh its faults. Lunn's concept of what can now be described as the 'new fantasy' (the intrusion of the supernatural into the everyday) was not only a first in Canada, but, of its type, it carries unusual conviction.

It was over twenty years (since Clark's *The Golden Pine Cone*) until another fantasist made use of Indian motifs and values. When Christie Harris's *Secret in the Stlalakum Wild* was published in 1972, she was already well known as a reteller of Indian legends with her *Once Upon a Totem* (1963). Her first fantasy, which is imbued with her knowledge and love of native culture, also introduced a rather bouncy and egotistical young protagonist, one common in realistic fiction by the 1970s but still rare in fantasy. The opening paragraph sets this modern tone:

> Life seemed only too predictable to Morann on the blistering hot day her father's sister Sarah was due to arrive. So much so that she took steps to start things off in a new direction. Determined to be somebody's favourite for a change, she went at the day head on. She brushed her hair hard, and she reeked of perfume when she finally emerged from the bathroom.

Morann is sidetracked from her clumsy attempts to make herself more visible and important to her family when, on a solitary excursion to the wild mountainous terrain of British Columbia adjacent to her home, she is visited by the 'Stlalakum sprites'. These are invisible Indian spirits who 'get inside you the way light gets into water. The way an electric current gets into a motor. They make you do things you hadn't thought of doing.' Through them Morann has a vision of the land as it was preserved by the Indians in the past and confronts a symbol of its destruction in the form of the double-headed Lake Snake. She then joins her aunt and her family in their ecological endeavours, having learned that healthy green and golden nature is more valuable than the green and gold in one's pockets.

Harris, like Catherine Anthony Clark, uses her knowledge of Indian lore and culture with skill and integrity; but the two writers differ greatly in their handling of fantasy. Clark's gentle (seemingly uncommitted) approach to the supernatural eventually gave each of her books an aura of 'faerie', not least because most of the plot is linked with enchantment. Harris's entries into the 'Stlalakum Wild' are few, jerky, and so obviously contrived for a lesson in conservation that the element of fantasy is minor, while the emphasis on Morann's sudden change of heart and personality diminishes the innate power of Indian thought. Harris's writing style is as uneven as her dual purpose, moving from modern conversation and colloquialisms to fine passages describing the landscape and the 'stlalakum'.

Personal problems and an Indian mythic background are also springboards for Joan Clark's *Wild Man of the Woods* (1985). Stephen arrives from Calgary for a month's summer vacation with his aunt and uncle and cousin Louie, who live in the foothills of the Rockies in a deliberately chosen simple home-craft style. Their livingroom is dominated by a sun-mask, carved by Old Angus, an Indian who camps intermittently in the forest across the lake. Stephen and Louie become friends, but their boyish innocent pleasures are interrupted by two neighbouring bullies, and this harassment develops into a war between two camps. In an early episode the two boys find Angus's animal masks in the forest; each dons one and frightens off the roughnecks. This confrontation gives Stephen a kind of courage he has not hitherto possessed; he has allowed himself to be bullied, not through a lack of courage, but rather through an inability to react in kind. In an alien environment, dominated by masks, Stephen has nightmares in which he is always conquering his enemies by violent means. In an even more violent dénouement, Stephen has access to, and dons the mask of, an ancient Indian cannibal, the 'Wild Man of the Woods', and in a ferocious burst of power tries to kill not only the bullies but his cousin Louie. In his rage he cannot distinguish between friend and foe.

In its themes of possession, and the release of unconscious, destructive energy, *Wild Man of the Woods* resembles two children's books by English authors—William Raynor's *Stag Boy* (1972) and

Penelope Lively's *The Wild Hunt of Hagworthy* (1972)—in which the boys are seized by the power of a stag when they don a headdress of antlers. The violence that ensues is also similar. But *Wild Man of the Woods* also has a psychological healing power: Stephen and Louie come to realize that they have indulged in actions and retaliations that, taken on a larger scale, have led countries to war. Stephen in particular recognizes his personal guilt and muses on it:

> Could wearing a mask make you tell the truth about yourself, things like violence and revenge that you'd rather hide in nightmares? . . . Was the truth that meanness wasn't just in the faces of other people but in your own as well, where you couldn't see it? It was this thought, that he was no better than the people who'd been bullying him, that depressed Stephen most of all.

The varied aspects of the plot are well integrated, thus lending inevitability to the outcome. The boys are real boys (twelve and eleven years of age) and the aspects of play, household chores, and daily summer living close to a resort area give a realistic relief to the thrust of the supernatural.

Joan Clark's companion fantasy, *The Moons of Madeleine* (1987), is a linked family story. As Stephen rides the bus in the foothills of the Rockies to visit his cousin Louie in a town called Inverary, Louie's sister Mad (short for Madeleine) is on her way to stay with her aunt and cousin Selena in Calgary on an exchange visit. Clark's two books are also linked through a mask that Selena is bringing to her relatives—a moon mask, carved by old Angus—and by a book, *Great Masks of the World*. Beyond these parallels the stories are individually plotted, although both end in the protagonists' attaining a new self-awareness.

Madeleine is unhappy in her new environment because her fourteen-year-old cousin Selena has changed so dramatically; she is no longer a child but a sophisticated teenager with 'mod' clothes, brilliantly coloured hair, and vivid make-up. 'What a weirdo, Mad thought.' The realistic components of the book—Mad's alienation from Selena, her wary relationship with her aunt (a busy professional woman), her worries about her grandmother who is ill in a nursing home, and the tug-of-war relationship between Selena and her mother—are all believable, although in no way dramatic or original or particularly moving. The fantasy element, however, is seriously flawed. While the Indian moon mask appears to begin the events when Mad puts it on in the moonlight, native myth is immediately and totally submerged in Greek mythology. Mad finds herself drawn into a circle of young Greek goddesses (who speak like modern teenagers) and becomes involved in initiation rites, the change from childhood to womanhood. While the Greek goddesses are an artificial intrusion into a Canadian setting (Clark makes no attempt to make them part of the environment, as Ruth Nichols did with dwarves in *A Walk Out of the World*), her use of masks has led her into some interesting symbolism. When Mad puts on a clown's face and costume for the Calgary Stampede parade, she feels an extraordinary sense of freedom, as if her real persona were being released. There is also some significance in Selena's use of heavy makeup; her real face is not shown until the end of the story. Yet it is somewhat puzzling that Selena should be named for the goddess of the moon, yet has no part in the moon rituals—unless the untidy rebel goddesses can be taken as her *alter ego*. All in all, Clark's mixture of fantasy and realism works much better in *Wild Man of the Woods* than in *The Moons of Madeleine*, partly because of the setting of the earlier book. Inverary, in the foothills of the Rockies, is a borderline place, existing comfortably on the edge of the real and the mythic, as well as with white and native cultures. Both fantasies are concerned with a symbolic transition for the young teenage protagonists, through initiation ceremonies, to maturity. *Wild Man of the Woods*, however, exhibits a clarity and force of style and theme lacking in *The Moons of Madeleine*.

Indian masks also provided the inspiration for Welwyn Wilton Katz's *False Face* (1987). Thirteen-year-old Laney McIntyre finds a cache of Iroquois relics in a wooded bog close to her home in London, Ontario. She is interrupted in her discovery by a half-Indian boy, Tom Walsh, who challenges her ownership of the artifacts. Laney gives Tom a pipe, keeps a comb, but hides in her pocket a minimask, one side of its face painted red and the other side black. On a later visit Tom finds a large mask (painted the same way) that is covering a skeleton. Tom flees from it in horror, for he recognizes it as the mask of the dark god Gaguwara. This mask is stolen by Laney's mother (an antique dealer), who intends to restore and sell both masks, although she knows that selling them is against the law that protects native artifacts. The masks' powers are released, however, causing supernatural tensions, violence, and terror.

But as in almost all modern fantasies in which the supernatural breaks into the real world, there are emotional and psychological determinants already present in the teenagers. Laney is unhappy at home. Her parents are divorced; she does not see enough of her father (an anthropologist teaching at the university) as she would like to, because the divorce has been bitter. The mother favours her elder daughter because Laney has a strong physical resemblance to her father. The two sisters are also at odds; Rosemary, attractive and clever and close to her mother, slides out of most of the housework, even leaving the care of her dog to Laney. Tom has even more difficulties. His father is dead and he and his mother have left the reservation. He is alienated at his London High School (if the other students speak to him at all, they greet him with 'How!'). He feels himself Indian, but when he visits the reservation to seek help about the masks, he is rejected; and worst of all, when he looks at his mother he sees only her whiteness.

Like the ring in Tolkien's The Lord of the Rings, the masks have an effect on their owners—Laney and her mother—and their power can be eroded only when they are voluntarily yielded. The large mask is evil and the small one is traditionally tied to the large one to hold its purpose in check. In the final dramatic confrontation the masks are united and (in the classical mould) disorder is returned to order, disunity to unity. The masks are not even given to a museum; Tom returns them to the bog from whence they came.

The not-too-obvious message is somewhat similar to that of Joan Clark's Wild Man of the Woods: behind the mask there is an individual. Tom has seen only his mother's whiteness, not her difficulties as a non-native on the reservation; he has only seen his father as an Indian, not as a man who loved, and had the courage to marry, a woman outside his race. Mrs McIntyre has only seen Laney in the image of her father; she has not looked behind the green eyes and the facial features to the child who loves her and has tried desperately to please her. The story also has an ecological component that becomes a natural part of the plot. The bog, slated for urban development, is important as an Indian archaeological site. In a brief coda the developer gives up the struggle and donates the land to the city.

Katz has the ability to make evil palpable. Tom and Laney break into Mrs McIntyre's antique shop to steal the large mask that is in her workroom floating in a restorative bath of acids. They cannot open the door:

> But behind the door, crashing on it like waves of soundless surf, something abruptly hit at them. The Doctor, the monster, the red-clawed beast. Tom reeled. His eyes began to run, droplets so hot they burned, branded themselves behind his flesh and his bone. He fell back against the other wall of the corridor. The flashlight dropped from his hand.

Yet although Katz can describe the knife-edge of terror—one of the attributes of this type of fantasy—she also gives her readers a choice of what to believe. Did Mrs McIntyre really harm Rosemary's dog in a fit of temper, or did it become ill through eating garbage? Did she really cause the illness of a rival antique dealer, so serious that he had to close his shop? Did Laney cure the dog through calling on the small mask for help, or was it her careful nursing of him? Katz always keeps a careful foot in reality. In fact the realistic component of the story is far stronger than the fantasy. We learn much about Laney and her family, her schoolwork, her chores, her mother's difficult temperament and the unhappy family relationships in general. Indeed, with a few strokes of the pen, the slight touch of fantasy could be swept away, leaving an interesting realistic novel with an archaeological background and conflict. Nevertheless, its touch of something beyond the real is an enrichment of the story, however one wants to interpret it; for the masks and their power are an expression of the primitive aggression that lurks in all of us and that needs a counterbalance.

For the most part Katz writes in a clear, straightforward manner, avoiding teenage colloquialisms and slang. She moves into what might be called psychedelic or surrealistic writing when she is describing Laney's dreams (Laney has nightmares after discovering the little mask), or when she is describing the impact of the Iroquois False Face Society upon the present. Here Laney is dreaming that she is in a hut of woven branches:

> Shouts. Someone entering the east door. Husk face! He—it?—crawled, crabbing along four-legged, heading for the fire. Corn-braided mask, long-nosed, funny and terrible. Tobacco and wood smokes blending.

Such brief passages, when pieced together, provide the mythic element underlying the plot, which is somewhat of a jigsaw puzzle and requires concentration from the reader. The 'Author's Note' at the end of the book is helpful and perhaps should have been put at the beginning.

Stories in which the protagonists travel into the past from the present—past-time fantasies—form a large sub-genre of fantasy in general, and in recent years this mode has attracted a number of Canadian writers. In such works there is usually only one magical premise: an entry into the past, which is generally accomplished by the use of a talisman, such as Dickie Harding's bauble in Edith Nesbit's *Harding's Luck* (1909); or a door opening in the mind of the protagonist, as in Alison Uttley's *A Traveller in Time* (1939); or, in a modern vein, a talisman plus the spur of unhappiness, as in *Playing Beattie Bow* (1980) by Ruth Park. But whatever the method of entry the result is the same; the novel becomes chiefly historical fiction. Writers of past-time fantasy, however, have more licence than do writers of historical fiction. With time-travellers as protagonists, contrasts can be made between the past and the present (the present being the time at which the book was written) and may even be commented upon. The use of such knowledge is forbidden to the writer of historical fiction. But both types of fiction operate under a major rule: the past cannot be altered. Still, the addition of magic allows the writer of past-time fantasy, more than any other type of fiction, to emphasize the universality of human needs and emotions.

Canadian past-time fantasy has developed greatly since John Buchan's didactic *Lake of Gold*, and a similar work by another visitor to Canada, Eva-Lis Wuorio's *Return of the Viking* (1955). Most recent writers have been more concerned with the social aspects of the past rather than with major and dateable events. Two exceptions are Karleen Bradford's *The Other Elizabeth* (1982) and Janet Lunn's *The Root Cellar* (1981)—time-slips to the War of 1812 and the American Civil War respectively. Of the two, Bradford's book is the more deliberately historical. The modern Elizabeth, on a school field trip to Upper Canada Village, is strangely drawn to enter Cook's Tavern (she has never shown any interest in history before) and finds herself over a hundred years in the past in the body of 'the other Elizabeth'. The background of the war and the immediate events leading to the fictional crisis are selectively and skilfully sketched in, while personal feelings about the war are not neglected. The plot involves two families—one Canadian (descendants of the United Empire Loyalists) and one American—who are close friends. The war does not tear them apart; in terms of their friendship and loyalty to one another it is remote. The social customs and family life of the past are unobtrusively described: the meals, the chores, and the modern Elizabeth's inability to work a sampler. Indeed, the whole package of information is tied up firmly and attractively. But the fantasy component is not compelling. The element of magic is absent, and this makes Elizabeth's entry into the past unconvincing. She was sent there to save a life, but we do not learn this until the end of the book. As a modern girl she is a trained swimmer, unlike her historical *alter ego*, and thus she can save the life of the American Jamie. He eventually marries 'the other Elizabeth', the great-great-great-grand-mother of the modern Elizabeth. Bradford's style is not as laboured as her fantasy, but it is without sparkle. The story is not for dedicated readers of fantasy, though it has merit as historical fiction.

Janet Lunn's past is the American Civil War and she uses it in its historical context and symbolically: a house divided against itself cannot stand. No battles are described, nor are the causes of the war given, but its aftermath is poignantly seen in the military hospitals of Washington, D.C., filled with wounded—in spirit as well as in body. Lunn treats the war through the plight of her heroine, Rose Larkin. She is a lonely twelve-year-old American orphan unused to close relationships, much like Mary Lennox in Frances Hodgson Burnett's *The Secret Garden*, which is Rose's favourite book. After the death of her guardian grandmother, Rose is sent to live with a large, boisterous family of Canadian relatives, whom she cannot relate to, in their decrepit old Ontario farmhouse close to the American border.

An old house is a convention in fantasy literature. Since it is a Canadian house it is in no way as old as the Elizabethan 'Thackers' in Alison Uttley's *A Traveller in Time* or Lucy Boston's Norman house, which admits the past into the present in *The Children of Green Knowe*. But it has always been a happy house and this atmosphere lingers. Rose is given a glimpse of it in its former well-cared-for state when she meets and converses with an old woman who gives her name as Mrs Morrissay and who assures Rose that she is not a ghost; she is simply and occasionally 'shifted' out of her time. The ground is thus well prepared for Rose herself to be shifted.

The 'root cellar' of the title provides her with an entry to the past. When the shadow of a hawthorn tree falls exactly between the cellar's two doors, Rose can escape through it from the life she hates into the midst of the American Civil War. Here she receives companionship and understanding from two young people, Susan and Will, and when Susan sets off to find Will, who has joined the American Union Army, Rose goes with her. Thus she takes her first step towards maturity as she sees the horror of war, and forgets herself in a kinship with others. Although she feels happier in the past than in the present, she comes to realize that she belongs in her own time with her Canadian family. Rose returns from her journey a changed person.

In an unnecessary coda Lunn's hitherto firm hold on fantasy slides into licence—as does so much of modern fantasy. Lunn tries to convince her readers that Rose's experiences have been as real as the Civil War itself. There are no metaphysical questions on the nature of time, reality, ghost-lives, and dreams, as in Phillippa Pearce's perfectly conceived fantasy *Tom's Midnight Garden*, in which we find that Tom has entered an old woman's dreams of her childhood and Tom's longings and hers have commingled. In the more matter-of-fact *Root Cellar* old Mrs Morrissay, now dead, was Susan and the house was her home. She returns to give Rose some very practical help. In a burst of familial feeling Rose insists on cooking the Christmas dinner by herself and ruins it. She then prepares her typical dinner of sausages and mashed potatoes. However, when she flings the kitchen door open to admit the large family, the goose is perfectly cooked, the table set with old-fashioned dishes and table linens, and the room is appropriately decorated. There are transformation scenes in other fantasies, but they are usually a part of the Other World, not the real one. The scene Lunn describes is in the order of the fairy godmother waving her wand over Cinderella. Apart from this extravaganza, the fantasy and the history exist comfortably with one another.

Lunn's themes are gently symbolic. Rose is a divided person. Her experiences in the past create an inner struggle over whether to remain or to return to the present. This is paralleled by Will (as a Canadian) realizing that he was involved in a war that was not his war. Symbolism can be noted in the title, *The Root Cellar*, which points to Rose's search for a family, and in Rose's name, a flower that combines thorns and beauty—much like her personality. Finally, the hawthorn tree that allows her to enter another century reverberates with magic from ancient legends. However, Lunn does not belabour her metaphors and allusions. They give some depth to the fantasy, but a knowledge of them is not necessary to a child's enjoyment of the story. Lunn's style is clear, flowing, and in the grim scenes of the war's aftermath very powerful indeed.

Kevin Major also draws on recorded history for his first venture into fantasy. *Blood Red Ochre* (1989) is based on one of the most tragic events in Canadian history—the disappearance from Newfoundland of the Beothuks in the early nineteenth century (although Major is not explicit about the time). He ingeniously uses a triple narrative pattern. That of the modern David is told in the third person and has, on the surface, the now fairly typical theme of a teenager's first love and search for identity. The plight of the last Beothuk family is told, in alternate chapters, by young Dauoodaset, who after travelling to what is now called Red Ochre Island to find food for his starving family, is killed by a white hunter. The penultimate chapter is also a first-person narrative by Nancy/Shanawdithit, who is Nancy in modern times and Shanawdithit in the final fantasy segment of the story. (The real Nancy Shanawdithit, the last of the Beothuks, died in St John's in 1829.)

The fantasy at first creeps only slightly into the story. At high school David is drawn to Nancy, a rather strange new girl, and seizes the opportunity to get to know her better because they are both doing a school project on the Beothuks. David's grandfather has lived on Red Ochre Island, has told him (rather vaguely) about the Beothuks, and has given him a bone pendant he had received from *his* grandfather. On a school field trip to the museum in St John's, David is bewildered when Nancy runs screaming from the museum; he sees only Beothuk artifacts and a reconstruction of a burial site. David is invited to Nancy's home and it is very uncomfortable, with contrasts of heat and cold, strange noises, and no family in evidence. David and Nancy become close (sharing embraces and kisses) and she persuades him to visit Red Ochre Island as a conclusion to their project. Here the fantasy begins in earnest: Dauoodaset appears from the past; Nancy tells David that she is Shanawdithit and that she was pledged to Dauoodaset (and still is). David has been brought to Red Ochre Island almost as a hostage for the white man's crimes against the Beothuks and because of his particular family link with the island. David at first is in terror for his life and is then enraged at Nancy's betrayal of his love for her. In a short space of time, almost moments, they all become friends, share food, and David and Dauoodaset build a shelter together. David gives Nancy his bone pendant, which in her past life she had given to Dauoodaset. Now the idyll is broken by the sudden appearance of the white hunter with a gun who had killed Dauoodaset long ago. The scene is repeated. 'I am Shanawdithit. I am the last of my people', Nancy says, and flees in a canoe out into the ocean. David watches her paddle away, and when he turns back to the campsite all evidence of it has disappeared.

David's story is told in Major's usual modern colloquial style, but with little use of the Newfoundland speech patterns that flavour his realistic novel *Hold Fast* (1978). Simple, rhythmic language is used by Dauoodaset for his moving and memorable account of the tragic despair of the Beothuks, and by Shanawdithit as she denounces the white man's ferocity towards the Beothuks ('It is your people who are the savages'). While the combination of realism and fantasy in the last chapter on the island is not altogether successful, Dauoodaset's telling of the terrible plight and destruction of the Beothuks stays in the reader's mind. Major's novel, on the whole, is compelling.

Both Lunn's *The Root Cellar* and Major's *Blood Red Ochre* draw on the built-in drama contained in the disasters of history. Quieter stories that take us back into the more fluid area of social history call for a sturdier fictional component. In particular the entry to the past must have a strong premise. Such is not the case with Ann Walsh's *Your Time, My Time* (1984), Florence McNeil's *All Kinds of Magic* (1984), and Heather Kellerhals-Stewart's *Stuck Fast in Yesterday* (1983), although the writers' research and interpretation of the past have considerable validity and interest. Elizabeth, of *Your Time, My Time*, is a rather ordinary, prickly young teenager at odds with her mother because she has to spend a summer with her in Barkerville, B.C. (away from her friends) while her mother works as a waitress trying to sort out her life after separating from her husband. Elizabeth has nothing to do, but in her aimless wanderings through the town she discovers the history of its gold-rush days through its museums, its lectures, and its tourist attractions. However, when she enters the past, through a talisman—a gold ring that she finds in the cemetery—she is not plunged into gold-rush events; rather she finds a young man of the past who becomes her first love. Elizabeth's time-slip can occur only in the cemetery, and when she tries to visit her friend when he is ill and dying in his home, to take him the modern medicine that can cure him, she finds herself to be a powerless phantasm. The theme of the modern time-traveller separated by death and centuries from the past-time lover has been treated with far more depth and credibility in Alison Uttley's *A Traveller in Time* and Ruth Park's *Playing Beattie Bow*.

Barkerville is also the setting for Florence McNeil's *All Kinds of Magic*. Jen, like Walsh's Elizabeth, is having an enforced summer holiday. It is being spent in Barkerville with her father, his new wife, and her stepbrother (whom she considers retarded). The children do not go into the past but help a ghost-like old woman, who may have lived on from gold-rush days, to establish her husband's name as a saviour of the town and a hero. In the process Jen discovers that her stepbrother is both likeable and intelligent.

Jennifer, of Heather Kellerhals-Stewart's *Stuck Fast in Yesterday*, is in the Royal Ontario Museum against her wishes viewing a photography exhibit with her parents instead of being at a Saturday matinée. As a result she is very cross indeed. The magic begins when she sees a life-size model of a photographer bent over an old-fashioned camera that is aimed at an equally life-size photograph of old-fashioned-looking children labelled 'Seen and Not Heard Children circa 1900'. In a swirl of events Jennifer is plunged back into family and child life in Ontario at the turn of the century, pursued by a sinister photographer, who, if he takes her picture, will make her into a perfect 'seen and not heard' child, imprisoned in time. In the past she is assisted by two children who live in a semi-rural setting close to Toronto. They are in no way 'goody-goody' children, but they do live a more disciplined life (especially in school) than Jennifer. There is a strong element of terror in the pursuit by the photographer, reminiscent of the undue child punishment that was so much a part of early children's literature. Though Jennifer has been presented as something of a brat in the museum, she really is quite normal. She hardly deserves the punishment that is inflicted on her.

The works of Walsh, McNeil, and Kellerhals-Stewart are slight fantasies—as slight in their intent and their dénouements as in their brevity—that do not allow for memorable contrasts between the past and the present, even though the periods chosen allow for such contrasts. It is obvious that the fantasies that deal with the social history of the past need as strong a hand on a past reality as do those that deal with wars, revolutions, or other external conflicts. These three novels (that of Walsh to a lesser extent) lack strength in both their fictional and historical components.

Cora Taylor's *The Doll* (1987) and Kit Pearson's *A Handful of Time* (1987) demonstrate the union of fantasy and social history at its best. Both also weave family history into the pattern of the past. Cora Taylor's ten-year-old Meg is a troubled child whose parents are on the brink of divorce. Recovering from rheumatic fever and disturbed by suspicions about her parents, she is propelled by the force of illness and emotional distress into an earlier era. Her talisman is a traditional family 'invalid' doll that has comforted sick children in Meg's family since her great-great-grandmother brought it across the Prairies. Now the doll's spirit transports Meg in her sleep into the pioneer past. There she enters the body of a pioneer girl and as Morag, her great-great-aunt, she fulfils her destiny—to save another child from fire who becomes her great-great-grandmother. Meg finds in the Red River pioneer family the warmth that is lacking in her own. In the round of daily activities and adventures she also finds a perseverance in herself that counteracts the pain of her own family breakup. Psychic power is present in a number of elements: the eerie, slightly sinister character of the doll, the fear of identity loss as Meg loses herself in the pioneer Morag, and in the coma-like lifelessness of Meg as she sleeps during the time-travel episodes, a coma that prefigures the death of her great-great-aunt. Balancing these supernatural events is the strong down-to-earth sense of family continuity and inheritance; of values, history, and even physical gestures transmitted across generations. Taylor writes with a subtle perception into human needs and behaviour, and with a nicety of language, that puts *The Doll* in the small company of Canadian children's books noted for their literary style.

In placing her story only thirty-five years in the past, Kit Pearson set herself a hard task in *A Handful of Time*. The difficulties of achieving bold contrast within such a short time-span are compounded by setting the plot in a summer-cottage milieu, where it can be expected that life and customs change more slowly than in an urban environment. Yet Pearson evokes the past by the unobtrusive inclusion of small but specific details: water has to be carried from a pump some distance away and heated on a wood stove, girls 'do up' their hair in pincurls, and the village store of the past carries less 'junk food' than that in the present.

A Handful of Time bears a resemblance to Philippa Pearce's *Tom's Midnight Garden*, and the epigraph is a quotation from it: 'You might say that different people have different times, although of course, they're really all bits of the same big Time.' There are two people and two times in *A Handful of Time*. Twelve-year-old Patricia is a shy, reserved Torontonian suffering from the conflicts of her parents' divorce and a seeming estrangement from her mother, Ruth, with whom she is to live; she has been closer to her father. She has been sent to live with her aunt and uncle and four cousins for the summer and her cousins make her feel an unwelcome outsider. In her isolation she seeks refuge in the guest cabin and there she finds an old pocket watch inscribed with her grandmother's first name (which is also Patricia's) and a last name that she does not recognize. The hands on her wrist-watch point to the same time as that on the old watch, and when she winds it, it starts ticking. Thus the magic begins. When Patricia emerges from the cabin she is in the same place but in her mother's time when she was Patricia's age. Pearson is obviously a fan of Edith Nesbit, the classic Edwardian writer of magical fantasy and the one who, in essence, defined its operational logic. Patricia must find out exactly how the watch works and plan her journeys to the past to fit in with her life in her own time. This talisman also makes her invisible, and so she is a ghost-like witness to her mother's summer. Patricia observes Ruth's hardships as she struggles against her mother's obvious favouritism for a younger sister and rebels against the family treatment of girls as subservient, docile, and deprived of the opportunities and freedom offered to boys. She sees how her mother's childhood has made her the brittle, determined person she has become. As a highly intelligent and fiery rebel, Ruth wins Patricia's understanding and compassion as a young adolescent as she never did as an adult.

The magic ends with the breaking of the watch and Ruth's unexpected arrival at the cottage. All the major characters are now present (including Ruth's mother), as they were in that summer not so long ago, but now it is time for reconciliation and understanding, especially between mothers and daughters. The women are fully developed even though their appearances are brief. At the heart of the story is Ruth's mother, embittered most of her life because the man she loved had died—he whose name was engraved on the watch. She has been dominating and manipulative—a common portrayal of motherhood in the American problem novel, but one rarely found in quality children's literature. An exception is the psychologically cruel grandmother in *Jacob Have I Loved* (1980) by the American writer Katherine Paterson.

The details of canoeing, horseback-riding, high-jinks, and conflicts among siblings are the perennial matter of many a summer-adventure story, but here they are an especially pleasant and realistic diversion from the problems created by adults that motivate the plot. However, it is the fantasy that makes this novel special; it is treated with some humour (Patricia as a ghost has some tricky moments), but also with the same quiet restraint and subtle control that is exhibited in the writing.

A slight and gentle story, beautifully written, is Margaret Laurence's *The Olden Days Coat* (1979). It is the most successful of her four books for children, chiefly because it is closest to her adult books, linking, as it does, the present with the past by bridging generations. Like *A Handful of Time*, it is a family-history fantasy narrating the experience of ten-year-old Sal, who travels back into her grandmother's childhood.

Sal is unhappy because she is being forced to spend Christmas in her country grandmother's home rather than her own. She misses the small traditions that are a part of her family's festivities, such as having an early Christmas present, and to while away the time she examines a chest of old photographs in a shed, stored away because, as her Gran says: 'The past is in my mind—I've got no need of photographs.' Sal dons an old coat she discovers in the chest and suddenly finds herself out in the snow in a village that resembles the one in the old photographs. She meets and talks with Sarah, a young girl, who is driving a sleigh, and finds that they have many things in common, including the opening of an early Christmas present. Sarah shows Sal a beautifully painted box that her parents made for her. Sal senses that she cannot remain too long in the past and excuses herself from an invitation to Sarah's home. As is befitting in a fantasy, Sal also realizes that she must return her talisman. At the last minute she throws the coat in Sarah's departing sleigh and finds herself back in the shed where she spies the coat neatly folded at the bottom of the trunk.

Christmas becomes a delight. Sal is offered the choice of an early present and chooses her grandmother's gift, which is the carved box that had been given to the grandmother at the age of ten, inscribed to Sarah. The fact that Sal is only subconsciously aware of her visit to the past and of the reality that Sarah is her grandmother is significant. Laurence values the present over the past because it is only in the present that the individual can work hard and live courageously.

A Canadian living in Ireland has written two fantasies that are a striking departure from the books discussed above, for they are epic in scope. The past in O.R. Melling's *The Druid's Tune*, (1983) and *The Singing Stone* (1986) is mythological. Legends of the Irish hero Cuchulain are the basis for *The Druid's Tune* and the tales of the Tuatha De Danaan, in which the fairy and supernatural folk of Ireland originated, inspired *The Singing Stone*. Both novels, in keeping with a trend in modern fantasy, have older teenage heroines and heroes (young women are here centre-stage) and inevitably deal with romantic love. Although Melling begins and ends her stories in the real world (in the tradition of 'there and back again'), the introduction of a love interest brings them close to the fantasies of the American Robin McKinley (*The Blue Sword*, 1982, and *The Hero and the Crown*,

1985), which also focus on spirited young women.

Rosemary and Jimmy of *The Druid's Tune* have been sent to Ireland from Toronto to spend the summer with their aunt and uncle on a farm because their father disapproves of Rosemary's friends. Here they are drawn into Ireland's legendary past through the powers of the mysterious hired man, Peter Murphy, who is seeking his Druidic roots. They find themselves in the midst of the Tain Bo Culange (Queen Maeve's cattle raid of Cooley), made famous by the stand of Cuculann (Cuchulain) at a ford where he single-handedly defended his province of Ulster against Queen Maeve's warriors from the rest of Ireland. Jimmy becomes Cuculann's charioteer, while Rosemary is at first assigned the more traditional female role of being beautifully dressed by Queen Maeve's daughter and winning the love of one of Maeve's sons, Maine. Rosemary searches for her brother and with help from a Druid (Peter Murphy) she finds him and joins Cuculann. She and Jimmy assist him, observe his berserk (bearsark) fits of rage (fortunately described much less horrifically than in the original legend) as he prepares for battle, and tend him when he is wounded. At the final battle, which Maeve wins, Rosemary and Jimmy are turned into birds, and Rosemary saves Maine's life by scratching out the eyes of his opponent. At this point the story returns to the present, and the hired man comes to realize that he does not have real Druidic powers because, we are told, he needed Jimmy's and Rosemary's help to enter the past. He will be satisfied with being a harper. (Presumably as a reward for their endeavours in the past he sings, and Rosemary and Jimmy are given a fleeting vision of civilization—past, present, and future.) As for the two young people, they are left only with indelible bonds—Jimmy with his hero Cuculann and Rosemary with her first love Maine—that are no less strong for being in memory.

The most positive aspect of *The Druid's Tune* is its vivid re-creation of some of the Celtic legends, with which Melling is well acquainted. The insertion of the two young Canadians in this alien environment, however, has little plausibility. They remain insistently modern teenagers, particularly in their speech, and are never really affected by the powerful mythological world they have entered. One exception occurs when Rosemary witnesses the ceremonies of Beltane, in which young lovers join hands and jump over a bonfire to pledge their betrothal:

[Rosemary] looked up at the night sky and around the shadowy hilltop. A pagan time. A pagan rite. The ancient magic was taking hold of her. She was no longer Rosemary from Canada, but Rose, a Celtic girl, a woman of the stone cairns, the timeless hills, the blood passions of a warrior race. In that moment she understood an oath purged in fire, a bonding under the sight of the great moon goddess. She threw back her head as the spirit flooded through her and her face was exultant.

Maine saw the change. With a wild cry he grasped her hand, and they ran toward the fire.

Melling's second fantasy is written with more assurance. Kay Warrick of *The Singing Stone* was left at an orphanage as a baby, and after living in a series of foster-homes strikes out on her own at age sixteen. When she receives a parcel of books from an anonymous source, concerned with legends of standing stones—some written in English and some in Gaelic—she spends a year studying Old Irish. She confides her story to Alan Manducca, a young man from Crete whom she meets the night before she leaves for Ireland to seek her destiny and to unravel the dreams and nightmares that have haunted her all her life.

Once in Ireland the magic begins quickly as Kay is drawn to the arched Singing Stone. As an exquisite note of music sounds, she is impelled to pass through it, and thus enters the mists of Irish history and legend. (Melling dates the historical events—taken from the *Lebor Gabala*, the 'Book of Conquests'—at 1500 BC.) Kay meets Aherne, who changes with unnatural speed from a child into a beautiful red-haired woman without any memory of her past. The two girls are given a task by Fintan the Mage; they must find and bring together the lost treasures of the Tuatha De Danaan—the Sword, the Spear, the Cauldron, and the Stone of Destiny. They retrieve the treasures—all but the sword. In the course of the search Kay develops psychic powers—she can read others' thoughts and move objects with her mind. At one point memory floods back to Aherne, and she realizes she is Eriu, the Rising Queen of the Tuatha de Danaan. To confirm her queenship and to possess the sword she has to run a race, which she wins. The Tuatha De Danaan move in a procession through the Singing Stone to become the faery folk of Ireland. But Eriu remains in the land (to be named Eire in her honour) and marries Amergin, king of a neighbouring hostile tribe. The startling dénouement of the story is Kay's discovery from Fintan that she is the daughter of Eriu and Amergin, sent back from the future to aid her parents:

> '. . . Why did you kidnap me?' 'Isn't that obvious?' Fintan said quietly. 'Didn't you read the books I sent you? I put everything in those stories to prepare you for what lay ahead. There were several, I'm sure, about children stolen from their cradles—spirited away to come back much later and save the fortunes of their house or city or land.'

Fintan tells Kay that she has become a Mage and that she will keep her powers in the real world. She also finds in Alan Manducca the love she would have had in the past.

This brief description of the complex *Singing Stone* has excluded the element of war. (Both this book and *The Druid's Tune* include excessive violence, but they are in a sense anti-war books—the chief protagonists do not approve of war.) In fact the plenitude of incident in *The Singing Stone* is its outstanding feature—it overwhelms and takes priority over the undifferentiated characterization and dialogue, and reduces the writing style to a form of serviceable exposition. Its greatest charm lies in the strong friendship between the two young women, who of course do not know (as we do not know) that they are mother and daughter.

Of all legends, those of King Arthur and his knights have appealed most strongly to modern adult writers as material to be reworked in novelistic form. Adult fantasies based either strongly or loosely on the tales from the Arthurian cycle would fill several bookshelves. Many English writers for children have also strengthened their fantasies by a minor and consistently similar use of the Arthurian tales. The Merlin figure (with a change of name) is obvious in Alan Garner's *The Weirdstone of Brisingamen* (1960) and *Elidor* (1965). He appears under his own name in Peter Dickinson's *The Weathermonger* (1968). The legend of the sleeping Arthur and his knights, ready to rise in England's time of need, is part of the plot of *The Weirdstone of Brisingamen* and William Mayne's *Earthfasts* (1966). King Arthur's sister, Morgan Le Fay, causes trouble in Penelope Lively's *The Whispering Knights* (1971), and the use of a sword with magic powers, such as Arthur's Excalibur, is a common fantasy device. Susan

Cooper's *The Dark Is Rising* quintet (1965-77) is strongly infused with Celtic lore: there is a dominant Merlin-figure, a magic sword, an appearance by King Arthur, and a twist to the legend in that Queen Guinevere is provided with a son whom she has brought into the twentieth century.

Welwyn Wilton Katz, in *The Third Magic* (1988), relates some of the components of Arthurian legend to a complex mythology of her own devising set in 'the world of Nwm'. There the twins Rigan and Arddu share a psychic communication, although they are socially set apart from each other. Rigan, as a girl and a Sister of the First Magic or the Circle, has a special status, while Arddu, male and inferior, is an outcast. Rigan is sent by the Sisters of the First Magic on a mission to Earth, where she is reborn as Morgan Le Fay, the sister of Arthur, over whom she is intended to gain control. In the present the young teenager Morgan LeFevre—a great reader of Arthurian legends, visiting England with her parents—is taken to Tintagel Castle, and standing on the ruins, she is swept into another time and dimension:

> An archway led into the ruined inner ward of the castle. Briefly she saw a number of low stone walls delineating what had once been rooms. And then a mist rolled in, but it was not a mist. It crumpled the world, pleating foreground and background like a piece of paper, so that one became the other, or half of each, dimensions folding in on themselves, blending.

In Nwm—a terrifying Secondary World—Morgan meets Arddu, whom she resembles, and the two engage in suspenseful struggles to escape from the warring factions of the female magic of the Circle and the male magic of the Line. In the course of their frightening adventures they encounter the great talismans of the Arthurian legend (and, seemingly, of the 'Third Magic'): the sword (Excalibur) and the Grail, which transport them back to Arthurian England. On Earth, Rigan's mission fails as she sees Arthur succumb to the powers of M'rlendd (Merlin), sent to Earth by the Line, whose child Mordred she bears. (Mordred and Arthur, of course, eventually kill each other—though this has no part in *The Third Magic*.) All these strands come together in the penultimate conclusion, with Arddu and

Morgan bringing the talismans to earth for the selection of 'the once and future king'. In a scene of destruction and transformation, the original Arthur is annihilated by Rigan's 'Death Spell', but Morgan salvages the history of Earth by bringing together two parts of a jade circlet and by her wish 'to make things the way they ought to be'. The 'Third Magic' is now Earth magic and the Arthurian legend will survive intact. Morgan becomes Morgan Le Fay and Arddu becomes Arthur. In the epilogue, Morgan Le Fay has brought the dead Arthur home to Nwm (Avalon?), and is reincarnated as the modern Morgan, whose conflicting loves for her father and mother are a faint echo of the conflict between the Circle and the Line.

The plot is so complicated that it defies easy summary and accurate interpretation. It even reduces Morgan to a somewhat puzzling summation at the end:

> . . . It's all coming together, don't you see? Excalibur was on Nwm. Someone had to bring it here. The sword in the stone. The hand coming out of the lake. All those legends had to have a start. We've brought them, you see? We're where it all came from. I suppose if we hadn't come, the legends would have started another way, and they would have been the same legends, they would have to be. But we did come, and so we're the cause.

The Third Magic contains some powerful scenes. The fierce world of Nwm and the relationship of Morgan and Arddu are well drawn. But it is flawed because the interplay of the invented narrative and the Arthurian subtext is not lucid or telling, and there is a sense that the author is not in control of her story. One may well ask: why should anyone be put to so much trouble figuring out a complicated plot that has little inner logic and contains no hint of the mythological and historical importance of the central figure, Arthur?

Both Katz's *False Face* and *The Third Magic* show a great development over her earlier two books, *Witchery Hill* (1984) and *Sun God, Moon Witch* (1986). The former is a story of modern witchcraft, set in one of the Channel Islands. Two young people (the boy is from Canada) uncover a modern witch's coven, with evil rituals that include murder. There is a power struggle for the headship of the coven that entails knowledge from an arcane book that can be obtained only through the death of its possessor. The violence is gratuitous, whether it is used in reality or through the supernatural, and the plot would not be out of place in a late-night television horror show. *Sun God, Moon Witch*, as its title suggests, is steeped in mythic material. As with most modern fantasies, it is combined with a strong dose of reality. Thorny (short for Hawthorn, a tree credited in legend with magic powers) has been sent to a small English village to live with her aunt and cousin for the summer. This is an enforced visit; Thorny's father has married again and he is honeymooning in Athens. Thorny has been close to her father and also dominated by him. She finds the village in an uproar because a new squire has decided to tear down Awen-Un, a circle of standing stones of great archaeological importance. But the stones are also important to the supernatural powers, the Sun God and the Moon Witch, and Thorny is caught between them. She is approached by a mysterious lady in white (the Moon Witch), who is the embodiment of the triple deity of birth, life, and death so extensively described in Robert Graves's mythological study *The White Goddess*. The squire is named Belman, a derivation of Bel, or Baal, the sun god and the son of the moon. Thorny feels attracted to him because he reminds her of her father. These mythic figures are struggling for power over the stones, but it is only a human force that can control and defeat both—which Thorny does. *Sun God, Moon Witch* is too short a book to encompass all the mythological, archaeological, and scientific matter that Katz introduces, along with Thorny's relationship with her father. The theme of the power struggle between male and female magic in the mythological domain is presented more effectively in *The Third Magic*.

In keeping with their material, Melling and Katz have set their books (with the exception of *False Face*) in Britain and have combined many strands of myth and legend (those of Melling, and Katz's standing stones, would make books themselves). Janet Lunn, in *Shadow in Hawthorn Bay* (1986), uses only two fantasy conventions: the lure of the demon-lover, and the concept of Celtic 'second sight', which may or may not be considered a use of the supernatural. *Shadow in Hawthorn Bay*, however, is completely based in a known past, Upper Canada of the 1830s—a carefully delineated background that gives it the right to be discussed as a historical novel as well as a fantasy.

In Scotland fifteen-year-old Mary Urqquhart hears her cousin Duncan (to whom she is betrothed) calling to her across the three thousand miles that separate Scotland from Upper Canada. She responds to his voice and, alone and poor, sets off to be with him on a journey that makes most recorded pioneer emigrations seem easy. She arrives at her destination to find that Duncan has died and that his family is already on its way back to Scotland. Mary makes a life for herself among the Loyalist immigrants, but her second sight and her belief in a spirit world, so natural in her native land, disturb the practical Yankees. The dead Duncan obsesses Mary, and night after night, by the bay in which he drowned, she hears his voice calling to her to come to him. Duncan is seen only as a wild, unstable boy in Scotland, but his presence haunts the book as it does Mary. The mysterious communion of the lovers (although never physical) evokes the relationship between Heathcliff and Cathy in Emily Brontë's *Wuthering Heights*. Like Heathcliff, Duncan casts a sinister shadow. He is the demon-lover, a figure in British ballads and Celtic folklore who lures young women to their deaths (often by drowning), and the spectre lover-bridegroom who returns to claim his betrothed. Although Duncan's ghost is calling to Mary from the depths of Hawthorn Bay, his presence also functions symbolically as a negative, demonic, animus figure, a destructive aspect of Mary's own psyche. Until she rejects once and for all his seductive invitation to join him in suicide, Mary can never build another close relationship, especially with the young settler (Luke) who has asked her to marry him. Luke has come to accept Mary's special gifts, but he has also had the acumen to point out to her that she may be so caught up in her 'ghosts and fairies and strange critters' that she cannot appreciate the natural world. With a release from the spirit of Duncan, Mary finds that she can even conquer her fear of the huge sunless forest of Upper Canada that is so different from the gentle banks and braes of her native Scotland, with their benign spirits. Still, at the end a mythic sense prevails over the historicity, the realism, and the practicalities of the story. On her wedding day Mary kneels at Duncan's grave:

'It is well, Duncan,' she said. 'And it will be well, for it is meant to be. It is not the same here for me as it was at home—as it was not the same for you. The burns that rush so swiftly down our hillsides are not the creeks that wander through these deep woods. The high hills are not these low lands and the spirits of our rocks and hills and burns, the old ones who dwell in the unseen world, are not here.'

'But we are not to grieve. The old ones came to our hills in the ancient times. It began somewhere. It began there long ago as it begins now here. We are the old ones here.'

Mary fell silent. She stood up. Then she said again, very softly, 'It is so, we are the old ones here.' She went back to her house to dress for her wedding.

Mary and Duncan are to be seen as the vessels through which ancient beliefs will become rooted in a new world that has been devoid of them. (Native myth, unknown to the settlers, is never acknowledged by the author.)

Because of the age of its heroine and its romantic overtones, *Shadow in Hawthorn Bay* could be considered a novel for young adults. Yet its plot and page-turning quality make it equally available to children; while its nuances in characterization, its classic style, and its rich portrayal of a pioneer society make it attractive to adults. It is indeed a book for everyone.

The child in Cora Taylor's *Julie* (1986) also possesses extra-sensory perception. By the age of three Julie Morgan (her father calls her his 'little Celtic child') experiences second sight, and as she grows to the age of ten she struggles to handle her special gift. She is surrounded by happy, normal brothers and sisters, but she feels estranged from her mother, who does not want to acknowledge Julie's second sight. At the climax of the story Julie's gift saves her father's life, but with a sudden addition to her powers—telekinesis: she is able to cause the tractor to move off her father's body. This second ability is an intrusion in an otherwise believable and moving story. The pictures of full family life and the atmospheric prairie setting build a foundation of realism that supports the psychic element.

Michael Bedard's *A Darker Magic* (1987) incorporates elements of black sorcery and demonic possession. In a small town that could be anywhere in North America the lives of three disparate characters become intertwined as they move towards August 8th, the date when a mysterious magic show, only for children, is to be performed by a sinister Professor Mephisto. There are two plots that eventually form a whole. There is Miss Potts, the elderly schoolteacher who remembers an August 8th magic show in her childhood when the magician was an agent of evil and murder. Enlisting the help of teen-aged Emily, she tries to stop the second arrival of the magic show. Their immediate concern is an older teenager, Craig. He seems to be endangering himself by becoming obsessed with another teenager, Scott, a kind of Pied Piper for Professor Mephisto, who can manipulate reality and illusion. As in so many modern fantasies, the fantasy itself is inexplicable. A second magic show takes place, its audience made up of the ghosts of the children who mysteriously died after participating in the performances of earlier years. The professor's machinations are resisted and foiled by Emily and Craig. But who is this sinister magician who wants to destroy children? Is he really to be taken as the devil? He hardly appears in the book, though he is the *deus ex machina* of the plot. Why is Craig a special target of malevolence? On the other hand, the realistic component is highly successful. For example, we are drawn into the humdrum routine of Miss Potts' life in a boarding-house and Emily's homelife in a lower-income family, with a harassed mother and boisterous, manic siblings. These scenes are often genuinely funny. *A Darker Magic* is much in the vein of the psychic fantasies by the New Zealand writer Margaret Mahy (*The Haunting*, 1983, and *The Changeover*, 1984). Mahy, however, is a superior stylist and her approach to the supernatural is far more restrained than that of Bedard.

David Day's *The Emperor's Panda* (1986) tells of the imaginary period of China's Celestial Empire when the world was magic and filled with dragons, unicorns, griffins, and gorgons. The rarest creature of all was the panda. The Master Panda is called Lord Beishung and he represents 'the essence of balance', because the panda is equal parts black and white. (Eric Beddows' fine drawings of the Chinese characters and setting emphasize this theme of Taoist life-balance through their light and dark tonal variations.) Lord Beishung guides the young flute player Kung (he has learned his art from 'the wind in the grass and bamboo') in his quest to find his uncle. *The Emperor's Panda* is basically an extended folktale, and has both the wisdom and humour that have kept such tales alive. David Day often has a poetic turn of phrase, which he combines with some modern colloquialisms and plays on words that appear to be deliberately anachronistic for humorous effect. (The Master Panda returns to the Emperor's court to save the kingdom from 'panda-monium'.) It is on the whole a delightful story, but some judicious cutting would have made it even better.

This is also true of Donn Kushner's *A Book Dragon* (1987). It begins in England five hundred years ago with a straightfaced account of the family of Nonesuch, the dragon, and particularly of his grandmother, who—like all good dragons—guarded a treasure in a cave. This first part of the book is a spoof of dragon lore, with stories of fierce dragons, foolish dragons, and even a revisionist explanation of the dragon who was killed by St George. When Nonesuch strangely shrinks to the size of a dragonfly he discovers a monk drawing beautiful pictures for a medieval Book of Hours. (The medieval aspect of the story is emphasized in Nancy Ruth Jackson's extended initial letters that begin each chapter in the tradition of the illuminated manuscript.) The monk glimpses Nonesuch and inserts glowing pictures of the little dragon in his illustrations, and the book becomes Nonesuch's own treasure to guard. When it is stolen he is trapped inside the box that contains the book and there he remains, with brief forays outside, for centuries. The book ends up in a modern bookstore in North America whose proprietor knows its value and cherishes it. When a developer wants to buy the site of the bookstore, Nonesuch turns back briefly into his former large dragon size and destroys him—regretfully, because he is a friendly dragon—thus saving the bookstore. He then reverts to his miniature size to stay with his book. This is a well-written fantasy, but it is filled with historical allusions and satire that seem to address the literate adult.

ANIMAL FANTASY AND BEAST TALES

Stories of talking animals have constituted one of the most popular and enduring forms of children's literature in the English language. This roster includes Rudyard Kipling's *The Jungle Book* (1894), Kenneth Grahame's *The Wind in the Willows* (1908), E.B. White's *Charlotte's Web* (1952), Robert O'Brien's *Mrs Frisby and the Rats of NIMH* (1971), and Richard Adams' *Watership Down* (1972). Basically these writers have taken animal characteristics that tend to reflect those of a certain type of human and transposed them to produce a mirror-image of human behaviour. The resulting picture of ourselves may be friendly, ironic, devastatingly cutting, or a combination thereof. Although both *The Wind in the Willows* and *Watership Down* contain these elements of animal/human life, Grahame and Adams are worlds apart in their concept of fantasy. Adams' rabbits are completely natural; they live in burrows and warrens, eat only what real rabbits eat, and do nothing that their kind could not do given a measure of human intelligence. Adams provides them with their own language (not human speech) and a kind of *lingua franca* for their converse with birds and other animals. In contrast, Grahame's Rat, Mole, Badger and Toad wear the clothes of English country gentlemen, have household goods, and consume human food and drink. This gives *The Wind in the Willows* the greater aura of fantasy, while *Watership Down* is better described as a beast tale—a descendant, though a complex one, of Aesop's *Fables*. However, each book is successful in its own way, owing to their writers' ability to command belief in their talking animals and to their insights into human nature. Grahame's restless Toad conveys the Edwardian spirit of change, while Adams' General Wormwort is a rabbit model of a fascist dictator. It is this interchange of human and animal personalities that distinguishes animal fantasy from stories in which the animals have supernatural powers—Day's Master Panda or Kushner's 'book dragon'.

The first Canadian animal fantasy was W.A. Fraser's *Mooswa and Others of the Boundaries* (1900), which has a large cast of talking animals, each with a distinct personality. They include:

MOOSWA, *the Moose*. Protector of the Boy

MUSKWA, *the Bear.*

BLACK FOX, *King of the Boundaries.*

ROF, *the Blue Wolf.* Leader of the Gray Wolf pack.

CARCAJOU, *the Wolverine.* Lieutenant to Black King, and known as the 'Devil of the Woods.'

. . .

and

ROD, *The Boy.* Son of Donald MacGregor, formerly Factor to Hudson's Bay Company at Fort Resolution.

When Rod was a little chap, Mooswa had been brought into Fort Resolution as a calf, his mother having been killed, and they became playmates. Then MacGregor was moved to Edmonton, and Rod was brought up in civilization until he was fourteen, when he got permission to go back to the Athabasca for a Winter's trapping with François, who was an old servant of the Factor's. This story is of that Winter. Mooswa had been turned loose in the forest by Factor MacGregor when leaving the Fort.

The animals are bound together by a covenant, the 'Law of the Boundaries', whose oath begins:

'We, Dwellers with the Boundaries, swear by the Spirit of Wiesahkechack, who is God of the Indians and all Animals, that, come Trap, come Ironstick, come White-powdered Bait, come Snare, come Arrow, come what soe'er may, we will help each other, and warn each other, and keep ward for each other; in the Star-time and the Sun-time, in the Flower-time and the Snow-time; that the call of one for help shall be the call of all; and the fight of one shall be the fight of all; and the enemy of one shall be the enemy of all. . . .'

Clearly influenced by Kipling's *Jungle Books*, published a few years before, and such Biblical conventions as the wandering tribe, the patriarch (Mooswa), and the covenant, Fraser wrote a rather lumbering but not uninteresting fantasy in which the talkative animals and their elevated discourse are offset by their naturalistic habits and actions and the believable atmosphere of the Boundaries—the 'great Spruce forests and Muskeg lands lying between the Saskatchewan River, the Arctic Ocean, and the Rocky Mountains'.

The few early recent Canadian animal fantasies have been an unbroken succession of failures, chiefly because their authors did not understand this special genre. Mazo de la Roche's *The Song of Lambert* (1955), Fred Lindsay's *Mouse Mountain* (1964), and Margaret Laurence's *Jason's Quest* (1970) offer only counterfeits of animals and parodies of humans; there is insight into neither. Margaret Laurence, for example, was satisfied with a simple transference of human externals to the animal world. Glitter La Fay, the mole singer, plays at the Mousedrome rather than the Hippodrome; paws are clapped rather than hands, and 'appearance is only fur-deep'. The result bears more resemblance to a cartoon than to a genuine fantasy.

The few recent animal fantasies are, on the whole, more successful than those of the past. Heather Kellerhals-Stewart with *The Whale's Way* (1988), M. Wylie Blanchet with *A Whale Named Henry* (1983), and Beatrice Culleton with *Spirit of the White Bison* (1985) are obvious followers of Adams rather than Grahame. The whales and the bison perform no acts that are beyond their mammal capabilities, and the fantasy (other than animal speech) is minimal. *The Whale's Way* has the most interesting structure as it combines the adventures of a bumptious young whale, a barnyard goose of great good sense, and the lives of a young boy, Jesse, and his autistic sister, Merle, who live on Quadra Island off the British Columbia coast. Raza the whale is shot and wounded by a hunter and takes refuge in an inlet where he is befriended by Flora the goose. Flora, although she has escaped butchering, likes and understands humans, and when she and Raza come in contact with the children she realizes that there is something special about Merle. She is right. Merle can communicate with Raza by making the same clicking sounds (somewhat like Morse code) by which whales communicate with each other. Like Raza, too, she can sense an approaching storm. In a satisfactory ending Raza saves Jesse from drowning, the children's lives are improved, Flora stays with Merle, and Raza, his wound healed, swims off to find his pod.

Some plot details of *A Whale Named Henry* are remarkably similar to Kellerhals-Stewart's story. Blanchet's Henry is a fifty-foot adolescent and behaves like one; he will not listen to his mother. As a result he is trapped in an inlet and only finds his way out with the help of a young wounded seagull. The text is a long short story, copiously illustrated and with detailed maps of the west coast of British Columbia, showing Henry at all stages of his adventures. Culleton's *Spirit of the White Bison* is set in the past, and with its intense (and accurate) descriptions of the white man's slaughter of the Prairie buffalo in the nineteenth century it could also be considered historical fiction. However, it is also reminiscent of the kind of animal autobiography that was made popular for a time by Anna Sewell's *Black Beauty* (1877) and Marshall Saunders' *Beautiful Joe* (1894), both of which are message books on behalf of the prevention of cruelty to domestic animals. The voice of Culleton's white buffalo is also a *cri de coeur*, but one that relates to a past disaster that cannot be rectified—the disappearance of the buffalo and the resulting disappearance of the traditional native way of life. *Spirit of the White Buffalo* is a tragic story.

On the whole the strengths of Kellerhals-Stewart, Blanchet, and Culleton lie in their realism. In both *The Whale's Way* and *A Whale Named Henry* there is no doubt about the authors' knowledge of whales and their ways (overly demonstrated in the latter book). Much of the appeal of the former lies in the family life of Jesse and Merle, living alone on the island with their lumberman father (their mother has abandoned them for the bright lights of Vancouver), and in Jesse's care of his young sister. The fantasy in both books is chiefly confined to the unusual relationship between a whale and a bird, with the birds showing a remarkable ability to cling to the backs of killer whales. The fantasy element of *Spirit of the White Bison* is even less evident. In spite of its title, the bison is not to be considered a spirit creature (the author disclaims any such mythic intent). Yet there are anomalies and hints of the supernatural that are not well integrated into the story. Considering its colouring, it is remarkable that the bison survived for so long, even though at times it appeared to be invisible to its enemies.

In animal fantasy it is to be expected that animals should be centre-stage, yet there is more to the genre than simply having them talk. Craftsmanship is of the utmost importance. Animals can all too easily become wooden symbols of humans, or they can become too naturalistic and remain merely animals who perform actions that cannot be credited. Basically *The Whale's Way* and *Spirit of the White Bison* are a step above the latter method, with their concerns that transcend the animal dimension. With the introduction of child and family life into the former and history into the latter, Kellerhals-Stewart and Culleton may have given Canadian animal fantasy a new direction.

LIGHT FANTASY

Humour and wit are the identifying marks of light fantasy, whose authors often poke fun at the very form they are using. Whether the humour is broadly cartoon-like, child-simple, or sophisticatedly adult, its presence removes the stories from the threatening struggles and the deep meanings of serious fantasy. Some of the most enduring (and endearing) fantasies for younger children fall into this category—Pamela Travers' *Mary Poppins* (1934), Astrid Lindgren's *Pippi Longstocking*, published in English in 1950, and Helen Cresswell's *The Piemakers* (1967).

A small group of Canadian writers have explored aspects of this sub-genre. Hazel Hutchins gently mocks the conventions of magic and fairy-tale wishes in *Anastasia Morningstar and the Crystal Butterfly* (1984), *The Three and Many Wishes of Jason Reid* (1983), and *Casey*

Webber the Great (1988). She depicts ordinary children whose orderly lives are disrupted by extraordinary people or talismans. *Anastasia* begins: 'On a bright morning in May the lady [Anastasia] at the corner grocery store turned Derek Henshaw into a frog.' The children, Anna and Ben, witness the transformation and take Anastasia as the subject of their science project. As a result of the friendship that develops they discover the mystery of Anastasia's nature. In *The Three and Many Wishes of Jason Reid* eleven-year-old Jason is offered three wishes by an elfish creature called Quicksilver, who comes 'stepping through' earth. Jason is a 'good thinker' and avoids the mistakes of the greedy careless folk in the fairy tales who have to use their third wish to undo their first two. Jason uses his third wish to request three more, and so on, endlessly. Anastasia is a kind of Mary Poppins, and the irritable Quicksilver resembles the grumpy Psammead in Edith Nesbit's *Five Children and It* (1902). The source of the magic in *Casey Webber the Great* is a jacket of invisibility. Like all Hutchins' children, Casey discovers the differences between 'real' magic, the power of the imagination, and the trickery and showmanship of being a magician. Hutchins' stories are also cautionary tales: the use of magic (or its talismans) is shown to be potentially dangerous, and the children wisely surrender the extraordinary for the ordinary, returning enriched to their everyday lives. As befits her play with fairy-tale motifs, her style is tongue-in-cheek, with touches of poetic invention.

The miniature Tom Thumb (of King Arthur's court) and his female counterpart, Hans Christian Andersen's Thumbelina, have been transferred from folklore to fantasy in many children's novels; one thinks immediately of Arrietty in Mary Norton's *The Borrowers* (1952) and Stuart in E.B. White's *Stuart Little* (1952), who is a human-like mouse. Tina, a diminutive of Peanutina, in Jane Jacobs' *The Girl on the Hat* (1989), is so tiny that 'if she curled up and scrunched her toes she could fit into a peanut shell'. Like Stuart Little, she is born into an ordinary family and escapes one disaster after another, always with the help of her beloved peanuts. Also like Stuart (who at one time becomes a teacher), Tina wants 'a useful life for herself' and becomes an 'Animal Photographer'. But unlike her counterparts in folklore and fantasy, Tina does not stay small forever; she begins to grow. Her family wonders why:

'Maybe it's because of your adventures,' said Tina's mother.
'Maybe it's because you work so hard,' said Ernest.
'Maybe it's because you wanted to,' said her father.
'Maybe it's because it was just time to,' said Tina.

The breezy tone and comic escapades bring to mind Astrid Lindgren's *Pippi Longstocking*. Tina is also like Pippi in her affirmation of child autonomy in a powerful adult world.

Mordecai Richler's Jacob of *Jacob Two-Two Meets the Hooded Fang* (1975) has received his name because he is 'two plus two plus two' years old and because, as the smallest child in the family, he has to say things twice to get the attention of anyone in his busy home. In a dream sequence he is incarcerated in the dungeon of Slimer's Isle, a children's prison, for allegedly insulting an adult by asking a question twice. Through a series of farcical events Jacob proves his worth. He discovers the secret childish heart of the dreaded jailer (The Hooded Fang), and with the help of his brother and sister rescues the other child prisoners. Richler achieves a raw comic-book appeal. Its 'Superman' imagery (Jacob's brother and sister are dressed in 'Day-Glo blue jeans and flying golden capes, the spine-chilling emblem *Child Power* emblazoned on their chests') is far less evident in its sequel, *Jacob Two-Two and the Dinosaur* (1987). It has a Canadian setting as opposed to the English one of the first book, and Richler has another original plot line (Jacob rescues a friendly dinosaur from extermination by self-serving politicians in a brave escape to the Rocky Mountains). But it is also a heavy-handed satire on politics and other aspects of contemporary life. Jacob's brother Daniel extols a rock group:

'Dracula and the Nose-Pickers are playing at the Palace tonight,' Daniel said. 'They're really great! They chop pianos to bits, whack each other over the head with guitars, and spray the crowd with hot pig's blood.'

This adult, mordant humour overpowers the childlike aspects of the plot, greatly to its detriment. The finely drawn pen-and-ink illustrations by Norman Eyolfson are also satirically adult.

Young Galahad of Morgan Nyberg's *Galahad Schwartz and the Cockroach Army* (1987) is also a child saviour, as befits his name. When his father and mother do not return from their balloon flight to transform the Sahara desert into a garden, he leaves his South

American jungle home to live with his Grandfather in the North American town of Glitterville. Here, through the power of his shaman-like friend from the jungle, he learns to communicate with insects and pigeons, and with their help he defeats the fascist villains who are using a disappearing gas on elderly citizens, and restores order and democracy to the town. The manic energy of the plot and the cast of stereotyped eccentrics align it with Richler's tales; and the helpful insects and birds are obviously akin to those in Roald Dahl's *James and the Giant Peach* (1961), but lack their individuality. Despite sporadic attempts at a 'magic realist' tone, *Galahad Schwartz* more accurately resembles light comic-book entertainment.

Kenneth Oppel's *Colin's Fantastic Video Adventure* (1985), written when he was fourteen, keeps to a now fairly ordinary realm of childhood. One day Colin's favourite video game of Meteoroids turns into magic as two miniature space pilots (Drogel and Snogel) pop out of the screen into Colin's pocket. In a clever conspiracy the three are able to manipulate the game and win all the Meteoroid contests. They are on their way to the world championship when Colin's conscience overtakes him and he deliberately loses the game. The simple, lively story is enriched by the contrasting characters of Drogel and Snogel, a few sly observations on adult behaviour—and a surprise ending.

All these works are best described as stories of magic rather than fantasy. They are basically in the tradition of the Edwardian Edith Nesbit, who brought this sub-genre of fantasy to its full flowering in such stories as *Five Children and It*. All take place in the real world, and their chief strength lies in the contrast between the ordinary and the fabulous. Due importance is given to the children's everyday lives, and in this respect they are contemporary stories of childhood. Still, their motivating force (and greatest charm) comes from the children's belief in magic and its momentary gracing of their lives.

Most of the fantasies discussed in this chapter were published in the 1980s. It is too soon to make predictions about which, if any, will last, but few stand out as shining examples of the genre. The younger tales of light fantasy and animal fantasy are modest in literary impact, compared to the larger group of more serious and ambitiously complex fantasies. They do, however, share a bright, contemporary tone and playful charm. The most noticeable trend within the serious fantasies—and one that links the new Canadian fantasies with those of Britain, the United States, Australia, and New Zealand—is the age of the protagonists: they now tend to be teenagers rather than children. This move of fantasy into the field of almost young-adult literature allows for the introduction of more complex subject matter, more subtle relationships between adults and the young, as well as romantic interest. The relative freedom implied by this wider scope has been taken by some writers to mean licence to indulge in the unrestrained and uncontrolled invention of ambitious swirling epics whose conundrums simply work against 'the willing suspension of disbelief'. Melling, Katz, and Bedard, for example, are certainly steeped in their mythological subjects, but this knowledge has led them, on occasion, into a dense thicket of foggy, contrived mysticism where credibility and emotional involvement are imperilled. Fantasy exacts a degree of discipline from its practitioners, far beyond the demands of realism, in order to compel what Tolkien, in his essay 'On Fairy-tales', has called 'A Secondary Belief':

> Anyone inheriting the fantastic device of human language can say *the green sun*. Many can then imagine it or picture it. But that is not enough. . . . . To make a Secondary World inside which the green sun will be credible, commanding Secondary Belief, will probably require labour and thought, and will certainly demand a special skill, a kind of elvish craft.

On the whole, Canadian fantasists are not elvish, and neither are their contemporaries in other countries. They are better realists than fantasists, creating their most memorable scenes in full reality—such as Emily's hectic family life in Bedard's *A Darker Magic* and Madeleine's family relationships in Clark's *The Moons of Madeleine*.

All the best fantasies of the past, whatever their sub-genre—past-time fantasy (Alison Uttley's *A Traveller in Time*), animal fantasy (E.B. White's *Charlotte's Web*), epic fantasy (Susan Cooper's *The Dark Is Rising* quintet)—have simple plots, with richness and complexity being supplied by the characters themselves and the author's view of life. In Canadian fantasy, too, the simpler fantasies work best and certainly carry the most conviction: Kit Pearson's *A Handful of Time*, Joan Clark's *Wild Man of the Woods*, and Janet Lunn's *Shadow in Hawthorn Bay*.

Locating the story outside Canada and in the far-distant (or mythic) past is another trend in recent books, although a minor one at present. Bedard's *A Darker Magic*, however, has no recognizable setting, a rarity in fantasy. Most writers name or identify subtly a specific locality. Ruth Nichols' setting for *A Walk Out of the World* is unnamed, but it is familiarly Canadian and (to a Vancouverite) recognizably Vancouver.

Another trend in non-Canadian fantasy is the endowment of the young with on-going special powers, ranging from simple ESP to destructive psychic ones. The teen-age protagonists can now also be witches or magicians. The children of earlier books, of course, were furnished with nothing but the occasional talisman, whose magic powers ended with the story, and had to rely on their innate abilities rather than on the supernatural. Canadian fantasists have kept to this older tradition. Two exceptions are Julie in Cora Taylor's *Julie* and Mary in Janet Lunn's *Shadow in Hawthorn Bay*. In both books the possession of extra powers is used with exemplary discretion and the two heroines are shown as ultra-sensitive to their surroundings and to other people. Thus credibility is maintained.

The plenitude of recent books tells us that fantasy is very much alive in Canada. Their inventiveness shows us that the scope of the genre has widened considerably; and their emphasis on characterization and overall sophistication (in comparison with earlier books) demonstrate that they are in step with fantasies from other English-speaking countries. Among all our recent fantasies, the best ones are rooted in the Canadian experience.

9

Science Fiction

C.S. Lewis pointed out the difficulties of defining science fiction when he wrote:

> You can, if you wish, class all science-fiction together; but it is about as perceptive as classing the works of Ballantyne, Conrad and W.W. Jacobs together as 'the sea story' and then criticising that.

Science fiction may be undefinable simply because of its wide perimeters. The *aficionados* of the genre who reject the term in favour of the abbreviation S/F are perhaps taking the more sensible approach. S/F can stand for Science Fiction, Science Fantasy, Space Fantasy, Speculative Fiction, or even the grotesque 'Schlock Fantasy'. It may be this breadth that inspired the science-fiction writer and critic Brian Aldiss to describe it as 'a wacky sort of fiction that grabs and engulfs anything new or old for its subject matter, turning it into a shining and often unsubstantial wonder'. It certainly does grab and engulf, taking in fantasy, realism, historical fiction, and social fiction, melding them frequently into a potpourri. Realistic fiction, historical fiction, and fantasy have more precise limits and are strengthened thereby.

The term science fiction, of course, suggests that some aspect of science or technology, or an extrapolation of them, should be included in the work, just as one expects history to be a strong component of the historical novel. But such is not generally the case, especially in modern science fiction, probably because most writers in this field, particularly those for children, are not scientists. Most science fiction, however, is promulgated on the future, and in this aspect it can be seen as the opposite of historical fiction. Entry into the unknown should give writers a tremendous freedom of movement for, as Walter de la Mare has noted in his children's fantasy, *The Three Mullah Mulgars* (1910), 'the future is easier to manage than the past'. The stories may take place in the future; they may take place on another planet; the characters may have advanced technology at their disposal and so have unusual life-styles. But whatever projections of worlds are described, the messages are for the here and now. In this aspect of the genre, science-fiction writers for children are continuing its basic tradition of issuing warnings about what may happen in the future if present society does not mend its ways.

Science fiction is thus not only the antithesis of historical fiction (the past cannot be changed); it is also in contrast to modern children's realistic fiction, which is premised on individuals and their personal concerns—often narrowly so. While some recent science fiction concentrates on character as well as on issues, the genre is still the only one that asks its readers to look at a society rather than at themselves. Its service here is a great one.

In many ways science fiction is allied to fantasy. Indeed, it has been called 'a branch of fantasy' by a critic of science fiction, Sam Moskowitz. Fantasy has its conventions, including the use of talismans, dreams, time-travel, and, latterly, extrasensory perception. Science fiction has also developed its own conventions: intergalactic travel that excludes scientific probabilities, time-machines, sentient computers, aliens, and above all atomic and ecological disasters, with causes either unexplained or broadly sketched. In both fantasy and science fiction, to be a little too picky about details is to 'strain at a gnat and swallow a camel'.

Science fiction written deliberately for the young came quite late into children's literature. Although children read Jules Verne's *Twenty Thousand Leagues Under the Sea* (1870), Conan Doyle's *The Lost World* (1912), and H.G. Wells's *The War of the Worlds* (1898), these were directed at an adult audience and were not, in their time, considered science fiction; the term was not coined until 1926, in the first issue of *Amazing Stories*. The first clearly identifiable American science-fiction novel for children is Robert A. Heinlein's *Rocket Ship Galileo* (1947), in which three high-school boys and a scientist travel, in a made-in-the-backyard rocket, to the moon, where they find and defeat a nest of Nazis who were preparing for world conquest. The first in England was David Craigie's *The Voyage of the Luna I* (1948), which, among other improbabilities, puts flora and fauna on the moon. In general this 'space opera' approach has disappeared from children's science fiction, being replaced by S/F, standing for 'speculative fiction'.

The first, and for a considerable time the only, Canadian science fiction for children was by the French-Canadian writer Suzanne Martel, *Surréal 3000*, translated into English as *The City Underground* (1964). The story is premised on what could happen after an atomic devastation (a theme dear to the hearts of science-fiction writers, whether for adults or children). Under the city that was once Montreal, a highly technical arid society develops, with its people forbidden to go above ground for fear of radiation effects. On the outside, a more primitive society that has kept close to the natural world struggles to exist. Through the curiosity and daring of a young teenager, the two disparate civilizations are brought together and discover that they need one another. The English translation is crisp and clean in style and the book has deservedly remained popular.

The more recent science-fiction scene in Canada has been the almost single-handed creation of Monica Hughes. Most other Canadian offerings, and indeed most science fiction from either England or the United States, do not measure up to her best works: *The Tomorrow City* (1978), *Beyond the Dark River* (1979), *Ring-Rise, Ring-Set* (1982), *The Keeper of the Isis Light* (1980) and its sequel *The Guardian of Isis* (1981), *Devil on My Back* (1984), and its sequel *The Dream Catcher* (1986). All Hughes' books contain very strong messages. These range from a concern for the environment (the more natural the better) to a plea for respect and tolerance for all people (differences among us should be celebrated, not feared). Monica Hughes is particularly interested in a contrast of cultures and, like many writers of science fiction, she appears to distrust technology. Her messages are all the more effective because they are contained within strong plots—she is a good storyteller—and have well-defined characters, chiefly young female teenagers.

The Tomorrow City is set in Thomsonville, which might be any future city in North America. Caro's father has invented a computer, C-Three, to handle all the problems of the city, such as directing traffic and collecting the garbage. The computer has also been programmed to care for the children, since they are the city's future. In addition the father has also programmed Caro's special needs into it, thus making her C-Three's 'dear' (or 'caro'). When there are complaints from the citizens about the computer's arbitrary ways, Caro is on the computer's side and says to it: 'If it were *my* city . . . I'd *make* people be sensible and want the right things.' C-Three does just that, and soon there is no need for opposition. Strange things begin to happen. Tramps disappear and elderly people are taken away to a Home and their houses are razed to make parks or playgrounds for the children; cigarettes and candy disappear from the shelves of stores; people appear to be hypnotized by television; and finally the weather is artificially controlled by a dome spread over the city. Caro realizes that she is responsible for C-Three's behaviour and determines to rectify it. She and her friend David, seemingly the only two in the city unaffected by the computer's hypnotic power, manage to break into its fortress-like room. The plan is for Caro to engage C-Three in conversation, trying to make it see the error of its ways, while David attempts to break its circuits. The ensuing conversation is philosophical, but also childlike, as Caro tries to explain to C-Three that children must be allowed to learn from experience: 'If they never see anything sad or ugly or dirty, how are they going to learn compassion?' By flinging herself in front of David when C-Three finally shoots a laser beam at him, she demonstrates her point that humans are made up of more than brains and body—against the computer's argument that humans must be forced to achieve cold logic in every action. The beam blinds Caro, and when the computer realizes that it has hurt the child it was created to protect, it self-destructs. Stories of intelligent computers are rife in science fiction for adults (especially in short-story form), but Hughes' novel has a particular freshness and depth because of the children's unselfish and decisive actions. If the melodramatic and naïve ending is reminiscent of many an episode in the TV serial *Star Trek*, it is still appropriate for this book.

The disparity between cultural groups in a future Canada forms the basic theme for *Beyond the Dark River* and *Ring-Rise, Ring-Set*. Both are also premised on disasters—apparently nuclear in the former, and the return of the Ice Age in the latter. The Hutterites of *Beyond the*

Dark River are still a closed society in the twenty-first century; indeed, they are even more reclusive than in the past and have lost all knowledge of technology. The children of the colony (the Bruderhof) are ill with a mysterious fever, and the elders reluctantly allow young Benjamin to leave the settlement to consult an Indian 'heathen witch'. Benjamin finds a young girl, Daughter-of-She-Who-Came-After, who is destined to succeed her grandmother as her tribe's Healer. She accompanies Benjamin to the Bruderhof and does her best for the children with her care and herbal remedies. Then Benjamin and the girl decide to make their way to the University Library in Edmonton—the City of the Dead—to try to find medical aid through books. They embark on a dangerous voyage downriver, only to encounter nightmarish adventures with bestial, misshapen humans who capture Benjamin and almost make him a human sacrifice to their god, and a half-crazed but cunning librarian who tries to send them to their deaths. Their quest is a failure (the medical books give the symptoms of illnesses, but medical remedies are unavailable). The strong implication of the plot is that back at the Bruderhof the simple native remedies are working a cure.

Although the story involves science fiction's usual stern messages—the Hutterites' isolation has made them more susceptible to disease—the story belongs to Benjamin and Daughter-of-She-Who-Came-After. Both have been seeking to take on adult roles, and in their rites of passage to adulthood, symbolized by the journey downriver to Edmonton, and in their fight for survival, they learn to value each other's heritage, spirit, and disparate personalities. This, or course, is a common theme in Canadian fiction, such as Farley Mowat's *Lost in the Barrens* (1956) and James Houston's *Frozen Fire* (1977). But here the poignancy of two young people, who have come to love one another and must part when they realize they have special roles to fulfil in their own cultures, adds a special dimension of both sadness and responsibility.

Ring-Rise, Ring-Set contrasts two societies: the 'Techs', the scientists who are living in almost an underground city in the Canadian Arctic, and the 'Ekoes' (Eskimos), who have reverted to the nomadic, igloo-building, hunting ways of their forebears. The Ekoes are described as warm, loving, and communal. The Techs also live a communal life, but one that is cold and highly organized; children rarely see their parents, food is chiefly synthetic, and no consideration is given to individual problems or needs. The Techs are desperately searching for a solution to control and eventually stop the imminent threat of a new Ice Age, which could overwhelm the whole of North America and eventually the world. They feel they have found a stop-gap, but it is destroying the environment upon which the Ekoes depend for their very existence. The question posed at the end of the book is whether a few thousand people must be sacrificed to save millions and even billions of people. The Ekoes have obviously adapted to the changing climate, but this would in no way be true of people in the southern cities.

The link between the two societies is teen-aged Liza who, in a fit of rebellion against the stifling atmosphere of the city, smuggles herself onto an outside expedition, is accidentally abandoned, and then rescued by an Ekoe family. Here she is assumed to be an Ekoe girl, Iriook, who had been taken away by spirits and is now miraculously returned to her mother, who receives her joyfully. At first Liza accepts her role to save her life. But gradually, over a year, she sheds her antiseptic, technical upbringing and psychologically merges her modern identity with that of Iriook. However, when she sees the devastation caused by the Techs (they are sprinkling the snow with a poisonous black substance that will absorb the sun's rays), she returns to the city to confront the scientists. Failing to convince them of their wrongdoing, she returns to her Ekoe family, who are equally determined not to join the Techs in their city to survive. The story ends in both romance and a question. Liza will marry the young Ekoe whom she has come to love as Iriook, and they will wait out their fate. But will they have happiness for more than a year? Given Hughes' general optimistic view of life, the answer must be yes.

Isis of *The Keeper of the Isis Light* is a habitable planet, with only two inhabitants: Olwen, age sixteen, and the 'keeper of the Isis Light', since her parents were killed in an accident when she was a baby, and a companion whom Olwen affectionately calls Guardian, not realizing that he is a robot, programmed by her parents to care for her. Olwen and Guardian live in the upper reaches of Isis, close to the Light that constantly sends out signals to passing space traffic and reports on weather conditions on Isis back to Earth. Now the planet is to be colonized by settlers who have arrived in a spaceship from overcrowded Earth. At first Olwen resents the settlers, but then wishes to be friendly, particularly when she is attracted to seventeen-year-old Mark London, who returns her affection. When Olwen first meets the newcomers, or when she is with Mark, she wears a protective suit that covers even her face. Guardian assures her that it is a necessary precaution against germs. Then one day Mark laboriously climbs up the rock-face to her home and sees Olwen standing with her back to him:

> She was like Isis as she stood there. She was alien, like the wonderful tangy drink, like the scented golden flower, like the rolling mountains. . . .
> 'Olwen.' He spoke again. This time she heard him and turned in a sudden swirl of copper hair and opalescent drapery.
> Mark staggered to his feet and took one totally involuntary step backward. . . . He was going over backward into space.

Olwen and Guardian save Mark's life, but he is injured and Olwen feels that she saw a look of horror on his face before he fell. Now Guardian explains that when she was a child, he altered her body and features to protect her from all the dangers on Isis and also so that she could breathe naturally the upper air of the mountains and withstand the sun's ultra-violet rays. The changes she has undergone are graphically described in the sequel, *The Guardian of Isis*:

> Her face was broad, with wide nostrils and thick lips, not unlike his own. The forehead, though high, was strangely shaped and bumpy. But these details were insignificant beside the one startling impossible fact that her skin was a deep and irridescent bronzy-green, and not smooth like a person's, but scaly like a snake's.

Olwen's relations with the settlers deteriorate, even though she saves the life of one of the children. She and the Captain of the spaceship do not get along, because he sees her as less than human and points out that the planet is no longer hers alone. When Mark sees photographs of Olwen (she has insisted on sending them to him), he rejects her completely. Bruised in spirit, she and Guardian withdraw to an inaccessible part of Isis, with Guardian as her representative to the colonists' council meetings when he is needed.

The clear message of the book is that we fear and hate those who are different from us. When the Captain tries to make excuses for the killing of Olwen's beloved pet, Hobbit, saying that the men thought it was a hairy dragon, Olwen replies: 'He couldn't help looking the way he did, you know!' It is also a story of adolescent rites of passage and decision-making. When the Captain suggests to Olwen that she return to earth where science might be able to turn her into a normal-looking person, she rejects the offer. With her face and body as they are, all of Isis is open to her and she refuses to give up this freedom of movement. The settlers are confined to the valley unless they wear special suits and masks.

The Keeper of the Isis Light is a rich story, as well as a page-turning one. The planet is different enough from Earth to give a sense of an alien setting;

> Olwen looked around her at the purple and orange mountains, at the silvery grey grass, at the empty sky, and she stretched out her arms as if she could embrace the world. Oh, how lucky she was to have a whole beautiful planet to herself.

Her love for her planet is never described sentimentally; she is simply at one with it.

In *The Guardian of Isis*, Mark is now the President of the colony and, particularly owing to his leadership, the colony has reverted to a primitive agricultural society and is stagnating. All the scientific knowledge and capabilities the first settlers had brought with them have been lost or are discredited. A strange mixture of myth and taboo has taken the place of technology. There is also a strict hierarchy, with women at the bottom.

Jody, the black grandson of the child Olwen once saved, is an anomaly in the settlement. He is curious, resourceful, and of an inventive cast of mind. Feeling threatened by Jody, Mark finds an excuse to have him banished—basically a death sentence, because the settlers have never travelled beyond their valley. Jody survives very well, eventually meets Guardian and is taken on a 'floater' (an air-raft) to meet Olwen. Here he learns that all he has been taught is a lie. Jody has already sensed that his village is in danger from the rising waters of the river and he and Guardian are able to rechannel it, with Jody accomplishing the most difficult and dangerous part of the task.

Jody has passed his initiation tests and feels that he has become a man. With determination, courage, and new-found knowledge he sets out, at the end, for his village: 'Then one day, not too far into the future, he would lead his people out of their narrow Valley and show them the rest of their new world.'

Although Jody is an appealing young hero, he is no match for Olwen in the first book, who appears here as an elderly woman. The reasons for the colony's decline are passed over quickly, although certainly Mark's dislike, even hatred, for Olwen appears to be at the root of it. The third volume, *The Isis Pedlar* (1982), is original enough in its plot, but disappointing as a conclusion to the trilogy. Captain Flynn, the childish adult space pedlar of the title who tries to 'con' the still-naïve Isis community, is too far removed from the superb characterization of Olwen to unify the three books. There is considerable humour at the end of the story when Flynn's daughter, Moira, wishes to stay on Isis to marry the nephew of Jody of *The Guardian of Isis*, but feels equally that she should travel on with her father to save him from future follies. Guardian offers himself as a guardian for Flynn in her place—a relationship of opposites that deserves a book to itself.

Three earth societies are contrasted in Hughes' *Devil on My Back*, and its sequel *The Dream Catcher*. The year is AD 2147 and (as stated in the second book) is the 141st year after 'the Age of Confusion that followed the End of Oil'. Two domed cities called Arks (somewhat similar to the enclosed city in *Ring-Rise, Ring-Set*) are, in essence, the guardians of what remains of civilization. Ark I of *Devil on My Back* has become completely computerized and totalitarian. At the top of the hierarchy are the Lords, who carry information paks that are implanted into their necks and linked to the computer. As the Lord Tutor tells the students: 'The computer is your memory and mine. With every pak you access you become closer to the ideal of a perfect thinking being. . . .' At the other end of the social structure are the soldiers, workers, and slaves who have no access to information and are all treated as outcasts. At age fourteen Tomi, the son of the Overlord, successfully achieves a rite-of-passage ceremony in which an additional pak is added to his neck (two of his friends fail and will become slaves). As a reward he is allowed a Recreation called 'Dreamland' and he dreams of being outside the Ark. Then the slaves revolt and Tomi, in a fast-paced series of events, finds himself in the outside world for the first time in his life.

In contrast to the dystopia of Ark I, Ark III of *The Dream Catcher* is presented as a utopia. Here for 141 years there has been a concentration on developing skills of 'telepathy, healing and empathic communication'. All the work is divided equally among the members of the community, including the Leaders. In particular they have developed a mind-link among themselves that is referred to as 'the Web', or the 'Great Pattern'. However, fifteen-year-old Ruth thinks herself an outsider in Ark III. She feels awkward, unattractive, and unloved (there is no family structure) and, most importantly, she is unable (not unwilling) to join in the Great Pattern. After Ruth tries to run away from the Ark, it is discovered that she is a special psychic—she has not only developed psychokinesis, but in her dreams she is communicating with someone outside the city. The community decides that she may be receiving messages from Ark I and a small expeditionary force, armed only with psychic powers, sets out to find it. The third society lives a primitive life in natural surroundings. It is composed of slaves who have escaped from Ark I (they were somehow not affected by the dictates of the computer) and now live a kind of early Indian tribal life without any aspect of technology. In *Devil on My Back* they rescue Tomi, remove his 'infopaks', and teach him about freedom. Eventually Tomi feels it his duty to return to Ark I, take up his appointed place, and secretly send agricultural implements and other artifacts to ensure an easier survival for the group. *The Dream Catcher* brings the strands of both stories together. Tomi and Ruth, for example, have entered each other's dreams of freedom and of the liberating outside world. Ruth is thus able to lead her group to Ark I and Tomi and the freed slaves. The ending is exciting (if rather incredible, even for science fiction). Both groups combine to liberate Ark I, but in order to release the computer's mind-control powers and yet not destroy its support systems, Ruth and her close friend Luke must *think* themselves small enough to enter the circuitry of the computer. Isaac Asimov's novelization of the film *Fantastic Voyage* (1966), in which scientists become minuscule in order to travel through a human body and effect a medical cure, seems almost realistic in comparison with the kind of exaggerated mysticism Hughes projects. The Ark III group, by forming a Web, can even drive out poison gas.

In the last analysis Hughes apparently means to indicate that the slaves who escaped from Ark I will form (or have formed) the ideal society. The society of Ark III, although based on humanitarian concerns, certainly appears rather rigid. For example, the young are selected for future careers by their teachers and elders at age fifteen, and thereafter their garments are colour-coded to identify their positions. Certainly it is a society in which it is expected that everyone will have extrasensory perception. Still, that Hughes intends Ark III to be seen as an admirable society is shown by both the care and understanding shown to Ruth and by the fact that the Ark III group, with the exception of Ruth and Luke (who elect to remain outside the dome), are anxious to return home and to the comfort of the Web, as if to a nest.

Hughes' contribution to science fiction is outstanding. She explores moral growth, both individual and societal, within gripping adventures. She manages to create flesh-and-blood characters set within a global dimension. But perhaps her greatest contribution has been to create—in *The Keeper of the Isis Light*—a shining touchstone for judging children's science fiction.

Douglas Hill is as opposite to Monica Hughes in his writing as he is in his life. Hill was born in Canada and now lives in England, whereas Monica Hughes was born in England and now lives in Canada. Hill's considerable body of work has adventure at its core, along with a great deal of violence, as exhibited in his Finn Ferral trilogy: *The Huntsman* (1982), *Warriors of the Wasteland* (1983), and *Alien Citadel* (1984). The stories are set about three hundred years into Earth's future after atomic devastation has destroyed most of the population. Some thousands survived to build anew, only to be conquered by ugly and cruel creatures from space who have powerful flame weapons, flying spy creatures called 'spywings', egg-shaped flying ships, and seemingly impregnable fortresses. Now there are only remnants of thousands who live a pre-agricultural existence, always in terror of the alien 'Slavers'.

The three volumes comprise a quest story as Finn searches for his foster-father and foster-sister who have been carried off by the aliens. In his search he makes use of his hunter's skills and his almost uncanny knowledge of the wilderness. He meets mutants, is enslaved, and penetrates the fortresses of the Aliens in which he uncovers horrible experiments on humans, carried out by a master of the 'Slavers'. He also discovers the secret of his own birth (he had been found as a naked three-year-old child living alone in the forest) and realizes that he was one of the Aliens' failed experiments, and so has become a superior human being rather than an inferior or a bestial one, such as the 'Bloodkin'. The Aliens are not completely defeated; however, they leave Earth when they find more lucrative planets to provide them with the metal they need.

Although Finn is highly intelligent, and the plots do not introduce the supernatural as in fantasy (the 'spywings', for example, are compounded of flesh and metal and advanced technology), the action of the book (fights, hunts, chases, and stress on physical prowess) is curiously reminiscent of Robert Howard's *Conan the Barbarian* pulps.

Douglas Hill is somewhat of a rarity today in children's science fiction. His concentration on physical skills and cliffhanging plots (also evident in his *Young Legionary*, 1982, and *Exiles of ColSec*, 1984) recalls nineteenth-century boys' adventure stories. His heroes, however, are not simply idealized; they are infallible.

Carol Matas projects three different future societies in her trilogy *The Fusion Factor* (1986), *Zanu* (1986), and *Me, Myself and I* (1987). They are linked through Rebecca Lepidus, a twelve-year-old Winnipeg girl of the present who travels by means of a time-machine into the future of Winnipeg, meant to represent the world as a whole, although the capital of Manitoba is curiously never shown in the grip of winter. Unlike most series books, the first is the weakest in concept and plot. When Rebecca sees her schoolmate, Lonney, kidnapped by men driving a black van, no one will believe her; when she sees another boy kidnapped, she follows the van on her bicycle to a warehouse, enters a booth that turns out to be a time-machine, and is catapulted into the year 2040. Here she finds herself in an underground city, built as a scientific research centre, that is apparently a survivor of a nuclear holocaust. Children who are unwanted or uncared for are being kidnapped to build a new society, since the centre's children are retarded. There are two additional, though not well-integrated, components to the story: an adjoining military group, headed by a Dr Strangelove-like General, and the hint of human mutants. Rebecca finds Lonney and returns with him back to their own time, with the help of two daring children who want to leave and are taken in (and presumably adopted) by Rebecca's parents.The key to all three stories comes at the end of this first book as the children decide to form peace groups and support groups for children who are uncared for or abused; however, this latter concern disappears from the sequels. Both *Zanu* and *Me, Myself and I* have simpler plots and are more descriptive of a definite future society. In *Zanu* the year is 2080, but is now described as the '40 Real Corporate Era', for everyone must work for the Corporation Zanu that has taken over all the governments of the world. Rebecca finds this Winnipeg of the future to be a consumer-based society and a police state. She learns that there are no separate countries, no wars, and no poverty. However, people are forced to buy goods (made by robots) and are punished severely for not filling their quota. In *Me, Myself and I* the year is also 2080, but it posits an alternative world. Rebecca finds it almost perfect, but while people may do as they please, they are ignored if they deviate from the norm.

In the second and third books the sins and spectres of the present—the threat of nuclear war, the 'greenhouse effect', pollution, and the use of pesticides (among other poisons)—are clearly but briefly pointed out. The future depends upon the present and the present will depend greatly on children like Rebecca and her friends. At the end of *Me, Myself and I*, Rebecca muses:

> She wasn't perfect and she knew it. She also knew that she, just the way she was, could help change the world into a better place, even though it too might never be perfect.

All three books are fast-paced adventure stories, with hunts, chases, and escapes, but with an underlying social seriousness. In the various societies described Matas cleverly makes some delineation through food—from pills in *The Fusion Factor* to ersatz food in *Zanu* to food grown without chemicals in *Me, Myself and I*. The time-switches between the future and the present are sometimes fuzzy, but there is always Rebecca to hold things together. She is courageous, loyal to her friends, an example of child-power—but, as she says herself, not always perfect.

A time-machine is also central to *Sudbury Time Twist* (1984) by

Wence Horai. This machine travels only to a specific point in time—the Proterozoic era whence, the author postulates, came the meteorite that formed the Sudbury Basin. In this story the geological details and the concept of the earth two billion years back in time are far more interesting than the characters or even the plot.

Martyn Godfrey's *The Vandarian Incident* (1981) and *Alien War Games* (1984) are both set on other planets and are filled with the exotic material of science fiction—aliens, strange flora and fauna, and wars. *The Vandarian Incident* begins as a survival story. Earthling Tyler Hobart is in his graduating year at a Space Academy on the desert planet of Tilyel, and now has to undergo a final test. He is left alone a hundred kilometres from the Academy, quite sure of his ability to make his way back but unaware that a sand blizzard, which is the x-factor in his test, is on its way. He gets back to his base (the survival experience is much the best part of the short book) to find the Academy blasted by a Vandarian warship. He is joined by another survivor, a clairvoyant girl from the planet Selgel, and together they set out for the northern part of the planet to prevent the Vandarians from sabotaging two other Galactic powers on a peace mission. Of course they succeed, and both young people will become 'fluxdrivers'—that is, pilots of the Galaxy's warships.

Alien War Games has a much more serious theme relating to colonization policies on Earth. The Terrans bring civilization (including drugs and nuclear energy) to the planet Jancan and determine to drive its 50,000 inhabitants, the Diljug, on to what might be called reservations. The Diljug, a peaceful people, want to be friends, but they are at first outmanoeuvred by surely the most despicable teenage character in children's fiction, Gravis Solaran, the son of the subGovernor of Jancan, who hates the planet and its natives from the moment he arrives. He is further affronted when he is beaten in single combat by a native girl, Darsa, who sees the contest as an amicable one. The Diljug at first try to follow the ways of their people to settle differences. One such is a war game, in which the object is to drive one's opponents from the field with clubs, but not to kill them. However, in the game the humans (in Godfrey's two books the people from earth are the humans), prompted by Gravis, turn their laser weapons ('flamurs') on the natives. Here the title of the book (*Alien War Games*) can be seen to be ironic. The natives take their revenge; they are now armed with flamurs, although it is unclear how they obtained them. Their second attack ends with what can be presumed to be an atomic explosion; the Diljugs do not understand modern technology. However, there is some hope at the end of the story. Gravis's machinations are unmasked and one of the Diljug people, who has tried to be an honest broker between the factions, may have a chance. As he tells Darsa: 'There are Terrans who believe in law and justice.'

Godfrey's *More Than Weird* (1987) is a long short story and, in its tall-tale quality, is somewhat of a spoof on science fiction. Cory Johnson, from Dawson Creek, describes himself as an average teenager: 'My parents hassled me enough so that I could complain about them to my friends.' His strange adventure begins simply because he is so average. He is chosen by a robot society, one that is 550 years in the future, to be an exemplar of a human in their zoo; the robots are nostalgic for the people who created them but who then left Earth to go adventuring in other solar systems. The robot agent is a beautiful female named Susie, who first asks Cory to come with her through the time gate, then demands that he do so, and then tries to force him. The humour lies in Cory's reactions to the robot and his methods of escape. The book is a light moment in Canadian science fiction, which for the most part is serious and even portentous, much like science fiction in general.

'Serious and portentous' are also words that can be applied to Peter Baltensperger's *Guardians of Time* (1984) as it contrasts two civilizations—Earth in the year 2263 and the planet of Kalimar. Earth is a highly technological, computerized, controlled society; Kalimar is inhabited by a race of gentle giants who can communicate by telepathy and whose needs are satisfied through a minimum of work. On Earth, fourteen-year-old Finnegan Turpin, the son of an important politician, is given a rigorous education (chiefly mathematical) by means of a Teaching Machine and a talking 'Wall' that seemingly controls his life. He is, however, given 'Periods of Relaxation' through dreams that take him into the past. On one such occasion he meets a boy playing with marbles and Finnegan desires marbles so much that he snatches them from the boy and causes his death. When he awakens, the marbles are but a handful of dust. Finnegan is a 'whizz kid' already in the process of overcoming the computer, but when he tries to have marbles manufactured for himself he is met with a 'Catch 22'. He finds that 'marbles are classified because they are a waste of time, and they are a waste of time because they are classified.'

The scene moves to Kalimar when Finnegan's father is sent there as an ambassador. Finnegan's education is continued, but in a very different way from that on Earth. Here it is psychic rather than mathematical—the expansion of the mind into telepathy and other awesome mental powers under mentors akin to Eastern gurus. He finds a beach strewn with coloured stones—at last he has his marbles. Finnegan grows in size to match that of the Kalimarians, meets and loves a Kalimarian girl, Shenondah, and discovers his destiny. He is to be one of the Kalimarian élite, the select group of Grand Masters who watch and guard the planets, scattered like marbles 'on the shores of time'. But first he has an assignment as a 'Guardian'. He and Shenondah, pooling their mental capacities, create a gigantic spaceship, control it, and set it for the planet Earth. Presumably Earth is to become a second Kalimar.

Guardians of Time exhibits many of the clichés, the faults, and yet the interest of science fiction. It is almost standard to have aliens superior in emotional and cultural development to that of Earth people. Another cliché is that humans can develop only through acquiring special powers. The faults of the story lie chiefly in the second half of the book, where a mystical sentimentality overrides even a modicum of believability. It is the earth scenes, worked out with the intricacy of technology, that give the story some validity.

With so few Canadian writers of science fiction, a generalization about the Canadians' contributions to the genre is hardly worth making. (Hill, who lives, writes, and publishes in England, may not belong here at all.) But one notices first that there is a difference between Hughes' flesh-and-blood characters—Olwen, Liza, Ruth (and even the robot Guardian)—and the rather wooden creations of Matas, Godfrey, Baltensperger, and certainly the young people of Wence Horai's *Sudbury Time Twist*. Still, it is clear that all our science fiction (as well as Canadian fantasy) tends to be more richly plotted than modern realistic fiction, which can often be described briefly as the young coming to terms with themselves within the context of a specific problem in their lives. In dealing with larger issues—future societies, disasters (past or incipient), life on other planets, as well as the emotional growth of a protagonist, Canadian writers of science fiction frequently incorporate minor imaginative details that linger in the mind sometimes more than the trajectory of the story. In Hughes' *The Keeper of the Isis Light* there is the golden, musical dress that Guardian makes for Olwen, and in *Ring-Rise, Ring-Set* there is the indelible image of the blackened snow that is destroying the naturalness of the Ekoes' lives. Even less memorable works have touches of creative imagination. There is the talking 'Wall' (halfway between an authoritarian and a reasonable instructor) in Baltensperger's *Guardians of Time*, and in Carol Matas's *Me, Myself and I* both the terror and the humour of meeting one's doppelgänger. One has to say, however, that with the exception of Hughes' *The Keeper of the Isis Light*, many such details are simply brief compensations for rather ordinary factual writing.

Most of our writers see the genre as a literature of change and ideas, as expressed by Monica Hughes:

> I think one of the functions of a good writer for children (besides, obviously, being entertaining) is to help them explore the world and the future. And to find acceptable answers to the Big Questions: 'What's life all about?' 'What is it to be human?'.... Those are questions that demand truthful answers, not pat ones.... One faces oneself in the darkest inside places of one's memory and one's subconscious, and out of that comes both joy and sorrow. But always . . . there must come hope.

Canadian science fiction for children is both optimistic and humanitarian, while showing the dark aspects of both life and technology. It joins the international stream of science fiction in proving that it can give children an intellectual awareness about the present and the future. In addition, it sometimes offers the aesthetic and personal emotional experiences that were once the prerogative of fantasy and realistic fiction. However, it must be said that even though these books appear to demonstrate the ill-effects of science and technology, like their British and American counterparts, they are virtually all devoid of scientific fact or probability. The term Science Fiction is therefore a misnomer. With all their use of time-machines, extrasensory perception, other planets, and dystopias, they are commentaries on the present with an imaginative rather than a scientific basis. Indeed, when one thinks of writers of adult scientific fiction from Jules Verne to Fred Hoyle, Isaac Azamov, and Arthur C. Clarke, these books for children should more properly be considered (as Moskowitz suggested) a branch of fantasy literature, although a very special one.

10
Poetry and Verse

Poetry defies definition, although many critics have speculated on it in terms of structure, language, and emotion. Some poets have more accurately described their feelings when reading genuine poetry. Emily Dickinson felt that 'If I read a book and it makes my whole body so cold no fire can ever warm me, I know that is poetry. If I feel physically as if the top of my head were taken off, I know that is poetry.' Randall Jarrell's chipmunk in his *The Bat-Poet* (1964) reacts in much the same way when he hears a poem: 'It makes me shiver. Why do I like it if it makes me shiver?'

It is an observed fact that babies and young children respond to the innate rhythms and musicality of folk poetry: lullabies, nursery rhymes, and street and game chants. The older child's response to poetry is less obvious, even mysterious. Some of their comments, as revealed in Harry Behn's *Chrysalis: Concerning Children and Poetry* (1968), a lyrical study of childhood and poetry, vary considerably. One child says: 'People are stories. A poem is something else. Something way out. Way out in the woods. Like Robert Frost waiting in a snowstorm with promises to keep.' Another feels that 'a poem should simply make music with words, that's all. The shorter the better. One of mine is only, *Clink, Clank, Clunk*. It's about a carpenter pounding nails in a new house.' These responses suggest that the young understand intuitively much that is unfamiliar and beyond their acquaintance. Certainly the full impact of some poetry escapes children when it deals with experiences particular to the adult world; nevertheless children take what they desire, leaving the rest until some moment of fruition occurs later in their lives. Authentic poetry operates on many levels, offering portions of itself to all readers of whatever age.

Most poetry deliberately written for the young should be described as verse rather than poetry. Religious and didactic verse entered children's literature early in its history, becoming props for children's spiritual education. John Bunyan's *A Book for Boys and Girls* (1686) is the harshest example of this type of verse. Yet once in a while the moral versifiers could envision the thoughts of a child and put them into a simple, effective form. One example is 'Twinkle, twinkle, little star' (first titled 'The Star'), which appeared in 1806 in Jane Taylor's *Rhymes for the Nursery*. The nonsense verses of Edward Lear (*Book of Nonsense*, 1846), and those in Lewis Carroll's *Alice's Adventures in Wonderland* (1865), were the first strong notes of levity in a highly moral climate. However, there was already a wealth of poetry available to children—William Blake's *Songs of Innocence*, William Wordsworth's nature poems, Samuel Taylor Coleridge's haunting dream-like ballads ('The Rime of the Ancient Mariner' and 'Kubla Khan') and Henry Wadsworth Longfellow's 'The Song of Hiawatha'. In this long and rich period, from the eighteenth to the end of the nineteenth century, poetry can be truly seen as a shared ground between adults and children.

Robert Louis Stevenson's *A Child's Garden of Verses* (1885) set the tone of verses specially written for the young for about the next seventy-five years. His word-pictures of small children engaged in imaginative play, going to bed or getting up in the morning, were joined some forty years later by A.A. Milne—in *When We Were Very Young* (1924) and *Now We Are Six* (1927)—who reinforced Stevenson's domestic verse with more humour and word-play. But the most original voice of the early twentieth century was that of Walter de la Mare in *Peacock Pie* (1913) and other collections. His musical poems ranged in tone from childlike humour to lyrical mystery, and are timeless.

As in other genres of children's literature, the 1960s brought some changes, most emanating from the United States. American poetry for children now spoke of concerns formerly deemed too adult for them—alienation, injustice, the effects of technology and war. Eve Merriam's collection, *Finding a Poem* (1970), is one such, among several others. Nature poetry was also transformed from gentle observations of the wind and the rain to a starker vision, as exemplified by the British poet Ted Hughes in *Season Songs* (1976). Other well-known and respected poets for adults have also entered the children's field—Robert Graves, Randall Jarrell, Charles Causley, Theodore Roethke, John Updike, and David McCord—although as yet not even one of their poems has reached the common coinage of Stevenson and Milne.

While poetry for adults was a potent force in the development of Canadian literature, none of its spirit can be found in early verses for children. They were all derivative, first of Stevenson's *A Child's Garden of Verses* and later of Milne's *When We Were Very Young*. Isabel Ecclestone MacKay's *The Shining Ship and Other Verse* (1918) projects the little-boy world of Stevenson with sentimentality rather than sentiment. Arthur Bourinot—in *Pattering Feet* (1925) and *Ottawa Lyrics, and Verses for Children* (1929)—echoed, in a very pale way, both Stevenson and Milne. Bourinot's 'Opening Parliament', which begins 'They're opening parliament up on the hill,/The soldiers are all dressed up for the drill' demonstrates its lineage from Milne's 'They're changing the guard at Buckingham Palace,/Christopher Robin went down with Alice'. Other children's verse of the period was simply inept. Grace Helen Mowat's *Funny Fables of Fundy and Other Poems for Children* (1928) was filled with Canadian content but lacked not only fun but the minimal expertise of a versifier ('To know the evil from the good/So in the coming generation/You'll be a blessing to the nation.')

Throughout this dismal period, Canadian children took what they wanted from the adult world and made it their own. This can be seen in the popularity of Pauline Johnson's *Flint and Feather* (1912). For many Canadian children 'The Song My Paddle Sings', encountered in textbooks, was their first pleasurable entrance into poetry. The first children's anthology—made up of Canadian poetry likely to appeal to children—seems to have been John W. Garvin's *Canadian Verse for Boys and Girls* (1930), containing poems by Pauline Johnson, Arthur Bourinot, Archibald Lampman, W.H. Drummond, and others. Three decades of such textbook anthologies were abruptly and thankfully brought to an end in 1968 with the appearance of *The Wind Has Wings: Poems from Canada*, selected by Mary Alice Downie and Barbara Robertson.

The first poem in the book—'Orders', by A.M. Klein, which ends 'Let me sit silent/Let me wonder'—establishes the atmosphere of the anthology, which is maintained from beginning to end in the carefully contrived succession of moods and subjects expressed by the poems and in the illustrations by Elizabeth Cleaver. Although some of these are in black-and-white, the total impression is one of a celebratory riot of colour. For many years it was our most beautiful children's book. In choosing poems that were not originally written for children but that had qualities the compilers thought would appeal to them, they found seventy-seven, ranging from Eskimo chants to poems by Irving Layton and James Reaney, and including Robert Service's 'The Shooting of Dan McGrew'. The popularity of the book was an indication of their good judgement—and of how an appealing collection for children can be compiled without deference to a limited, outdated stereotype of poems children will like. *The New Wind Has Wings* (1984) has a few deletions from the first edition, with fifteen poems added, including two deliberately written for children by Dennis Lee and sean o huigin.

Poetry written for children, especially young children, usually comes in the form of light-hearted versifying, but even this was scarce from about the 1940s to the 1970s. Only Desmond Pacey's *The Cow With the Musical Moo* (1952) and *Hippity Hobo and the Bee* (1952)—later brought together, with additions, as *The Cat, the Cow, and the Kangaroo* (1968)—filled the gap.

More recent versifiers have followed in Pacey's tradition, although they go far beyond him in verbal wit and occasionally create poetry rather than verse. Dennis Lee, Robert Heidbreder, Lois Simmie, and Sheree Fitch write for pre-schoolers and children of the early elementary grades. sean o huigin and Dennis Lee write less domestic, more grotesque and macabre nonsense for slightly older children, as well as longer narrative poems. Nature poetry is surprisingly scanty, when one considers the impact of the environment upon poetry for adults and the children's novel. George Swede's haiku poetry is an exception. Jean Little has produced a book of domestic and lyric poetry for older readers, while some of Raymond Souster's adult poetry has been selected and published for young readers. Numerous picturebooks in verse range from lullabies and jaunty rhymes to serious narrative poetry, and the last decade has seen collections of poetry written by children.

It is somewhat ironic that Dennis Lee—a scholar and a Governor General's Award-winning poet for adults—should have penned 'Alligator pie, alligator pie,/If I don't get some I think I'm gonna die', thus becoming a household name in Canadian families with young children. His avowed intention in his first collection of nonsense and light verse, *Alligator Pie* (1974), was to give Canadian children (his own at first) a sense of their particular time and space—a feat that cannot be accomplished in writing from other countries, no matter how excellent it is. Lee's verses in *Alligator Pie* and in his later books, *Garbage Delight* (1977) and *Jelly Belly* (1983), are predominantly nonsensical—including domestic, narrative, and lyric elements— and are written with crafted simplicity. Their roots lie in the oral traditions of early childhood literature: the lullabies, nursery rhymes, and action verses that accompany fingerplays, dandling games, and the tickling of babies; and the incantatory rhymes, chants, and taunts of children's street- and game-lore. In their repetitive, pounding beat and compelling, satisfying rhymes Lee's verses echo Mother Goose and the poems of Stevenson and Milne. Lee's sound patterns make his verses come alive when read aloud.

Like Stevenson and Milne, Lee observes closely the self-absorbed inner life of the very young. His intermittent use of a child-narrator's point of view emphasizes the importance of friendship and play, of imagination and emotion. This gentle tone is exemplified in 'The Coming of Teddy Bears' in *Garbage Delight*:

> The air is quiet
> Round my bed.
> The dark is drowsy
> In my head.
> The sky's forgetting
> To be red.
> And soon I'll be asleep.

The warmth of Lee's domestic poems is counterpointed by the wild, anarchic spirit of his nonsense verse, which breaks parental social taboos and behavioural codes, explores children's primal fantasies, and flirts with the forbidden and the risqué.

As well as casting light on the emotional life of young children, Lee delineates Canada's urban landscape. His poems are often rich in allusions to skyscrapers and laundromats, and his images are often consciously and uniquely Canadian: they include place names (from Chicoutimi to Mississauga), historical characters (William Lyon Mackenzie King), and national pastimes (in a parody of a Milne poem, a unique hockey game is played by a worm, a flea, an elephant, and a bore). None of these details are self-consciously patriotic; the Canadian words and images are transformed into incantatory tongue-twisters and onomatopoeic talismans and charms, so that in the magical recital of emblems of Canadian culture, Moose Jaw becomes as mythic as Banbury Cross. Lee has been dubbed Canada's 'Father Goose'. Children who enjoy his poetry will certainly absorb the inflections of a Canadian sensibility, of a folklore poetic that is grounded in a real time and place and, in its own way, is as satisfying as that of Mother Goose.

Jelly Belly is directed to an even younger group than *Alligator Pie* or *Garbage Delight*. The cadences and metre of the verses do not recall Stevenson or Milne, but rather finger plays, game rhymes, and Mother Goose. For example, the traditional nursery rhyme, 'Elsie Marley is grown so fine,/She won't get up to feed the swine' is simply reworked for Lee's 'Lazy lousy Liza Briggs/Wouldn't get up to feed the pigs.' The modernization of traditional rhymes has always been part of Lee's repertoire, but here it dominates the collection—though there is a sprinkling of domestic realism and his witty and often adult, and Canadian, references, as in 'The Tiny Perfect Mayor', whose title refers to Toronto's mayor of the 1970s, David Crombie. Lee has had two illustrators. For *Alligator Pie, Nicholas Knock and Other People* (1974), and *Garbage Delight*, Frank Newfeld created bright, crisp vignettes that have a formality that does not fully complement the surreal fun of Lee's verses. *Jelly Belly* is illustrated by Juan Wijngaard, who lives in England. His pastel-toned drawings give the rhymes the folk-charm of an updated Mother Goose.

Lee's influence can be seen in two different streams of verse—the domestic and light, and the more black-humoured. In the former group are Robert Heidbreder (*Don't Eat Spiders*, 1985), Lois Simmie (*Auntie's Knitting a Baby*, 1984 and *An Armadillo Is Not a Pillow*, 1986), the late bp Nichol (*Giants, Moosequakes & Other Disasters*, 1985), and Tim Wynne-Jones (*Mischief City*, 1986). Heidbreder's rhymes (illustrated with clever, lively collages by Karen Patkau) are similar to those of Lee in their colloquial voice and catchy rhythms. In *Don't Eat*

Spiders he has fun with subjects of young children's daily life, with the dragon/witch/ghost figures of their imagination, and offers humorous Canadian references. (Contemporary British and American poets do not generally introduce local place-names or national or local figures, and certainly not with the humour of Lee and Heidbreder.) In 'Sticky Maple Syrup' Hiedbreder converts a national product into farce:

> Sticky maple syrup
> Dripping from your tree.
> You spread across the Prairies
> the Maritimes
> B.C.
> You cover up all Canada
> From sea to sticky sea.
> Sticky maple syrup
> Don't stick all over me.

Like Heidbreder, Sheree Fitch, in *Toes In My Nose and Other Poems* (1987), depicts the world of young children, from messing about with food to family closeness and general observations of the outside world. There are gentle experiments with concrete verse-play, with typography and shapes (for example, the stairs in 'Step Away') and the verses are brightened by a chanting quality, but many are uneven in metre and rhyme. Mollie Bobak's impressionistic sketches energize the collection. Lois Simmie is a more sophisticated versifier for older readers. Several poem cycles, on various themes, are interwoven throughout her two books, creating patterns of recurring characters and running gags, as in 'Mary McBickle One':

> Mary McBickle choked on a pickle
> And turned up her thin little toes;
> Mary dying at dinner that way
> Made Father feel quite indisposed.

Like Lee and Heidbreder, Simmie incorporates Canadian place-names, along with a tongue-in-cheek treatment of the grotesque in verses about monsters and nightmares. Simmie's two collections are illustrated by Anne Simmie's line drawings.

bp Nichol, in *Giants, Moosequakes & Other Disasters*, melded domestic verse with nonsense, adding nursery lyrics and elaborate narrative farces. There is a musical lullaby quality in his youngest verses, and, as in his poetry for adults, Nichol's experiments with punctuation, spelling, and typography add a stream-of-consciousness edge to the rhymed and free-verse. Maureen Paxton's illustrations provide a mortar of light wit that holds together these disparate poems.

Tim Wynne-Jones's *Mischief City* is an unusual poem cycle, using the first-person point of view of a young boy. In his musings on Winchell's self-absorbed parents, his wild baby sister, and his imaginary friend, Maxine, Wynne-Jones dramatizes his emotions and imagination. The poems attest to the psychological power of childhood fantasizing that resolves stress and frustration. This aspect of child life is happily shown in the last poem, 'The Arrangement':

> The day dreams of night,
> And the night dreams of day.
> And that's how they keep
> Out of each other's way.

Victor Gad's sophisticated illustrations suggest a formal stage-setting for this mini-opera.

The second stream of poetry following Dennis Lee's model is that of grotesque, black-humoured verse. Iconoclastic parodies and nonsense reversals that poke fun at adult society have tremendous appeal for children, who are also fascinated by the bizarre and the taboo, and enjoy being titillated by their own fears and fantasies. For younger children, Lee and Heidbreder temper these irresistible images of nightmare with a bright, sunny wit. Simmie and Wynne-Jones use the figures of monsters for comic effect and symbolic significance. But verse of gothic horror for older children is best exemplified in sean o huigin's collection, *Scary Poems for Rotten Kids* (1982, revised in 1988), illustrated by John Fraser and Scott Hughes, and in his single poem *The Dinner Party* (1984), illustrated by Maureen Paxton. His long narrative poems of monsters of the imagination are often parodies of cautionary verse, but they sometimes slide into gratuitous violence and mild scatology. Like bp Nichol, o huigin shows an inventive use of experimental verse-forms, such as concrete, sound, and visual poetry. His colloquial free-verse poems, which abandon the conventions of punctuation and capitalization, are unusual in the traditionally conservative field of children's poetry. Despite their often inventive concepts and satisfyingly macabre twists, however, o huigin's verses do not have the bite and strength of the masters of macabre verse—the British Roald Dahl and the American Jack Prelutsky.

Lee, Heidbreder, and Simmie share an intuitive understanding of the nature of nonsense poetry. Like Edward Lear and Lewis Carroll, they understand that order and logic are needed to create convincing nonsense, and that there is a fine line between gentle irony and bleak satire, between fantastical light verse and unmodified surrealism. The nonsense verse of sean o huigin and Irving Layton does not achieve this crucial precision and balance. Layton's evocative imagery and subtle metre in *A Spider Danced a Cosy Jig* (1984), illustrated by Miro Malish, give his work an arresting figurative and musical presence, but the misanthropic parodies of human behaviour in these poems of animal beauty and suffering, and Layton's cynical vision, betray the work's true spirit: it is adult social satire, rather than children's nonsense or nature poetry.

Dennis Lee, bp Nichol, and sean o huigin have each included in their collections long narrative poems tinged with fantasy or farce. However, the single-book narrative poem, with a serious theme and a specific Canadian setting, has appeared only rarely. o huigin's *The Ghost Horse of the Mounties* (1983) is based on an incident in the early days of the Northwest Mounted Police—a summer lightning storm that caused a horse stampede at Dufferin, Manitoba, in 1874. A young Mountie dies and his beloved horse searches for him across the prairie. Their spirits are reunited years later in a fantasy sequence when the horse is old and dying. The narrator's voice sets the tone for the drama in cadenced free-verse:

> imagine if you will the empty plains
> imagine if you will a sultry summer night
> imagine if you will a brilliant edge
> of gold on the horizon
> and a silence getting deeper all the time

The poem rings with the command 'imagine', and so the poet conveys both the feelings of the young man and the horse at their mutual loss and the ecstasy of their reunion. o huigin conveys a vivid sense of the desolate prairie, with its natural beauty and wild storm. It is as much a nature poem as it is a storytelling one.

The Ghost Horse has a romantic lyricism and folk quality that are also found in Ellen Bryan Obed's gothic narrative, *Borrowed Black: A Labrador Fantasy* (1988), also intended for older children, yet retaining a picturebook format. Borrowed Black, an amalgam of human and animal, steals the moon and buries it 'deep off the Labrador'. In legend-like fashion he is overcome by the crew of a boat, 'built in the back of a whale', and the moon is returned to the sky. The text suffers from both a lack of clarity and by overwriting, but its faults are somewhat ameliorated by Jan Morgensen's dark, lowering washes that yet have a romantic aura and a strong sense of place.

These two narrative poems reflect the regionalism of Canada, the diversity of landscape, and of plant and animal life, all of which are strong presences in children's fiction. By contrast, it is surprising that nature poetry written specifically for children—poems of the seasons, of flora and fauna, of Canada's physical geography—has been rare and, usually, mediocre, despite the strengths of Canadian adult poetry in this area. Robert Heidbreder and George Swede have both treated nature, but not in a way that is as specifically Canadian as, for example, Wilfred Campbell's 'Indian Summer' ('Along the line of smokey hills/The crimson forest stands'). Heidbreder's nature lyrics, such as 'Sun, Sun' and 'Falling Leaves', possess a gentle music, and there is clarity and precision in Swede's haiku in *Tick Bird: Poems for Children* (1983), *Time Is Flies: Poems for Children* (1984), and *High Wire Spider* (1986). Swede's deceptively simple poems include free and concrete verse, but are strongest in the nature haiku:

> Among the yellow roses
> the yellow butterfly
> grows still

Many of Dennis Lee's narrative and lyric poems for older children in *Nicholas Knock and Other People* have a philosophical and thought-provoking quality, and no other children's collection has yet appeared to equal it. Since 1975 the most powerful collection of contemplative poetry for older children and teenagers is Raymond

Souster's *Flight of the Roller-Coaster: Poems for Young Readers* (1985), composed of works originally written for adults. (The title poem, like Layton's 'A Spider Danced a Cosy Jig', was first presented to children in *The Wind Has Wings* in 1968.) Whether Souster's brief lyrics describe the hockey games of his childhood, a morning-glory, or his cat, he projects a crystal-clear celebration of felt experience.

Unlike Souster, Jean Little has written specially for the young adolescent in *Hey World, Here I Am!* (1986). Her poetic voice is translated through thirteen-year-old Kate Bloomfield, who first appeared in Little's two novels of friendship, *Look Through My Window* (1970) and *Kate* (1971). Kate's thoughts are earnest, sentimental, and at times shrewd and ironic, as she observes people and relationships from a naturally egotistical perspective, with moments of genuine understanding:

> Our History teacher says, 'Be proud you're Canadian.'
> My father says, 'You can be proud you're Jewish.'
> My mother says, 'Stand up straight, Kate. Be proud you're tall.'
>   So I'm proud.
> But what I want to know is,
> When did I have the chance to be
>   Norwegian or Buddhist or short?

The poems of Kate's quest for identity and meaning in life are interspersed with diary-like prose pieces.

Little creates a convincingly natural, colloquial, teen-age voice for Kate, and the poems in *Hey World* are close in spirit to the poetry and prose actually written by children and young adults in anthologies such as *Children of the Great Muskeg* (1985) and *Come With Us: Children Speak For Themselves* (1978). Despite some reservations about the literary and artistic value of poetry written by children, and the question about whether such works are of more interest to adults than to children, collections of Canadian children's poetry do provide examples of their ability to use language freshly and inventively, and also open a window on their thoughts, emotions, and imagination. *Children of the Great Muskeg* is a compilation of verse and artwork by Cree and Métis children in northern Ontario, and reveals a love for the sub-Arctic land and wildlife, as well as the conflict between old and new traditions. Conflict is also a major element in *Come With Us*, comprising both verse and prose, in which new-Canadian children give snapshot images of arriving in Canada and establishing a new identity.

POETRY PICTUREBOOKS

The international trend of illustrating a single poem is new to Canada, beginning in the 1980s. Most of these publications are for very young children and are designed to be read aloud. Some have a chanting lullaby quality, sliding in and out of formal rhyme, for bedtime reading and singing. *Once: A Lullaby* (1983, 1986) by bp Nichol is a soothing poem about young animals going to sleep. It has been illustrated twice: first by Ed Roach in simple line drawings, and later by the American Anita Lobel, whimsically, with elaborate detail. Dayal Kaur Khalsa's *Sleepers* (1988) is more humorous as it chronicles, in partial rhyme, a young child's observations of the sleeping habits of a variety of humans and animals. Khalsa's flat shapes and bright colours pack considerable detail into this small book. Her child is fighting sleep, as is the baby in Teddy Jam's *Night Cars* (1988), in which the partially rhymed text has touches of onomatopoeia, alliteration, and repetition. The paintings of Eric Beddows (a.k.a. Ken Nutt) show the baby, warm and safe, observing the night life of the city street through his window. Equally nursery-oriented is Rose Robart's *The Cake That Mack Ate* (1986), a light-hearted parody of 'The House That Jack Built'. The cumulative text and thumping rhythm detail the creation of a cake that abruptly ends in the stomach of Mack the dog. It is illustrated in expansive cartoon style by Maryann Kovalski.

Phoebe Gilman and Marie-Louise Gay write domestic verse recounting children's daytime play and night-time imaginings. Gilman's *Jillian Jiggs* (1985) and *The Wonderful Pigs of Jillian Jiggs* (1988) are composed of somewhat strained rhyming couplets that detail Jillian's antics. The cartoon drawings in blocks of colour tell the stories more effectively than the verse. Gay's *Rainy Day Magic* (1987) and *Moonbeam on a Cat's Ear* (1986) suffer from the same imbalance. The dynamic illustrations of children playing frenetically, moving in and out of fantasy and dream, eclipse the banal rhyming texts. Gay has also illustrated one of the few successful picturebooks in narrative verse—Dennis Lee's *Lizzy's Lion* (1984). It is a humorously macabre tale, similar in tone to many of the exaggerated tales in Lee's other collections. The controlled metre and rhyme provide an excellent vehicle for Gay's pictorial interpretation of Lizzy's watch-dog lion devouring a wicked robber.

Two verse-stories in picturebook format have an outdoor setting: Patricia Sillers' *Ringtail* (1987) and Hazel Hutchins' *Ben's Snow Song: A Winter Picnic* (1987). The adventures of Ringtail, a racoon who lives in a Toronto ravine, are treated in bouncy rhyme and are made vivid by Karen Patkau's collage art. In *Ben's Snow Song* Hutchins loosely blends simple free verse, inner rhyme, and onomatopoeia to describe a family's ski outing. Lisa Smith's coloured drawings, however, do not capture the verses' celebration of the magic of the ordinary. *Atmosfear* (1985), by sean o huigin, is also environmental, but the theme is one of protest. Although pollution is treated metaphorically, in an amalgam of free verse and rhyme, its message is very clear. Barbara Di Lella's too-literal illustrations do not add any dimension to the poem.

Ted Harrison's psychedelic evocation of the North gives an unearthly resonance to two poems by Robert Service: *The Cremation of Sam McGee* (1986) and *The Shooting of Dan McGrew* (1987). But classical children's verse by non-Canadians is now attracting Canadian illustrators. For Eugene Field's *Wynken, Blynken and Nod* (1985), Ron Berg has created soft representational drawings in dreamy muted tones and has given Edward Lear's *The Owl and the Pussycat* (1984) a whimsical Edwardian setting. Erica Rutherford has illustrated the same poem, *The Owl and the Pussycat* (1986), with a naïve primitive look. Gilles Tibo has made Edgar Allan Poe's famous poem of love and yearning, *Annabel Lee* (1987), both appealing and highly accessible to young readers. It has a strong Canadian setting: Quebec's Gaspé Peninsula, including Percé Rock, is depicted with the same magical, haunting quality that surrounds the ghostly children.

There have been few poets for children, at any time or in any country, whose names are immediately recognizable in the world of children's literature. The great exception is Walter de la Mare of England, who has been rightly called 'the children's poet'. His poems—whether humorous ('Ann, Ann!/Come quick as you can?/There's a fish that *talks*/In the frying-pan!'), or narrative ('Nicholas Nye'), or mysterious and evocative ('Some one came knocking/At my wee small door')—are as fresh and compelling as the day they were written. In modern times there are Ted Hughes and Charles Causley of England, and Myra Cohn Livingston and David McCord of the United States, who are genuine poets. In general the trend today is towards domestic, light, nonsensical versifying for quite young children, with a sprinkling of the macabre or the satirical for slightly older children. This pattern is clearly being followed in Canada. The seminal influence has come from Dennis Lee, whose *Alligator Pie* began the modern school of Canadian verse for children, in which low-keyed wit and self-reflective irony allow us to laugh at ourselves. However, the work of Lee and the writers that followed him, although always showing some originality, is basically derivative of nursery rhymes and of Robert Louis Stevenson, A.A. Milne, or Heinrich Hoffman's cautionary verse *Strüwwelpeter* (1848). Most of their publications are produced in picturebook format and are greatly enhanced by their illustrators.

The success of these collections of lighthearted, delightfully anarchic verse should not, however, suggest that children have no liking for more mature poetry. Those of us who were bored at school by textbooks that included Shakespeare, Blake, and Tennyson and yet hold in our minds such poems as Coleridge's 'Kubla Khan' and Alfred Noyes' 'The Highwayman', and such lines as Blake's 'Tyger, tyger! burning bright/In the forests of the night', and Tennyson's 'The splendour falls on castle walls', will not find it hard to believe that children can enjoy far more than easy, quirky rhymes of everyday experience. The long life of *The Wind Has Wings* in its two editions—still our best anthology of Canadian adult poems selected for children, and certainly the most attractively illustrated—attests to this.

There is no question that there are talented Canadians writing verse for children, but there are few voices speaking to them and for them while also giving them a sense of the power of poetry to

articulate sensation and experience—as in Robert Hogg's 'Song' in
The New Wind Has Wings:

> The sun is mine
> And the trees are mine
> The light breeze is mine
> And the birds that inhabit the air
> are mine
> Their voices upon the wind
> are in my ear

11
Canadian Publishing for Children
and How It Grew

During much of the nineteenth century, Canadian writers of fiction sometimes found first publication in monthly magazines or newspapers, but they usually sought book publication in London or New York, where the market was large and good distribution was ensured. Among children's books, Catharine Parr Traill's *Canadian Crusoes: A Tale of the Rice Lake Plains* (1852), for example, was published in London, as were most of the works of James MacDonald Oxley. James de Mille and Marshall Saunders were published in the United States, while L.M. Montgomery did not have a Canadian publisher until 1916. This publishing trend brought, of course, greater financial rewards to these early authors, but not recognition as Canadian writers—Marshall Saunders' *Beautiful Joe* (1894) is listed in an American bibliography of first editions. Many of these early writers were highly prolific. De Mille wrote nine books for boys, Oxley thirty-one, Saunders penned innumerable talking-animal stories, and L.M. Montgomery not only produced seven sequels to *Anne of Green Gables* (1908), but also eight other girlhood romances as well as short stories and poems.

This season of fruitfulness, as far as numbers were concerned, was not to last. Productivity dropped. From records extant it would appear that only ten children's books were published between 1921 and 1923, and until 1950 there were only about nine or ten each year. There was a slow increase until the 1960s and early 1970s, when about fifty or sixty were published annually. This latter period also saw the appearance of some well-designed and well-illustrated children's books. For the first time they could compete in physical attractiveness with imported works. Here most of the credit can be given to Oxford Canada and to the then recently established firm of Tundra Books of Montreal. Oxford employed several artists who worked imaginatively in black and white—Theo Dimson, Leo Rampen, and Donald Grant—and then moved into full colour with Frank Newfeld, Elizabeth Cleaver, and Laszlo Gal. Tundra brought Ann Blades and William Kurelek to international notice and expanded with a full panoply of exciting illustrators.

The seeds of change are first noticeable in the late 1970s with the first books by writers such as Monica Hughes, Brian Doyle, Barbara Smucker, and Kevin Major, who have continued to write and who heralded the flood of new authors and illustrators in the 1980s, a period that so far represents the high point in Canadian children's publishing. Though many factors combined to stimulate the industry, there can be little doubt that the influx of government moneys was the most potent force in the release of new writers and illustrators.

In spite of these modest gains, publishing for children by 1975 seemed to be in a holding position. The major problems besetting the publishing industry as a whole were magnified in the children's-book field. Most difficulties remain stumbling blocks today. Briefly stated, they are: a small population divided by language (indeed languages) and scattered across a vast distance, making distribution and promotion erratic and expensive; smaller print-runs and higher printing costs than for imported books, resulting in higher prices for indigenous works; and always, of course, severe competition from imports (Canada is the largest book-importing country in the world). Added difficulties besetting publishing for children were, in the past, a lack of children's-book editors; the modest buying policies of school and public libraries for Canadian children's books; a paucity of grants and awards for writers and illustrators of children's books; and the absence of mass-audience reviewing media. Most importantly, Canadian publishers had no popular backlists, the bread and butter of any firm. (The publishers of *Winnie-the-Pooh* (1926) or *Charlotte's Web* (1952), for example, will continue to rake in a tidy sum each year indefinitely, with little or no effort.) Thus, with small markets and no steady profits, Canadian publishers for children could rarely afford to take risks with new or unknown writers or illustrators.

Changes are easy enough to tabulate, but not so easy to rank in order of importance. In terms of publishing for children, many factors appeared to arise, or at least became evident, almost simultaneously. Much credit is due to innumerable people, chiefly children's librarians, school librarians, library associations, publishers, and booksellers who worked unknown and unsung to further the cause of Canadian children's books. Their efforts resulted in the appointment of a children's specialist at the National Library of Canada in 1976, the formation of the Canadian Children's Book Centre in the same year, and the informal establishment of Children's Literature Round Tables across the country. In 1975 the first journal devoted exclusively to serious criticism of Canadian children's literature was founded at the University of Guelph by a group of academics; the success of *Canadian Children's Literature/Littérature canadienne pour la jeunesse* has proved that our children's literature is worthy of serious study. Although there is now some coverage of children's books in newspapers (the Toronto *Globe*, for example), there is an unfortunate gap left by the demise of our most important journal, *In Review*, in 1982. In addition to reviews and articles in national book-trade and reviewing journals—such as *Books in Canada, Quill & Quire*, and *CM: Canadian Materials*—*Children's Book News* (published by the Canadian Children's Book Centre) provides up-to-date information on authors and lists of recommended books, and *Emergency Librarian* reviews children's paperbacks and books about children's literature. In the 1980s the proliferation of new Canadian titles was recognized by well-known American reviewing journals. The *Horn Book Magazine* instituted a regular column, 'News From the North', and a similar column is included in the *Children's Literature Association Quarterly*. However, there is no journal that supplies the comprehensive and comparative reviewing necessary to evaluate our books in the context of an international children's literature. Children's book prizes and awards also increased dramatically from the two offered by the Canadian Association of Children's Librarians before the 1970s, many carrying financial rewards. The Canada Council played an increasingly important role, not only with its Children's Literature Prizes, established in 1976 (now part of the prestigious Governor General's literary awards), but also with its grants to authors, illustrators, and publishers, and financial support for author readings in public and school libraries. This is an area of promotion that is also sponsored by the Canadian Children's Book Centre through its annual Children's Book Festival. In 1974 The Children's Book Store, the first Canadian book store devoted exclusively to children's books, opened in Toronto. It has since become famous worldwide and has been joined by approximately fifty such stores across the country.

All these developments, taken together, produced unprecedented excitement about our children's literature. Other major influences were also at work. In a political sense there was a rising tide of nationalism in the late sixties and early seventies. One aspect of this was demonstrated by the Committee for an Independent Canada, formed to promote cultural and economic independence from the United States. The problems of the publishing industry came to the fore in 1970 with the sale of the financially troubled Ryerson Press to an American firm. Ryerson had almost symbolized Canadian publishing; founded in 1890 as an arm of the United Church, it had expanded into Canadian culture in general and into the publication of Canadian poetry in particular. Publishing concerns were documented in the 1971 report of the *Royal Commission on Book Publishing* and in studies of the industry, such as the Secretary of State's *The Publishing Industry in Canada* in 1977.

Much of the debate centred on the ownership of publishing firms in Canada; many more were now completely Canadian-owned. It was suddenly the age of the small nationalist presses, many of which were consciously created as alternatives to mainstream publishing. Some, such as House of Anansi, Oberon, and James Lorimer, were committed to the publication of Canadian adult writing; others, such as The Women's Press, Kids Can Press, Annick Press, and Tundra Books published only children's books. These, along with the small regional publishers, such as Tree Frog Press, and larger regional presses such as Douglas and McIntyre, who rapidly specialized in children's books under its Groundwood imprint, combined to increase the number of children's books published annually to over two hundred in the late 1980s. Much of this publication was supported by grants from the Canada Council and from provincial Arts Councils, such as the Ontario Arts Council. In the early 1980s publishing was also supported through grants from the Federal

Department of Communication. The Canadian Book Publishing Development Program was formed in 1976 to stimulate the Canadian-controlled sector of the publishing industry. This program provides funds to publishers, to be used to increase the overall profitability of a firm and the book-publishing industry in general. Naturally, such grants also foster publishing for children.

Although the economics may still be discouraging, publishers have risen to the challenge with determination and imagination; the industry is not only surviving but expanding. This is partly due to more aggressive marketing and promotion. Since the late 1970s many publishers have followed the lead of Tundra Books in establishing high profiles at international book fairs, such as the Bologna Children's Book Fair and the Frankfurt Book Fair. Children's book publishers are seeking, with success, co-publication and the sale of foreign rights, particularly in the field of picturebooks, which sometimes travel better than novels. This development has provided some solutions to common publishing problems, including greatly enlarged (and therefore less expensive) print runs—sometimes as high as 15,000 to 25,000, as opposed to runs of 3,000 to 5,000 that were the norm in the past.

Then there were the children of the postwar baby boom who marched off to university—the best-educated generation in Canadian history. There they found burgeoning courses in their own country's literature, and these became so popular that not all student demands could be met. CAN LIT had been discovered. In 1943, writing about Canadian poetry—though his comment applied to other genres—Northrop Frye pointed out that '. . . there is an interest for Canadian readers much deeper than what the achievement itself justifies.' But now Canadian literature was being recognized, and for its *innate* worth as well as for being a valuable and viable method of learning about ourselves. While courses in children's literature had regularly been offered in Library Schools and Faculties of Education (almost from their beginnings), they were added to the syllabus of many university English Departments in the late 1960s. These gradually developed more Canadian content and today courses in Canadian children's literature are offered in many institutions of higher learning. Conferences on children's literature have gone the same route. In 1976, at the First Pacific Rim Conference on Children's

Literature (held under the aegis of the School of Librarianship at the University of British Columbia), one day out of five-and-a-half days was devoted to Canadian authors, illustrators, and publishers. In 1986 a two-and-a-half-day conference (sponsored by the Manitoba School Library Audio-Visual Association as Canadian Images Canadiennes) concentrated solely on Canadian children's books and their creators. A second is to be held in 1990. Both courses and conferences have meant a higher profile for authors and illustrators, media coverage (at least locally), and increased sales.

The baby-boom children, as adults, take a great interest in their children's exposure to books, especially where their pre-school children are concerned. They are more consciously interested than their forebears were in Canadianism. Either by choice or necessity, modern parents make use of day-care and nursery-school facilities, most of which use picturebooks to a great extent and employ nursery lore. And almost every public library now has its programs for infants: 'Books for Babes', 'Books for Toddlers', etc. These social changes have certainly helped to foster the Canadian 'picturebook boom'.

There was another strong force at work over a fairly long period. This was the growth, popularity, and finally the international acclaim of our writers of fiction for adults. In the late 1970s Margaret Atwood, Robertson Davies, Timothy Findley, Margaret Laurence, and Alice Munro (to name but a few) were saluted internationally for their excellence. And at this point, two axioms came into play: first, children's literature generally follows that for adults in growth and stature; and second, as in our adult literature, the more books that are written and published, the greater the likelihood that a significant number will be of worth.

There is some debate surrounding the exportability of books with a strong Canadian content. But this factor does not appear to concern picturebooks to any great extent, since pictures speak a universal language. We have examples of successes both with and without a local background and ambience. William Kurelek's *A Prairie Boy's Winter* (1973) and *A Prairie Boy's Summer* (1975) were welcomed abroad as works of art, while it can be presumed that Ann Blades' *Mary of Mile 18* (1971) has crossed borders because of its major theme—a child and a pet—although it is strongly rooted in a specific place and life-style. But the greatest modern success story in moving beyond Canadian borders belongs to Robert Munsch, with his tall tales of feisty, generic children and absolutely no local colouring. Some American editors, or publishers, do demand changes—the Manitoba setting of Betty Waterton's *Pettranella* (1980) became in the American edition the midwestern United States. Some novels appear to travel better than others. Brian Doyle's *Angel Square* (1984), with its pronounced Ottawa setting and Canadian-style irony, has not been appreciated in the United States, while Jean Little's family stories, which are almost completely without background, have long been popular in other countries. One surmises that the less Canadian content there is, the greater the chance of a Canadian book's being accepted abroad. And yet it may be that theme, characterization, and storytelling qualities matter most. Probably no Canadian children's book is as firmly rooted in place as L.M. Montgomery's *Anne of Green Gables*, yet Anne's personality and escapades have appealed (and continue to appeal) to millions of readers around the world. Perhaps the fact that Canada is not seen as exotic was established in the nineteenth century. The great success of the prolific writer for boys, R.M. Ballantyne, was his *Coral Island* (1858), set on a Pacific Ocean island, not his northern-Canadian adventure story, *Snowflakes and Sunbeams; or The Young Fur Traders* (1856). Still, the important point about a fine Canadian children's book is not its potential for export, but that it makes its way in its own country.

Although most major publishers have children's lists, a trend towards specialization is noticeable: picturebooks from Tundra Books, Annick Press, Groundwood Books, and Oxford; young-adult novels from Irwin Publishing and Groundwood Books; Indian legends from the small native presses; works emphasizing multiculturalism from James Lorimer and Tundra Books; and non-fiction from Greey de Pencier and Kids Can Press. Although not in the numbers that one would wish, there has been an increase in translations from French to English—primarily picturebooks published by James Lorimer and Annick Press. There have also been notable changes within publishing houses. Tundra Books appears to be much less sophisticatedly art-oriented and more childlike, moving from John Lim's *Merchants of the Mysterious East* (1981) to alphabet books. Kids Can Press, at first known for simple child-oriented tales, has enlarged its publishing program to include such distinguished productions as Robert Service's *The Cremation of Sam McGee* (1986) and *The Shooting of Dan McGrew* (1987), with artwork by Ted Harrison.

The publication of the *Canadian Children's Treasury* in 1988, an anthology that ranges from native legends to selections from recent writers such as Monica Hughes and Barbara Smucker, may herald a new publishing trend. It is the first such collection since *Kanata* (1976), an equally interesting pot-pourri of selections from published works chosen by Mary Rubio and Glenys Stow. Anthologies have inbuilt weaknesses; no compiler will ever please everyone, and selections from novels, unless they are episodic in their structure, may give a false impression of the whole work. Still, it may be said that anthologies give a kind of cachet to a literature and that there is now certainly enough excellent creative writing to fill several of them.

Among the many other keen observations in Ecclesiastes is the remark that 'Of making many books there is no end'. This certainly applies today to children's books, and even to Canadian children's books. The last ten years are remarkable in that there have been more books published than in the 150 years before. Indeed there is a frenetic quality to the publishing scene. One sign of this is that among the books of quality, there are now so many innocuous and forgettable books, perhaps best described as 'disposables'; but this, of course, has always been true of both British and American publishing. Much of the increased productivity is certainly due to talented writers and illustrators, to imaginative and aggressive publishers, to parents, teachers, and librarians who are concerned to root children in their own place and time and history, and to young readers who have never been more receptive to Canadian books. Branches of non-Canadian publishing houses have played a major role in the past in nurturing an indigenous literature and they continue to do so. But today the most important and notable aspect in the development of publishing (and in the writing of literature) has been the injection of public money. An examination of the acknowledgements in children's books published by Canadian-owned firms reveals that we do not have complete laissez-faire economics in the business of publishing for children. Book after book recognizes a debt to the Canada Council, provincial Arts Councils, or both. Their support can thus be clearly seen as the prime influence in bringing about the rapid growth of Canadian children's-book publishing in the last decade, thus fostering the many admirable works of literature and art that have so recently appeared. Nevertheless, it took such government intervention to prove something about Canada itself: that this relatively small and individualistic society, historically conditioned to being dominated by the cultures of Britain and America, does not need to accept a situation in which foreign imports determine the cultural development of its children.

Bibliography

1. CANADIAN CHILDREN'S LITERATURE AND HOW IT GREW

BALLANTYNE, ROBERT MICHAEL. *Snowflakes and Sunbeams; or, The Young Fur Traders.* Illustrated by the author. London, T. Nelson, 1856.

_____. *Ungava; A Tale of Esquimaux-Land.* Illustrated by the author. London, T. Nelson, 1858.

BARBEAU, MARIUS. *The Golden Phoenix and Other French-Canadian Fairy Tales.* Retold by Michael Hornyansky. Illustrated by Arthur Price. Toronto, Oxford, 1958. Reprinted under the title: *The Golden Phoenix and Other Fairy Tales from Quebec*, 1980.

BAYLEY, MRS. H. *Henry; or, The Juvenile Traveller.* London, Simpkin, 1836.

_____. *Improvement; or, A Visit to Grandmama.* London, Simpkin, 1833.

BELANEY, ARCHIBALD STANSFELD. *The Adventures of Sajo and Her Beaver People* by Grey Owl (pseud.). Toronto, Macmillan, 1935. Published as *The Adventures of Sajo and the Beaver People*, 1986.

BLADES, ANN. *Mary of Mile 18.* Illustrated by the author. Montreal, Tundra, 1971.

BURNHAM, JOHN. *Jack Ralston; or, The Outbreak of the Nauscopees: A Tale of Life in the Far North-East of Canada.* London, T. Nelson, 1901.

CLARK, CATHERINE ANTHONY. *The Golden Pine Cone.* Illustrated by Clare Bice. Toronto, Macmillan, 1950.

_____. *The Hunter and the Medicine Man.* Illustrated by Clare Bice. Toronto, Macmillan, l966.

CLUTESI, GEORGE. *Son of Raven, Son of Deer: Fables of the Tse-Shaht People.* Illustrated by the author. Sidney, B.C., Gray's Pub., 1967.

CONNOR, RALPH (pseud.). See Gordon, Charles W.

DE MILLE, JAMES. *Among the Brigands.* Boston, Lee and Shepard, 1872 (The Young Dodge Club series).

——————. *The 'B.O.W.C.'; A Book for Boys.* Boston, Lee and Shepard, 1869.

——————. *The Boys of Grande Pré School.* Boston, Lee and Shepard, 1871 (The 'B.O.W.C.' series).

——————. *Fire in the Woods.* Boston, Lee and Shepard, 1871 ('B.O.W.C.' series).

——————. *Lost in the Fog.* Boston, Lee and Shepard, 1870 ('B.O.W.C.' series).

——————. *Picked Up Adrift.* Boston, Lee and Shepard, 1872 ('B.O.W.C.' series).

——————. *The Seven Hills.* Boston, Lee and Shepard, 1873 (Young Dodge Club).

——————. *The Treasure of the Seas.* Boston, Lee and Shepard, 1873 (The 'B.O.W.C.' series).

——————. *The Winged Lion.* Boston, Lee and Shepard, 1877 (Young Dodge Club).

DOWNIE, MARY ALICE and BARBARA ROBERTSON, eds. *The Wind Has Wings: Poems from Canada.* Illustrated by Elizabeth Cleaver. Toronto, Oxford, 1968.

DUNCAN, NORMAN. *The Adventures of Billy Topsail.* New York, Revell, 1906.

GORDON, CHARLES W. *Glengarry School Days: A Story of Early Days in Glengarry* by Ralph Connor (pseud). Toronto, Westminster, 1902; Toronto, McClelland, 1975 (New Canadian Library).

GOSSE, PHILIP H. *The Canadian Naturalist. A Series of Conversations on the Natural History of Lower Canada.* London, J. Van Voorst, 1840.

GREY OWL. See Belaney, Archibald Stansfeld.

GROVE, MISS. *Little Grace; or, Scenes in Nova-Scotia.* Halifax, C. Mackenzie, 1846.

HAIG-BROWN, RODERICK L. *Saltwater Summer.* New York, Morrow, 1948.

——————. *Starbuck Valley Winter.* Illustrated by Charles de Feo. New York, Morrow, 1943.

——————. *The Whale People.* Illustrated by Mary Weiler. London, Collins, 1962; Toronto, Totem, 1982.

HARRIS, CHRISTIE. *Raven's Cry.* Illustrated by Bill Reid. Toronto, McClelland, 1966.

HAYES, JOHN. *Buckskin Colonist.* Illustrated by Fred J. Finley. Toronto, Copp, 1947.

——————. *Bugles in the Hills.* Illustrated by Fred J. Finley. Toronto, Copp, 1955.

HENTY, G.A. *With Wolfe in Canada.* Illustrated by Gordon Browne. London, Blackie, 1887.

HEWITT, MARSHA and CLAIRE MACKAY. *One Proud Summer.* Toronto, Women's Press, 1981; Markham, Ont., Puffin, 1988.

HORNYANSKY, MICHAEL. See Barbeau, Marius.

HOUSTON, JAMES. *Tikta'Liktak: An Eskimo Legend.* Illustrated by the author. Don Mills, Ont., Longmans, 1965.

_____. *The White Archer: An Eskimo Legend.* Illustrated by the author. Don Mills, Ont., Longmans, 1967.

HUGHES, MONICA. *Hunter in the Dark.* Toronto, Clarke, 1982; Toronto, Avon, 1984.

HUNTER, BERNICE THURMAN. *Lamplighter.* Richmond Hill, Ont., Scholastic-Tab, 1987.

KURELEK, WILLIAM. *A Prairie Boy's Summer.* Illustrated by the author. Montreal, Tundra, 1975.

_____. *A Prairie Boy's Winter.* Illustrated by the author. Montreal, Tundra, 1973.

LEE, DENNIS. *Alligator Pie.* Illustrated by Frank Newfeld. Toronto, Macmillan, 1974.

_____. *Nicholas Knock and Other People.* Illustrated by Frank Newfeld. Toronto, Macmillan, 1974.

McCLUNG, NELLIE. *Sowing Seeds in Danny.* New York, Doubleday, Page, 1908.

MACMILLAN, CYRUS. *Canadian Fairy Tales.* Illustrated by Marcia Lane Foster. London, John Lane The Bodley Head, 1922.

_____. *Canadian Wonder Tales.* Illustrated by George Sheringham. London, John Lane The Bodley Head, 1918. Reissued, with *Canadian Fairy Tales,* as *Canadian Wonder Tales.* Illustrated by Elizabeth Cleaver. London, Bodley, 1974.

The Maple Leaf. Montreal, Robert W. Lay, 1852-4.

MARRYAT, FREDERICK. *The Settlers in Canada; Written for Young People.* London, Longman, 1844. 2 vols.

MELZAK, RONALD. *The Day Tuk Became a Hunter and Other Eskimo Stories.* Illustrated by Carol Jones. Toronto, McClelland, 1967.

MONTGOMERY, LUCY MAUDE. *Anne of Green Gables.* Boston, Page, 1908; Toronto, Seal, 1976.

MOWAT, FARLEY M. *The Dog Who Wouldn't Be.* Illustrated by Paul Galdone. Toronto, Little, 1957; Toronto, Seal, 1980.

_____. *Lost in the Barrens.* Illustrated by Charles Geer. Boston, Little, 1956; Toronto, McClelland, 1973.

_____. *Owls in the Family.* Illustrated by Robert Frankenberg. Boston, Little, 1961; Toronto, McClelland, 1973.

NICHOLS, RUTH. *The Marrow of the World.* Illustrated by Trina Schart Hyman. Toronto, Macmillan, 1972; Toronto, Gage, 1977.

_____. *A Walk Out of the World.* Illustrated by Trina Schart Hyman. Toronto, Longman, 1969.

OXLEY, JAMES MACDONALD. *Up Among the Ice Floes*. London, T. Nelson, 1890.

_____. *The Wreckers of Sable Island*. London, T. Nelson, 1894.

A Peep at the Esquimaux; or, Scenes on the Ice ... By a Lady. London, H.R. Thomas, 1825.

PHILLIPPS-WOLLEY, CLIVE. *Gold, Gold in Cariboö A Story of Adventure in British Columbia*. Illustrated by Godfrey C. Hindley. London, Blackie, 1894.

ROBERTS, CHARLES G.D. *The Kindred of the Wild: A Book of Animal Life*. Illustrated by Charles Livingston Bull. Boston, Page, 1902.

SAUNDERS, MARSHALL. *Beautiful Joe; An Autobiography*. Philadelphia, American Baptist, 1894 ; Toronto, McClelland, 1985.

SETON, ERNEST THOMPSON. *Two Little Savages; Being the Adventures of Two Boys Who Lived as Indians and What They Learned*. Illustrated by the author. New York, Doubleday, 1903; New York, Dover, 1962.

_____. *Wild Animals I Have Known*. Illustrated by the author. New York, Scribner, 1898; Toronto, McClelland, 1977 (New Canadian Library).

SHARP, EDITH L. *Nkwala*. Illustrated by William Winter. Boston, Little, 1958; Toronto, McClelland, 1977. (New Canadian Library)

The Snow Drop; or, Juvenile Magazine. Montreal, Lovell and Gibson, 1847-53.

TAYLOR, CORA. *Julie*. Saskatoon, Sask., Western, 1985.

TOYE, WILLIAM. *The Mountain Goats of Temlaham*. Illustrated by Elizabeth Cleaver. Toronto, Oxford, 1969.

_____. *How Summer Came to Canada*. Illustrated by Elizabeth Cleaver. Toronto, Oxford, 1969.

TRAILL, CATHARINE PARR (STRICKLAND). *Canadian Crusoes: A Tale of the Rice Lake Plains*. London, A. Hall, Virtue, 1852; Ottawa, Carleton University, 1986 (Early Canadian Texts).

_____. *Lady Mary and Her Nurse; or, A Peep Into the Canadian Forest*. London, A. Hall, Virtue, 1856. (Later published as *Afar in the Forest; or, Pictures of Life and Scenery in the Wilds of Canada*. London, T. Nelson, 1869).

_____. *The Young Emigrants; or, Pictures of Canada*. London, Harvey and Darton, 1826; Pontefract, W. Yorkshire, Lofthouse/E.P.Pub., 1969 (Early Children's Books).

TRUSS, JAN. *Jasmin*. Vancouver, Douglas, 1982 (A Groundwood Book).

YEE, PAUL. *The Curses of Third Uncle*. Toronto, Lorimer, 1986.

YOUNG, EGERTON RYERSON. *Children of the Forest: A Story of Indian Love*. New York, Revell, 1904.

_____. *Three Boys in the Wild North Land, Summer*. Illustrated by J.E. Laughlin. New York, Eaton & Mains, 1896.

_____. *Winter Adventures of Three Boys in the Great Lone Land*. Illustrated by J.E. Laughlin. New York, Abingdon, 1899.

2. REALISTIC FICTION

The Outdoor Survival Story

BELANEY, ARCHIBALD STANSFELD. *The Adventures of Sajo and Her Beaver People* by Grey Owl (pseud.). Toronto, Macmillan, 1935. Published as *The Adventures of Sajo and the Beaver People*, 1986.

DUNCAN, NORMAN. *The Adventures of Billy Topsail*. New York, Revell, 1906.

GREY OWL (pseud.). See Belaney, Archibald Stansfeld

HAIG-BROWN, RODERICK L. *Starbuck Valley Winter*. Illustrated by Charles de Feo. New York, Morrow, 1943.

_____. *Saltwater Summer*. New York, Morrow, 1948.

HALVORSON, MARILYN. *Let It Go*. Toronto, Irwin, 1985.

_____. *Nobody Said It Would Be Easy*. Toronto, Irwin, 1987.

HOUSTON, JAMES. *Black Diamonds: A Search for Arctic Treasure*. Illustrated by the author. Toronto, McClelland, 1982; Markham, Ont., Puffin, 1983.

_____. *Frozen Fire: A Tale of Courage*. Illustrated by the author. Toronto, McClelland, 1977; Markham, Ont., Puffin, 1979.

_____. *Ice Swords: An Undersea Adventure*. Illustrated by the author. Toronto, McClelland, 1985.

_____. *Long Claws: An Arctic Adventure*. Illustrated by the author. Toronto, McClelland, 1981.

_____. *River Runners: A Tale of Hardship and Bravery*. Illustrated by the author. Toronto, McClelland, 1979; Markham, Ont., Penguin, 1981.

_____. *Tikta'Liktak: An Eskimo Legend*. Illustrated by the author. Don Mills, Ont., Longmans, 1965.

_____. *The White Archer: An Eskimo Legend*. Illustrated by the author. Don Mills, Ont., Longmans, 1967.

_____. *Wolf-Run: A Caribou Eskimo Tale*. Illustrated by the author. Don Mills, Ont., Longmans, 1971.

HUGHES, MONICA. *Hunter in the Dark*. Toronto, Clarke, 1982; Toronto, Avon, 1984.

_____. *Log Jam*. Toronto, Irwin, 1987; Don Mills, Ont., Collins, 1988.

MAJOR, KEVIN. *Hold Fast*. Toronto, Clarke, 1978.

MARKOOSIE. *Harpoon of the Hunter*. Illustrated by Germaine Arnaktauyok. Montreal, McGill-Queen's, 1970.

MOWAT, FARLEY M. *The Black Joke*. Illustrated by Douglas Johnson. Toronto, McClelland, 1962.

_____. *The Curse of the Viking Grave*. Illustrated by Charles Geer. Boston, Little, 1966; Toronto, McClelland, 1973.

_____. *Lost in the Barrens*. Illustrated by Charles Geer. Boston, Little, 1956; Toronto, McClelland, 1973.

PHILLIPPS-WOLLEY, CLIVE. *Gold, Gold in Cariboo! A Story of Adventure in British Columbia*. Illustrated by Godfrey C. Hindley. London, Blackie, 1894.

SETON, ERNEST THOMPSON. *Two Little Savages; Being the Adventures of Two Boys Who Lived as Indians and What They Learned*. Illustrated by the author. New York, Doubleday, 1903; New York, Dover, 1962.

STEFANSSON, VILHJALMUR AND VIOLET IRWIN. *Kak, the Copper Eskimo*. Toronto, Macmillan, 1924.

TRAILL, CATHARINE PARR (STRICKLAND). *Canadian Crusoes: A Tale of the Rice Lake Plains*. London, A. Hall, Virtue, 1852; Ottawa, Carleton University, 1986 (Early Canadian Texts).

TRUSS, JAN. *Jasmin*. Vancouver, Douglas, 1982. (A Groundwood Book).

WILKINSON, DOUGLAS. *Sons of the Arctic*. Illustrated by Prudence Seward. Toronto, Clarke, 1965.

Stories of Child and Family Life

BELANEY, ARCHIBALD STANSFELD. *The Adventures of Sajo and Her Beaver People* by Grey Owl (pseud.). Toronto, Macmillan, 1935; Published as *The Adventures of Sajo and the Beaver People*, 1986.

BILSON, GEOFFREY. *Hockeybat Harris*. Toronto, Kids Can, 1984.

CHETIN, HELEN. *The Lady of the Strawberries*. Illustrated by Anita Kunz. Toronto, PMA, 1978; Agincourt, Ont., Book Society of Canada, 1982.

COLLURA, MARY-ELLEN LANG. *Sunny*. Toronto, Irwin, 1988.

_____. *Winners*. Saskatoon, Sask., Western, 1984.

COOK, LYN. *The Bells on Finland Street*. Illustrated by Stanley Wyatt. Toronto, Macmillan, 1950.

_____. *The Little Magic Fiddler*. Illustrated by Stanley Wyatt. Toronto, Macmillan, 1951.

DE MILLE, JAMES. *The 'B.O.W.C.': A Book for Boys*. Boston, Lee and Shepard, 1869.

DOYLE, BRIAN. *Angel Square*. Vancouver, Douglas, 1984 (A Groundwood Book).

_____. *Hey, Dad!* Toronto, Groundwood, 1978.

_____. *Up to Low*. Vancouver, Douglas, 1982 (A Groundwood Book).

_____. *You Can Pick Me Up at Peggy's Cove*. Illustrated by Heather Collins. Toronto, Groundwood, 1979.

DUNHAM, BERTHA MABEL. *Kristli's Trees*. Illustrated by Selwyn Dewdney. Toronto, McClelland, 1948.

ELLIS, SARAH. *The Baby Project*. Vancouver, Douglas, 1986 (A Groundwood Book).

_____. *Next-Door Neighbours*. Vancouver, Douglas, 1989 (A Groundwood Book).

HALVORSON, MARILYN. *Cowboys Don't Cry*. Toronto, Clarke, 1984.

_____. *Let It Go*. Toronto, Irwin, 1985.

_____. *Nobody Said It Would Be Easy*. Toronto, Irwin, 1987.

HEFFRON, DORIS. *Crusty Crossed*. London, Macmillan, 1976.

HUNTER, BERNICE THURMAN. *As Ever, Booky*. Richmond Hill, Ont., Scholastic-TAB, 1985.

_____. *A Place for Margaret*. Richmond Hill, Ont., Scholastic-TAB, 1984.

_____. *That Scatterbrain Booky*. Richmond Hill, Ont., Scholastic-TAB, 1981.

_____. *With Love From Booky*. Richmond Hill, Ont., Scholastic-TAB, 1983.

KAPLAN, BESS. *The Empty Chair*. Saskatoon, Sask., Western, 1986.

KOGAWA, JOY. *Naomi's Road*. Illustrated by Matt Gould. Toronto, Oxford, 1986.

LITTLE, JEAN. *From Anna*. Illustrated by Joan Sandin. Toronto, Fitzhenry, 1972.

_____. *Home From Far*. Illustrated by Jerry Lazare. Toronto, Little, 1965.

_____. *Listen for the Singing*. Toronto, Clarke, 1977.

_____. *Mama's Going to Buy You a Mockingbird*. Markham, Ont., Viking, 1984; Markham, Ont., Puffin, 1985.

_____. *Lost and Found*. Illustrated by Leoung O'Young. Markham, Ont., Viking, 1985; Markham, Ont., Puffin, 1986.

_____. *Mine For Keeps*. Illustrated by Lewis Parker. Toronto, Little, 1962.

MAJOR, KEVIN. *Hold Fast*. Toronto, Clarke, 1978.

MATAS, CAROL. *Lisa*. Toronto, Lester, 1987.

MONTGOMERY, LUCY MAUDE. *Anne of Avonlea*. Boston, Page, 1909; Toronto, McGraw, 1968.

_____. *Anne of Green Gables*. Boston, Page, 1908; Toronto, Seal, 1976.

_____. *Emily Climbs*. Toronto, McClelland, 1925; Toronto, Seal, 1983.

_____. *Emily of New Moon*. Toronto, McClelland, 1923; Toronto, Seal, 1983.

_____. *Emily's Quest*. Toronto, McClelland, 1927; Toronto, Seal, 1983.

_____. *Pat of Silver Bush*. Toronto, McClelland, 1933; Toronto, Seal, 1988.

_____. *Rainbow Valley*. Toronto, McClelland, 1919; Toronto, Seal, 1987.

_____. *Rilla of Ingleside*. Toronto, McClelland, 1921; Toronto, Seal, 1987.

MOWAT, FARLEY M. *Owls in the Family*. Illustrated by Robert Frankenberg. Boston, Little, 1961; rev. ed., Toronto, McClelland, 1973.

PAPERNY, MYRA. *The Wooden People*. Illustrated by Ken Stampnick. Toronto, Little, 1976; Toronto, Overlea, 1987.

PEARSON, KIT. *The Daring Game*. Markham, Viking, 1986; Markham, Puffin, 1987.

_____. *The Sky Is Falling*. Markham, Viking, 1989.

SMUCKER, BARBARA. *Amish Adventure*. Toronto, Clarke, 1983; Markham, Puffin, 1984.

_____. *Jacob's Little Giant*. Markham, Ont., Viking, 1987.

STREN, PATTI. *There's a Rainbow in My Closet*. Illustrated by the author. Toronto, Fitzhenry, 1979.

TAKASHIMA, SHIZUYE. *A Child in Prison Camp*. Illustrated by the author. Montreal, Tundra, 1971.

TENNANT, VERONICA. *On Stage, Please*. Illustrated by Rita Briansky. Toronto, McClelland, 1979.

TRUSS, JAN. *Red*. Vancouver, Douglas, 1988 (A Groundwood Book).

_____. *Summer Goes Riding*. Vancouver, Douglas, 1987 (A Groundwood Book).

Light Realism

HODGINS, JACK. *Left Behind in Squabble Bay*. Illustrated by Victor Gad. Toronto, McClelland, 1988.

KORMAN, GORDON. *Don't Care High*. New York, Scholastic, 1985.

_____. *This Can't Be Happening at Macdonald Hall*. Richmond Hill, Ont., Scholastic-TAB, 1978.

McNEIL, FLORENCE. *Miss P. and Me*. Toronto, Clarke, 1982; Richmond Hill, Ont., Scholastic-TAB. 1984.

ROBERTS, KEN. *Hiccup Champion of the World*. Illustrated by Victor Gad. Vancouver, Douglas, 1988 (A Groundwood Book).

_____. *Pop Bottles*. Vancouver, Douglas, 1987 (A Groundwood Book).

SCHWARTZ, ELLEN. *Starshine!* Winlaw, B.C, Polestar, 1987.

Bibliography: Realistic Fiction | 323

WATERTON, BETTY. *Quincy Rumpel.* Vancouver, Douglas, 1984 (A Groundwood Book).

_____. *Quincy Rumpel, P.I.* Vancouver, Douglas, 1988 (A Groundwood Book).

_____. *Starring Quincy Rumpel.* Vancouver, Douglas, 1986. (A Groundwood Book).

Mystery and Detective Stories

CLARK, JOAN. *The Hand of Robin Squires.* Illustrated by William Taylor and Mary Cserepy. Toronto, Clarke, 1977; Markham, Ont., Puffin, 1986.

COLLINS, ROBERT. *The Mystery at the Wildcat Well.* Toronto, Seal, 1981 (first published as *Rory's Wildcat*, 1965).

CROOK, MARION. *The Hidden Gold Mystery.* Toronto, Overlea, 1987.

_____. *Payment in Death.* Toronto, Overlea, 1987 (A Susan George Mystery).

_____. *Stone Dead.* Toronto, Overlea, 1987 (A Susan George Mystery).

DOYLE, BRIAN. *Angel Square.* Vancouver, Douglas, 1984 (A Groundwood Book).

GORDON, SARAH. *The Dangerous Dollhouse.* Vancouver, Stoneberry Books, 1988 (A Julie Dare Mystery).

_____. *Eyes of the Lion.* Vancouver, Stoneberry Books, 1988 (A Julie Dare Mystery).

HARRIS, CHRISTIE. *Mystery at the Edge of Two Worlds.* Illustrated by Lou Crockett. Toronto, McClelland, 1978.

HOWARTH, MARY. *Could Dracula Live in Woodford?* Toronto, Kids Can, 1983.

HUGHES, MONICA. *The Ghost Dance Caper.* London, Hamilton, 1978; Toronto, Methuen, 1986.

MACKAY, CLAIRE. *The Minerva Program.* Toronto, Lorimer, 1984 (Time of Our Lives).

MANUEL, LYNN. *The Mystery of the Ghostly Riders.* Illustrated by Sylvie Daigneault. Toronto, Gage, 1982 (Jean Pac).

READ, ELFREIDA. *Race Against the Dark.* Illustrated by Tony Heron. Toronto, Gage, 1983 (Jean Pac).

SUTHERLAND, ROBERT. *The Loon Lake Murders.* Richmond Hill, Ont., Scholastic-TAB, 1987.

_____. *Mystery at Black Rock Island.* Richmond Hill, Ont., Scholastic-TAB, 1983.

WALKER, DAVID H. *Pirate Rock.* Toronto, Collins, 1969.

WEIR, JOAN. *Balloon Race Mystery and Other Stories.* Toronto, Grolier, 1988 (Mystery Club).

_____. *Ski Lodge Mystery and Other Stories.* Toronto, Overlea, 1988 (Mystery Club).

WILLIAMS, JERRY. *The Ghost of Pirate Walk*. Illustrated by Barry Rubin. Toronto, Gage, 1982 (Jean Pac).

WILSON, ERIC. *Disneyland Hostage*. Toronto, Clarke, 1982; Toronto, Totem, 1983 (A Liz Austen Mystery).

—————. *The Kootenay Kidnapper*. Toronto, Collins, 1983; Toronto, Totem, 1984 (A Tom Austen Mystery).

—————. *Murder on the Canadian*. Illustrated by Tom McNeely. Toronto, Clarke, 1976; Toronto, Totem, 1982.

—————. *Terror in Winnipeg*. Illustrated by Gavin Rowe. Toronto, Clarke, 1979; Toronto, General, 1982 (A Tom Austen Mystery).

—————. *Vampires of Ottawa*. Toronto, Collins, 1984; Toronto, Totem, 1985 (A Liz Austen Mystery).

—————. *Vancouver Nightmare*. Toronto, Clarke, 1978; Toronto, Totem, 1982 (A Tom Austen Mystery).

WOODWARD, LUCY BERTON. *Kidnapped in the Yukon*. Illustrated by Maria Jursic. Don Mills, Ont., Burns, 1968; Scarborough, Ont., Nelson, 1984.

Young-Adult Novels

BELL, WILLIAM. *The Cripples' Club*. Toronto, Irwin, 1988.

BROCHMANN, ELIZABETH. *What's the Matter, Girl?* New York, Harper, 1980.

BROOKS, MARTHA. *Paradise Café and Other Stories*. Sakatoon, Thistledown, 1988.

CRAIG, JOHN. *No Word for Good-bye*. Illustrated by Harry Alto. Toronto, Martin, 1969; Toronto, Clarke, 1979.

CULLETON, BEATRICE. *April Raintree*. Winnipeg, Pemmican, 1984 (Cut version of *In Search of April Raintree*).

—————. *In Search of April Raintree*. Winnipeg, Pemmican, 1983.

DALE, MITZIE. *Round the Bend*. Vancouver, Douglas, 1988 (A Groundwood Book).

DAVIES, PETER. *Fly Away Paul*. New York, Crown, 1974; Don Mills, PaperJacks, 1976.

DOYLE, BRIAN. *Angel Square*. Vancouver, Douglas, 1984 (A Groundwood Book).

—————. *Easy Avenue*. Vancouver, Douglas, 1988 (A Groundwood Book).

—————. *Hey, Dad!* Toronto, Groundwood, 1978.

—————. *Up to Low*. Vancouver, Douglas, 1982 (A Groundwood Book).

—————. *You Can Pick Me Up at Peggy's Cove*. Illustrated by Peggy Collins. Toronto, Groundwood, 1979.

DUNCAN, FRANCES. *Kap-Sung Ferris*. Toronto, Burns, 1977; Toronto, Macmillan, 1982.

HAIG-BROWN, RODERICK L. *Starbuck Valley Winter*. Illustrated by Charles de Feo. New York, Morrow, 1943.

HALVORSON, MARILYN. *Cowboys Don't Cry*. Toronto, Clarke, 1984.

_____. *Let It Go*. Toronto, Irwin, 1985.

HENEGHAN, JIM. *Promises to Come*. Markham, Ont., Overlea,1988.

HOUSTON, JAMES. *Tikta'Liktak: An Eskimo Legend*. Illustrated by the author. Don Mills, Ont., Longmans, 1965.

_____. *Whiteout*. Toronto, Greey, 1988.

LITTLE, JEAN. *Little by Little: A Writer's Education*. Markham, Ont., Viking, 1987; Markham, Ont., Puffin, 1988.

McNEIL, FLORENCE. *Catriona's Island*. Vancouver, Douglas, 1988 (A Groundwood Book).

MAJOR, KEVIN. *Dear Bruce Springsteen*. Toronto, Doubleday, 1987.

_____. *Far from Shore*. Toronto, Clarke, 1980.

_____. *Hold Fast*. Toronto, Clarke, 1978.

_____. *Thirty-six Exposures*. Toronto, Doubleday, 1984.

MONTGOMERY, LUCY MAUDE. *Anne of Green Gables*. Boston, Page, 1908; Toronto, Seal, 1976.

_____. *Emily of New Moon*. Toronto, McClelland, 1923; Toronto, Seal, 1983.

MOWAT, FARLEY M. *Lost in the Barrens*. Illustrated by Charles Geer. Boston, Little, 1956; Toronto, McClelland, 1973.

RAZZELL, MARY. *Salmonberry Wine*. Vancouver, Douglas, 1987 (A Groundwood Book).

_____. *Snow Apples*. Vancouver, Douglas, 1984 (A Groundwood Book).

RICHMOND, SANDRA. *Wheels for Walking*. Vancouver, Douglas, 1983 (A Groundwood Book).

SADIQ, NAZNEEN. *Camels Make You Homesick and Other Stories*. Illustrated by Mary Cserepy. Toronto, Lorimer, 1985 (Time of Our Lives).

SMUCKER, BARBARA. *Amish Adventure*. Toronto, Clarke, 1983; Markham, Ont., Puffin, 1984.

WIELER, DIANA J. *Bad Boy*. Vancouver, Douglas, 1989 (A Groundwood Book).

YEE, PAUL. *Teach Me to Fly, Skyfighter! and Other Stories*. Illustrated by Sky Yee. Toronto, Lorimer, 1983 (The Adventure in Canada Series).

3. THE REALISTIC ANIMAL STORY

BELANEY, ARCHIBALD STANSFELD. *The Adventures of Sajo and Her Beaver People* by Grey Owl (pseud.). Toronto, Macmillan, 1935. Published as *The Adventures of Sajo and the Beaver People*, 1986.

BODSWORTH, FRED. *Last of the Curlews*. Illustrated by T.M. Shortt. Toronto, Dodd, 1955; Toronto, McClelland, 1963 (New Canadian Library).

BURNFORD, SHEILA. *The Incredible Journey: A Tale of Three Animals*. Illustrated by Carl Burger. Boston, Little, 1960; New York, Bantam, 1977.

GREY OWL. See Belaney, Archibald Stansfeld.

HAIG-BROWN, RODERICK L. *Ki-Yu: A Story of Panthers*. Illustrated by Theyre Lee-Elliott. Boston, Houghton, 1934. (Also published under the title *Panther*. London, Collins, 1934.)

_____. *Silver: The Life Story of an Atlantic Salmon*. Illustrated by Capt. J.P. Moreton. London, Black, 1931.

KASSIAN, OLENA. *Flip the Dolphin Saves the Day*. Illustrated by the author. Toronto, Greey, 1984.

_____. *Slip the Otter Finds a Home*. Illustrated by the author. Toronto, Greey, 1984.

LANGFORD, CAMERON. *The Winter of the Fisher*. Toronto, Macmillan, 1971.

MOWAT, FARLEY M. *The Dog Who Wouldn't Be*. Illustrated by Paul Galdone. Toronto, Little, 1957; Toronto, Seal, 1980.

_____. *Never Cry Wolf*. Toronto, McClelland, 1963; Toronto, Seal, 1982.

Owl: The Discovery Magazine for Children. Toronto, Young Naturalist Foundation, 1976.

ROBERTS, CHARLES G.D. *The Feet of the Furtive*. Illustrated by Paul Bransom. London, Ward Lock, 1912.

_____. *The Haunters of the Silences*. Illustrated by Charles Livingston Bull. Boston, Page, 1907.

_____. *Jim: The Story of a Backwoods Police Dog* [and other stories]. New York, Macmillan, 1919.

_____. *The Kindred of the Wild: A Book of Animal Life*. Illustrated by Charles Livingston Bull. Boston, Page, 1902.

_____. *Red Fox: The Story of His Adventurous Career in the Ringwaak Wilds and of His Final Triumph over the Enemies of His Kind*. Illustrated by Charles Livingston Bull. Boston, Page, 1905; illustrated by John Schoenherr. Richmond Hill, Ont., Scholastic-TAB, 1986.

_____. *Thirteen Bears*. Chosen and edited by Ethel Hume Bennett. Illustrated by John A. Hall. Toronto, Ryerson, 1947.

ROSSER, ERIC. *Snow Babies*. Illustrated by Olena Kassian. Toronto, Greey, 1985.

RUSSELL, ANDY. *Andy Russell's Adventures With Wild Animals.* Illustrated by Harry Savage. Edmonton, Hurtig, 1977.

SAUNDERS, MARSHALL. *Beautiful Joe; An Autobiography.* Philadelphia, American Baptist, 1894; Toronto, McClelland, 1985.

SETON, ERNEST THOMPSON. *Bannertail: The Story of a Gray Squirrel.* Illustrated by the author. New York, Scribner, 1922.

_____. *The Biography of a Grizzly.* Illustrated by the author. New York, Century, 1900; Folcroft, P.A., Folcroft, 1977.

_____. *Wild Animals I Have Known; Being the Personal Histories of Lobo, Silverspot, Raggylug, Bingo, The Springfield Fox, The Pacing Mustang, Wully and Redruff.* Illustrated by the author. New York, Scribner, 1898; Toronto, McClelland, 1977 (New Canadian Library). Many of Seton's stories have been published separately.

SMITH, DAVID ALLENBY. *Sharptooth: A Year of the Beaver.* Illustrated by Robert Kebic. London, Martin, 1974; Toronto, Irwin, 1978.

WIDELL, HELENE. *The Black Wolf of River Bend.* New York, Farrar, 1971.

4. HISTORICAL FICTION

ALLAN, IRIS. *John Rowand, Fur Trader: A Story of the Old Northwest.* Illustrated by Doug Sneyd. Toronto, Gage, 1963 (Frontier Books).

BELLINGHAM, BRENDA. *Storm Child.* Toronto, Lorimer, 1985.

BILSON, GEOFFREY. *Death Over Montreal.* Toronto, Kids Can, 1982.

_____. *Goodbye Sarah.* Illustrated by Ron Berg. Toronto, Kids Can, 1982.

BRADFORD, KARLEEN. *The Nine Days Queen.* Richmond Hill, Ont., Scholastic-TAB, 1986.

BRANDIS, MARIANNE. *The Quarter-Pie Window.* Illustrated by G. Brender à Brandis. Erin, Ont., Porcupine's Quill, 1985.

_____. *The Tinderbox.* Illustrated by G. Brender à Brandis. Erin, Ont., Porcupine's Quill, 1982.

CHALMERS, JOHN W. *Horseman in Scarlet: Sam Steele of the Mounties.* Illustrated by Lex Bell. Toronto, Gage, 1961 (Frontier Books).

CLARK, CATHERINE ANTHONY. *The Man With Yellow Eyes.* Illustrated by Gordon Rayner. Toronto, Macmillan, 1963 (Buckskin Books).

CLARK, JOAN. *The Hand of Robin Squires.* Illustrated by William Taylor and Mary Cserepy. Toronto, Clarke, 1977; Markham, Ont., Puffin, 1986.

COOK, LYN. *Rebel on the Trail.* Illustrated by Ruth M. Collins. Toronto, Macmillan, 1953.

DENISON, MURIEL. *Susannah: A Little Girl with the Mounties.* Illustrated by Marguerite Bryan. New York, Dodd, 1936.

DOWNIE, MARY ALICE. *The King's Loon.* Toronto, Kids Can, 1979.

_____. *The Last Ship*. Illustrated by Lissa Calvert. Toronto, PMA, 1980 (Northern Lights).

DOWNIE, MARY ALICE and GEORGE A. RAWLYK. *A Proper Acadian*. Illustrated by Ron Berg. Toronto, Kids Can, 1980.

DOWNIE, MARY ALICE and JOHN DOWNIE. *Honor Bound*. Toronto, Oxford, 1980.

FREEMAN, BILL. *Danger on the Tracks*. Toronto, Lorimer, 1987.

_____. *First Spring on the Grand Banks*. Toronto, Lorimer, 1978.

_____. *Harbour Thieves*. Toronto, Lorimer, 1984.

_____. *The Last Voyage of the Scotian*. Toronto, Lorimer, 1976.

_____. *Shantymen of Cache Lake*. Toronto, Lorimer, 1975.

_____. *Trouble at Lachine Mill*. Toronto, Lorimer, 1983.

FRYER, MARY BEACOCK. *Escape: Adventures of a Loyalist Family*. Illustrated by Stephen Clarke. Don Mills, Ont., Dent, 1976; Toronto, Dundurn, 1982.

GERMAN, TONY. *Tom Penny*. Toronto, McClelland, 1977.

GOODSPEED, DONALD J. and HERBERT F. WOOD. *Redcoat Spy* by John Redmayne (pseud.). Illustrated by John Lawrence. Toronto, Macmillan, 1964.

GREENWOOD, BARBARA. *A Question of Loyalty*. Richmond Hill, Ont., Scholastic-TAB, 1984.

HAIG-BROWN, RODERICK L. *The Whale People*. Illustrated by Mary Weiler. London, Collins, 1962; Toronto, Totem, 1982.

HAMILTON, MARY. *The Sky Caribou*. Illustrated by Debi Perna. Toronto, PMA, 1980 (Northern Lights).

_____. *The Tin-Lined Trunk*. Illustrated by Ron Berg. Toronto, Kids Can, 1980.

HARRIS, CHRISTIE. *Forbidden Frontier*. Illustrated by E. Carey Kenney. New York, Atheneum, 1968.

_____. *Raven's Cry*. Illustrated by Bill Reid. Toronto, McClelland, 1966.

HAYES, JOHN. *The Dangerous Cove*. Illustrated by Fred J. Finley. Toronto, Copp, 1957.

_____. *A Land Divided*. Illustrated by Fred J. Finley. Toronto, Copp, 1951.

_____. *On Loyalist Trails*. Illustrated by J. Merle Smith. Toronto, Copp, 1971.

_____. *Rebels Ride at Night*. Illustrated by Fred J. Finley. Toronto, Copp, 1953.

_____. *The Steel Ribbon*. Illustrated by Fred J. Finley. Toronto, Copp, 1967.

_____. *Treason at York*. Illustrated by Fred J. Finley. Toronto, Copp, 1949.

HEWITT, MARSHA and CLAIRE MACKAY. *One Proud Summer*. Toronto, Women's Press, 1981; Markham, Ont., Puffin, 1988.

HUDSON, JAN. *Sweetgrass*. Edmonton, Tree Frog, 1984.

HUNTER, BERNICE THURMAN. *Lamplighter*. Richmond Hill, Ont., Scholastic-TAB, 1987.

KNOX, OLIVE. *Black Falcon*. Illustrated by Clarence Tillenius. New York, Bouregy and Curl, 1955.

_____. *The Young Surveyor*. Toronto, Ryerson, 1956.

LEITCH, ADELAIDE. *The Great Canoe*. Illustrated by Clare Bice. Toronto, Macmillan, 1962 (Buckskin Books).

LUNN, JANET. *Shadow in Hawthorn Bay*. Toronto, Lester, 1986; Markham, Ont., Puffin, 1988.

McSWEENEY, SUSANNE. *The Yellow Flag*. Illustrated by Brenda Clark. Toronto, PMA, 1980 (Northern Lights).

RAWLYK, GEORGE. *Streets of Gold*. Illustrated by Leung O'Young. Toronto, PMA, 1980 (Northern Lights).

REANEY, JAMES. *The Boy with an R in His Hand*. Illustrated by Leo Rampen. Toronto, Macmillan, 1965; rev. ed., Erin, Ont., Porcupine's Quill, 1984.

SASS, GREGORY. *Redcoat*. Erin, Ont., Porcupine's Quill, 1985.

SHARP, EDITH. *Nkwala*. Illustrated by William Winter. Boston, Little, 1958; Toronto, McClelland, 1974.

SMITH, T.H. *Cry to the Night Wind*. Markham, Ont., Viking, 1986.

SMUCKER, BARBARA. *Days of Terror*. Toronto, Clarke, 1979; Markham, Ont., Puffin, 1981.

_____. *Underground to Canada*. Illustrated by Tom McNeely. Toronto, Clarke, 1977; Markham, Ont., Puffin, 1978. (Published in the United States under the title: *Runaway to Freedom*.)

SWAINSON, DONALD and ELEANOR SWAINSON. *The Buffalo Hunt*. Illustrated by James Tughan. Toronto, PMA, 1980.

SWAYZE, BEULAH GARLAND. *Father Gabriel's Cloak*. Illustrated by Douglas Sneyd. Toronto, Macmillan, 1962 (Buckskin Books).

SWAYZE, FRED. *Iroquois War Trail*. Toronto, Ryerson, 1965.

_____. *Tonty of the Iron Hand*. Toronto, Ryerson, 1957.

TAIT, HERBERT. *Redwulf the Outlander*. Toronto, Clarke, 1972.

TANAKA, SHELLEY. *Michi's New Year*. Illustrated by Ron Berg. Toronto, PMA, 1980 (Northern Lights).

TURNER, D. HAROLD. *To Hang a Rebel*. Illustrated by Merle Smith. Toronto, Macmillan, 1977.

WEAVER, EMILY. *The Only Girl: A Tale of 1837*. Toronto, Macmillan, 1925.

YEE, PAUL. *The Curses of Third Uncle*. Toronto, Lorimer, 1986.

5. PICTUREBOOKS AND PICTURE-STORYBOOKS

ALDERSON, SUE ANN. *Bonnie McSmithers, You're Driving Me Dithers*. Illustrated by Fiona Garrick. Edmonton, Tree Frog, 1974; rev. ed., 1987.

_____. *Ida and the Wool Smugglers*. Illustrated by Ann Blades. Vancouver, Douglas, 1987.

ANDERSEN, HANS CHRISTIAN. *The Little Mermaid*. Retold by Margaret Crawford Maloney. Illustrated by Laszlo Gal. Toronto, Metheun, 1983.

ANDREWS, JAN. *Very Last First Time*. Illustrated by Ian Wallace. Vancouver, Douglas, 1985 (A Groundwood Book).

ASKA, WARABÊ. *Who Goes to the Park*. Illustrated by the author. Montreal, Tundra, 1984.

_____. *Who Hides in the Park/Les Mystères du parc*. Illustrated by the author. Montreal, Tundra, 1986.

BARBEAU, MARIUS. *The Princess of Tomboso: A Fairy-Tale in Pictures*. Retold by Michael Hornyansky. Illustrated by Frank Newfeld. Toronto, Oxford, 1960.

BIANCHI, JOHN. *The Bungalo Boys: Last of the Tree Ranchers*. Illustrated by the author. Newburgh, Ont., Bungalo, 1986.

BIRCH, DAVID. *The King's Chessboard*. Illustrated by Devis Grebu. New York, Dial, 1988.

BLADES, ANN. *A Boy of Taché*. Illustrated by the author. Montreal, Tundra, 1973.

_____. *By the Sea: An Alphabet Book*. Illustrated by the author. Toronto, Kids Can, 1985.

_____. *Mary of Mile 18*. Illustrated by the author. Montreal, Tundra, 1971.

BODGER, JOAN. *Belinda's Ball*. Illustrated by Mark Thurman. Toronto, Oxford, 1981.

BOSWELL, HAZEL. *French Canada: Pictures and Stories*. Illustrated by the author. New York, Viking, 1938; rev. ed., Toronto, McClelland, 1967.

BOURGEOIS, PAULETTE. *Big Sarah's Little Boots*. Illustrated by Brenda Clark. Toronto, Kids Can, 1987.

_____. *Franklin in the Dark*. Illustrated by Brenda Clark. Toronto, Kids Can, 1986.

CHASE, EDITH. *The New Baby Calf*. Illustrated by Barbara Reid. Richmond Hill, Ont., Scholastic-TAB, 1984.

CHISLETT, GAIL. *The Rude Visitors*. Illustrated by Barbara Di Lella. Toronto, Annick, 1984 (Annick Toddler series).

CLARK, JOAN. *The Leopard and the Lily*. Illustrated by Velma Foster. Lantzville, B.C., Oolichan, 1984.

CLEAVER, ELIZABETH. *ABC*. Illustrated by the author. Toronto, Oxford, 1984.

_____. *The Enchanted Caribou*. Illustrated by the author. Toronto, Oxford, 1985.

_____. *The Miraculous Hind; A Hungarian Legend*. Illustrated by the author. Toronto, Holt, 1973.

_____. *Petrouchka*. Adapted from the ballet by Igor Stravinsky and Alexandre Benois. Illustrated by the author. Toronto, Macmillan, 1980.

CLIMO, LINDEE. *Chester's Barn*. Illustrated by the author. Montreal, Tundra, 1982.

_____. *Clyde*. Illustrated by the author. Montreal, Tundra, 1986.

CUTLER, EBBITT. *If I Were a Cat I Would Sit in a Tree*. Illustrated by Rist Arnold. Montreal, Tundra, 1985.

DE ROUSSAN, JACQUES. *Beyond the Sun/Au-delà du Soleil*. Illustrated by the author. Montreal, Tundra, 1972.

_____. *If I Came from Mars/Si j'étais Martien*. Illustrated by the author. Montreal, Tundra, 1977.

DENTON, KADY MACDONALD. *Granny Is a Darling*. Illustrated by the author. Toronto, Kids Can, 1988.

DOWNIE, MARY ALICE and BARBARA ROBERTSON, comps. *The New Wind Has Wings: Poems from Canada*. Illustrated by Elizabeth Cleaver. Toronto, Oxford, 1984.

_____. *The Wind Has Wings: Poems from Canada*. Illustrated by Elizabeth Cleaver. Toronto, Oxford, 1968; rev. ed., *The New Wind Has Wings*, 1984.

EYVINDSON, PETER. *Chester Bear, Where Are You?* Illustrated by Wendy Wolsak-Frith. Winnipeg, Pemmican, 1988.

_____. *Kyle's Bath*. Illustrated by Wendy Wolsak. Winnipeg, Pemmican, 1984.

_____. *Old Enough*. Illustrated by Wendy Wolsak. Winnipeg, Pemmican, 1986.

GAITSKELL, SUSAN. *Emily*. Illustrated by Kellie Jobson. Toronto, Three Trees, 1986.

GALE, DONALD. *Sooshewan: Child of the Beothuk*. Illustrated by Shawn Steffler. St John's, Nfld., Breakwater, 1988.

GALLOWAY, PRISCILLA. *Seal Is Lost*. Illustrated by Karen Patkau. Toronto, Annick, 1988.

_____. *When You Were Little and I Was Big*. Illustrated by Heather Collins. Toronto, Annick, 1984 (Annick Toddler series).

GARRETT, JENNIFER. *The Queen Who Stole the Sky*. Illustrated by Linda Hendry. Richmond Hill, Ont., North Winds, 1986.

GAY, MARIE-LOUISE. *Angel and the Polar Bear*. Illustrated by the author. Toronto, Stoddart, 1988.

_____. *Moonbeam on a Cat's Ear*. Illustrated by the author. Toronto, Stoddart, 1986.

_____. *Rainy Day Magic*. Illustrated by the author. Toronto, Stoddart, 1987.

GILMAN, PHOEBE. *The Balloon Tree*. Illustrated by the author. Richmond Hill, Ont., North Winds, 1984.

GORDON, ROBERT KAY. *A Canadian Child's ABC*. Illustrated by Thoreau Macdonald. Toronto, Dent, 1931.

HAMMOND, FRANKLIN. *Ten Little Ducks*. Illustrated by the author. Vancouver, Douglas, 1987 (A Groundwood Book).

HARPUR, TOM. *The Mouse That Couldn't Squeak*. Illustrated by Dawn Lee. Toronto, Oxford, 1988.

HARRIS, DOROTHY JOAN. *Four Seasons for Toby*. Illustrated by Vlasta van Kampen. Richmond Hill, Ont., North Winds, 1987.

_____. *The House Mouse*. Illustrated by Barbara Cooney. Toronto, Saunders, 1973.

HARRISON, TED. *The Blue Raven*. Illustrated by the author. Toronto, Macmillan, 1989.

_____. *Children of the Yukon*. Illustrated by the author. Montreal, Tundra, 1977.

_____. *A Northern Alphabet*. Illustrated by the author. Montreal, Tundra, 1982.

HEARN, EMILY. *Good Morning Franny, Good Night Franny*. Illustrated by Mark Thurman. Toronto, Women's Press, 1984.

HEIDBREDER, ROBERT. *Don't Eat Spiders*. Illustrated by Karen Patkau. Toronto, Oxford, 1985.

HOWARD-GIBBON, AMELIA FRANCES. *An Illustrated Comic Alphabet*. Illustrated by the author. Toronto, Oxford, 1966.

HUTCHINS, HAZEL J. *Leanna Builds a Genie Trap*. Illustrated by Catharine O'Neill. Toronto, Annick, 1986.

JAM, TEDDY. *Night Cars*. Illustrated by Eric Beddows. Vancouver, Douglas, 1988 (A Groundwood Book).

KHALSA, DAYAL KAUR. *How Pizza Came to Our Town*. Illustrated by the author. Montreal, Tundra, 1989.

_____. *I Want a Dog*. Illustrated by the author. Montreal, Tundra, 1987.

_____. *My Family Vacation*. Illustrated by the author. Montreal, Tundra, 1988.

_____. *Sleepers*. Illustrated by the author. Montreal, Tundra, 1988.

_____. *Tales of a Gambling Grandma*. Illustrated by the author. Montreal, Tundra, 1986.

KOVALSKI, MARYANN. *Brenda and Edward*. Illustrated by the author. Toronto, Kids Can, 1984.

_____. *Jingle Bells*. Illustrated by the author. Toronto, Kids Can, 1988.

_____. *The Wheels on the Bus*. Illustrated by the author. Toronto, Kids Can, 1987.

KURELEK, WILLIAM. *Lumberjack*. Illustrated by the author. Montreal, Tundra, 1974.

_____. *A Northern Nativity: Christmas Dreams of a Prairie Boy*. Illustrated by the author. Montreal, Tundra, 1976.

_____. *A Prairie Boy's Summer*. Illustrated by the author. Montreal, Tundra, 1975.

_____. *A Prairie Boy's Winter*. Illustrated by the author. Montreal, Tundra, 1973.

LASKER, DAVID. *The Boy Who Loved Music*. Illustrated by Joe Lasker. New York, Viking, 1979.

LEE, DENNIS. *Lizzy's Lion*. Illustrated by Marie-Louise Gay. Toronto, Stoddart, 1984.

LEMIEUX, MICHELE. *What Is That Noise?* Illustrated by the author. London, Methuen, 1984.

LEVCHUK, HELEN. *The Dingles*. Illustrated by John Bianchi. Vancouver, Douglas, 1985 (A Groundwood Book).

LIM, JOHN. *At Grandmother's House*. Illustrated by the author. Montreal, Tundra, 1977.

_____. *Merchants of the Mysterious East*. Illustrated by the author. Montreal, Tundra, 1981.

LIM, SING. *West Coast Chinese Boy*. Illustrated by the author. Montreal, Tundra, 1979.

LOEWEN, IRIS. *My Mom Is So Unusual*. Illustrated by Alan Pakarnyk. Winnipeg, Pemmican, 1986.

LOTTRIDGE, CELIA BARKER. *One Watermelon Seed*. Illustrated by Karen Patkau. Toronto, Oxford, 1986.

LUNN, JANET. *Amos's Sweater*. Illustrated by Kim LaFave. Vancouver, Douglas, 1988 (A Groundwood Book).

_____. *The Twelve Dancing Princesses*. Illustrated by Laszlo Gal. Toronto, Methuen, 1979.

MALONEY, MARGARET CRAWFORD. *The Goodman of Ballengiech*. Illustrated by Laszlo Gal. Toronto, Methuen, 1987.

MAY, DAVID, C., ed. *Byron and His Balloon: An English-Chipewyan Counting Book*. Illustrated by the children of La Loche and friends. Edmonton, Tree Frog, 1984.

MOAK, ALLAN. *A Big City ABC*. Illustrated by the author. Montreal, Tundra, 1984.

MORGAN, ALLEN. *Matthew and the Midnight Money Van*. Illustrated by Michael Martchenko. Toronto, Annick, 1987 (Matthew's Midnight Adventure series).

_____. *Matthew and the Midnight Tow Truck*. Illustrated by Michael Martchenko. Toronto, Annick, 1984 (Matthew's Midnight Adventure series).

_____. *Matthew and the Midnight Turkeys*. Illustrated by Michael Martchenko. Toronto, Annick, 1985 (Matthew's Midnight Adventure series).

MORGAN, NICOLA. *The Great B.C. Alphabet Book*. Illustrated by the author. Markham, Ont., Fitzhenry, 1985.

_____. *Pride of Lions*. Illustrated by the author. Markham, Ont., Fitzhenry, 1987.

MOTHER GOOSE. *Sing a Song of Mother Goose*. Illustrated by Barbara Reid. Richmond Hill, Ont., Scholastic-TAB, 1987.

MULLER, ROBIN. *Little Kay*. [Illustrated by the reteller.] Richmond Hill, Ont., North Winds, 1988.

_____. *The Lucky Old Woman*. [Illustrated by the reteller.] Toronto, Kids Can, 1987.

_____. *Mollie Whuppie and the Giant*. [Illustrated by the reteller.] Richmond Hill, Ont., North Winds, 1982; Richmond Hill, Ont., Scholastic-TAB, 1983.

_____. *The Sorcerer's Apprentice*. [Illustrated by the reteller.] Toronto, Kids Can, 1985.

_____. *Tatterhood*. [Illustrated by the reteller.] Richmond Hill, Ont., North Winds, 1984; Richmond Hill, Ont., Scholastic-TAB, 1984.

MUNSCH, ROBERT. *I Have To Go*. Illustrated by Michael Martchenko. Toronto, Annick, 1987.

_____. *Jonathan Cleaned Up—Then He Heard a Sound, or Blackberry Subway Jam*. Illustrated by Michael Martchenko. Toronto, Annick, 1981.

_____. *Love You Forever*. Illustrated by Sheila McGraw. Scarborough, Ont., Firefly, 1986.

_____. *Mortimer*. Illustrated by Michael Martchenko. Toronto, Annick, 1983; rev.ed., 1985.

_____. *Murmel, Murmel, Murmel*. Illustrated by Michael Martchenko. Toronto, Annick, 1982.

_____. *The Paper Bag Princess*. Illustrated by Michael Martchenko. Toronto, Annick, 1980.

_____. *Pigs*. Illustrated by Michael Martchenko. Toronto, Annick, 1989.

_____. *Thomas' Snowsuit*. Illustrated by Michael Martchenko. Toronto, Annick, 1985.

MUNSCH, ROBERT and MICHAEL KUSUGAK. *A Promise Is a Promise*. Illustrated by Vladyana Krykorka. Toronto, Annick, 1988.

NEWLANDS, ANNE. *Meet Edgar Degas*. Toronto, Kids Can/National Gallery of Canada, 1988.

OBERMAN, SHELDON. *The Lion in the Lake/Le Lion dans le lac*. Illustrated by Scott Barham. Winnipeg, Peguis, 1988.

)'NEILL, CATHARINE. *Mrs. Dunphy's Dog*. Illustrated by the author. Markham, Ont., Viking, 1987.

)PPENHEIM, JOANNE. *Have You Seen Birds?* Illustrated by Barbara Reid. Richmond Hill, Ont., North Winds, 1986; Richmond Hill, Ont., Scholastic-TAB, 1986.

)TTO, MARYLEAH. *Tom Doesn't Visit Us Anymore*. Illustrated by Jude Waples. Toronto, Women's Press, 1987.

'ACHANO, JANE and J. RABBITT OZORES. *James Bay Cree ABC in Song and Picture*. Illustrated by J. Eitzen and others. Chisasibi, P.Q., James Bay Cree Cultural Education Center, 1983.

PAGE, P.K. *A Flask of Sea Water*. Illustrated by Laszlo Gal. Toronto, Oxford, 1989.

PASTERNAK, CAROL AND ALLEN SUTTERFIELD. *Stone Soup*. Illustrated by Hedy Campbell. Toronto, Canadian Women's Educational, 1974.

POULIN, STÉPHANE. *Ah! Belle Cité!/A Beautiful City ABC*. Illustrated by the author. Montreal, Tundra, 1985.

_____. *Can You Catch Josephine?* Illustrated by the author. Montreal, Tundra, 1987.

_____. *Could You Stop Josephine?* Illustrated by the author. Montreal, Tundra, 1988.

_____. *Have You Seen Josephine?* Illustrated by the author. Montreal, Tundra, 1986.

RICHARDS, JACK. *Johann's Gift to Christmas*. Illustrated by Len Norris. Vancouver, Douglas, 1972.

ROACHE, GORDON. *A Halifax ABC*. Illustrated by the author. Montreal, Tundra, 1987.

ROBART, ROSE. *The Cake That Mack Ate*. Illustrated by Maryann Kovalski. Toronto, Kids Can, 1986.

ROTHSTEIN, ETHO. *Jill and the Big Cat*. Illustrated by Maureen Paxton. Windsor, Ont., Black Moss, 1984.

SALTMAN, JUDITH. *Goldie and the Sea*. Illustrated by Kim LaFave. Vancouver, Douglas, 1987 (A Groundwood Book).

SERVICE, ROBERT W. *The Cremation of Sam McGee*. Illustrated by Ted Harrison. Toronto, Kids Can, 1986.

_____. *The Shooting of Dan McGrew*. Illustrated by Ted Harrison. Toronto, Kids Can, 1988.

SILLERS, PATRICIA. *Ringtail*. Illustrated by Karen Patkau. Toronto, Oxford, 1987.

SPEAR, JEAN. *A Candle for Christmas*. Illustrated by Ann Blades. Vancouver, Douglas, 1986.

SPRAY, CAROLE. *The Mare's Egg: A New World Folk Tale*. Illustrated by Kim LaFave. Camden East, Ont., Camden, 1981.

STAUNTON, TED. *Simon's Surprise*. Illustrated by Sylvie Daigneault. Toronto, Kids Can, 1986.

STINSON, KATHY. *Big or Little?* Illustrated by Robin Baird Lewis. Toronto, Annick, 1983 (Annick Toddler series).

_____. *Mom and Dad Don't Live Together Any More*. Illustrated by Nancy Lou Reynolds. Toronto, Annick, 1984.

_____. *Red Is Best*. Illustrated by Robin Baird Lewis. Toronto, Annick, 1982 (Annick Toddler series).

_____. *Teddy Rabbit*. Illustrated by Stéphane Poulin. Toronto, Annick, 1988.

STREN, PATTI. *Hug Me*. Illustrated by the author. Toronto, Fitzhenry, 1977; New York, Harper, 1984.

_____. *Sloan and Philamina; or, How to Make Friends with Your Lunch*. Illustrated by the author. Toronto, Clarke, 1979.

TAKASHIMA, SHIZUYE. *A Child in Prison Camp*. Illustrated by the author. Montreal, Tundra, 1971.

TANAKA, SHELLEY. *Michi's New Year*. Illustrated by Ron Berg. Toronto, PMA, 1980 (Northern Lights).

THOMPSON, RICHARD. *Jenny's Neighbours*. Illustrated by Kathryn E. Shoemaker. Toronto, Annick, 1987.

THORNHILL, JAN. *The Wildlife ABC: A Nature Alphabet*. Illustrated by the author. Toronto, Greey, 1988.

TIBO, GILLES. *Simon and the Snowflakes*. Illustrated by the author. Montreal, Tundra, 1988.

TOYE, WILLIAM. *Cartier Discovers the St Lawrence*. Illustrated by Laszlo Gal. Toronto, Oxford, 1970.

_____. *The Fire Stealer*. Illustrated by Elizabeth Cleaver. Toronto, Oxford, 1979.

_____. *How Summer Came to Canada*. Illustrated by Elizabeth Cleaver. Toronto, Oxford, 1969.

_____. *The Loon's Necklace*. Illustrated by Elizabeth Cleaver. Toronto, Oxford, 1977.

_____. *The Mountain Goats of Temlaham*. Illustrated by Elizabeth Cleaver. Toronto, Oxford, 1969.

WALLACE, IAN. *Chin Chiang and the Dragon's Dance*. Illustrated by the author. Vancouver, Douglas, 1984 (A Groundwood Book).

_____. *Morgan the Magnificent*. Illustrated by the author. Vancouver, Douglas, 1987 (A Groundwood Book).

_____. *The Sparrow's Song*. Illustrated by the author. Markham, Ont., Viking, 1986.

WALLACE, IAN and ANGELA WOOD. *The Sandwich*. Illustrated by Ian Wallace. Toronto, Kids Can, 1975; rev. ed., 1985.

WATERTON, BETTY. *Pettranella*. Illustrated by Ann Blades. Vancouver, Douglas, 1980.

_____. *A Salmon for Simon*. Illustrated by Ann Blades. Vancouver, Douglas, 1978; Richmond Hill, Ont., Scholastic-TAB, 1986.

WHEELER, BERNELDA. *A Friend Called "Chum"*. Illustrated by Andy Stout. Winnipeg, Pemmican, 1984.

_____. *I Can't Have Bannock, But the Beaver Has a Dam*. Illustrated by Herman Bekkering. Winnipeg, Pemmican, 1984.

_____. *Where Did You Get Your Moccasins?* Illustrated by Herman Bekkering. Winnipeg, Pemmican, 1986.

WILSON, BARBARA. *ABC et/and 123*. Illustrated by Gisèle Daigle. Toronto, Porcépic, 1980.

WISEMAN, ADELE. *Kenji and the Cricket*. Illustrated by Shizuye Takashima. Erin, Ont., Porcupine's Quill, 1988.

WOOD, ANGELA. *Kids Can Count*. Toronto, Kids Can, 1976.

WYNNE-JONES, TIM. *Architect of the Moon*. Illustrated by Ian Wallace. Vancouver, Douglas, 1988 (A Groundwood Book).

_____. *I'll Make You Small*. Illustrated by Maryann Kovalski. Vancouver, Douglas, 1986 (A Groundwood Book).

_____. *Mischief City*. Illustrated by Victor Gad. Vancouver, Douglas, 1986 (A Groundwood Book) .

_____. *Zoom at Sea*. Illustrated by Ken Nutt. Toronto, Douglas, 1983 (A Groundwood Book).

_____. *Zoom Away*. Illustrated by Ken Nutt. Toronto, Douglas, 1985 (A Groundwood Book).

WYSE, ANNE and ALEX WYSE, eds. *Alphabet Book*. Designed by Allan Fleming. Toronto, University of Toronto, 1968.

_____. *The One to Fifty Book*. Toronto, University of Toronto, 1973.

ZOLA, MEGUIDO. *My Kind of Pup*. Illustrated by Wendy Wolsak. Winnipeg, Pemmican, 1985.

_____. *Only the Best*. Illustrated by Valerie Littlewood. London, MacRae, 1981.

ZOLA, MEGUIDO and ANGELA DEREUME. *Nobody*. Illustrated by Wendy Wolsak. Winnipeg, Pemmican, 1983.

6. NATIVE LEGENDS

Indian Legends

AHENAKEW, FREDA, tr. and ed. *How the Birch Tree Got Its Stripes: A Cree Story for Children.* Illustrated by George Littlechild. Saskatoon, Sask., Fifth House, 1988.

_____. *How the Mouse Got Brown Teeth: A Cree Story for Children.* Illustrated by George Littlechild. Saskatoon, Sask., Fifth House, 1988.

AYRE, ROBERT. *Sketco the Raven.* Illustrated by Philip Surrey. Toronto, Macmillan, 1961.

CAMERON, ANNE. *How Raven Freed the Moon.* Illustrated by Tara Miller. Madeira Park, B.C., Harbour, 1985.

_____. *How the Loon Lost Her Voice.* Illustrated by Tara Miller. Maderia Park, B.C., Harbour, 1985.

_____. *Lazy Boy.* Illustrated by Nelle Olsen. Madeira Park, B.C., Harbour, 1988.

_____. *Orca's Song.* Illustrated by Nelle Olsen. Madeira Park, B.C., Harbour, 1987.

CAMPBELL, MARIA. *Little Badger and the Fire Spirit.* Illustrated by David Maclagan. Toronto, McClelland, 1977.

CLUTESI, GEORGE. *Son of Raven, Son of Deer: Fables of the Tse-Shaht People.* Illustrated by the author. Sidney, B.C., Gray's Pub., 1967.

COATSWORTH, EMERSON and DAVID COATSWORTH, comps. *The Adventures of Nanabush: Ojibway Indian Stories.* Told by Sam Snake, Chief Elijah Yellowhead, Alder York, David Simcoe, and Annie King. Illustrated by Francis Kagige. Toronto, Doubleday, 1979.

DAWE, TOM. *Winter of the Black Weasel: A Tale Based on a Newfoundland Micmac Legend.* Illustrated by Anne Macleod. St John's, Nfld., Breakwater, 1988.

ELSTON, GEORGE, comp. and ed. *Giving: Ojibwa Stories and Legends from the Children of Curve Lake.* Lakefield, Ont., Waapoone, 1985.

FISHER, OLIVE M. and CLARA L. TYNER. *Totem, Tipi and Tumpline: Stories of Canadian Indians.* Illustrated by Annora Brown. Toronto, Dent, 1955.

FRASER, FRANCES. *The Bear Who Stole the Chinook and Other Stories.* Illustrated by Lewis Parker. Toronto, Macmillan, 1959.

_____. *The Wind Along the River.* Illustrated by Lewis Parker. Toronto, Macmillan, 1968.

GRISDALE, ALEX. *Wild Drums: Tales and Legends of the Plains Indians.* As told to Nan Shipley. Illustrated by Jim Ellis. Winnipeg, Peguis, 1972.

HARRIS, CHRISTIE. *Mouse Woman and the Mischief-Makers.* Illustrated by Douglas Tait. Toronto, McClelland, 1977.

_____. *Mouse Woman and the Muddleheads*. Illustrated by Douglas Tait. Toronto, McClelland, 1979.

_____. *Mouse Woman and the Vanished Princesses*. Illustrated by Douglas Tait. Toronto, McClelland, 1976.

_____. *One More Upon a Totem*. Illustrated by Douglas Tait. Toronto, McClelland, 1973.

_____. *Once Upon a Totem*. Illustrated by John Frazer Mills. McClelland, 1963.

_____. *The Trouble with Adventurers*. Illustrated by Douglas Tait. Toronto, McClelland, 1982.

_____. *The Trouble with Princesses*. Illustrated by Douglas Tait. Toronto, McClelland, 1980.

HILL, KATHLEEN L. *Glooscap and His Magic: Legends of the Wabanaki Indians*. Illustrated by Robert Frankenberg. Toronto, McClelland, 1963.

_____. *More Glooscap Stories: Legends of the Wabanaki Indians*. Illustrated by John Hamberger. Toronto, McClelland, 1970.

HOOKE, HILDA M. *Thunder in the Mountains: Legends of Canada*. Illustrated by Clare Bice. Toronto, Oxford, 1947.

How Food Was Given: An Okanagan Legend. Illustrated by Ken Edwards. Penticton, B.C., Theytus, 1984.

How Names Were Given: An Okanagan Legend. Illustrated by Ken Edwards. Penticton, B.C., Theytus, 1984.

How Turtle Set the Animals Free: An Okanagan Legend. Illustrated by Ken Edwards. Penticton, B.C., Theytus, 1984.

JOHNSON, EMILY PAULINE. *Legends of Vancouver*. Illustrated by Ben Lim. New ed., Toronto, McClelland, 1961. (First published 1911 in a privately printed edition.).

JOHNSTON, BASIL H. *By Canoe and Moccasin: Some Native Place Names of the Great Lakes*. Illustrated by David Beyer. Lakefield, Ont., Waapoone, 1986.

_____. *Tales the Elders Told: Ojibway Legends*. Illustrated by Shirley Cheechoo. Toronto, Royal Ontario Museum, 1981.

JOHNSTON, PATRONELLA. *Tales of Nokomis*. Illustrated by Frances Kagige. Toronto, Musson, 1970.

MACMILLAN, CYRUS. *Canadian Fairy Tales*. Illustrated by Marcia Lane Foster. London, John Lane The Bodley Head, 1922.

_____. *Canadian Wonder Tales*. Illustrated by George Sheringham. London, John Lane The Bodley Head, 1918. Reissued, with *Canadian Fairy Tales*, as *Canadian Wonder Tales*. Illustrated by Elizabeth Cleaver. London, Bodley, 1974.

_____. *Glooskap's Country and Other Indian Tales.* Illustrated by John A. Hall. Toronto, Oxford, 1955.

NOWLAN, ALDEN. *Nine Micmac Legends.* Illustrated by Shirley Bear. Hantsport, N.S., Lancelot, 1983.

REID, DOROTHY M. *Tales of Nanabozho.* Illustrated by Donald Grant. Oxford, 1963.

SCRIBE, MURDO. *Murdo's Story: A Legend from Northern Manitoba.* Illustrated by Terry Gallagher. Winnipeg, Pemmican, 1985.

SKOGAN, JOAN. *Princess and the Sea-Bear and Other Tsimshian Stories.* Illustrated by Claudia Stewart. Prince Rupert, B.C., Metlakatla Band Council, 1983.

Stories from Pangnirtung. Illustrated by Germaine Arnaktauyok. Edmonton, Hurtig, 1976.

Tales from the Longhouse. By Indian Children of British Columbia. Sidney, B.C., Gray's Pub., 1973.

TOYE, WILLIAM. *The Fire Stealer.* Illustrated by Elizabeth Cleaver. Oxford, 1979.

_____. *How Summer Came to Canada.* Illustrated by Elizabeth Cleaver. Toronto, Oxford, 1969.

_____. *The Loon's Necklace.* Illustrated by Elizabeth Cleaver. Oxford, 1977.

_____. *The Mountain Goats of Temlaham.* Illustrated by Elizabeth Cleaver. Toronto, Oxford, 1969.

WEATHERBY, HUGH. *Tales the Totems Tell.* Illustrated by the author. Toronto, Macmillan, 1944.

Inuit Legends

AYRE, ROBERT. *Sketco the Raven.* Illustrated by Philip Surrey. Toronto, Macmillan, 1961.

CASWELL, HELEN. *Shadows from the Singing House: Eskimo Folk Tales.* Illustrated by Robert Mayokok. Edmonton, Hurtig, 1968.

CLEAVER, ELIZABETH. *The Enchanted Caribou.* Illustrated by the author. Toronto, Oxford, 1985.

HEWITT, GARNET. *Ytek and the Arctic Orchid: An Inuit Legend.* Illustrated by Heather Woodall. Vancouver, Douglas, 1981.

HOUSTON, JAMES. *Kiviok's Magic Journey: An Eskimo Legend.* Illustrated by the author. Toronto, Longman, 1973.

MELZAK, RONALD. *The Day Tuk Became a Hunter and Other Eskimo Stories.* Illustrated by Carol Jones. Toronto, McClelland, 1967.

_____. *Raven, Creator of the World: Eskimo Legends.* Illustrated by Laszlo Gal. Toronto, McClelland, 1970.

MÉTAYER, MAURICE, ed. and tr. *Tales from the Igloo*. Illustrated by Agnes Nanogak. Edmonton, Hurtig, 1972.

NANOGAK, AGNES. *More Tales from the Igloo*. Illustrated by the author. Edmonton, Hurtig, 1986.

SCHWARTZ, HERBERT T. *Elik and Other Stories of the Mackenzie Eskimos*. Illustrated by Mona Ohoveluk. Toronto, McClelland, 1970.

7. FOLK AND FAIRY TALES

ANDERSEN, HANS CHRISTIAN. *The Little Mermaid*. Retold by Margaret Crawford Maloney. Illustrated by Laszlo Gal. Toronto, Methuen, 1983.

AUBRY, CLAUDE. *The Magic Fiddler and Other Legends of French Canada*. Translated by Alice E. Kane. Illustrated by Saul Field. Toronto, Martin, 1968.

BARBEAU, MARIUS. *The Golden Phoenix and Other French-Canadian Fairy Tales*. Retold by Michael Hornyansky. Illustrated by Arthur Price. Toronto, Oxford, 1958; reprinted under the title: *The Golden Phoenix and Other Fairy Tales from Quebec*, 1980.

BARKHOUSE, JOYCE. *The Witch of Port LaJoye*. Illustrated by Daphne Irving. Charlottetown, Ragweed, 1983.

DOWNIE, MARY ALICE. *How the Devil Got His Cat*. Illustrated by Jillian Hulme Gilliland. Kingston, Ont., Quarry, 1988.

_____. *The Wicked Fairy-Wife: A French Canadian Folktale*. Translated and adapted from the French. Illustrated by Kim Price. Toronto, Kids Can, 1983.

_____. *The Witch of the North: Folk Tales of French Canada*. Illustrated by Elizabeth Cleaver. Ottawa, Oberon, 1975.

ELLIS, SARAH AND BILL RICHARDSON. *Mud & Gold*. Vancouver, First Avenue, 1986 (Audiocassette).

_____. *Pebbles & Porridge Pots*. Vancouver, First Avenue, 1986 (Audiocassette).

FASICK, ADELE MONGAN. *The Beauty Who Would Not Spin*. Illustrated by Leslie Elizabeth Watts. Richmond Hill, Ont., North Winds, 1989.

FINNIGAN, JOAN. *Look! The Land Is Growing Giants: A Very Canadian Legend*. Illustrated by Richard Pelham. Montreal, Tundra, 1983.

FOWKE, EDITH. *Ring Around the Moon: Two Hundred Songs, Tongue Twisters, Riddles and Rhymes of Canadian Children*. Illustrated by Judith Gwyn Brown. Toronto, McClelland, 1977; Toronto, NC Press, 1987.

_____. *Sally Go Round the Sun: Three Hundred Songs, Rhymes and Games of Canadian Children*. Illustrated by Carlos Marchiori. Toronto, McClelland, 1969.

FRANKO, IVAN. *Fox Mykyta*. English version by Bohdan Melnyk. Illustrated by William Kurelek. Montreal, Tundra, 1978.

HAMILTON, MARY. *A New World Bestiary.* Illustrated by Kim LaFave. Vancouver, Douglas, 1985.

GREGORY, NAN and MELANIE RAY. *Moon Tales.* Vancouver, First Avenue, 1989 (Audiocassette).

HARBER, FRANCES. *My King Has Donkey Ears.* Illustrated by Maryann Kovalski. Richmond Hill, Ont., North Winds, 1986.

KANE, ALICE. *Tales from an Irish Hearth.* Toronto, Storytellers School, 1985 (Audiocassette).

KONG, SHIU L. and ELIZABETH K. WONG. *Fables and Legends from Ancient China.* Illustrated by Michele Nidenoff and Wong Yin. Toronto, Kensington Educational, 1985.

LUNN, JANET. *The Twelve Dancing Princesses.* Illustrated by Laszlo Gal. Toronto, Methuen, 1979.

LUNN, JENNI. *The Fisherman and His Wife: A Grimm's Fairytale.* [Illustrated by the reteller.] Toronto, McGraw, 1982.

MacEWEN, GWENDOLYN. *The Honey Drum: Seven Tales from Arab Lands.* Oakville, Ont., Mosaic, 1983.

McNEILL, JAMES. *The Double Knights; More Tales from Round the World.* Illustrated by Theo imson. Toronto, Oxford, 1964.

_____. *The Sunken City and Other Tales from Round the World.* Illustrated by Theo Dimson. Toronto, Oxford, 1959.

MALONEY, MARGARET CRAWFORD. *The Goodman of Ballengiech.* Illustrated by Laszlo Gal. Toronto, Methuen, 1987.

MARTIN, EVA. *Canadian Fairy Tales.* Illustrated by Laszlo Gal. Vancouver, Douglas, 1984 (A Groundwood Book).

MOTHER GOOSE. *Sharon, Lois and Bram's Mother Goose.* Illustrated by Maryann Kovalski. Vancouver, Douglas, 1985.

_____. *Sing a Song of Mother Goose.* Illustrated by Barbara Reid. Richmond Hill, Ont., North Winds, 1987.

MULLER, ROBIN. *Little Kay.* [Illustrated by the reteller.] Richmond Hill, Ont., North Winds, 1988.

_____. *The Lucky Old Woman.* [Illustrated by the reteller.] Toronto, Kids Can, 1987.

_____. *Mollie Whuppie and the Giant.* [Illustrated by the reteller.] Richmond Hill, Ont., North Winds, 1982; Richmond Hill, Ont., Scholastic-TAB, 1983.

_____. *The Sorcerer's Apprentice.* [Illustrated by the reteller.] Toronto, Kids Can, 1985.

_____. *Tatterhood.* [Illustrated by the reteller.] Richmond Hill, Ont., North Winds, 1984; Richmond Hill, Ont., Scholastic-TAB, 1984.

NAKAMURA, MICHIKO. *Gonbei's Magic Kettle: A Folktale in Japanese and English.* Illustrated by San Murata. Toronto, Kids Can, 1980 (Folktale Library).

NEWFELD, FRANK [and WILLIAM TOYE]. *Simon and the Golden Sword*. Illustrated by Frank Newfeld. Toronto, Oxford, 1976.

QUINTON, LESLIE, (pseud.). *The Lucky Coin and Other Folk Tales Canadians Tell*. Illustrated by David Shaw. Toronto, McClelland, 1972.

SPRAY, CAROLE. *The Mare's Egg: A New World Fairy Tale*. Illustrated by Kim LaFave. Camden East, Ont., Camden, 1981.

SYMCHYCH, VICTORIA and OLGA VESEY. *The Flying Ship and Other Ukrainian Folk Tales*. Illustrated by Peter Kuch. Toronto, Holt, 1975.

THIEBAUX, TAMARA LYNN. *Goldilocks and the Three Bears*. [Illustrated by the reteller.] Markham, Ont., Fitzhenry, 1989.

YU, CHAI-SHIN, SHIU L. KONG, and RUTH W. YU. *Korean Folk Tales*. Illustrated by Bang Hai-ja. Toronto, Kensington Educational, 1986.

ZIMMERMAN, H. WERNER. *Henny Penny*. [Illustrated by the reteller.] Richmond Hill, Ont., North Winds, 1989.

8. FANTASY

BEDARD, MICHAEL. *A Darker Magic*. Don Mills, Ont., Collier, 1987.

BERTON, PIERRE. *The Secret World of Og*. Illustrated by William Winter. Toronto, McClelland, 1961. (Reissued 1974, with illustrations by Patsy Berton.)

BLANCHET, M. WYLIE. *A Whale Named Henry*. Illustrated by Jacqueline McKay Mathews. Madeira Park, B.C., Harbour, 1983.

BRADFORD, KARLEEN. *The Other Elizabeth*. Illustrated by Deborah Drew-Brook. Toronto, Gage, 1982.

BUCHAN, JOHN. *Lake of Gold*. Illustrated by S. Levenson. Toronto, Musson, 1941.

CLARK, CATHERINE ANTHONY. *The Diamond Feather; or, The Door in the Mountain: A Magic Tale for Children*. Illustrated by Clare Bice. Toronto, Macmillan, 1962.

_____. *The Golden Pine Cone*. Illustrated by Clare Bice. Toronto, Macmillan, 1950.

_____. *The Hunter and the Medicine Man*. Illustrated by Clare Bice. Toronto, Macmillan, 1966.

_____. *The One-Winged Dragon*. Illustrated by Clare Bice. Toronto, Macmillan, 1955.

_____. *The Silver Man*. Illustrated by Clare Bice. Toronto, Macmillan, 1958.

_____. *The Sun Horse*. Illustrated by Clare Bice. Toronto, Macmillan, 1951.

CLARK, JOAN. *The Moons of Madeleine*. Markham, Ont., Viking, 1987; Markham, Ont., Puffin, 1988.

_____. *Wild Man of the Woods*. Markham, Ont., Viking, 1985; Markham, Ont., Puffin, 1986.

CULLETON, BEATRICE. *Spirit of the White Bison*. Illustrated by Robert Kakaygeesick Jr. Winnipeg, Pemmican, 1985.

DAY, DAVID. *The Emperor's Panda*. Illustrated by Eric Beddows. Toronto, McClelland, 1986.

FRASER, WILLIAM ALEXANDER. *Mooswa and Others of the Boundaries*. Illustrated by Arthur Heming. Toronto, Briggs, 1900.

HARRIS, CHRISTIE. *Secret in the Stlalakum Wild*. Illustrated by Douglas Tait. Toronto, McClelland, 1972.

HUGHES, MONICA. *Sandwriter*. London, MacRae, 1985; London, Methuen, 1986.

HUTCHINS, HAZEL. *Anastasia Morningstar and the Crystal Butterfly*. Illustrated by Barry Trower. Toronto, Annick, 1984.

_____. *Casey Webber the Great*. Illustrated by John Richmond. Toronto, Annick, 1988.

_____. *The Three and Many Wishes of Jason Reid*. Illustrated by John Richmond. Toronto, Annick, 1983.

JACOBS, JANE. *The Girl on the Hat*. Illustrated by Karen Reczuch. Toronto, Oxford, 1989.

KATZ, WELWYN WILTON. *False Face*. Vancouver, Douglas, 1987 (A Groundwood Book).

_____. *Sun God, Moon Witch*. Vancouver, Douglas, 1986 (A Groundwood Book).

_____. *The Third Magic*. Vancouver, Douglas, 1988 (A Groundwood Book).

_____. *Witchery Hill*. Vancouver, Douglas, 1984 (A Groundwood Book).

KELLERHALS-STEWART, HEATHER. *Stuck Fast in Yesterday*. Vancouver, Douglas, 1983 (A Groundwood Book).

_____. *The Whale's Way*. Illustrated by John Hodges. Winslaw, B.C., Polestar, 1988.

KUSHNER, DONN. *A Book Dragon*. Illustrated by Nancy Ruth Jackson. Toronto, Macmillan, 1987.

LAURENCE, MARGARET. *Jason's Quest*. Illustrated by Staffan Torell. Toronto, McClelland, 1971; illustrated by Leslie Morriil. Toronto, Seal, 1981.

_____. *The Olden Days Coat*. Illustrated by Muriel Wood. Toronto, McClelland, 1979; rev. ed., 1982.

LUNN, JANET. *Double Spell*. Illustrated by A.M. Calder. Toronto, Martin, 1968; Markham, Ont., Puffin, 1986. (Published in the United States as *Twin Spell*.)

_____. *The Root Cellar*. Toronto, Lester, 1981; Markham, Ont., Puffin, 1983.

_____. *Shadow in Hawthorn Bay*. Toronto, Lester, 1986; Markham, Ont., Puffin, 1988.

McNEIL, FLORENCE. *All Kinds of Magic*. Vancouver, Douglas, 1984 (A Groundwood Book).

MAJOR, KEVIN. *Blood Red Ochre*. Toronto, Doubleday, 1989.

MELLING, O.R. *The Druid's Tune*. Markham, Ont., Viking, 1983; Markham, Ont., Puffin, 1984.

_____. *The Singing Stone*. Markham, Ont., Viking, 1986; Markham, Ont., Puffin, 1988.

NICHOLS, RUTH. *The Marrow of the World*. Illustrated by Trina Schart Hyman. Toronto, Macmillan, 1972; Toronto, Gage, 1977.

_____. *A Walk Out of the World*. Illustrated by Trina Schart Hyman. Toronto, Longman, 1969.

NYBERG, MORGAN. *Galahad Schwartz and the Cockroach Army*. Vancouver, Douglas, 1987 (A Groundwood Book).

OPPEL, KENNETH. *Colin's Fantastic Video Adventure*. Illustrated by Tony Blundell. Harmondsworth, Middlesex, Puffin, 1985.

PEARSON, KIT. *A Handful of Time*. Markham, Ont., Viking, 1987; Markham, Ont., Puffin, 1988.

RICHLER, MORDECAI. *Jacob Two-Two and the Dinosaur*. Illustrated by Norman Eyolfson. Toronto, McClelland, 1987.

_____. *Jacob Two-Two Meets the Hooded Fang*. Illustrated by Fritz Wegner. Toronto, McClelland, 1975; Toronto, Seal, 1981.

TAYLOR, CORA. *The Doll*. Saskatoon, Sask., Western, 1987.

_____. *Julie*. Saskatoon, Sask., Western, 1985; Richmond Hill, Ont., Scholastic-TAB, 1987.

WALSH, ANN. *Your Time, My Time*. Toronto, Porcépic, 1984.

WILKINSON, ANNE. *Swann & Daphne*. Illustrated by Leo Rampen. Toronto, Oxford, 1960.

WUORIO, EVA-LIS. *Return of the Viking*. Illustrated by William Winter. Toronto, Clarke, 1955.

9. SCIENCE FICTION

BALTENSPERGER, PETER. *Guardians of Time*. Toronto, Three Trees, 1984.

GODFREY, MARTYN. *Alien War Games*. Richmond Hill, Ont., Scholastic-TAB, 1984.

_____. *More Than Weird*. Don Mills, Ont., Collier, 1987.

_____. *The Vandarian Incident*. Richmond Hill, Ont., Scholastic-TAB, 1981.

HILL, DOUGLAS. *Alien Citadel*. London, Heinemann, 1984.

_____. *Exiles of ColSec*. London, Gollancz, 1984.

_____. *The Huntsman*. London, Heinemann, 1982.

_____. *Warriors of the Wasteland*. London, Heinemann, 1983.

_____. *Young Legionary: The Earlier Adventures of Keill Randor*. London, Gollancz, 1982.

HORAI, WENCE. *Sudbury Time Twist*. Toronto, Three Trees, 1984.

HUGHES, MONICA. *Beyond the Dark River*. Don Mills, Ont., Nelson, 1979.

_____. *Devil on My Back*. London, MacRae, 1984; London, Methuen, 1986.

_____. *The Dream Catcher*. Toronto, Methuen, 1986.

_____. *The Guardian of Isis*. London, Collins, 1981; London, Magnet, 1982.

_____. *The Isis Pedlar*. London, Collins, 1982; London, Magnet, 1983.

_____. *The Keeper of the Isis Light*. Toronto, Nelson, 1980; London, Collins, 1985.

_____. *Ring-Rise, Ring-Set*. London, MacRae, 1982; London, Heinemann, 1986.

_____. *The Tomorrow City*. London, Hamilton, 1978; London, Magnet, 1982.

MARTEL, SUZANNE. *The City Undergound*; tr. by Norah Smaridge. Illustrated by Don Sibley. New York, Viking, 1964; tr. by David Homel. Vancouver, Douglas, 1982 (A Groundwood Book).

MATAS, CAROL. *The Fusion Factor*. Saskatoon, Sask., Fifth House, 1986.

_____. *Me, Myself and I*. Saskatoon, Sask., Fifth House, 1987.

_____. *Zanu*. Saskatoon, Sask., Fifth House, 1986.

10. POETRY & VERSE

BOURINOT, ARTHUR S. *Ottawa Lyrics and Verses for Children*. Ottawa, Graphic Publishers, 1929.

_____. *Pattering Feet: A Book of Childhood Verses*. Illustrated by Alan B. Beddoe. Ottawa, Graphic Publishers, 1925.

DOWNIE, MARY ALICE and BARBARA ROBERTSON, comps. *The New Wind Has Wings: Poems from Canada*. Illustrated by Elizabeth Cleaver. Toronto, Oxford, 1984.

_____. *The Wind Has Wings: Poems from Canada*. Illustrated by Elizabeth Cleaver. Toronto, Oxford, 1968. Rev. ed. under the title: *The New Wind Has Wings*, 1984.

FERRIS, SEAN, ed. *Children of the Great Muskeg*. Windsor, Ont., Black Moss, 1985.

FIELD, EUGENE. *Wynken, Blynken and Nod*. Illustrated by Ron Berg. Richmond Hill, Ont., North Winds, 1985.

FITCH, SHEREE. *Toes In My Nose and Other Poems*. Illustrated by Molly Bobak. Toronto, Doubleday, 1987.

GARVIN, JOHN W., ed. *Canadian Verse for Boys and Girls*. Toronto, Nelson, 1930.

GAY, MARIE-LOUISE. *Moonbeam on a Cat's Ear*. Illustrated by the author. Toronto, Stoddart, 1986.

_____. *Rainy Day Magic*. Illustrated by the author. Toronto, Stoddart, 1987.

GILMAN, PHOEBE. *Jillian Jiggs*. Illustrated by the author. Richmond Hill, Ont., North Winds, 1985.

_____. *The Wonderful Pigs of Jillian Jiggs*. Illustrated by the author. Richmond Hill, Ont., North Winds, 1988.

HEIDBREDER, ROBERT. *Don't Eat Spiders*. Illustrated by Karen Patkau. Toronto, Oxford, 1985.

HUTCHINS, HAZEL. *Ben's Snow Song: A Winter Picnic*. Illustrated by Lisa Smith. Toronto, Annick, 1987.

JAM, TEDDY. *Night Cars*. Illustrated by Eric Beddows. Vancouver, Douglas, 1988 (A Groundwood Book).

JOHNSON, EMILY PAULINE. *Flint and Feather*. Toronto, Musson, 1912.

KHALSA, DAYAL KAUR. *Sleepers*. Illustrated by the author. Montreal, Tundra, 1988.

LAYTON, IRVING. *A Spider Danced a Cosy Jig*. Edited by Elspeth Cameron. Illustrated by Miro Malish. Toronto, Stoddart, 1984.

LEAR, EDWARD. *The Owl and the Pussycat*. Illustrated by Erica Rutherford. Montreal, Tundra, 1986.

_____. *The Owl and the Pussycat*. Illustrated by Ron Berg. Richmond Hill, Ont., North Winds, 1984.

LEE, DENNIS. *Alligator Pie*. Illustrated by Frank Newfeld. Toronto, Macmillan, 1974.

_____. *Garbage Delight*. Illustrated by Frank Newfeld. Toronto, Macmillan, 1977.

_____. *Jelly Belly*. Illustrated by Juan Wijngaard. Toronto, Macmillan, 1983.

_____. *Lizzy's Lion*. Illustrated by Marie-Louise Gay. Toronto, Stoddart, 1984.

_____. *Nicholas Knock and Other People*. Illustrated by Frank Newfeld. Toronto, Macmillan, 1974.

LITTLE, JEAN. *Hey World, Here I Am!* Illustrated by Barbara Di Lella. Toronto, Kids Can, 1986.

McCLARD, JUDY and NAOMI WALL, eds. *Come With Us: Children Speak for Themselves*. Toronto, Women's Educational, 1978.

MACKAY, ISABEL E. *The Shining Ship and Other Verse for Children*. Illustrated by Thelma Cudlipp. Toronto, McClelland, Goodchild & Stewart, 1918.

MOWAT, GRACE HELEN. *Funny Fables of Fundy and Other Poems for Children*. Illustrated by the author. Ottawa, Ru-mi-lou Books, 1928.

NICHOL, BP. *Giants, Moosequakes & Other Disasters*. Illustrated by Maureen Paxton. Windsor, Ont., Black Moss, 1985.

_____. *Once: A Lullaby*. Illustrated by Ed Roach. Windsor, Ont., Black Moss, 1983; illustrated by Anita Lobel. New York, Greenwillow, 1986.

OBED, ELLEN BRYAN. *Borrowed Black: A Labrador Fantasy*. Illustrated by Jan Morgensen. rev. ed. St John's, Nfld., Breakwater, 1988.

O HUIGIN, SEAN. *Atmosfear*. Illustrated by Barbara Di Lella. Windsor, Ont., Black Moss, 1985.

_____. *The Dinner Party*. Illustrated by Maureen Paxton. Windsor, Ont., Black Moss, 1984.

_____. *The Ghost Horse of the Mounties*. Illustrated by Phil McLeod. Windsor, Ont., Black Moss, 1983.

_____. *Scary Poems for Rotten Kids*. Illustrated by John Fraser and Scott Hughes. Windsor, Ont., Black Moss, 1982; rev. ed., 1988.

PACEY, DESMOND. *The Cat, the Cow, and the Kangaroo: The Collected Children's Verse of Desmond Pacey*. Illustrated by Mary Pacey. Fredericton, N.B., Brunswick Press, 1968.

_____. *The Cow With the Musical Moo and Other Verses for Children*. Illustrated by Milada Horejs and Karel Rohlicek. Fredericton, N.B., Brunswick Press, 1952.

_____. *Hippity Hobo and the Bee and Other Verses for Children*. Illustrated by Milada Horejs and Karel Rohlicek. Fredericton, N.B., Brunswick Press, 1952.

POE, EDGAR ALLAN. *Annabel Lee*. Illustrated by Giles Tibo. Montreal, Tundra, 1987.

ROBART, ROSE. *The Cake That Mack Ate*. Illustrated by Maryann Kovalski. Toronto, Kids Can, 1986.

SERVICE, ROBERT W. *The Cremation of Sam McGee*. Illustrated by Ted Harrison. Toronto, Kids Can, 1986.

_____. *The Shooting of Dan McGrew*. Illustrated by Ted Harrison. Toronto, Kids Can, 1987.

SILLERS, PATRICIA. *Ringtail*. Illustrated by Karen Patkau. Toronto, Oxford, 1987.

SIMMIE, LOIS. *An Armadillo Is Not a Pillow*. Illustrated by Anne Simmie. Saskatoon, Sask., Western, 1986.

_____. *Auntie's Knitting a Baby*. Illustrated by Anne Simmie. Sakatoon, Sask., Western, 1984.

SOUSTER, RAYMOND. *Flight of the Roller-Coaster: Poems for Younger Readers*. Selected by Richard Woollatt. Ottawa, Oberon, 1985.

SWEDE, GEORGE. *High Wire Spider*. Illustrated by Victor Gad. Toronto, Three Trees, 1986.

_____. *Tick Bird: Poems for Children*. Illustrated by Katherine Helmer. Toronto, Three Trees, 1983.

_____. *Time Is Flies: Poems for Children*. Illustrated by Darcia Labrosse. Toronto, Three Trees, 1984.

WYNNE-JONES, TIM. *Mischief City*. Illustrated by Victor Gad. Vancouver, Douglas, 1986 (A Groundwood Book).

Notes

Page

4 Judith St. John, 'Peeps at the Esquimaux Through Early Children's Books', *The Beaver*, Winter, 1965. p. 43.

4 Mrs. H. Bayley in *Bibliotheca Canadensis*, G.E. Desbarats, Ottawa, 1867. p. 22.

5 Northrop Frye, 'Conclusion to a *Literary History of Canada*', *The Bush Garden: Essays on the Canadian Imagination* (Toronto, Anansi, 1971), p. 214.

9 Northrop Frye, *op.cit.*, p. 232.

9 Northrop Frye, *op.cit.*, p. 225.

9 Margaret Atwood, *Survival: A Thematic Guide to Canadian Literature* (Toronto, Anansi, 1972).

10 Edward Salmon, *Juvenile Literature As It Is* (London, Henry J. Drane, 1888), p. 184.

21 Northrop Frye, *op. cit.*, p. 232.

21 Nina Bawden, 'Emotional Realism in Books for Young People', *The Horn Book Magazine*, 1980, p. 56.

29 J.R.R. Tolkien, 'On Fairy-Stories', *Tree and Leaf* (London, Unwin Books, 1973), p. 50.

36 Mary Rubio and Elizabeth Waterston, eds, *The Selected Journals of L.M. Montgomery*, Vol. II. (Toronto, Oxford University Press, 1987), pp. 39-40.

36 *Op.cit.*, p. 41.

36 *Op.cit.*, p. 44.

37 *Op.cit.*, p. 390.

37 Wilfrid Eggleston, ed., *The Green Gables Letters from L.M. Montgomery to Ephraim Weber 1905-1909* (Toronto, Ryerson, 1960), p. 64.

59 E.M. Forster, 'What I Believe', in *Two Cheers for Democracy* (New York, Harcourt, Brace and World, 1951), p. 68.

119 Hester Burton. 'The Author as Historical Novelist: One of the Elite,' in *The Cool Web: The Pattern of Children's Reading*, ed. by Margaret Meek and others (London, The Bodley Head, 1977), p. 161.

129 Alfred T. Sheppard, *The Art & Practice of Historical Fiction* (London, Humphrey Toulmin, 1930), p. 15.

130 Erik Christian Haugaard, *The Rider and His Horse* (Boston, Houghton, 1968), p. [ix].

183 Marc Lescarbot, *The History of New France* (Toronto, The Champlain Society, vol. 2, 1911), p. 170.

187 Penny Petrone, 'Indian Legends and Tales' in William Toye, ed., *The Oxford Companion to Canadian Literature* (Toronto, Oxford University Press, 1983), p. 379.

187 Wilson D. Wallis and Ruth Sawtell Wallis, *The Micmac Indians of Eastern Canada* (Minneapolis, University of Minnesota Press, 1955), p. 330.

188 Fraser Symington, *The Canadian Indian* (Toronto, McClelland and Stewart, 1969), p. 233.

197 Diamond Jenness, *The Indians of Canada* (Ottawa, The Queen's Printer, 1960), p. 317.

204 Katharine B. Judson, *Myths and Legends of British North America* (Chicago, McClurg & Co., 1917), p. 109.

205 J.W. Powell, *Eighteenth Annual Report of the Bureau of American Ethnology: Part 1, 1896-97* (Washington, Government Printing Office, 1899), pp. 452-3.

207 Knud Rasmussen, *Intellectual Culture of the Hudson Bay Eskimos* (Copenhagen, Gyldendalske Boghandel, Nordisk Forlag, 1930), p. 56.

208 Knud Rasmussen, *op. cit.*, p. 124.

208 Franz Boas, 'The Eskimo of Baffin Land and Hudson Bay', *Bulletin of the American Museum of Natural History*, Vol. XV, Part I (New York, The Museum, 1907), pp. 165-7.

215 Catharine Parr Traill, *The Backwoods of Canada* (London, Natali and Bond, 1839), p. 153.

229 J.R.R. Tolkien, 'On Fairy-Stories', in *Tree and Leaf* (London, Unwin Books, 1964), p. 36.

229 Joseph Campbell, *The Hero With a Thousand Faces* (Princeton University Press, 1973).

230 Tolkien, *op. cit.*, p. 50.

271 Tolkien, *op. cit.*, p. 45.

273 C.S. Lewis, *An Experiment in Criticism* (Cambridge University Press, 1961), p. 109.

273 Brian W. Aldiss, *Billion Year Spree* (London, Weidenfeld & Nicolson, 1975), p. 2.

274 Sam Moskowitz, *Explorers of the Infinite* (Westport, Conn., Hyperion Press, 1963), p. 11.

289 Monica Hughes, 'The Writer's Quest' in *Canadian Children's Literature: A Journal of Criticism and Review*, No. 26 (1982), p. 20-1.

291 Emily Dickinson, 'Letter to Colonel T.W. Higginson' in Martha Dickinson Bianchi, *The Life and Letters of Emily Dickinson* (Boston, Houghton Mifflin, 1924), p. 276.

291 Harry Behn, 'Poetry for Children,' in *Chrysalis: Concerning Children and Poetry* (New York, Harcourt, Brace & World, 1968), pp. 55-6.

310 Northrop Frye, 'Canada and Its Poetry', in *Canadian Forum* (December 1943).

Index

OF AUTHORS, TITLES, AND ILLUSTRATORS